Chinese Philosophy of History

Bloomsbury Studies in World Philosophies

Series Editor:

Monika Kirloskar-Steinbach

Comparative, cross-cultural and intercultural philosophy are burgeoning fields of research. Bloomsbury Studies in World Philosophies complements and strengthens the latest work being carried out at a research level with a series that provides a home for thinking through ways in which professional philosophy can be diversified. Ideal for philosophy postgraduates and faculty who seek creative and innovative material on non-Euroamerican sources for reference and research, this series responds to the challenges of our postcolonial world, laying the groundwork for a new philosophy canon that departs from the current Eurocentric sources.

Forthcoming Titles in the Series:

Chinese Philosophy of History, by Dawid Rogacz

Chinese and Indian Ways of Thinking in Early Modern European Philosophy, by Selusi Ambrogio

Chinese Philosophy of History

*From Ancient Confucianism to the End
of the Eighteenth Century*

Dawid Rogacz

BLOOMSBURY ACADEMIC
LONDON • NEW YORK • OXFORD • NEW DELHI • SYDNEY

BLOOMSBURY ACADEMIC
Bloomsbury Publishing Plc
50 Bedford Square, London, WC1B 3DP, UK
1385 Broadway, New York, NY 10018, USA
29 Earlsfort Terrace, Dublin 2, Ireland

BLOOMSBURY, BLOOMSBURY ACADEMIC and the Diana logo are trademarks
of Bloomsbury Publishing Plc

First published in Great Britain 2020
This paperback edition published in 2022

For legal purposes the Acknowledgements on p. vi constitute an extension
of this copyright page.

Series design by Louise Dugdale
Cover image © Olga Kurbatova/Getty Images

A catalogue record for this book is available from the British Library.

Library of Congress Cataloging-in-Publication Data
Names: Rogacz, Dawid, author.
Title: Chinese philosophy of history : from Ancient Confucianism to the end of the
Eighteenth Century / Dawid Rogacz.
Other titles: From Ancient Confucianism to the end of the Eighteenth Century
Description: London ; New York : Bloomsbury Academic, 2020. | Series: Bloomsbury
studies in world philosophies | Includes bibliographical references and index.
Identifiers: LCCN 2020026787 | ISBN 9781350150096 (hardback) |
ISBN 9781350150102 (ebook) | ISBN 9781350150119 (epub)
Subjects: LCSH: China–History–Philosophy. | China–Historiography.
Classification: LCC DS736.5 .R64 2020 | DDC 901–dc23
LC record available at https://lccn.loc.gov/2020026787

ISBN: HB: 978-1-3501-5009-6
        PB: 978-1-3502-1534-4
      ePDF: 978-1-3501-5010-2
      eBook: 978-1-3501-5011-9

Series: Bloomsbury Studies in World Philosophies

Typeset by RefineCatch Limited, Bungay, Suffolk

To find out more about our authors and books visit www.bloomsbury.com
and sign up for our newsletters.

Contents

Acknowledgements

This book would not have seen the light of the day without the help of many institutions and people. The research leading to these results has been supported by the Polish National Science Center (Narodowe Centrum Nauki) under grant agreement no. 2015/19/N/HS1/00977. I have also received all the necessary funding from the Department of Philosophy of Adam Mickiewicz University in Poznań, for which I am very grateful. The consultations with philosophers and Sinologists conducted as a part of the European Research Council grant 'Narrative Modes of Historical Discourse in Asia' have also been invaluable.

The book is a modified version of my PhD thesis from Adam Mickiewicz University in Poznań, which was written in Polish under the title 'The Idea of Historiosophical Holism in the Classical Chinese Thought' and defended with a *summa cum laude* on 25 March 2019. I would like to express my profound gratitude to my supervisor, Andrzej Wawrzynowicz, for all the remarks on the original version of the dissertation. I would also like to thank the other Poznań professors who helped me with my research: Krzysztof Brzechczyn, Ewa Domańska and Ulrich Timme Kragh. This book, however, would not have been possible without the help of scholars of Chinese philosophy from outside my university and Poland. Here I would like to single out for special thanks Achim Mittag (for the time devoted) and Philip J. Ivanhoe (for the materials provided). My thanks go to all those who have changed my way of interpreting the Chinese philosophy of history due to their comments to my papers: Selusi Ambrogio, Federico Brusadelli, Bart Dessein, Carine Defoort, Fabien Heubel, Yong Huang, JeeLoo Liu, John Makeham, Eric S. Nelson, Bryan W. Van Norden, Jana Rošker, Jörn Rüsen, Masayuki Satō, Sung Chia-fu and Mercedes Valmisa. I am indebted to Jens Østergård Petersen for sharing with me some of the classical sources that were necessary for completing this book, and to Małgorzata Bródka from the AMU Library for almost unlimited acquisition of all the needed secondary literature. I am very grateful to Stephen Dersley for helping with the copy-editing. I have great appreciation for Bloomsbury Press and its editors, Colleen Coalter and Becky Holland, for assisting to bring this book into print. All the mistakes occurring in this book are my own responsibility. Last but not least, I wish to express my gratitude to my wife Beata and my whole family for their encouragement.

INTRODUCTION

The Topic of the Book

Chinese civilization, alone among world civilizations, could glory in continuous five-thousand-year history. In fact, not only in history, but also, within a slightly more modest period of time, reflection on it – whether in the form of historiography or, as it will be shown in this book, the philosophy of history. In the face of this impressive continuity and the central position of historical works in Chinese culture, the question about the character of Chinese philosophy of history touches the foundations and sources of Chinese thought. This fact translates into the extraordinary variety and, at the same time, a certain coherence of the philosophies of history that were created and developed in China over the centuries.

The aim of this work is the reconstruction and philosophical interpretation of Chinese philosophy of history from its beginnings to the end of the eighteenth century. Philosophical interpretation means that, following a careful historical study, the common premises and the dynamics of transformation of analysed ideas will be interpreted by framing it in terms of a philosophical interpretative key, namely the notion of 'holism'. The meaning of this concept is explained in Chapter 1.

The exclusion of Chinese philosophy of history from the nineteenth and twentieth centuries from the scope of this book results from the aspiration to grasp the original Chinese philosophy of history preceding the reception of philosophical themes from Western thought. This period is referred to here as 'classical', in the traditional and broad meaning of the Chinese term 古代 *gǔdài*. The continuity of the motifs undertaken within 2,500 years of the development of Chinese philosophy of history shows the validity of such a postulate. In fact, any study of modern Chinese historical thinking should be preceeded by a careful analysis of the traditional Chinese views of history.

Buddhist thought is also excluded from the research area. First, Buddhist philosophy in China is rooted in Indian philosophical categories, some of which are also pre-Buddhist, the discussion of which goes beyond the scope of this book and would lead us away from the task of reconstructing the original Chinese philosophy of history. Second, as shown in the examples cited at the beginning of Chapter 5, the Buddhist vision of history is religious in its nature, closer to what is known in the West as the 'theology of history'. As a result, it did not have a significant and direct impact on the later, by definition Confucian, philosophy of history; hence its omission does not effect the reconstruction undertaken here.

The issues related to the history, methodology and political determinants of Chinese historiography will be covered only as far as they are indispensable for understanding Chinese philosophy of history. However, the philosophy of history in China was always connected with historiography in both an objective and meta-reflective way. Objective, because Chinese historiography, especially in its early period, implicitly contained many historiosophical elements and schemes; meta-reflective, since historiography was also the direct object of philosophical analysis conducted by Chinese thinkers.

The philosophy of history is understood here as both the philosophy of historical process and the philosophy of historiography. In general, the philosophy of history poses a question concerning the meaning (sense) of history, as opposed to the historical sciences, which posit this sense, putting forward particular sensible narratives and historical explanations. If a philosopher asks about the meaning of history and undertakes a speculative, historiography-independent interpretation of historical process, this is a philosophy of history *per se*; while if interest is devoted only to the meaning present in the histories (meaning *in* history), this is a philosophy of historiography. Non-philosophical visions of history present in the works of art and literature will be called, on the other hand, 'historiosophy'. The detailed understanding of these terms, together with their location in the context of contemporary debates, is presented in Chapter 1.

Terminology issues

From a purely linguistic perspective, the question naturally arises as to whether the term 'philosophy of history' or its analogue was used in classical Chinese before the nineteenth century. A negative answer to this question, however, cannot entail denial of the existence of the entire tradition of Chinese philosophy of history, the wealth of which is shown in this study. It has to be noticed that this sort of problem also concerns such Western concepts as 'aesthetics', 'ontology' or 'epistemology'. Technical terms denoting isolated areas of thought often come into existence along with the maturation, if not conclusion, of given intellectual traditions. An impatient proclamation of various '-isms', '-logies' or 'posts-' in the hope of attracting someone who would take it up is an idiosyncratic feature of our times. The lack of a separate term indicates at most the lack of a *separate* sphere of philosophical reflection. In this case, the philosophy of history in China was closely related to the philosophy of nature, political philosophy and ethics.

This notwithstanding, it has to be stressed that the Chinese had their own distinctive term for philosophy, the source of which was not so much 'love of wisdom' as 'search for the pattern' 窮理 *qiónglǐ*, and the concept of history, whether in the sense of a historical work (史 *shǐ*, originally 'a historian'), or a historical process (technical term 古今 *gǔjīn*, literally 'past-and-present'). In addition, Chinese philosophers frequently aimed at investigation into history/histories (考古今 *kǎo gǔjīn* or 考史 *kǎoshǐ*), or even more often at 'comprehending' or 'encompassing' 通 *tōng* history. All these terms become technically used only with the rise of Neo-Confucianism, which was incidental to the formation of the imperial examination system. After that time, even the titles of philosophical treatises were explicitly devoted to the study of the 'comprehensive meaning' 通義 *tōngyì* of history.

The term 'philosophy of history' 历史哲学 *lìshǐ zhéxué* has already been applied to the classical thought by the main Chinese authorities in this field, including one of the most eminent modern Confucians, Mou Zongsan 牟宗三, who juxtaposed it with the Hegelian philosophy of history,[1] and Stanislas Lo Kuang 羅光, who compared it with Western philosophy of history after St. Augustine.[2] It is worth noting that apart from the term *lishi zhexue*, Chinese academic literature also uses, in fact quite interchangeably, terms such as 'historical thought' 历史思想 *lìshǐ sīxiang*, 'historiographical thought' 史学思想 *shǐxué sīxiang* and 'conception of history' 历史观 *lìshǐ guān* (the term 历史理论 *lìshǐ lǐlùn* usually means, on the other hand, 'theory of history'). In the People's Republic of China, the context of the reception of historical materialism and the tendency towards looking for materialist currents in the history of Chinese thought has also been conducive to the progressive popularization of research into the native philosophy of history.

In the light of these findings, it is surprising that so far there has been no monograph in any Western language devoted to a comprehensive treatment of the classical Chinese philosophy of history. This only strengthens the already strong illusion that the philosophy of history is a specifically Western 'invention'. This opinion has found a powerful ally in the form of Karl Löwith, who, by showing that the Western philosophy of history is rooted in Christian eschatology, openly rejected the possibility of the existence of a philosophy of history in China.[3] However, Löwith's analysis implies only that it is impossible to comprehend the Western philosophy of history without the history of Western culture, but not that no other culture could create a philosophy of history. This view fits into the long tradition of interpretation of Chinese thinking, which began already before Hegel, putting an end to the Enlightenment Sinophilism.[4] The paradoxical implication of this book is the statement that in terms of metaphilosophical assumptions, the holistic philosophies of history of Hegel and Chinese thinkers are more similar than dissimilar, as Mou Zongsan accurately observed. This work therefore aims not only to fill an important gap in studies on Chinese philosophy, but also to broaden the area of reflection on the philosophy of history in general by restoring its intercultural character, analogously to processes that took place in ethics or ontology.

State of the art

Despite the apparent neglect of the studies on Chinese philosophy of history, there are several exceptions to this rule. In Western scholarship, the first and most important of these is David S. Nivison, a pioneer in the application of the methods of analytic philosophy to the study of classical Chinese thought. The philosophy of history is analysed in the three chapters of his celebrated monograph *The Life and Thought of Chang Hsüeh-ch'eng (1738–1801)* from 1966;[5] Nivison also applied the notion of 'philosophy of history' to earlier Chinese philosophers, such as Mencius.[6] Nivison was repeatedly returning to Zhang Xuecheng's philosophy of history, as evidenced by the unpublished manuscripts of his papers,[7] while in 2003, his entry 'Philosophy of History' appeared in the *Encyclopedia of Chinese Philosophy*, being an abbreviated version of the

69-page essay *Chinese Philosophies of History*, completed in 2006.[8] As Nivison writes, 'questioning about what the pattern of the past is, and where we all are in it, is conspicuous in Chinese philosophy from its beginning. Eventually one begins to see the Chinese were attending also to questions we will have to call 'critical' ones'.[9] Nivison's studies on Chinese philosophy of history were followed up by one of his students, Philip J. Ivanhoe, the author of the entry 'Chinese theories of history' in the *Routledge Encyclopedia of Philosophy*, who, just like Nivison, considers Zhang Xuecheng as the culmination of the development of the classical Chinese philosophy of history.[10] Chinese philosophy of history is also, though not directly, an important part of the research of Michael Puett, while particular concepts from the field of philosophy of history have been studied by such different Sinologists as Sarah Allan, Roger Ames, François Jullien, JeeLoo Liu, Achim Mittag, Yuri Pines, Conrad Schirokauer, Hoyt Tillman and Sarah Queen, all of whom are cited in this book. Ideas openly associated with the philosophy of history are also discussed in some parts in *Mirroring the Past: The Writing and Use of History in Imperial China* by Q. Edward Wang and On-cho Ng,[11] as well as in the recent study *The Politics of the Past in Early China* by Vincent S. Leung.[12]

In Chinese scholarship, in addition to the above-mentioned Mou Zongsan and Luo Guang, one should refer to Huang Chun-chieh 黃俊傑, author of *Rujia sixiang yu Zhongguo lishi siwei* (*Confucian Thought and Chinese Historical Reflection*), a synthetic study of the Confucian philosophy of history focused on Zhu Xi's thought, who was a co-editor of several volumes devoted to the broadly understood 'Chinese historical thinking': *Time and Space in Chinese Culture* (1997, with Erik Zürcher), *Notions of Time in Chinese Historical Thinking* (2006, with John B. Henderson) and *Chinese Historical Thinking. An Intercultural Discussion* (2015, with Jörn Rüsen).[13] On the one hand, the term 'Chinese historical thinking' includes not only the philosophy of history, but also the theory and history of historiography; on the other hand, it displaces the concept of the philosophy of history or narrows it down, as shown in an example of one of the articles in the volume *Notions of Time in Chinese Historical Thinking*, which states that Wang Fuzhi is the only 'genuine' pre-modern philosopher of history in China.[14] Most Chinese historians of Chinese philosophy, however, incorporate the philosophy of history into their reconstruction of the history of Chinese thought from its very beginnings. Feng Youlan 馮友蘭 in his *Zhongguo zhexue shi* (*History of Chinese Philosophy*) of 1934 (English translation of Derke Bodde of 1983, short version of 1948) was already using the term 'philosophy of history' in relation to the concepts of Chinese thinkers before the common era.[15] Surprisingly, the popularity of his interpretation did not have an impact upon discerning the existence and continuity of Chinese philosophy of history. Discussions of particular concepts in the field of the philosophy of history are also incorporated into the work of Ren Jiyu 任继愈: the four-volumed *Zhongguo zhexue shi* (*History of Chinese philosophy*) from 1985, as well as the four-volumed *Zhongguo zhexue fazhan shi* (*History of the development of Chinese philosophy*) from 1998.[16] *Zhongguo gudai zhexue* (*Classical Chinese philosophy*) by Fang Litian 方立天, a book organized not historically but thematically, includes an almost seventy-page chapter entitled 'Zhongguo gudai lishi guan' ('Classical Chinese views of history') reviewing thirty-three different positions in the field of the philosophy of history up to Wang Fuzhi.[17] The most comprehensive study of Chinese philosophy of history, integrated into a wider project of reconstructing Chinese theory of history and historiography, is the ten-volume *Zhongguo shixue sixiang tongshi* (*Comprehensive history of Chinese historiography*) edited by Wu Huaiqi 吴怀祺, eight volumes of which concern pre-nineteenth century thought. To this should be added numerous Chinese-language papers and diploma theses on particular philosophies of history, the number of which significantly increased at the beginning of this century.

The method

Nonetheless, those who do not read Chinese still lack a philosophically synthetic and historically comprehensive analysis of classical Chinese philosophy of history. This fact influences the method of this book, which uses both Sinological apparatus and philosophical conceptual analysis. Hence, in terms of the structure of presentation, the book resembles a syllogism. After explaining in Chapter 1 what is meant by the philosophy of history and holism in the philosophy of history (the 'major term'), these elements are found in the material of Chinese philosophy (the 'minor term'), which leads to the expanded conclusion that Chinese philosophy developed a philosophy of history, including the specific idea (ideas) of holism. In the proposed model of demonstrating the validity of this thesis, its middle and main part is of an 'empirical' character, which consists of five chapters. As in the Aristotelian method, also in this book the syllogistic structure of the presentation of research results is complemented by an inductive approach in terms of arriving at these conclusions. Unlike the Aristotelian method, however, this induction is deliberately guided by the theoretical criterion for the selection of material and explication of the concepts in question.

Chinese philosophical (and partly historical) works, as written and transmitted in classical Chinese, have been read from the perspective of their relationship with the broadest possible connection with the philosophy of history. To this end, the vast majority of works of classical Chinese thought were examined. The basic reference point in the translation of Chinese quotations for me was *A Student's Dictionary of Classical and Medieval Chinese* by Paul W. Kroll.[18] For comparative purposes, I consulted the existing translations into Western languages and Mandarin. Then, a 'list' of quotes relevant for the topic was ordered in a coherent narrative, in a sense in which historians of ideas collate the thoughts expressed in different places of the same work. Only then is the interpretation obtained in this way confronted with the subject literature. After acquiring the image of the philosophy of history in a given work, and more broadly – of a given philosopher, generalizations concerning a given era and, finally, the entirety of classical Chinese thought are made.

Importantly, in a situation in which the Western conceptual apparatus does not find a proper term reflecting the essence of a given Chinese concept, new terms, such as 'historical populism', 'historical fatalism' or 'prospectivism', are introduced. Accordingly, also the scope of meaning of existing concepts, such as 'historical materialism' (which is treated now almost as a synonym of Marx's position), have been extended. Each thesis, including the most general ones, refers therefore to specific statements, cited in numerous footnotes, which are basically addressed to Sinologists and a critical reader focused on revising the translation or interpretation of a given quotation. Key terms are always highlighted in the text by adducing their characters and reading according to the *pinyin* romanization. For the terms that are in operation in the subsequent paragraphs and chapters, only its transcription without tones is provided; with the exception of terms written in capital letters, i.e. 'Tian' and 'Dao', the rest are italicized.

Description of the chapters

Chapter One discusses the meaning of the term 'philosophy of history' and its relation to the term 'historiosophy', as well as the relation of the philosophy of history to the theory of history on the one hand and other philosophical disciplines on the other. When outlining the problems of philosophy of history, its fundamental contemporary division into continental and analytical philosophy of history is described. This leads to sketching the possibly broadest scheme of questions a philosophy of history answers to, including the ones that imply holistic positions (in six different meanings), which are eventually applied to the analysed material.

Chapter Two examines the pre-imperial Confucian philosophy of history, the basic categories of which remained a benchmark for later thinkers. The sources of these categories are to be found already in the bronze inscriptions and, then, in the historiosophy of the *Book of Songs* and the *Book of Documents*. The intermediate phase between this historiosophy and the Confucian philosophy of history in the strict sense was marked by the ethics of history in the *Analects* and the 'peripheries' of Confucianism that offered alternative views of history, such as the concept of the Great Unity in the chapter 'Destiny of rituals' in the *Book of Rites*. The philosophies of history of Mencius and Xunzi became a mature expression of all these tendencies: the former proposed a developed cyclical vision of history governed by the moral principle, while the latter opposed the newly established theory of the Mandate of Heaven and the belief in an undifferentiated cognitive unity of the past and present.

Chapter Three elaborates on the alternative, non-Confucian philosophies of history in the Warring States Period, focusing on the Legalist philosophy of history of Shang Yang and Han Fei, which introduces the key concept of the propensity of history (*shi*), proposing the interpretation of history through the prism of social and technological development. Another distinctive view of history, although not so contrasted to Confucianism in its basic premises, was propounded by the Mohists. The Daoists, in turn, defended the idea of returning to the pre-social state of nature, manifesting their critical (and ironic) attitude towards speculative philosophy of history. This speculative character was not lacking in the philosophy of history of the Yin-Yang School, which built its thought based on the categories present in the *Book of Changes*. In addition to Zou Yan, these ideas can also be found in the eclectic *Lüshi Chunqiu*.

Chapter Four analyses the philosophy of history of the Han dynasty, especially the philosophy of history resulting from the combination of the Confucian ethics of history and the theory of the Mandate of Heaven with the philosophy of nature, as it was reflected in the philosophy of history of Dong Zhongshu and other Confucian thinkers of this paradigm. The broader idea of a correlation between nature and human history was also common to earlier Confucians, who did not assume the mediation of Heaven (Lu Jia) and the Daoist authors of the *Huainanzi*. On the other hand, many philosophers of the time have turned against the synthesis of cosmology and the philosophy of history, seeing the only driving force of history in man, either in the individual sense (Yang Xiong) or collective (Jia Yi and Zhong Changtong); the others separated the natural and social laws of history, finding the causes of historical changes in positive laws (Cui Shi and Huan Tan) or the natural ones (Wang Chong). The chapter ends with the analysis of the historiosophy of Sima Qian and Ban Gu, which accompanied the birth of official historiography.

Chapter Five, the longest in this book, is devoted to the Medieval Chinese philosophy of history from the third to the twelfth century. The Early Middle Ages are shown as a period of opposition to correlative meta-narrations, whether in the form of the idea of historical heroes, or the millenarian philosophy of history enunciated in the Neo-Daoist *Taipingjing*, or, finally, in the philosophy of historiography of Liu Zhiji. Then the Neo-Confucian philosophy of the Tang and Song era is discussed, which, depending on the approach to the presence of timeless principles in history, is divided into idealist positions, including spiritualist ones, as represented by Shao Yong, Wang Anshi, Sima Guang, the Cheng brothers and Zhu Xi, and realistic standpoints, including the materialist ones, as proposed by Liu Zongyuan, Li Gou, Ouyang Xiu, Su Xun and Chen Liang. Historical idealism includes both linear and cyclical, developmental and regressive views; in the case of historical materialism, its various versions – social, economic and natural – are distinguished and differentiated from historical realism.

Chapter Six expounds the development of Chinese philosophy of history from the thirteenth to the eighteenth century. In the Ming era, the philosophy of history was approached from a viewpoint of specific individualism and historism, as testified by Wang Yangming's thought, contemporaneous philosophy of historiography (Wang Shizhen, Hu Yinglin), the relativism of Li Zhi and prospectivism of Wang Tingxiang and Zhang Juzheng. In the initial phase of the Qing dynasty, the philosophy of history became even more rooted in the evidential scholarship (*kaozheng*) and prospectively oriented thought, which is shown in the example of Gu Yanwu and Huang Zongxi, and which culminated in the systems of Wang Fuzhi and Zhang Xuecheng, the former being a synthesis closer to historical realism, while the latter approached historical idealism. It was also Zhang Xuecheng who finally integrated the philosophy of historical process and the philosophy of historiography into a coherent and holistic synthesis.

In the conclusion of the book, following a diachronic presentation of the transformations of classical Chinese philosophy of history, a synchronic interpretation from the perspective of the idea of holism in the philosophy of history is put forward. This does not mean that Chinese philosophy of history taken as a whole expresses a specific idea of holism in unison, but that the holistic view of history has resulted in the most comprehensive concepts in Chinese philosophy of history, transformations of which, causing a specific reaction and opposition, determined the dynamics of this thought. Finally, this interpretative body of classical Chinese philosophy of history is compared with the main premises of the Western philosophy of history, which leads to some suggestions for further comparative studies.

What is the Philosophy of History?

Introduction

An attempt to define the subject matter of the philosophy of history is just as necessary as it is burdensome, in the face of fundamental disagreements over the scope of, issues associated with – and even the term for – philosophical reflection on history. To avoid an arbitrary or even normative definition, I will try to present the different ways of understanding this notion and outline a view of the philosophy of history that is closest to the Chinese conceptions under examination here. Since this is an explicitly interdisciplinary field, the relationship between the philosophy of history and other disciplines, both historical (such as theory of history and methodology of history) and philosophical, cannot be overlooked. The meaning of the term 'philosophy of history' is also highly ambiguous, especially in English, where the word 'history' can refer to both a process and a story. Awareness of this basic difference becomes much clearer, however, in contemporary philosophy, which some time ago divided itself into the analytic and continental (or substantial) branches of the philosophy of history. Taking all of this into consideration, I will try to delineate the issues associated with the philosophy of history in the most general manner, as they are reflected in a diversity of particular standpoints. One of those viewpoints, namely holism in the philosophy of history, plays a crucial role in the proposed interpretation of the Chinese philosophy of history.

Philosophy and the theory of history

To explicate the difference between the philosophy of history and the theory/ methodology of history, some larger fields to which they belong need to be clearly acknowledged: the philosophy of history has always been a part of philosophy, while the theory and methodology of history are assigned to be a part of science. This idea would not have been alien to the Greeks, those fathers of Western historiography, and it was not without reason that Herodotus titled his work Ἰστορίαι (*Inquiry*), for his studies involved travels to historical places and collecting reliable evidence of the past. Understandably, at the very outset questions were posed concerning which sources were reliable, and generally what kinds of sources are reliable, or what methods should be used to scrutinize these sources, and how to create a historical narrative that will not 'lose' its credibility. General reflection of this nature, originating from the practice of writing history, is quite different from proper historiography. In the face of the ambiguity of the concept of history, which means both history in the sense of past events (*res gestae* in Latin) and history in the sense of a narrative (*historia rerum gestarum*), a great deal of time was devoted to searching for a distinctive term that would encompass general scientific research on history. In 1815, the Polish historian Joachim Lelewel introduced the concept of 'historica' in his book *Historyka, tudzież o łatwym i pożytecznym nauczaniu historii* (*Historica, or easy and useful teaching of history*), which was popularized by Johann Gustav Droysen (*Grundriss der Historik*, 1868). Importantly, Lelewel distinguished historica from the philosophy of history:

> Comments of a philosophical or political character and moral lessons are not allowed here, because they usually could become the motive, or at least give the writer the suspicion that he narrated the circumstances, distending them to his views.[1]

In the work *Historica. The principles of the methodology and theory of historical knowledge*, another Polish historian, Marceli Handelsman, defined 'historica' as a science devoted to: (1) the theory of historical knowledge, and (2) the creative process of writing about history, as well as (3) a method for historical research.[2] In fact, under the pressure of time, the programme of 'historica' became further diversified, differentiated and divided. Contemporary scholars usually use the term 'theory of history' to name the first domain, and 'methodology of history' to denote the third domain, whereas reflection on the creative process of writing history (2) often goes by the name of 'metahistory', from the celebrated work of Hayden White, *Metahistory: The Historical Imagination in Nineteenth-Century Europe* (1973). Interestingly, as part of the reaction to this diversification, the term historica has returned to favour, for example in Jörn Rüsen's *Historische Vernunft: Grundzüge einer Historik* from 1983.

The difference between the theory and the methodology of history is neither clear nor established. Generally speaking, the methodology of history is more concerned with the cognitive actions of historical research, while the theory of history addresses the results of these activities. Yet, when employing a programme of contemporary analytic philosophy of history, the boundary between the theory and philosophy of history gradually fades. For this reason, some researchers, such as Jerzy Topolski, have proposed a new definition of the methodology of history that also includes inquiry into the subject of history, which is usually treated as part of the philosophy of history.[3]

The discussion on the subject of the theory (or methodology) of history proves that professional historians are insistent that there should be a clear difference between even the theoretical part of historical research and philosophical reflection on history. This trend is an extension of the dissenting vote against the philosophy of history that was cast by the fathers of modern historical research: Leopold von Ranke and Jacob Burckhardt. The latter proclaimed a total divergence between philosophy and history, denying the existence of any general idea of history.[4] Note, however, that regardless of these declarations, historians tend to make assessments of historical events in the light of the value systems rooted in their own (often unrealized) views of history. After the criticism of positivism, such 'axiologically neutral' procedures as selection of sources and explanation turned out to be deeply rooted in the preceding theories. Hayden White claims that even the form of emplotment has an affinity to the specific idea of history and its process.[5] These arguments show that not only the theory of history, but also historiography, is entangled in the philosophy of history.

The philosophy of history and other philosophical disciplines

A similar ambiguity is found in the relation between the philosophy of history and other philosophical disciplines. The first point to stress is that the philosophy of history does not belong to the classical branches of philosophy. At first glance, the philosophy of history is closest to political philosophy, but the analytic philosophy of history falls within the scope of the philosophy of science (or the philosophy of language), whereas narrativism or the hermeneutic philosophy of history is closer to the aesthetics and philosophy of literature. The speculative philosophy of history is, on the other hand, often identified with the 'metaphysics of history'. It is this polysemy of the term 'history' that ultimately makes the status of the philosophy of history so unclear. There is no doubt that the philosophy of history is essentially linked with each of the traditional branches of philosophy. Ontological concepts of time, change and development significantly shape our understanding of history. Issues in the domain of philosophical anthropology, such as views on human nature or man's place in nature and society, influence the philosophy of history to no less a degree (and in the case of this book, perhaps have the greatest influence). The relationship between epistemology and the philosophy of history was already evident in the philosophy of Giambattista Vico, Georg W.F. Hegel and Wilhelm Dilthey. It then grew even stronger with analytic philosophy, which focused on the problems of historical explanation, historical narrative, representation of the past and the status of historical experience. Axiology is present in the philosophy of history primarily as a basis for the evaluation of the past. And in a special way, the philosophy of history is affected by political philosophy, as historiography deals mainly with the political history of states and nations. The most important systems of the philosophy of history, including Hegelianism and Marxism, interpret history through the prism of their own political project, whose implementation crowns the historical process. This association was so strong that many contemporary political philosophers (Karl R. Popper, Isaiah Berlin, François Lyotard) blamed the philosophy of history as such (or 'historicism'[6]) for the twentieth-century totalitarianisms of Nazism and Communism.

This notwithstanding, it seems that the central position among determinants of the philosophy of history is occupied by historical factors themselves. This can be both the fall of empires (Rome in the case of St. Augustine, the Ming China for Wang Fuzhi and the Soviet Union for Francis Fukuyama), as well as the emergence of outstanding individuals initiating a new era (Liu Bang for Jia Yi, St. Francis for Joachim of Fiore, Napoleon for Hegel). The decisive impulse that gave rise to the Western philosophy of history is often considered to be the Lisbon earthquake of 1755, which shook people's faith in divine providence: in 1765 Voltaire published *La Philosophie de l'histoire*, in which the term 'philosophy of history', as opposed to 'theology of history', was used for the first time.

The philosophy of (the) history, philosophy of (a) history, historiosophy

The ambiguity of the English term 'philosophy of history' is caused by the fact that there are no rival or alternative terms. In Polish, for instance, there are three different terms that denote the philosophy of history, and in two of them different words for 'history' are used: one for history as a process (*dzieje*) and another for history in the more general sense, including history as a narrative (*historia*). This is similar to German, in which *Geschichte* tends to mean history as the past, while *Historie* refers to scientific or literary accounts.[7] Hence the term *Geschichtsphilosophie* might be identified with a speculative philosophy of history, claiming to have an insight into the nature of the historical process. In his *Culture and History* (1959), Phillip Bagby tries to coin the term 'a history' for the work of historians and 'the history' for the events of the past.[8] Hence what there should be is 'philosophy of a history' and 'philosophy of the history'. However, this division is not commonly accepted and probably seems odd to most proficient speakers of English. Accordingly, I will continue using the term 'philosophy of history' as the most general form, denoting both *res gestae* and *historia rerum gestarum*, since – especially in the case of pre-modern thinkers, Chinese included – it is hard to maintain a strict demarcation between these two areas. Should it become necessary to stress the systematic and independent character of this thought, I will opt for the term 'speculative philosophy of history'. Although I treat this notion as identical with the German *Geschichtsphilosophie*, I shall not restrict its reference to Hegelianism and Marxism, as I hold it is theoretically acceptable to construct an independent philosophical view of historical processes, usually devoid of any 'logic of history' (putting aside the issue of a *scientific* character of such a view). As Emil Angehrn shows, there are at least three main periods in the development of the Western *Geschitsphilosophie*: from its beginnings and St. Augustine to modern times; its classical period in the times of Hegel and Marx; and the reformulations of speculative philosophy of history in the twentieth century.[9]

There is also another term denoting this area of philosophical reflection, namely 'historiosophy'. This was coined by the Polish philosopher August Cieszkowski in his *Prolegomena zur Historiosophie* (1838). With historiosophy, Cieszkowski intended to make a transition from Hegel's philosophy of history to the 'wisdom of history'. As Wawrzynowicz points out, despite the fact that this work was published in Berlin (the mecca for Hegelians), it did not find any follow-up:

> In turn, the third of the terms coming here into play – 'historiosophy' – has contemporarily even more capacious meaning (…) It includes within its scope all, also purely literary, visions of history, not necessarily of any philosophical or scientific nature. In this broad sense one can therefore speak of a historiosophy of

some classic twentieth-century texts of world literature (such as Samuel Beckett's *The Lost Ones*), or of e.g. Nostradamus' historiosophy of centuries. In our case, we will be interested only in historiosophical conceptions that have a thread of connection with philosophical, historical or generally academic discourse.[10]

Following this proposition, I will use the term 'historiosophy' to designate all the implicit interpretations of history embodied in art, literature and historical writing, in contrast to the philosophy of history as an explicit reflection of both a speculative and critical character.[11]

Analytic and continental philosophies of history

This, however, does not end the terminological controversy. The contemporary philosophy of history has adopted a division of twentieth-century philosophy into analytic and continental branches. The problems of the analytic philosophy of history were largely determined by Carl Gustav Hempel's 1942 article, *The function of general laws in history*. This area of reflection is dominated by issues of historical explanation and causality in history, or more broadly, the justification of historical knowledge (W.H. Walsh, William Dray, Patrick L. Gardiner, Arthur C. Danto). It is much more difficult to define the continental philosophy of history. First, because the geographical criterion is inadequate (there are both European analytic philosophers of history, such as Ankersmit, and Anglo-Saxon hermeneutic philosophers of history, such as Robin G. Colingwood). Second, there is no common denominator for such diverse philosophers of history as Paul Ricœur, Oswald Spengler, Walter Benjamin, Alexandre Kojève and Reinhart Koselleck that is defined as clearly as in the case of analytic philosophy. Third, in the Baden School of Neo-Kantianism (Wilhelm Windelband, Heinrich Rickert), the issue of historical knowledge, including historical explanation, was taken up long before it was in the analytic philosophy of history. The creator of the term 'analytic philosophy of history', Danto, contraposed it to 'substantive philosophy of history'. The latter is a comprehensive approach to history that does not grow out of the practice of historiography, but rather involves the specific 'prophecy' that extends historical schemes to the future. The substantive philosophy of history originates therefore from theological thinking, and is not connected with philosophy at all, or at least no more than history itself is.[12] The point is, however, that many – if not most – twentieth-century continental philosophers of history were not substantive philosophers of history in this sense.

Eventually, however, the analytic philosophy of history was also shaken at its foundations, first by Louis Mink's contribution and then thanks to Hayden White: if only the texts written by historians are subjected to analysis, and these are part of the literature, special attention should be given to the literary figures constructing the narrative rather than to artificially imputed laws or models. Once narrativism had reduced the ranks of the Anglo-Saxon philosophy of history, bringing it closer to the continental current (not without the help of Neopragmatism), the analytic philosophy of history became no less antiquated than the substantive philosophy of history. For this reason, the notion of the 'philosophy of historiography' proposed by Aviezer

Tucker seems to be the most adequate and neutral.[13] From this perspective, we can talk about both the continental philosophy of historiography (e.g. Ricoeur) and the analytic philosophy of history (e.g. Daniel Little). Hence the vocabulary used in this book can be depicted as follows:

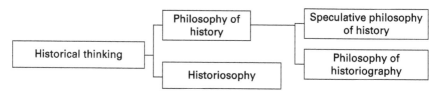

Figure 1 Terminology employed in the book.

Historical thinking implicitly expressed in works of art, literature and historiography will be called 'historiosophy'; philosophical – that is, *explicitly* philosophical – forms of historical thinking will be named 'philosophy of history', regardless of whether it is speculative philosophy of history, directly reflecting upon the past, or philosophy of historiography, analysing representations of the past. The latter differs from the theory of history just as philosophy does from historiography: it is not a part of science.

The problems of the philosophy of history

The attempt to use the term 'philosophy of history' in the most general and neutral manner, so as to also cover Chinese philosophical expressions of historical thinking, cannot be fixated on terminological issues and should make a step from purely formal accounts to descriptions of content. The easiest way to perform this task without any prior and privileged definition of the philosophy of history (which usually condemns some concepts as scientific but not philosophical, or theological but not philosophical, whereas they are always neither scientific nor religious), is to prepare a list of questions to which views generally recognized as the philosophy of history correspond as answers. Having such a list, the discovery of new or unrecognized philosophies of history will be manageable.

The fundamental question of the philosophy of history is: in what way does history have meaning? ('Meaning' here is used to denote both the 'meaning of the word' and the 'meaning of life', as in the German *Sinn*.) This question does not preordain whether it is history as a process or history as a story that makes sense; and thus neither does it assume that this sense or meaning could only be conceptualized as some 'logic'. Danto distinguished, respectively, the 'meaning *of* history' and 'meaning *in* history'.[14] The belief that history does have meaning is thus accepted. Actually, it is also accepted by historians, although their task is not to explain this postulate, but rather to build on it by means of constructing 'meaningful' narratives.

According to Marek Wichrowski,[15] six basic questions, which are derived from the basic question about the meaning of history, can be distinguished (in this case, mainly in the field of the speculative philosophy of history):

1. Can history (as *res gestae*) be the subject of knowledge?
2. If yes, is there any specific scheme of historical change?
3. If yes, is this scheme knowable?
4. If yes, is the direction of historical change reversible?
5. Can this scheme be objectively evaluated?
6. If yes, does the direction of historical change coincide with an increase in the desired values?

Different answers to these questions result in differing views of history. A positive answer to the fourth question implies a cyclical model of history, while a negative answer suggests a linear model. A positive answer to the sixth question creates a model of progress, while a negative one constructs a model of decline. But then we get only three paradigms of history: one cyclical and two linear. It is possible, however, to synthesize the model of the cycle and the line within a specific 'spiral' model, such as that represented by, for example, Vico in the West, Ibn Khaldun in the Near East, and many Chinese philosophers of history (as we shall see) in the Far East. As Koselleck argues, the opposition linear/circular is ideologically burdened, because each historical sequence contains both linear and recursive elements.[16] Apart from monolinear views of history there are also multilinear conceptions. The second point should have already led to the question of whether the scheme of historical change is the only one. In this sense, the multiplicity of schemes would also include multi-cyclical visions of history, etc. The omission of that possibility by Wichrowski shows that philosophers are still deeply influenced by the monolinear idea of progress, and even particularly irreversible progress, as though a positive answer to the fourth question would be a prerequisite for the cyclical vision of history, as if any linear change was irreversible (e.g. Max Weber speaks of the possibility of re-enchantment of the world).[17] This makes us aware that these basic questions should be understood as a compass (or a torch) showing the entire range of problems covered by the philosophers of history, rather than a 'yes/no' questionnaire, a yardstick for what is already given.

All these questions combined (and adequately problematized) imply the core qualities of the philosophy of history, which will guide us in the extraction, exploration and explication of the premodern Chinese philosophy of history. All philosophies of history investigate the problem of the meaning (sense) of history, when history is understood either as the meaningful past, as in the case of the speculative philosophy of history, or as meaningful knowledge (narrative) of the past, as with the philosophy of historiography. Philosophies of history also address the problem of the source of the meaning of history, namely what specific being, principle or factor makes history meaningful. Importantly, such a source usually functions as a general point of orientation that distinguishes irrelevant historical events from those that are imbued with a universal meaning. Typically, philosophies of history examine the structure of this meaning, that is, the structure of historical process or the elements of historical knowledge, providing, of course, that the knowability of history or its scheme is not denied by them, which in itself constitutes a philosophical standpoint that offers a negative answer to one of the first three questions proposed by Wichrowski. As for the detailed presentation of the structure of historical process, philosophies of history can assume that history unfolds in a linear or cyclical manner, or both, or neither. This process may be reversible or irreversible, mono- or multilinear (-cyclical). Furthermore, with regard to the evaluation of the direction of historical process (providing that such evaluation is not rejected), meaningful historical events can follow on from one another regressively or progressively, or by combining these two ways, or in some other distinctive way. This shifts emphasis to the meaning of the beginning of history, or the end of history, including the possible idea of the goal of history, or any other limitrophe moment of historical process. In the philosophy of historiography, analogous questions are asked regarding the structure of making historical sense, the priority and sequence of respective procedures of sense-making, the causes and purposes of historical writing and their influence upon the structure of historical narrative. It should be noted, however, that these are only the most general problems that are to be assigned to the philosophy of history. Such specific issues as, for instance, the way of combining linear and cyclical approaches or the postulate of necessity or the mere possibility of the end of history will not be touched upon here. All such standpoints belong to the domain of the philosophy of history, but they are not necessary to define it. And, yet again, we should be constantly open to enlarging the list of possible answers. It cannot be presumed that the examined material will not teach us anything new, especially in terms of Chinese thought.

Holism in the philosophy of history

One of the standpoints often developed or criticized by philosophers of history is generally known as holism in the philosophy of history (hereafter: HPH). Unfortunately, it is much more often adopted than explained. Since this term will be applied to the proposed *interpretation* of Chinese philosophy of history, I shall endeavour to explicate its different meanings. It has to be emphasized, however, that respective views of history do not have to evince themselves as holistic in order to be considered philosophies of history. HPH is rather one among many possible views of understanding history, and as such it needs to be clarified.

The term 'holism' was coined by a South African philosopher, Jan Christian Smuts (1870–1950), who based it on the idea of a 'unity of parts which is so close and intense as to be more than the sum of its parts (...) [so] the whole and the part therefore reciprocally influence and determine each other'.[18] Accordingly, holism in the philosophy of history would be 'a (w)holistic approach to history'. However, depending on what is meant by 'whole' and 'part', different variants of HPH could be distinguished. Because they can overlap, some views might be deemed more holistic than others. They could be enumerated as follows:

1. *HPH regarding space*: A philosophical interpretation of the history of as many states or world civilizations as possible. In this way, philosophers try to go beyond the environs of their location, creating a philosophy of world history. Holism of this kind was represented by Hegel in his *Lectures on the Philosophy of World History*, and even more by Arnold Toynbee, who considered the history of

twenty-one civilizations, including many that have collapsed. Hegel's HPH-1, which assumes one universal human civilization, may be called 'universalist', while Toynbee's HPH-1, which recognizes many civilizations, may be called 'pluralist'.

2. *HPH regarding time*: A philosophical interpretation of the totality of historical time: the past, the present and – crucially – the future. In this way, philosophers try to show that the rules they apply to historical process are 'inscribed in' the nature of the world in general, not only in the domain of what is past, thus they must also apply to the future (and in this context, Danto's thesis that speculative philosophy of history entails a prophecy, is right). This view was explicitly held by the previously mentioned Cieszkowski.[19]

3. *HPH regarding causality*: A philosophical interpretation of history that gives priority to the totality of historical social relations over their parts. Philosophers of history thereby claim that a community, not individuals, is endowed with historical causality. This meaning of HPH is often used in the analytic philosophy of history.[20] Also, as Popper pointed out, 'the well-known theory of the existence of a group-spirit, as the carrier of the group traditions, although not necessarily itself a part of the historicist argument, is closely related to the holistic view'.[21]

4. *HPH regarding substance*: A philosophical interpretation of history that does not search for the essence of history only in one ontological category and the factors belonging to it. Philosophers try, in this way, to move beyond the antinomy between historical idealism and materialism. This can be done in at least two ways: by creating some sort of monism with a single substance of history, or by considering both ideal and material factors as equal, under an 'organic, holistic vision of man and of history', as in the case of the contemporary Indian philosopher of history, T.M.P. Mahadevan.[22]

5. *HPH regarding reason*: A philosophical interpretation of history that transcends the division into theoretical and practical historical reason, which holds that the presented view of history is not merely a theory formulated on the descriptive level, but also a set of rules of a normative nature. This view is similar to the position of the Young Hegelians (including Karl Marx), who called for the transition to a 'theoretical practice' of history.

6. *HPH regarding meaning*: A philosophical interpretation of historical writing that gives priority to the meaning of a whole narration over its parts, i.e. sentences. This understanding of holism is close to Willard V.O. Quine's holism and, according to Jouni-Matti Kuukkanen, is typical for narrativism, especially that of Frank Ankersmit.[23] In this approach, holistic representations of (aspects of) the past cannot be decomposed without the past losing its meaning.

Three or more dimensions of holism can be combined in the thought of some philosophers; to take this to an extreme, all of these dimensions could be merged together. This, of course, never means a mechanical combination of the above-discussed types of holism, but rather their creative, and thus qualitatively new, combination. Therefore, even if the proposed method is to apply the above-described notions: from philosophy of history in general to holism in the philosophy of history in particular, all these ideas will be modified in the light of the examined sources. In principle, I shall uphold that the analysed Chinese categories are, at least to some extent, translatable and comparable with Western ideas, although many of them do not have any direct Western counterparts. Due to this fact, classical Chinese philosophy of history should be introduced to the whole community of philosophers.

Following the Past

The Philosophy of History in Ancient Confucianism

Introduction

This chapter discusses the Confucian philosophy of history in pre-imperial China. The decision to devote a separate chapter to ancient Confucianism results from the fact that the vast majority of Chinese philosophies of history in the imperial era share Confucian premises, either in a 'Neo-Confucian' or a 'Post-Confucian' way. Our study of the classical Confucian philosophy of history starts with the views on history implicitly expressed in the literary and historical masterpieces of early Chinese culture, namely bronze inscriptions, the *Book of Songs* and the *Book of Documents*. This is followed by an analysis of philosophical ideas about history propounded in the Spring and Autumn Period and the Warring States Period, in such works as *the Analects*, the *Book of Rituals* and some of the so-called Guodian texts. Finally, the chapter examines mature and systematic philosophies of history created by Mencius and Xunzi, whose thought culminates in the development of pre-imperial Confucianism.

The historiosophy of the sources of Confucianism

Looking for the sources of the Confucian philosophy of history, we should go back to the historiosophy of the bronze inscriptions, the *Book of Songs* and the *Book of Documents*. I prefer to use the term 'historiosophy' here, because the subject of the analysis proposed in this part of the chapter are religious, artistic, literary and historiographical visions of history. Since they are enunciated implicitly, they need to be explicated. The way their historiosophy connects with the philosophy of history in mature Confucianism will become fully visible after the discussion of the latter. It should be emphasized that those works, common to Chinese culture in its entirety, have in no way been 'appropriated' by any particular philosophical school. However, the case of Confucianism is somewhat unique. The school known in the West as 'Confucianism' was originally named the 'school of scholars' 儒家 *rújiā*. Some researchers even prefer the term 'Ruism'. Those scholars, also known as 'literati', were experts in, as well as the most likely authors of, both the *Book of Songs* and the *Book of Documents*. As a social group devoted not only to education, but also to the performance of rituals, they could have originated from the layer of shamans and dance masters, as has been suggested by, among others, Robert Eno and Yan Buke.[1] Without addressing these investigations in any more depth, it suffices to notice that the inscriptions on the bronzes might also be genetically associated with (later) Confucianism, and to provide a partial explanation of the lifespan of their historiosophy.

Historiosophy in the Shang and Western Zhou dynasties

Tradition holds that the first dynasty ruling China was the Xia dynasty, which is said to have reigned between 2070 and 1600 BC. However, the lack of any references to this dynasty in the oldest inscriptions on oracle bones, or even to its conquest by the later Shang dynasty (1600–1046 BC), makes it semi-legendary. These inscriptions are the oldest relics of literature in China and East Asia in general. The main and most troublesome character appearing in these inscriptions is Di 帝 *dì*, later known under the expanded name, 'The Lord on High', 上帝 *Shàngdì*. Di wields rain, wind and thunder. During the settling or (quite frequent) change of the capital, divinations of the will of Di were prepared. Interestingly, in contrast to the ancestral spirits, Di did not have a temple, nor were sacrifices made in his honour. Michael Puett states that Di was not part of the pantheon, but something in the nature of a powerful god that could not be controlled by ritual.[2] However, there are also phrases stating that Di approved of the king or that 'Di will bring an end to this city'.[3] Why did Di not approve of their king? And how did the writer know that that city would be brought to an end? In this regard, the terse inscriptions on the bones are silent. It is even unknown what underlies the character *dì*, whether it is the image of a god, another name of a Shang ancestor also known as Ku (or Kui), the personification of a celestial pole or a collective name for all the spirits of the ancestors.[4] Hence, it is not possible to decide whether Di actively intervened in human history, as is suggested by one of the above quotations. The phrase referring to Di bringing an end to a city could well be a ritual formula, nothing but a concluding omen.[5]

The change of (or rather the birth of) historical thinking was caused by history itself. As a result of the Battle of Muye in 1046 BC, the Shang dynasty was defeated and overthrown by Wu Wang, the Valorous King, who established the Zhou dynasty. The Zhou needed to justify laying violent hands on the previous authorities, to legitimize its reign and thereby discourage potential followers from fomenting rebellion against the Zhou. For this purpose, they used a specific interpretation of history.

This was done in two ways. As Sarah Allan claims, the Shang themselves believed in the existence of people who were opposed to them, characterized as being 'dark' and living 'underwater', and who had allegedly been beaten by the ancestors of the Shang.[6] According to Allan, the Zhou's deployment of this myth called the Xia dynasty into existence, which was said to have been overthrown, just like the Shang: 'by thus transforming a Shang myth of an earlier people who were their opposite into "history," a repeating cycle of three dynasties was established.'[7] In this way, two fundamental steps were taken. First, the present, the nearer and the further past (the Xia Dynasty) were combined into a single, continuous scheme, later known as 'history'. Second, it was implicitly recognized that the sense of history lies in the repeatability of its constituent sub-structures, namely the dynasties. Before this conviction was explicated in philosophy, it was incorporated into historiographical practice: henceforth the Xia dynasty, about which all oracle bones are silent, will be represented with the same degree of precision and according to the same rules as the Shang and Zhou dynasties.

Another way to legitimize power was not to explain 'how', but 'why' this historic event had happened. The Zhou answer was that a being called 天 *Tiān* (usually translated as 'Heaven') withdrew its previous decree 命 *ming*, which had allowed the Shang to reign, and transferred it to the Zhou. Thus was born the famous concept of the Mandate of Heaven 天命 *Tiānming*, which will be a recurring element in this book.

Prior to delineating the conceptions which developed the idea of the Mandate of Heaven, two issues should be considered. First, did this idea introduce an important novelty in relation to Shang culture? Second, did the inscriptions on the ancient bronze vessels that are the main source of knowledge of the Western Zhou Dynasty (1045–771 BC) already present a theory of the Mandate of Heaven? With regard to the first issue, opinions are divided, and the truth probably lies somewhere in between: some elements of Shang culture have been preserved, others have changed. In the first instance, the language was changed: Tian took up Di's duties. The nature of this 'replacement' remains a matter of conjecture, however. Robert Eno is of the opinion that whereas the Shang king was only a priest of Di, the King of Zhou identified himself with Tian, considering himself a contractor of Tian's judgements on Earth.[8] The Zhou rulers are thus held to have believed that the legitimacy of their power came directly from Tian, while the legitimacy of the Shang power sprung from divination, assigned to Di.[9] If this is true, it perhaps leads to the main difference between these two approaches. The Shang settled for sacrifices offered to the ancestors and auguries through which they sought the knowledge accessible to Di. The Zhou rulers, in turn, would have assumed that there was also a reciprocal 'top-bottom' movement: Tian has regard for the virtue of rulers, actively giving them support, so that the principles of ancestors should be emulated in the life of every ruler.[10] In a sense, it would have been a move that combined metaphysical, ritual and normative factors.

The continuity of both cultures is attested to by the fact that Di did not completely disappear from the inscriptions on the bronzes, and even from the *Book of Documents* or the later *Book of Rites*. On the *Hou Xing gui* inscription, the phrase 'Di will not bring an end to the mandate of Zhou' appears.[11] This is also the only inscription that equips Di with such prerogatives. Perhaps Di and Tian coexisted with one another for some time?[12] At any rate, the idea of the Mandate of Heaven was new.

This leads to the question of whether the concept of the Mandate of Heaven had already been expressed in the inscriptions on the bronze relics. The *zun* bronze from the times of the Western Zhou reads:

> And so king Wen received this great mandate. It was after king Wu had conquered the great city Shang, then [he] respectfully reported to Heaven, saying: 'I shall inhabit this central state [and] from it govern the people'.[13]

Strictly speaking, the 'great mandate' is not the same as the Mandate of Heaven. Mercedes Valmisa observes that the phrase *Tiānming* is not present on any of the

Western Zhou bronzes. There are, instead, such phrases as 'big order' 大令 *dàlìng*, 'great mandate' 大命 *dàmìng* or 'order of Heaven' 天令 *Tiānlìng*.[14] These phrases occur in a general context, and with one exception there are no mentions of any practical or discernible signs indicating that there is an actual order of Heaven. In other words, it is not known what orders stem from the original act of the mandate. This 'great mandate' might simply mean a general right to rule, while subsequent orders are rendered by the king. In this sense, its primary function would be a legitimization of Zhou power, not a metaphysical interpretation of history. There are also no mentions of the Xia on the bronzes from the Western Zhou, which shows that the idea of dynastic cycles might be a later invention.[15] If this is so, the discovery of the 'history' and associated vision of the Mandate of Heaven was not the work of the Western, but of the Eastern Zhou (770–476 BC). This could be confirmed by the fact that the phrase *Tianming* appeared directly several times, without the above-listed equivalents, on the *Qin gong gui* and *Qin gong zhong* inscriptions of the seventh century BC,[16] namely from the time when the oldest parts of the *Book of Documents* were formed, which definitely represent a fully developed conception of the Mandate of Heaven.

On the other hand, this shows that these ideas had been introduced before, albeit gradually and continuously. The *Mao Gong ding* inscription reads as follows:

> Greatly illustrious were Wen and Wu. August Heaven was greatly content with their charismatic power (德 *dé*). They were worthy of our blessed Zhou, and so they received the great appointment.[17]

Even if it is unclear what the 'great appointment' was, it is certain that it comes from Tian: the creation of the term *Tianming*, especially in the face of the existence of similar *Tianling*, did not have to constitute a revolution. Also present at this stage was the belief that human virtue (charismatic power) affects Tian, which in turn gives the ruler warrant to rule, and in this context leads to significant change in history. For instance, the inscription *Da Yu ding* states that the reason Tian withdrew its appointment of the Shang was their drunkenness.[18]

If, therefore, the idea of the Mandate of Heaven existed even then in embryonic form, how did it differ substantially from later developments? Valmisa makes an important observation, noting that only the founders of the Zhou dynasty, the kings Wen and Wu, are the recipients of the Mandate. Later rulers are in the position of making ordinary, continuous efforts to maintain power. Hence, the inscriptions suggested following the path of the 'former kings' 先王 *xiānwáng*.[19] Those commands express not just pragmatic hope for the efficiency of the well-trodden paths of the former kings, but also appeal to 'a meaningful relationship between past and present by which the present achieves recognition, power and legitimacy'.[20] The situation changed when the Zhou stopped ruling over China in real terms: when other rulers, such as the ruler of the Qin, started to claim that they had been appointed by Tian, the Mandate of Heaven ceased to be a general validation of the power of the Zhou, and became the collective name for a series of individual commands by particular rulers. As a result of assigning the Mandate of Heaven to the rulers of respective Chinese states, the commands of Tian became, as Eno remarks, as changeable as the weather.[21] The unpredictability and irrationality of Heaven's interventions in the history of Chinese states created a fear that found magnificent expression in the first masterpiece of Chinese culture, the *Book of Songs*.

Historiosophy in the *Book of Songs*

The *Book of Songs* 詩經 *Shījīng*, or rather simply *The Songs* 詩 *Shī*, is an anthology of 305 Chinese poems written between 1000 and 600 BC.[22] As Michael Nylan points out, the *Book of Songs*, along with other Classics, is Confucian only in the sense that tradition attributed to Confucius a compilation of the Classics, which were a major point of reference in the teachings of his followers.[23] Therefore, it has to be stressed once again that the *Book of Songs* and the *Book of Documents* are here called 'Confucian' first and foremost in the logical sense, as containing the seeds of the later, mature Confucian conceptions.

It should also be clarified in what sense the songs transmit any historiosophy. Basically, some historiosophical ideas were expressed directly in the odes, and especially in the hymns – official songs from within the circle of the court. Others were expressed indirectly, as evidenced, for example, by descriptions of the talks from the *Zuo Commentary*, where each side responds to the others using quotations from the *Book of Songs*. Similar interpretations, though open, were made in the commentaries that sought a political allegory even in the amorous poems. Confucius says in the *Analects* that the recitation of three hundred songs from memory without knowledge of their political message is useless.[24] Also the *Great Preface* 大序 *Dàxù* to the *Book of Songs* by Wei Hong (first century CE) reads as follows:

> By means of *feng*, rulers transformed their subjects, and subjects rebuked rulers using *feng* (...) When the Kingly Way collapsed, morality and justice were discarded; when there were no government instructions, each state began to have its own rule, and families – to differ in customs, then changes in *feng* and *ya* were made. State historians clearly grasping guides for the success and defeat, grieving over the changes in the relationships and mourning the severity of the penalties and orders, expressed their feelings in the odes to rebuke their rulers. Realizing the changeability of the circumstances, they were still attached to the old customs.[25]

Of course, the concept of the fall of the Kingly Way is of later origin, not to mention the breakup of the Zhou monarchy into lesser states, which had not been witnessed by many authors of *The Songs*. It is intriguing, though, that Wei Hong attributed the authorship of the songs to state historians 國史 *guóshǐ*, and not poets. The ideas of which they were aware when composing the *Songs* included the concept of success and defeat 得失 *dé-shī*. This shows that elements of historiosophy can also be traced in the *Book of Songs*, especially since these historians were said to be reflecting upon the variability of events 事變 *shì biàn*.

The theme of the collapse of the Zhou frequently appears in the pages of the *Book of Songs*. It is not perceived as a result of historical necessity, but it does create disappointment with history: 'how magnificent was formerly our great house,/ but now at every meal there is nothing left./ alas! it cannot be continued [as it began].'[26] Yet, the course of history itself is not the subject of reproaches: 'not because of the wind that blows,/ not because of the hurtling cart,/ but looking back at the way of Zhou/ I feel pain deep in my heart.'[27] It might be said that the authors of the *Book of Songs* accept the historicity as a factuality, the 'winds of history', but not its moral overtone and consequences. This caused an idealization of the past, in particular the founder of the dynasty, Zhou Wenwang (c. 1112–1050 BC), who was to embody all the great features of the previous order.

The main philosophical contribution of the book was, however, the development of the concept of Heaven. Some part of the reflection had a metaphysical nature, regarding Tian as the source of bounties that people receive: 'Heaven guards and protects you,/ and its care is constant;/ it makes you generous,/ every blessing comes from it.'[28] Those blessings are independent of human will, like the good harvest mentioned later in the same ode.

In the context of the clearly declared role and position of Heaven, many places in the *Book of Songs* that condemn Tian are almost blasphemous. 'Merciless great Heaven' is helpless in the face of growing chaos, punishing people without any guilt.[29] Tian is hardly propitious to the people – it is Heaven that sends down death and disruption[30]:

> Great and wide Heaven,
> How is it you have contracted your kindness,
> Sending down death and famine,
> Destroying all through the kingdom?
> Compassionate Heaven, arrayed in terrors,
> How is it you exercise no forethought, no care?
> Let alone the criminals:
> They have suffered for their offences;
> But those who have no crime,
> Are indiscriminately involved in ruin.[31]

The fact that Heaven sends down hunger or death should not arouse indignation on the basis of metaphysical assumptions. If Tian is behind things that are beyond human control, such as the fate of the crops, it is also responsible for natural disasters. 'Divine wrath' stems from the irrationality of Heaven's will, which is either unjustified ('no forethought'), or simply unjust (punishing the innocent). If so virtuous a family as the Zhou fell and their state declined, there is no reason to accept the impact of Heaven on history with optimism. This criticism may reveal a certain 'secularization' of the religious image of the mysterious Tian, which had formerly been worshipped regardless of what happened to the people.[32] The *Book of Songs* therefore formulates the problem of fatalism with which the *Book of Documents* will struggle: if Heaven does not take account of virtue, human actions have no effect on history – the innocent share the same fate as the felons.

Historiosophy in the *Book of Documents*

The *Ancient Documents* 尚書 *Shàngshū*, also known as the *Book of Documents* 書經 *Shūjīng*, is the most important monument of early Chinese literature.[33] Sometimes called the *Book of History*, according to tradition it was a historical book, like the *Spring and Autumn Annals*. But while the *Annals* were only a record of deeds, the *Documents* compiled speeches. This scheme might be considered well-grounded only in respect of the *Annals*. This is so because in addition to the speeches, the *Shangshu* contains many historical narratives and philosophical passages that were included in the speeches. The latter were, of course, far from faithful records of actual speeches from thousands of years before. Hence, they form an important source of the historiosophy contained therein.

The historiosophy of the *Shangshu* is centred on the idea of Tian. On the one hand, Heaven gives some people such a nature that without any ruler they fall into chaos, while prominent people are given the ability to govern them.[34] On the other hand, 'Heaven hears and sees as our people hear and see.'[35] This means that the order guaranteed by Heaven is aimed at the preservation of the people: Tian 'invisibly secures the people, making them harmonious with their position'.[36] The personification of Heaven has its limits though – Tian is unerring in its decisions, and does not manifest any bias.[37] The will of Heaven is thus ultimately an unknowable object of fear.[38] But if so, does not Tian absorb some of the properties of Di?

In fact, the term 'Shangdi' appears in the *Book of Documents* thirty-two times. Shangdi is often used interchangeably with Tian, and it transpires that Di decided to destroy the Shang dynasty – the same dynasty that formerly worshipped him.[39] Elsewhere, the text reads that it was the 'divine' Di who felt compassionately about innocent people threatened with death.[40] Taking into account the occurrence of the phrase 'Supreme Spirit of Heaven' 上天神 *Shang Tiānshén* in the *Tanggao* chapter,[41] it might reasonably be asked whether there is here a trace of the concept of a personal, intangible god. In his work on historical thought in the *Shangshu*, Wang Can shows that although Tian is the highest spirit, it is neither the creator of the world nor of man, and it does not transcend the world, contrasting this vision with the historical dualism of the Old Testament.[42] This opinion is in line with most of the text of *Shangshu*.

However, a definitive answer to the question of Tian's status in the *Shangshu* is impossible to arrive at, as long as Heaven is an object of direct discourse only in relation to mankind – Heaven in and of itself does not arouse such interest as its presence in human history does, the most explicit expression of which was the granted or withdrawn 'mandate', *ming*. Withdrawal of the legitimation of the power offered to one dynasty and its transfer to another is openly extended to the period preceding the reign of the Zhou. The *Speech of Tang* records that Heaven had instructed the founder of the Shang to bring an end to the Xia because of its faults.[43] And not only did it instruct him, but it also sent down calamities on the Xia to expose their sins.[44] Also, with regard to the Shang, this sequence is repeated:

> Relentless Heaven sent down ruin on the Yin [i.e. the Shang]. As soon as the Yin has lost its appointment, our House of Zhou has received it. I do not dare, however, to say, as if I knew it, that founded [dynasty] will ever last in prosperity.[45]

This passage reveals some important features of the *Tianming* idea. First, the Mandate has an exclusive character – at any one time there can only be one dynasty.

Secondly, the mandate cannot remain unassigned – someone always has to have it, and as soon as one clan loses it, another clan immediately receives it. Thirdly, the mandate is temporary; no dynasty can rule endlessly. Thus, if anything is infinite, it is this variability. In this way, the *Shangshu* lays the foundations for a concept of historical cycles, although the notion of the cycle does not explicitly appear here, and the terms for dynasties – proper names – are not theoretically generalized. On the other hand, the above conditions are strict and define some kind of structure. Hence, it is claimed that although the mandate changes, its principle is constant.[46] It might be said that the Mandate is variable in its content, but not its form. This variation stems from the situation to which it is applied: the mandate references a concrete time and is specific;[47] this time (in the sense of the Greek καιρός) is called 'heavenly time' 天時 *Tiānshí*.[48] The process of changing the Mandate has an implicit structure, too. The chapter *Commander of the Western expedition to Li (Xibo Kanli)* presents the following sequence:

1. A ruler committed too many crimes and his bad deeds were 'registered above';[49]
2. Heaven decides to bring an end to the dynasty;
3. Heaven locks the stores and sends famine;
4. There is chaos among the people, who want the dynasty to fall.[50]

Another element not listed there, which ultimately leads to the fall of the dynasty, is the executors of Heaven's will, also known as 'the shepherds of Heaven' 天牧 *Tiānmù*.[51] Such persons are somehow exempt from moral responsibility, as they mete out the punishment prescribed by Heaven.[52] Heaven sends its punishments 'as if using a hand' of the one putting an end to the ruling dynasty.[53] If for a long time there was no viable man, Heaven waited until the right person came into sight.[54] But how that person knows they are the one remains a mystery. If Heaven says nothing, the lack of revelation implies the absence of the category of vocation. It is instead replaced by a recognition: Tian appoints the ruler who recognized the Mandate was withdrawn due to the misery of the people. The legitimization of power itself is moral, not political. 'Virtue moves Tian and there is no distance, which it would not reach',[55] thus 'august Heaven is not biased and helps only the virtuous'.[56] The character translated here as bias, 親 *qīn*, literally means 'relative' and 'affinity', so it might be said that Tian has 'no relatives'. It seems that in the *Shangshu*, moral principles stand over blood relations: if a new state whose rulers are more moral should hove into view, Heaven will abandon the existing rulers. Wang Can, for instance, contrasts this universalism with the Jewish idea of the chosen people.[57] The concept of the direct reason for the withdrawal of the Mandate of Heaven being the ruler's lack of virtues has other important implications. If the conduct of the king affects the granting (or withdrawal) of *Tianming*, it transpires that the accusation of historical determinism that appeared implicitly in the *Book of Songs* is baseless. 'Punishments sent by Heaven can be avoided, but those caused by thyself cannot', reads *Tai Jia zhong*.[58] The people themselves determine their own destiny (*ming*), so if it was entirely dependent on the determinations of Heaven, no government would survive for long.[59]

This also has a didactic dimension. If the Shang repeated what happened to the Xia, in order to avoid their fates, a lesson should be learned from what happened to both of them. 'If we are not to follow antiquity today, we will not even know that Heaven's Mandate has ended.'[60] Antiquity should be examined before taking office.[61] The specific term coined in the *Shangshu* for the study of antiquity, 稽古 *jīgǔ*, means – as David Schaberg believes – 'the citation of historical precedents and language in the construction of deliberative and philosophical arguments'.[62] It should be noted, however, that this had little to do with any scientific research on history. On the contrary, it was a strictly normative act, which was aimed at finding patterns in antiquity that would confirm the historiosophical scheme, and therefore was considered to be followed by successive generations of rulers. The first four chapters of the *Shangshu*, including two 'canons', begin with the same formula: 曰若稽古 *yuē ruò jīgǔ* 'studying antiquity [we see that]', after which the names of the legendary rulers are listed and attributed with such qualities as wisdom, self-control, etc. The most important part of the narrative of the emperors Yao and Shun is the moment when Yao, having abdicated, refused to hand power over to his own son and instead transferred it to the virtuous Shun. As Allan convincingly proves, this narration has its own structure, repeated in the histories of Shun and Yu, Jie and Tang, Zhou and Wu Wang, which differs from the dynastic model of hereditary transfer, serving as an argument for government by virtue.[63]

Interestingly, the former kings were not attributed with any superhuman capabilities. Their only distinguishing feature was their unusual virtue, as opposed to the parallel ideals of the Hebrew prophets who had superhuman knowledge and the Greek heroes who possessed superhuman strength or skills.[64] This does not change the fact that eminent individuals were assigned a role in determining the course of history. 'The collapse of the state depends on one man, the glory and peace of the country are also the result of the nobility of one man', reads the last sentence of the *Book of Documents*.[65] Outstanding individuals are contrasted with the homogeneous people 民 *mín*. It is the people who show that Tian withdrew the Mandate, so the ruler has to cherish the people and keep them safe. When this is done, the people respect and praise the ruler, acting in accordance with the hierarchy established by Tian. This vision may have its roots in an older concept, dating back to the Shang era or even earlier, to be found in the opening 'Canon of Yao'. This states that people, birds and wild animals behave in accordance with a given season. For example, 'in summer people are distracted, birds and wild animals mate'. As has been convincingly shown by Martin Kern, this is the image of the 'primordial order – the order of human and animal life before history'.[66]

To fully confirm this interpretation, it has to be argued whether, strictly speaking, the *Book of Documents* has the notion of 'history'. Since the rules for granting and withdrawing the Mandate of Heaven are fixed and the same goes for three consecutive dynasties, and the power of the Zhou will also come to an end sometime, awareness of the continuity of political changes and their relation to the present was clear. This is confirmed by the following passage:

Examining the people of ancient times, there was [the founder of] the Xia dynasty. Heaven led him and protected his successors. He recognized Tian and obeyed him. But *over time*, the mandate favouring him has been withdrawn. That's why *we examine now* [the founder of] the Yin Dynasty. Heaven *similarly* led him and protected [his successors], and he recognized Tian and obeyed him, but *over time*, favouring mandate has been withdrawn. Here is our current king who ascended the throne in his youth, and although he lacks the age and experience [literally: wrinkles], it may be said that he *scrutinizes the virtue of the ancients*, and even that is able to examine their advice in the light of [the way] of Heaven.[67]

This twofold 'examining the people of ancient times' indicates that the topic is a description of history. The identical scheme ('similarly') of the dynastic history repeats itself 'over time'. Thus, this scheme becomes a subject of study, precisely because it is the ruler of the Zhou dynasty who wishes to perpetuate the rule of his predecessors, studying their virtuous conduct, for which Heaven has bestowed the Mandate upon them. The ontological, historical, moral and political dimensions are here all linked together. As Yi Ning and Wang Xianhua observe:

> The awareness of historical change as represented by the records in these sections of the *Shangshu* was limited to the change of royal power between the proceeding and the following but consecutive royal families (. . .) For the people of Zhou, the future is open to change and not predictable, and this was how the Zhou people related the future to the present when seeing the present in the light of the past. It is quite a holistic view of history.[68]

Interestingly, what Yi and Wang call 'a holistic view of history' perfectly fits our notions of HPH regarding time and substance, showing the ultimate implications of the way the *Book of Documents* addresses the problem of the meaning of history.

Nevertheless, the notion of 'history' does not appear here explicitly. For this reason, it is still better to refer to the 'historiosophy' of the *Book of Documents*, although it already stood at the threshold of mature philosophical reflection. The character 史 *shǐ*, which will later mean 'history', denotes in the *Shangshu* the office of a diviner who interprets the signs sent by Tian.[69] But even then, *shi* was closer to the office of 'historiosopher' than historian.

Conclusion

The earliest monuments of Chinese culture set great store on the meaning of the transition from one dynasty to another, searching for its pattern in a way that already contained the seeds of later, explicitly philosophical speculation on the meaning of history. It was implicitly assumed that the meaning of history lies in the repeatability of its constituent sub-structures, namely the dynasties. The source and warrant of this meaningfulness was seen as lying in a being known as *Tian* (Heaven), which took the place of god Di. Originally, it was believed that Heaven intervened in history by granting the power only to the founders of the Zhou dynasty. However, along with the faltering position of the Zhou, the rulers of other Chinese states also arrogated to themselves the support of the mysterious Tian. In this manner, a carefully constructed view soon came to be ridiculed and openly undermined, as testified by some of the blasphemous parts of the *Book of Songs*. As a result, the authors of the *Book of*

Documents strove to recover the rationality of historical change. They were sure that although Tian does not speak and acts in history only 'as if using the hand' of eminent (yet not supernatural) individuals, the rules for granting and withdrawing the Mandate of Heaven (*Tianming*) are fixed. The Mandate is exclusive, temporary and cannot remain unassigned, whereas the basis of Heaven's decisions lies in the moral standards of the rulers, expressed (or not) in their care for the people. Metaphysical, historical, moral and political factors are thereby synthesized: political care for the people is moral perfection, which has a historical effect, which is in turn guaranteed by a being called Heaven. In combination with the didactic expectations from history that require the present to be seen in the light of the past, all this resulted in the holistic view of history that inspired the Confucian philosophy of history until the eighteenth century.

The origins of the Confucian philosophy of history

Early Chinese historiosophy had a great impact on the first philosophical views of history that could be associated with Confucian tradition. Nonetheless, the incipient Confucian philosophy of history introduced an important innovation in understanding the meaning of history, as testified by the *Analects*, the *Book of Rituals*, and the excavated Guodian texts, which are the topic of this part of the chapter. This novelty consisted in the essentially ethical approach to the meaning of history. This ethical turn led Confucius to the discovery of the Dao of history, whereas the later utopianisms from the *Book of Rituals* and the excavated texts carefully traced the historical process of departure from this Dao and the original unity.

Ethics of history in the *Analects*

Analysis of the philosophical views of history in early Confucianism could not begin anywhere other than with the *Analects* 論語 *Lùnyŭ*. Generally speaking, the *Analects* are a collection of anecdotes and statements attributed to historical Master Kong 孔子 *Kŏngzĭ* (551–479 BC) and his disciples. Still, the *Lunyu* are neither the only nor perhaps the earliest source on the life and thought of Kongzi.[70] The authorship, authenticity and dating of the *Lunyu* are also the subject of debate among Sinologists.[71] However, for ease of reading and in accordance with academic practice, instead of phrases such as 'the authors of *the Analects* ascribe to Confucius the words..', I will instead write 'Confucius believes that..', and so forth.

Liu Fengchun identifies three main issues that frame what might be called the philosophy of history of the *Lunyu*: the concept of Tian and *ming*, the historical role of rituals 禮 *lĭ*, and Confucius' attitude towards specific historical figures.[72] Importantly, it is worth noting that the second problem did not appear in the previous historiosophy. The third issue, in turn, is grounded in the belief that is unrecognized by Liu Fengchun: Confucius' ethical approach to the past and the idea of the Dao of history.

Confucius is interested in history primarily for didactic reasons. For him, only one who takes a fresh look at antiquity to gain new knowledge can become a teacher.[73] Hence, Confucius believes that he does not create anything, but only transmits the ideals of antiquity, which he trusts and loves.[74] However, this declaration was all too often treated as an expression of simple conservatism, while in fact it reflects Confucius' selective attitude to the past, which he treats as a source of examples to illustrate his moral views. These moral rules also define 'the Way' 道 *Dào*, which was said to still be alive in the people's hearts.[75] As the *Lunyu* reads,

> The Master said, 'When it comes to people, I condemn some of them and praise the others. If I have praised someone, there are grounds for it. This is exactly because of such people that Dao has been continuously implemented throughout the Three Dynasties.'[76]

Confucius explicitly uses a general concept to denote the Xia, Shang and Zhou, emphasizing that only some people – those who should be held up as an example to follow – implemented Dao. The Dao, which is the proper Way of moral, ritual and social conduct, lies immanently in history, which means it has to be drawn forth from the totality of historical changes, and only then could it become the subject of teaching.

If a historical period that followed the Dao in the fullest way had to be singled out, for Confucius this would be the times of the Zhou, who had already learned from the history of the two previous dynasties. The second reason Confucius prefers the ideals of the recent past is epistemological. Confucius claimed he could not treat the rituals of the Xia and Shang as being equally credible to those of the Zhou, because in the states where the descendants of these dynasties still lived there was a lack of sufficient records.[77] He praises the historians who, in the absence of sources, left a hiatus (闕文 *quēwén*), which could be later filled by those who would find the information.[78] Confucius was therefore far from being a naive historical moralist. In these few passages that constitute an embryo of the Chinese philosophy of historiography, Confucius stresses the role of sources and the adjudication of their reliability – the foundation of all subsequent source criticism, from the Han to the Qing.

As part of 'refreshing' the Dao of history, Confucius openly approves selected historical figures. In particular, Confucius praised the first legendary rulers of China: Yao, Shun and Yu. According to the *Lunyu*, Yao and Shun refrained from transferring power to their sons and offered it to the person of the greatest virtue instead. Approval of that legendary act, described in the *Book of Documents*, expresses Confucius' support for governance based on virtue, and at the same time directly justifies the need to emulate the old, perfect rulers:

> Master said: How majestic! Shun and Yu possessed the entire world and yet had no need to actively manage it. How great was Yao as a ruler! So majestic! It is Heaven that is great, and it was Yao who modeled himself upon it. So vast! Among the common people there were none who were able to find words to describe him. How majestic in his accomplishments, and glorious in cultural splendor! Shun had five ministers and the world was well governed (. . .) Virtue flourished as never before after the reigns of Yao and Shun.[79]

Note that the fragment is not a normative statement: to convince his audience that there should be as few ministers as possible, Confucius says that the ideal ruler had five, which was enough for the whole world. In addition to these emperors, Confucius had extraordinary esteem for the regency of Zhou and his great ministers.[80] Dozens of other historical figures were the object of his praise or rebuke.[81] When there are no proper names, Confucius praises the virtue of 'ancient kings',[82] or even ancient people, as opposed to his contemporaries.[83] In this way, he also depicts the fall of historical values – the collapse of Dao.

However, if these historical figures are imitable because they followed Dao, it is not enough to just enlist them in order to understand Confucius' view of history – it has to be understood what Dao consists in and of. On the basis of the *Analects*, it seems that the historical presence of Dao is manifested not only in moral attitudes, but also in the rituals, which is an important novelty in relation to the historiosophy of the *Book of Documents*:

> Confucius said: When Dao prevails in the world, rituals, music, punitive expeditions, and attacks issue from the Son of Heaven. When Dao does not prevail in the world, these things issue from the feudal lords. When they issue from the feudal lords, within no more than ten generations the lords will lose the power.[84]

This passage is usually understood as a manifesto of political philosophy: the superiority of the Way of Kings above the Way of Hegemons. Attributing the fall of states to a change of rituals suggests the historical role, or even power, of the latter. It also means that ostentatious ritualism does not guarantee success: as an example, Confucius holds up the severity of ancient people in this regard.[85] Had it not been for the rituals common to the Three Dynasties, there would have been no continuity of Chinese history, and it is only thanks to them that we know why the Xia and Shang dynasties gained and lost their power. Finally, what will happen in future generations is knowable in the same way.[86]

The interpretation of Dao as a set of appropriate moral and ritual attitudes that are present in history lies between two interpretations proposed by scholars investigating this issue. In his recent book, Vincent S. Leung aptly observes that for Confucius 'the past is painted as a repertoire of cultural practices' and that there is no logic of replacing one practice by another. At the same time, he is silent on the issue of Dao, which in my opinion leads him to the conclusion that 'the *Analects* conceives of an open, much more expansive, historical field with a diverse repository of exemplary cultural practices', with no 'objective set of standards',[87] an image that ultimately results in relativism and is hardly reconcilable with the didactic function that Confucius ascribed to the examples from the past he had chosen. Herbert Fingarette, in turn, argues that for Confucius there is actually one *lǐ*, which remains in harmony with the cosmic Dao.[88] Understanding Dao as a cosmic being that is different from the conduct of rituals is, however, a misuse, and a foreign idea even to the Neo-Confucians.[89]

But is Confucius' philosophy of history actually free of metaphysics? To answer this question, his concept of *Tianming* has to be examined. What catches the eye when reading the *Lunyu* is the personal, subjective context in which Heaven appears. Tian is said to have used Confucius,[90] though he himself admits that he understood the commands of Heaven at the age of fifty.[91] As Confucius states, Heaven is the source of the virtue he finds in himself.[92] For this reason, he does not dare to blame it for his own mistakes.[93] On the contrary, it is Tian that might scorn him.[94] Hence, although Ivanhoe is right in seeing Heaven as endowing people with virtue,[95] at the same time people and people alone are responsible for developing this potential: Heaven does not intervene in history to support them nor to punish them. It is therefore stressed that Heaven does not say anything, but only manifests itself through the course of events.[96] Zi Gong concludes that one cannot hear the Master discussing the nature of Heaven.[97] But if the category of Heaven is understood in the *Lunyu* in this way, how should one grasp *ming*? If Tian is recognized in a manner so different from the above-discussed *Book of Documents*, could the phrase *Tianming* be translated as the 'Mandate of Heaven'?

One of the basic meanings of the character *ming* is, in addition to 'command' or 'permit', also 'destiny', and this latter meaning can be found in the *Analects*. 'Death and life: this is *ming*; riches and honours depend on the Tian', it says.[98] It is not known, however, whether death as such or its precise time is predestined. Similarly, the *Lunyu* states twice that one cannot blame the past 往 *wǎng*.[99] The question is whether it cannot be blamed because it has passed, or whether it cannot be blamed because something happened one way and not the other? Both questions arise from a dispute that dates back to the Mohists: was Confucius a fatalist? Confucius says, for example, that if Heaven wants to save the culture of Zhou, the people of Kuang could not prevent it.[100] Or simply:

> The Master said: If Dao is to be put into practice, this is because of *ming*. If Dao is to fall down, such is the *ming*. What power has Gongbo Liao to affect *ming*![101]

Reviewing several interpretations of Confucius' concept of *ming* in the light of the text of the *Analects*, Ning Chen argues that complete fatalism is alien to Confucius. The idea of *ming* rather demarcates what is dependent on, and independent of, human activity.[102] *Tianming* from the *Analects* should not be translated as the 'Mandate of Heaven'. There is no passage in the *Lunyu* that provides a cyclical narrative of the gain and loss of *Tianming*, like in the *Shangshu*. It might be said that if Tian is the source of morality, *ming* is its boundary, therefore what lies beyond it – namely metaphysics – is not of interest to Kongzi. As a result, the Dao of history in the *Analects* should be understood only as referring to the standards of conduct, and Confucius' philosophy of history as an approach to the issue of the meaning of history (and meaning in histories) from the perspective of ethics.

Utopias on the periphery of Confucianism

The Analects, along with the works of Mencius and Xunzi, which are analysed in the next section, have always been the starting point (and often the end point) of studies on ancient Confucian philosophy. The thought of the 'school of scholars' covers, however, many more perspectives, including the field of the philosophy of history, which due to archaeological discoveries are nowadays becoming a topic of heated discussion among historians of Chinese philosophy. These findings often blur the line between Confucian and non-Confucian thought, or rather constitute a broader background, if not a periphery of Ruism. A distinctive feature of some of these texts is utopianism, which is complementary to the belief in the collapse of the former order.

A good example of this approach to the meaning of history could be found in the *Book of Rituals* 禮記 *Lǐjì*, particularly in the chapter *On the Channelling of Rituals* 禮運 *Lǐyùn* and its vision of 'Great Unity' 大同 *dàtóng*. The following fragment of the celebrated description of *datong* (put into the mouth of Confucius) depicts the utopia and what happened thereafter:

> When Great Dao was practiced, everything under Heaven was common and public. Only the worthy and able men were promoted: their words were full of good faith, they cultivated the harmony [in their deeds]. Hence, they did not regard as parents only their own parents, nor as sons only their own sons (. . .) Thieves and rebels did not arise, so the outer gates of the houses were continually open. This age is called the Great Unity. Now Great Dao has become hid and the world has been divided into families. Each regards as parents only his own parents and as sons only his own sons (. . .) Rituals and righteousness came to life in order to regulate the relationship between ruler and subject, to ensure relation between father and son, peace between brothers and harmony between husband and wife (. . .) Emperor Yu, Kings Tang, Wen, Wu, Cheng, and the Duke of Zhou were chosen for this reason (. . .) If any ruler does not abide by these principles, but instead relies on his power, the people treat it as a danger. This age is called the Small Prosperity.[103]

The passage is quite surprising in the light of the views analysed so far: the situation in which the rituals and the social hierarchy is established is not the ideal nor primordial state. Great Unity preceding Small Prosperity 小康 *xiǎokāng* is not only a state of harmony and peace, but also of the absolute equality and commonality of all property. It is therefore not surprising that this view attracted the Communists, and most of all Kang Youwei – a social reformer and philosopher of history at the turn of the nineteenth century.[104] The idea that in the perfect state people love each other to the same extent, regardless of their blood relationship, was typical of the Mohists (see next chapter), who were the main rivals of the Confucians, and it is possible that they were the authors of this view. This would partially explain the unpopularity of the *Liyun*'s utopianism until the nineteenth century.

On the other hand, further sentences of the *Liyun* show that the transition to the era of the Small Prosperity was not in any way a disaster. On the contrary, due to the rituals, the former kings regulated human nature. The era of Great Unity is also a time when people did not have houses but lived in caves, dressed in animal skins and were not able to use fire. Thanks to outstanding later rulers they mastered fire, built houses and began to make offerings to the spirits and to Di.[105] The creation of rituals was therefore, for the authors of the *Liyun*, preceded by the rise of organized religion and collective life. The Great Unity is considered an irrevocably lost era. As Michael Ing rightly observes,

It is notable that throughout the 'Liyun' chapter Confucius makes no attempt to advocate a return to the era of Grand Unity; rather, he consistently seeks to understand and argue for the rituals of the Three Dynasties, which are part of the era of Modest Prosperity. Confucius, in short, realizes that humanity *will not*, and more importantly *should not*, return to a period of Grand Unity. Contrasting this with Mircea Eliade's notion of a 'nostalgia for paradise,' Confucius exhibits no 'desire to live in the world as it came... fresh, pure and strong.' While the era of Grand Unity is a development from the beginning of civilization where human beings lived in caves and nests, it is not simply a paradise. This is a central difference from texts usually labeled 'Daoist', which advocate a return to or an 'embracing' of simplicity.[106]

The perception of the era of Great Unity as strictly historical (past) means that the above passage should be interpreted from the perspective of the philosophy of history, not political philosophy. Clearly, *datong* may be called a utopia in only one sense: as an original state (the golden age), in which there was peace, equality and no evil. In European philosophy, the term 'utopia' meant both a (pre-)historical status, as well as the perfect political project that had yet to be put into practice. *Datong*, until the nineteenth century, was not a utopia in the latter sense. Hence, it is ultimately doubtful that this vision came from the Mohists – the core of the Confucian critique of the idea of universal love, proclaiming that the concept was unrealistic and impossible to apply, was maintained (although the *Liyun* might have been created by a wing of the school of scholars sympathizing with the Mohists). With regard to our criteria of constructing the meaning of history, the vision of the *Liyun* is that of an irreversible, linear fall. If there is an eclecticism in the *Liyun*, it is of a different kind.

Some parts of the *Liyun* are in fact heavily influenced by the Yin-Yang School. The *datong-xiaokang* philosophy of history is placed in a broader cosmogony, according to which the Great One 大一 *Dà Yī* was divided into Heaven and earth, which put in motion *yin* and *yang*. People originated from the combination of the power of Heaven and earth, the *yin* and *yang*, animal soul and spirit, and the five elements of matter.[107] Hence, the history of the world has gone through the stages presented in Figure 2.

Incorporating the history of mankind into the history of nature could be the result of the deformation which this text received during the Han Dynasty. On the other hand, the fundamental direction of historical change in this perspective – the gradual distancing from the unity and progressive differentiation of society – completely complied with the Confucian belief in the collapse of the principles of the Zhou. This view of history preceding the reign of former kings could also be found in other pre-Han sources.

These sources have become available to us thanks to the latest archaeological discoveries: the unearthed literary monuments of the state of Chu, written on silk and excavated in 1974 in Mawangdui (Hunan province). Above all, these treasures include the texts written on bamboo slips, which were discovered in Guodian (Hubei Province, near the former capital of the Chu) in 1994. The so-called Chu bamboo-slips are still being transcribed – some of them ended up in the collections of the Shanghai Museum and Qinghua University in Beijing as a result of illegal excavations. For our purposes, I

Stage name	Description
Great One 大一	The undifferentiated cosmos
creation of Heaven and earth	Isolation of the forces of yin and yang
creation of men	Combination of Heaven and earth, yin-yang, soul, spirit, and matter
Great Unity 大同	State of good, equality, peace and practice of Great Dao; people live in caves, do not use fire
Small Peace 小康	The reign of great rulers, creation of rituals, building of houses, use of fire, creation of religion
	Current times of practice of old-time rituals

Figure 2 The history of the cosmos and mankind according to the *Liyun* chapter of the *Book of Rituals*.

will focus on those texts from Guodian that are important from the perspective of the philosophy of history.

One of the texts, *The Way of Tang and Yu* 唐虞之道 *Táng-Yú zhī dào*, developed the legend of the abdication of the former kings, who refrained from transferring power to their sons in favour of giving it to the most virtuous. By virtue of these acts, they achieved sagacity in its fullness, which took the virtue of *ren* to its climax.[108] They served all the people, sacrificing their own profit – such was the past, since people had come into existence.[109] The text teaches, however, that humbly waiting for the mandate (*ming*) and practice of the virtue of *ren* is not enough, as one needs a proper 'big moment' 大時 *dàshí*, which cannot be controlled – one cannot make it happen.[110] This idea, expressing belief in the existence of the objective historical moment, which is beyond the control of even the greatest men, was brought up in another text from Guodian, *Failure and Success Appear at Their Respective Times* 窮達以時 *Qióng dá yǐshí*. The text states that if people are moral, but do not live to the proper time, they cannot do anything, whereas time itself is a sufficient condition.[111] The text presents the profiles of historical figures who appeared at the right moment, then says that the emergence of a favourable time depends on Heaven, which is the main difference between Heaven and man (Heaven sends the proper time, to which people are only subjected).[112]

The utopian portrayal of the reign of former rulers can be also found in the text *Rongchengshi* 容成氏 *Róngchéngshì*, which enumerates the names of the nine kings who would have ruled before Yao and Shun. Each of these rulers is said to have abdicated and handed power over to the most virtuous. In these times, people loved each other regardless of their social differences, there was peace, and the disabled were not cast aside.[113] As a whole, society was still harmonious and free from criminals even under Yao, there were still no epidemics or natural disasters under Shun; evil appeared in the times of Yu, but was eradicated by him, yet after a few generations, under the reign of Jie, it dominated the world and was only defeated thanks to Cheng Tang, the founder of the Shang Dynasty.[114] The last ruler of the Shang did not follow the Dao of the ancient kings and was replaced by the Zhou. In this way, the *Rongchengshi* integrates in its narrative both linear (first of abdication, then of inherited throne) and cyclic (the Xia, Shang, Zhou) schemes, starting from the utopia of the golden age. Pines takes the *Rongchengshi* to be the first Chinese text that embraces various eras in a historical narrative. In this respect it was pioneering in relation to Sima Qian, even in its proposition of a vision of a single, coherent history of the world.[115] Allan believes, in turn, that the text is a manifesto of political philosophy.[116] It seems that the truth lies in between: because of its size and vagueness, the *Rongchengshi* is not a chronicle, but neither is it an abstract political philosophy. Instead, it is an amalgam of the two, namely a form of historiosophy. Interestingly, the oldest history of mankind is still perceived there as a period of monarchy and only the achievements of individual people led to the development of culture. The utopianism of all the Guodian texts differs in this respect from the concept of the Great Unity. Furthermore, the vision of the *Liyun* is linear, while the *Rongchengshi* combines periodicity and linearity. Yet the core of both views, namely the idea of gradual distancing from the golden age of unity, is common, showing the importance of utopianism in the ancient Confucian view of history.

Conclusion

Early Confucian philosophy was characterized by a variety of views on history. Interestingly, none of these views advocated the idea of Heaven intervening in history. This was in a way compensated by introducing the concept of rituals (*li*) and their historical efficacy. It was not until the *Analects* that morality and rituals alone, embodied in the idea of 'Dao', became treated as a principle immanently governing history. This translated into the motif of drawing moral lessons from the past (specifically from the heroes of Confucian historical narratives), and generally – into a search for the meaning of history from the perspective of ethics (instead of metaphysics). Confucius' understanding of history was followed by such utopianisms as that from the *Rongchengshi* and, most importantly, the image of the 'Great Unity' (*datong*) from the *Book of Rituals*, which traced the dynamics of the historical change of moral principles themselves. These dynamics were conceptualized as a departure from the original era of peace and unity, purely linear in the case of *datong*, and both linear and cyclical in *Rongchengshi*.

The philosophies of history of Mencius and Xunzi

With the figures of Mencius (孟子 *Mèngzǐ*, orig. 孟轲 *Mèng Kē*, 372–289 BC) and Xunzi (荀子 *Xúnzǐ*, orig. 荀况 *Xún Kuàng* or 荀卿 *Xún Qīng*, 320–235 BC), early Confucian philosophy of history entered a decisive and systematic phase, characterized by an explicit philosophical view of history. The authenticity of the treatise *Mengzi* is still a subject of animated debate, whereas the *Xunzi* is believed to have mostly been written by the philosopher of the same name. The philosophies of history of both Mencius and Xunzi evince themselves as relatively independent and self-standing philosophical views of history. However, the vast majority of innumerous studies and comparisons of their thought are focused on conceptions of virtue, human nature, moral feelings, ritual and politics, and with few exceptions[117] omit their philosophy of history. This part of the chapter attempts to fill this gap.

Mencius' philosophy of history

Mencius builds on Confucius' didactic use of the past and relates it to the concept of the Mandate of Heaven by introducing *ren* as the principle of history and Heaven as a guarantor of its historical efficacy. Doing so, he also combines linear and cyclical views of history.

One of the most striking features of Mengzi's thought in general is the idealization of the past, particularly the times of the great founders of the Shang and Zhou dynasties, as well as the times of the legendary emperors Yao and Shun. Idealization means here, firstly, that the words and decisions of these rulers perfectly applied Confucian norms. Importantly, they are ideal not because their patterns of conduct could not be achieved, but because such conduct should be followed by all people at all times: 'Shun was a human; I, too, am a human. Shun was a model for the world, one that could be transmitted to the following generations.'[118] It is said, for instance, that Shun completely fulfilled the duties of what constitutes filial piety, and moreover the same Shun is said to have regarded good as a common property of the people.[119] The latter example credits Shun with some sort of moral theory, and one that is notably close to Mencian ethics. In fact, the moral theory of Mencius was projected back onto the times of Yao and Shun, and this is the second sense of the idealization of the past in his philosophy: modelling the past according to certain philosophical principles, as in the following sentence: 'Mencius discoursed upon the goodness of human nature, constantly referring to Yao and Shun.'[120] Not only an act of attribution with regard to the purely Mencian doctrine of human nature, but also an explicit mention of Mencius himself (probably made by one of his disciples), shows that Yao and Shun served as important rhetorical figures. In other words, in order to justify his views, Mencius put them into the mouths of Yao and Shun: 'I dare not set forth before the king anything but the Way of Yao and Shun.'[121] The figures of Yao and Shun were also invoked in order to promote concrete solutions, for example the ideal tax system.[122]

However, so far this concerns nothing but Mengzi's attitude towards great rulers. It seems that even if idealized, supposing such views still broadly agree with historical records, they do not propose any independent philosophy of history that would not be rooted in general, historical views. Indeed, Mencius stresses the necessity of learning histories, as can be seen from the following:

> When he feels that being a friend of all the good scholars of the world is not enough, he will go back in time to consider the people of antiquity, repeating their

poems and reading their books. Not knowing what they were like as persons, he considers what they were like in their own time.[123]

But even a superficial review of the ancient Chinese chronicles does not allow one to share Mengzi's optimism on this point, as kings often killed and betrayed their allies. How can such a problem be solved? Mengzi's answer is so much the worse for the facts. The sentence attributed to *Mengzi* – that it would be better not to have the *Book of Documents* than to give it full credence – shows that Mencius gave priority to his own philosophy, yet never totally rejected the *Shangshu* as a source of historical knowledge.[124] This attitude constitutes the third meaning of the idealization of the past: the more we idealize history, the more we wander off the account of *wie es eigentlich gewesen*.[125]

Apart from references to particular rulers, Mencius discusses former kings (*xianwang*) in general. Their hearts were full of compassion for the people, and their politics followed this attitude;[126] they loved virtue and therefore refrained from immoral use of their political power.[127] And although Mencius wrote that the influence of noble man ends in the fifth generation, this did not prevent him from stating that the principles of both earlier and later kings were the same,[128] which would be the key bone of contention between him and Xunzi. In similar contexts, Mencius also used the term 'the people of antiquity'. This shows that he was not interested in praising singular individuals, but all rulers and all people of ancient times, and thus his idealization of the past was very broad. The ancients are portrayed as a pure ideal of conduct, which makes them exemplars to be followed by all the following ages. People who repeat that 'born in this age, we should be of this age', have the moral standards of eunuchs.[129] This shows that the three kinds of idealization are in fact one and the same way of thinking: one has to read the chronicles (the third kind) as a manual of proper conduct (the second kind), as embodied in the figures of the ancients (the first kind). This constitutes Mengzi's critical view of history and historiography.

The moral use of the histories, however, does not exhaust Mencius' thought. The idealization (or the constructing) of the past poses a question of how Mencius interpreted history: what was his speculative philosophy of history?[130]

Mencius accepted and developed the doctrine of the Mandate of Heaven. He is convinced that only by receiving the favour of Heaven can one achieve significant results with any endeavour.[131] There is no way, for example, to besiege a city, if Heaven did not send down the right moment for doing so.[132] Accordingly, not being equal to the task that Heaven has placed before us at a particular time and place results in the disasters that it visits upon us. Mencius states that Heaven cares for those who obey its commands, by preserving their states and helping them conquer the world.[133] Those who rebel against the will of Heaven, will surely pass away.[134] Although Mencius agrees with his Master that Tian does not speak, but only manifests its will through the course of events, he credits Heaven with features making it responsible for all events happening objectively, mostly those unexplained rationally. He provides specific criterion to see which actions are caused by Heaven:

1.   What man cannot make, comes from Heaven;
2.   That which is done without any agent, comes from Heaven;

3. That which does not have a [recognized] purpose, comes from the command of Heaven.[135]

This triple criterion also includes seemingly random factors enabling the seizure of power: the right time, a favourable combination of events or the right people encountered on life's path.

All of this notwithstanding, this is only one side of the Mencian theory of Tian. The other is the moral condition for receiving Heaven's appointment. One has to receive any gift of Heaven in humility, because what is sent by Heaven comes naturally. Heaven's gift is more the culmination of the way than a ready solution (*deus ex machina*): 'when Heaven intends to confer a great responsibility upon a person, it first visits his mind and will with suffering, toils his sinews and bones, subjects his body to hunger, exposes him to poverty, and confounds his projects.'[136] As Mencius believes, it is thus sometimes necessary to wait hundreds of years until the desired, outstanding individual called by Heaven reveals himself. Only a person who faithfully serves Heaven is able to overcome all these difficulties.[137] He is also able to overthrow all his opponents, with the result that there are no enemies left in the state.[138] This is the reason why several scholars claim that the theory of Heaven is nothing but a theory of the legitimization of power. On the one hand, it is also a theory of moral legitimacy – Mencius in no way condones the possibility of a murderer effecting a political takeover solely on the basis of *Realpolitik*. If someone came to power and established a new dynasty, then he was able to do so because Heaven had previously tested him. On the other hand, Mencius never answered the question of what kind of being Tian was exactly. He does not provide a clear explanation, because he defines Heaven through functions ('creates', 'rewards', 'listens to'), and not by predicates. In a way, Tian intervenes in history, no matter what Tian is.

In a long dialogue with Wan Zhang, Mencius explains how the sages had received their thrones, and notes that, on closer examination, nobody had given another person the throne:

> The Son of Heaven can present a man to Heaven, but he cannot cause Heaven to give him the realm (…) In antiquity Yao presented Shun to Heaven, and it was Heaven that accepted him. He displayed him to the people, and the people accepted him. (…) When Heaven gave the power to rule to the worthiest, it was given to the worthiest (…) A common man who comes to possess all-under-Heaven must have virtue comparable to that of Shun and Yu and also the recommendation of the Son of Heaven. This is why Confucius never possessed all-under-Heaven. One who has inherited all-under-Heaven is put aside only by Heaven if he is like Jie or Zhou.[139]

This passage shows a connection between two dimensions of Mengzi's historical thinking which seem to be separate: idealization and the moral use of the past, and a quasi-ontological theory of Heaven being a historical agent. As appointed by Tian, these historical heroes could serve as moral examples. Counter-examples of cruel rulers or righteous people who did not obtain the throne (like Confucius) do not falsify Mencius' thesis, they only show that one of the conditions was not fulfilled. For instance, that Confucius was not presented as a candidate, and tyrants were not accepted by Heaven.

We can go further and ask which principle makes a king a king – a person who changes the course of history. Mencius' answer is the virtue of benevolence 仁 *rén*. All those who conquered the world can be called benevolent.[140] This statement is found in several sentences describing how Yao, Shun and Yu ordered the world and made China so different from the barbarian countries. Sometimes this is made even more explicit: 'There have been cases of individuals without benevolence who possessed a single state, but never an instance of one who got the world without benevolence.'[141] What Mencius attempts to say here is that the past should be followed not because it is the past, but rather because it was benevolent. Antiquity alone is not a pattern of conduct, thus the Mencian idealization of the past is not naïve; accordingly, *ren* alone is not sufficient to have historical influence, as one must also comply with ancient laws:

> If one had the Way of Yao and Shun but lacked humane government, one would not be able to rule the world. Though he may have a humane heart and a reputation for humaneness, one from whom the people receive no benefits will not serve as a model for later generations because he does not practice the Way of the former kings. Therefore it is said, 'Goodness alone does not suffice for the conduct of government; Laws alone do not implement themselves'. The *Ode* says, 'Not transgressing, not forgetting, But following the statutes of old'. No one has ever erred by following the laws of the former kings.[142]

It could be said that for Mencius *ren* is the principle of history. If the conduct of the ancients was benevolent, they were respected by Heaven and hence able to do what seems beyond human power and change the history of the world. But if *ren* is the principle of history, then the question arises of whether *ren* remains the same throughout history, but still has to change things – there is no 'history' without change – what is there to be changed? This problem is so apparent that some interpreters, such as Vincent Leung, go too far and state that 'for the *Mengzi*, history is at best idle knowledge (...) it was not mere indifference to the idea of history, but a deliberate, measured distancing from it.'[143]

Change is determined by differences, and this is also true in this case. Rulers are either benevolent or they are not, and the possession or lack of benevolence does have a historical impact: 'It was by benevolence that the Three Dynasties gained the throne, and by not being benevolent that they lost it.'[144] Cyclical 'transformations' of *ren* are therefore identical to dynastic cycles. In this way, Mencius laid the foundations for this influential idea. In the last remaining passage of the *Mencius*, the Chinese philosopher determined the length of each cycle, estimating it at 500 years. However, in order to conform his calculations to history he treats Confucius as a king (without a crown), which means that his contemporaries would have had to wait another four centuries for the end of the cycle.

The difference between the beginning and end of each cycle is called the 'period of order and period of chaos' 一治一亂 *yīzhì yīluàn*,[145] But even in the latest periods of order, the moral standards of the people were not as high as those in the times of Yao and Shun. This leads not only to a cyclical change of order and chaos, but also to a linear and graduating decay of the principles so strongly stressed by idealization of the past:

> From Tang down to Wuding there were six or seven worthy and sagely rulers. (...) The interlude between Zhou and Wuding was not long, and the inherited customs of the old families and the legacy of good government still persisted. (...) In the present time, it would be easy [to attain royal dignity]. In the flourishing periods of the Xia, Yin, and Zhou, the domain did not exceed a thousand *li*, and Qi has this much land (...) Never a time when the people's sufferings from tyrannical government have been so great [than now].[146]

In fact, this is not only an interpretation that is used in order to connect a more cyclical approach with the linear view of gradual collapse. Mencius himself gives such an account:

> Once Yao and Shun were no more, the Way of the sages declined, and oppressive rulers arose one after another. (...) When it came down to the time of the tyrant Zhou, the world was once again in great chaos. The Duke of Zhou assisted King Wu and destroyed Zhou (...) Again the world declined, and the Way was concealed. Deviant speech and oppressive actions again became prevalent. There were cases of ministers murdering their rulers and of sons murdering their parents. Confucius was afraid, and so wrote the *Spring and Autumn Annals*. (...) Once again sages and kings do not appear, the lords have become arbitrary and intemperate, and unemployed scholars indulge in uninhibited discussions. The words of Yang Zhu and Mo Di flow throughout the world. (...) When the path of humaneness and rightness is blocked, animals are led to devour people, and people will be led to devour one another (...) If a sage should arise again, he would not change my words.[147]

This passage gives us the most comprehensive exposition of the Mencian philosophy of history, combining the idea of the decay of the ancient principles with the cycles of arising sages. Mencius encapsulates all the dimensions of his philosophy of history, including the moral use of the past, in this one passage. In this respect, his philosophy of history is quite holistic in nature. Xu Wentao states that the Mencian philosophy of history is based on the idea of 'moral cosmos', embodied by Tian as an objective factor and force of history.[148] However, such a reading runs the risk of imputing to Mencius a belief in the impersonal force of history, whereas for him the course of history ultimately depends upon the moral or immoral conduct of the ruler. In fact, it is precisely this idea that makes Mencius' philosophy of history holistic: according to our terminology, it represents HPH regarding reason that unifies descriptive and normative dimensions of history.

Xunzi's philosophy of history

In contrast to Mencius, Xunzi strives to save the idea of following the past from the image of Heaven intervening in history. For this reason, he focused on the historical role of rituals and culture in general, conceived as a tool of transformation of nature that was performed by the sages.

Xunzi was not an exception to other Confucians interested in the moral use of the past: 'If one observes happenings from the past, in order to give oneself forewarning, then order and chaos and right and wrong are within reach of one's recognizing.'[149] This recognition is not different from education: 'If you never hear the words transmitted from the former kings, you will not know the richness of learning.'[150] Knowledge that does not fit with the standards of the ancient kings is said to be that of a vile mind.[151] What is more, learning does not here refer to purely intellectual activity, but implies the practice of rituals and music in ways created by the ancient kings. In the commentary to the *Xunzi*, John Knoblock aptly notes:

> Xunzi shares with most of his contemporaries the belief that history provides the basis on which any philosophy of government must be based (...) Political philosophy, then, is inseparable from the study of history and, in Xunzi's particular view, of ritual principles (...) The model left behind by the sages is the starting point for any analysis of the proper form and function of the government.[152]

The keyword of that last sentence is 'model'. Here, model means not only something on which the analysis is being modelled, but also a representation which consists of numerous items structured in proper order. It is not a single instance, but a set of examples. Thus Xunzi writes that being in opposition to ritual is the same as lacking a model 法 *fǎ*.[153] Consequently, 'well ordered' refers to ritual and moral principles, and 'chaotic' refers to what is contrary to them.[154] And again, not just any kind of rituals but concrete rituals of antiquity, as they are described in the Classics: 'One who is both spirit-like and firm in this state is called the sage (...) The ways of the hundred kings are unified in him. Thus, the principles of the *Songs, Documents, Rituals*, and *Music* are summed up in him.'[155] However, an imitation of the model of the ancient kings has to be full of benevolence, because their conduct was *ren* to the utmost extent: 'how much more important are the ways of the former kings, the principles of benevolence and justice, and the social divisions given in the *Songs, Documents, Rituals*, and *Music*. They surely contain the greatest thoughts in the world.'[156] The Classics are much more than a handbook:

> When does learning begin? When does learning end? I say: Its order begins with reciting the Classics, and ends with studying ritual.[157]

The goal of education is expressed in the most conservative way: one has to read and learn nothing but the Classics, focusing on the rituals. From the point of view of the individual, one has to make progress in learning, but from the perspective of society nothing could change the state of knowledge. After achieving one's own purpose, the final result of the process of education is still identical to what previous generations had already obtained. One has to be attentive enough to see the meaning of the Classics, but not to find new principles.

Xunzi states this positively: the model of the sages is the first and last pattern of conduct. It guarantees the continuity and maintenance of civilization:

If each dawn begins a new day and each day a man begins anew, then how is it that there are states that have lasted a thousand years tranquilly through this? I say it is because the state is succoured by a trustworthy model, itself a thousand years old.[158]

The greatest danger to the state is breaking this continuity – when a dynasty is removed and new regulations are created, danger can arise. The introduction of new laws results in chaos but holding on to the ancient regulations implies harmony. In this respect, Xunzi idealizes the past. Xunzi upholds the Confucian legends of Yao and Shun. He even writes that they governed so well that in their times robbers did not steal and thieves did not burgle anywhere.[159] Sometimes Xunzi 'uses the past' purely rhetorically, e.g. writing that even Yao and Shun could not have added more.[160] In fact, Antonio Cua distinguished as many as four kinds of use of the past in Xunzi: pedagogical, rhetorical, elucidative and evaluative.[161]

The distinctive feature of Xunzi's idealization of the past is his effort to show that sages and ancient kings, albeit magnificent, were still people of the same nature as us:

> All people share something (. . .) This is what Yu and Jie have in common (. . .) Yao and Yu were not born already possessing [all advantages], but they began to transform their old selves, becoming perfect through cultivation and only after the extreme effort.[162]

Ancient kings do not represent an unapproachable ideal: anyone could and should follow them, because they transformed their original nature in the same way as everyone ought to. 'Anyone on the street could become a Yu (. . .) people on the streets all have the potential for knowing benevolence, righteousness, legality, and propriety.'[163] The appearance of eminent individuals in history is thus normal and regular, and there is no need to appeal to Heaven in order to explain their existence. It is even 'statistically' certain that some of the people will follow the model. 'In every generation there were such individuals. Born in the present age, such a proper man focuses his mind on the way of the ancients.'[164] This does not necessarily mean that people following the sages have the status of sages. They could simply be emulating their conduct in the belief that they have to do so, while thinking it difficult to fully realize their principles, or that some of their regulations are hard to understand. The ancient principles are present today first and foremost because they are transmitted from father to son. This partially explains why Xunzi so stresses the role of education – it has historical impact:

> The reason that the model of the Three Dynasties still exists even though they have perished is that officers and bureaucrats have meticulously observed the rules and laws, the weights and measures, criminal sanctions and penalties, and maps and registers. This has been accomplished even when they no longer understood the meaning because they conscientiously safeguarded the calculations and out of prudence never presumed either to increase or diminish them. Rather, they handed them from father to son.[165]

This kind of reflection leads Xunzi to the fundamental statement about the unity of history: past and present are not separate dimensions, guided by different principles. 'The beginning of Heaven and Earth is still present today, the way of Hundred Kings is in that of the Later Kings.'[166] As a result, Xunzi criticizes those who claim that it is impossible to follow the rules of the past in present times. 'Fools say: the circumstances of the past and the present are quite different, and the Way by which to bring order to the anarchy of today must be different.'[167] But Xunzi does not agree with this premise, thus largely denying that there is any 'category mistake' in his reasoning:

> The sage uses men to measure men, circumstances to gauge circumstances, each class of thing to measure that class, the persuasion to measure the achievement, and the Way to observe the totality, so that for him the ancient and modern are one and the same. Things of the same class do not become contradictory even though a long time has elapsed because they share an identical principle of order.[168]

Xunzi argues not only for the unity, but also for the holistic character of history, as it appears from the perspective of Dao. As has been shown by Masayuki Satō, the formal categories of 'one' (*yī*) and 'the same kind' (*tónglèi*) are the basis for the integration of the moral and natural order in the philosophy of Xunzi.[169] Because different epochs share the same principles and can be further used as a gauge of proper conduct, they also create a negative criterion: 'Whatever words do not agree with the former kings or do not comply with norms of ritual and righteousness should be called nefarious words.' Theories not created by ancient kings, but falsely attributed to them, are pernicious as well, just like the theory of Five Phases.[170]

But Xunzi is not naïve, and he sees the differences between the ancient times and his own on the epistemological level, rather than on ontological and ethical levels. Despite the unity of principles (ethics), and belonging to one category of events (ontology), the third subject of comparison – knowledge of the past – is not the same in both cases. The ancients knew more about their own times than we know about them now. Moreover, the more ancient the times, the less we know about them. 'There are reports of the government of Yu and Tang, but they are not as precise as those regarding the Zhou.'[171] This does not mean that Xunzi looks for historical truth ('what really happened'), which is different from moral principles, because moral truth is what really happened. 'That before the Five Ancestors there are no traditions concerning individuals is not because of the absence of sages during that time, but because of the extreme antiquity of the period.'[172] The model of the sages had been existing even before the first such sages were mentioned. The moral unity of history is the indisputable truth, even though we do not know much about extreme antiquity or why the past and our own times constitute one totality.[173]

The distinction between earlier and later kings has normative implications: since the principles of early and late antiquity are identical, but those of late antiquity are more accessible to us, we should follow the principles of later kings. 'If you want to trace the tracks of the sage kings, then look to the clearest of them, namely that of the later kings.'[174] From this point of view, Xunzi condemns those thinkers who follow the ancient kings only in a fragmentary manner, such as Mencius, who sees no difference between our knowledge of the ways of former and later kings. Thinkers following the model of the former kings are called vulgar Confucians 俗儒 *sùrú*, while those following the later kings but not knowing why they should, are called cultivated *ru* 雅儒 *yárú*. Meanwhile, the great scholars 大儒 *dàrú* intentionally model themselves on the later Kings.[175]

However, the biggest difference between Xunzi's philosophy of history and the view of Mencius does not lie in the prioritization of later kings over earlier ones, but rather in the lack of any concept of the Mandate of Heaven and historical cycles. Xunzi denies the doctrine of *Tianming* by denying its very premise: 'There is a regularity in the activity of Tian. It did not persist because of Yao, it did not perish because of Jie.'[176] Regardless of the moral or immoral conduct of rulers, Tian has never changed course and intervened in history, it has never been a historical agent, but a background to all historical actions. Consistently, only people are 'history-makers'. 'Since Yu achieved order and Jie brought chaos, order and chaos are not due to Heaven.' People are fully responsible for history, and if they become sages, it is due to their own effort. If the way of Heaven is constant, it is also understandable and rational – what are perceived as miracles or unique events can thus be explained rationally:

> The falling of stars and the groaning of the trees are simply rarely occurring things among the changes of Heaven and Earth and the transformation of *yin* and *yang*. To marvel at them is permissible, but to fear them is wrong.[177]

For such a precise mind as Xunzi's, the rationality of nature implies certain conclusions about how it is used. As he puts it in his famous poem, 'to obey Heaven and praise it – how can this compare to overseeing what Heaven has mandated and using it?'[178] In this respect, 'Tian' should rather be translated as 'Nature' (as Knoblock did). The question of the use of Nature was central to Xunzi's philosophy of history. Although Xunzi refutes the doctrine of the Mandate of Heaven, he still agrees that the sages played a significant role in history because they successfully employed nature in order to prevent chaos. In other words, the ancient kings regulated nature, and continued those regulations in their own conduct.[179]

By 'transformation of nature', not only the natural world is meant, but also people's nature. Sages transform original nature, both their own and that of other people. The tools used for the transformation of one's own nature are rituals and moral duties, which form a basis for the system of laws and standards. The sage's relation to rituals and moral principles is like that of the potter to his pots.[180] The reason for the transformation of human nature was that it was originally evil:

> In antiquity the sage kings took man's nature to be evil, to be inclined to prejudice and prone to error, to be perverse and rebellious, and not to be upright or orderly. For this reason they invented ritual principles and precepts of moral duty.[181]

It is the rituals and rules used by the kings that explain the causes of chaos in the world.[182] In this manner, Xunzi found a way to provide a historical basis for the educational programme of the Confucians that did not require any references to historical agency of Heaven.

Conclusion

The philosophical views of history of Mencius and Xunzi surmount the development of Confucian philosophy of history in pre-imperial China. For Mencius, who returns to the ideas delineated in the *Shangshu*, Heaven is a powerful historical agent, giving and withdrawing its Mandate. For Xunzi, Tian is rather a synonym for 'nature', constant in its course and understandable in its transformations, employed by sages and 'prolonged' in rituals. Both thinkers also differed in their way of addressing the question of the historical role and realization of moral principles. Mencius sees no difference between the earlier and later sages: all realized the same principle, *ren*. History is only a repetitive process of respecting, or not respecting, benevolence. Each cycle is a reincarnation of the previous period, although every next cycle expresses the progressive disrespect of moral principles. Xunzi, on the other hand, is fully aware of the 'historicity' of history, especially the limitations of our knowledge of the past. Then, although they stressed the historical role of morality and rituals, *ren* plays a central role in the Mencian view of history, which has little interest in rituals. In Xunzi, the reverse is the case.[183] Both of them, however, shared a belief in the moral use of the past (the rationale for learning from history is the idealization of the past). Both Mencius and Xunzi were proponents of the moral unity of the past and present (the latter explicitly), treating history as history only because of its everlasting principle. What made them Confucians was their ethics rather than the metaphysics of history, which demonstrates the common ground of all Confucian philosophies of history.

Quest for the Trend of History

The Philosophy of History in Other Schools of Thought in the Warring States Period

Introduction

The flourishing of philosophy in the Warring States Period, which was unique on the scale of Chinese history, and as Karl Jaspers pointed out, comparable only to the Indian or Greek, had many reasons. Of these, the first was the disintegration of the Zhou monarchy, which led to the questioning of old patterns, and encouraged philosophers to find political solutions that would put an end to the ubiquitous war. In the face of China's breaking up, the mobility of its scholars increased, and this was conducive to both polemics and the emergence of schools.

This period is also known as the time of the 'Hundred Schools of Thought' 諸子百家 *zhūzǐ bǎijiā*. The number is symbolic, since even Chinese sources do not agree on the final number of schools. The first description of the main schools, along with their names, is to be found in the essay *On the Essentials of the Six Schools* 論六家要旨 *Lùn liù jiā yàozhǐ* by Sima Tan (司馬談, 165–110 BC), included in the *Records of the Grand Historian*. These were: the Scholars of *yin-yang* (陰陽 *yīnyáng*), the Confucians (儒者 *rúzhě*), Mohists (墨者 *Mòzhě*), the School of *Fa*, i.e. Legalism (法家 *fǎjiā*), the School of Names (名家 *míngjiā*) and the School of Dao, i.e. Daoism (道家 *dàojiā*).[1] The *Yiwenzhi* catalogue from the *Book of Han* also mentions the School of Diplomats (literally: the School of Vertical and Horizontal Alliances, 縱橫家 *zònghéngjiā*), the School of Eclectism (杂家 *zájiā*), the School of Agriculture (農家 *nóngjiā*)[2] and the School of Minor Talks (小說家 *xiǎoshuōjiā*).[3] Yet both classifications omit such schools as the School of Strategists or Militarists (兵家 *bīngjiā*), represented by the famous *Art of War*, or the hedonism of Yang Zhu. The last chapter of the *Zhuangzi* mentions other philosophers that cannot be assigned to any of abovementioned schools,[4] thus the metaphor of the 'Hundred Schools of Thought' is to some extent justified.

At this point it is good to make some methodological remarks, for one of the more common trends in contemporary Sinology is a departure from the use of the term 'philosophical schools'. First, it is argued that since the division was created in the Han dynasty, its application to the Warring States Period is anachronistic and erroneous.[5] Second, diversified thought of particular representatives of the 'schools' and numerous syncretisms, especially in light of recent archaeological discoveries, seems to question the well-established divisions. The answer to the first ('temporal') argument can be seen in the analysis of Danto, who showed that predication of true narrative statements about the past requires a time gap, and that the narrator's knowledge must be greater than the knowledge of the participant: the sentence 'The Thirty Years War began in 1618' was not true either at the outbreak of the war nor even 29 years later.[6] The owl of Minerva spreads its wings only with the falling of the dusk. This applies to our case: Sima Tan wrote his essay a century after the burning of the books, which practically put an end to Mohism, the School of Names and the *Nongjia*, just to name the few, leading to the fusion of Confucianism, Legalism and the Yin-Yang School. The relatively short distance on the scale of history travelled by these ideas, and the fact that it was a Chinese philosopher and historian with access to the archives who made this division, speaks for its credibility.

The argument for scope, referring to differentiation and syncretism, results from misunderstanding the nature of philosophical schools, if not even confusing them with sects. Philosophical schools are intellectual formations that connect similar thinkers who remain original philosophers – the diversity and fluidity of the boundaries are natural. In the cases of China and India (for example, the classical *darśanas* or Buddhist schools), as well as Greece (the Hellenic schools), reflection of this fact can be easily found.[7] The fluidity of the periphery has no effect on the 'centre': no one will conclude that Zhuangzi was Confucian. In addition, both Mencius and Xunzi recognized themselves as *ru*. Therefore, the debate is not so much about the existence of the schools, but how and whom to classify by the schools.

Most importantly, philosophical school is not defined here in terms of an established institution, all the more that the most eminent Chinese philosophers – Confucians Mencius and Xunzi, Legalist Shen Dao, Mohist Song Xing, Logician Shunyu Kun, Yin-Yang Scholar Zou Yan, and possibly Daoist Zhuangzi – debated with each other in the famous Jixia Academy 稷下學宮 *Jixià xuégōng* in Linzi, Qi's capital. Hence, philosophical school is understood here as a group of thinkers, whose thought is focused around the same core concepts and key points of reference, including the texts. In other words, logical connections between the members of a given philosophical school are often closer than the historical ones. For instance, Shen Dao, Shang Yang and Han Fei are considered Legalists. Han Fei quotes Shen Dao's words about power/ tendency of a state (*shi*), developing his view on *shi* in general accordance with how the category of *shi* is understood in the *Shangjunshu*, the book attributed to Shang Yang. At the same time the Legalist reading of *shi* corresponds to some extent to the Militarist interpretation to be found in the *Art of War* (one chapter of which is devoted to the exposition of the concept of *shi*). On the other hand, the character *shi* itself does not appear at all in the most important texts of the Confucian legacy, namely the *Book of Songs*, *the Analects* and the *Spring and Autumn Annals*, along with the *Zuo Commentary*. Finally, the Legalists are highly critical of Confucian solutions (and *vice versa*), validating their criticism in a way different from, for instance, the Daoists and the Mohists. It is clear therefore that we deal here with different bodies of thought.

In a similar way the views of history created within respective schools of Chinese philosophy can be distinguished. This chapter focuses on philosophy of history in the

Warring States Period of schools other than Confucianism. Generally speaking, Legalism offers a comprehensive alternative to the Confucian view of history, while Mohism shares certain assumptions of Confucianism in this respect; the Yin-Yang School contains the germs of the Han interpretation of history, while Daoism distances itself from the philosophy of history as such. The last passage of the chapter discusses eclectisms and syncretisms, which links the thought of that time to its later developments.

Legalist philosophy of history

The common feature of the first Legalists and the intellectuals close to them was the fact that most of these thinkers conducted extensive social reforms aimed at strengthening the state: Zi Chan (子產, d. 522 BC) in Zheng; Li Kui (李悝, 455–395 BC) in Wei; Wu Qi (吳起, 440–380 BC) in Chu; and Shang Yang (商鞅, 390–338 BC) in the state of Qin. The reforms of Shang Yang, the alleged author of the *Book of Lord Shang* 商君書 *Shāngjūnshū*[8], resulted in a flourishing of the Qin and indirectly to the foundation of the Qin empire. In addition to Shang Yang and Han Fei (韓非, 280–233 BC), the author of the *Hánfēizǐ* 韓非子, Shen Buhai (申不害, 400–337 BC), Shen Dao (慎到, 350–275 BC) and Li Si (李斯, 280–208 BC) are usually mentioned among the Legalist philosophers. The philosophy of history of Shang Yang and Han Fei is discussed in the following sections. The works of Shen Buhai and Shen Dao, in turn, are focused solely on the political philosophy.[9] Li Si, adviser to the First Emperor, who flung Han Fei into prison, has not left any works behind.

Legalism was an element of a larger intellectual movement that could be described as a critique of the political idealism of the Mohists and Confucians, with concurrent rejection of the equally utopian naturalism of Daoists or *nongjia*, and might be framed in terms of political realism – a political theory assuming that power alone is the primary end of political action ('might is right'). This current embraced the School of Militarists with the famous Sunzi, the School of Diplomacy and the eclecticism of such texts as the *Guanzi*, *Shizi* and *Yinwenzi*. It also produced the alternative historical narratives, contained in the *Bamboo Annals* 竹書紀年 *Zhúshū Jìnián* and the *Strategies of the Warring States* 戰國策 *Zhànguó cè*.[10] For instance, the *Bamboo Annals* states that Shun imprisoned Yao and banished his son, and Yu killed the minister in order to give power to his son,[11] which directly conflicts with the Confucian and Mohist legends. However, since the thought of these political realists intersects with historical, political and military discourse (which is quite technical in its nature), this chapter focuses only on what can be counted as a coherent philosophical view of history, namely the philosophies of history of Shang Yang and Han Fei.

Shang Yang's philosophy of history

Shang Yang offered a linear interpretation of history through the prism of transformations of political power that contested Confucian idealization of the past.

Shang Yang's philosophy of history is both a condition and continuation of his political philosophy. He believes that a strong state bases its rule on law (*fa*).[12] Shang

Yang gives a number of conditions that make the law right and effective. As not every kind of law fulfils these conditions, Legalism cannot be considered a form of legal positivism. For example, the law should be in line with the customs and nature of the people, otherwise it will be ineffective.[13] The law should also be impartial, and instead of satisfying private interests, ought to serve the public order. For this purpose it should also be clearly formulated[14] Finally, the law should respond to the specific needs and circumstances of a given time:

> The former kings established laws as appropriate to the times; they measured tasks and then regulated undertakings. When laws are appropriate to their times, there is orderly rule; when undertakings correspond to their tasks, there is success. Now the times have changed, but the laws have not yet been altered. When one strives to change but continues to maintain affairs according to the past, this means that laws contradict the times, and one's undertakings differ from one's tasks.[15]

Hence, the illustriousness of great rulers is not testified to by the content of their decisions, but by their function – that they have always been consistent with their times.[16]

Shang Yang opposes the Confucian interpretation of history, according to which all rulers and dynasties realized one and the same principle. The Three Dynasties and hegemons changed their rituals and laws, and the legendary rulers were essentially different from each other in their means of governance.[17] Discrepancies were fundamental and involved such issues as whether to rule on the basis of knowledge or strength.[18] What is more, the change of principles took place also during a single rule, depending on whether the ruler had just gained power or was trying to hold on to it.[19] This observation leads Shang Yang to a very important conclusion:

> There is more than one way to govern the world and there is no necessity to imitate antiquity, in order to take appropriate measures for the state. Tang and Wu succeeded in attaining supremacy without following antiquity, and as for the downfall of Shang and Xia — they were ruined without rites having been altered. Consequently, those who acted counter to antiquity do not necessarily deserve blame, nor do those who followed established rites merit praise.[20]

This passage shows that Shang Yang not only criticized the Confucian ideals of modelling on the past, but also did so on the basis of premises foreign to most of the philosophers of the Warring States Period: that there was no one sure way of introducing order. In this way Shang Yang desubstantialized political philosophy, and consistently also the philosophy of history.[21] As Yuri Pines argues, Shang Yang's approach contrasts with the contemporaneous Confucian approach, which allows only minor and superficial changes in history.[22] For Shang Yang, history is a collection of floating, if not unrepeatable, factors.

As a result, it is not enough to say that imitation of antiquity is erroneous because of different circumstances. Furthermore, an imitation of the present, that is any form of imitation obscuring a reading of the signs of the times, leads to a 'casting out of history':

A sage does not imitate antiquity, nor does he follow the present time. If he were to imitate antiquity, he would be behind the times; and if he follows the present time, he is obstructed by circumstances. The Zhou dynasty did not imitate the Shang dynasty, nor did the Xia dynasty imitate the period of Yu; the Three Dynasties encountered different circumstances, but all three succeeded in attaining supremacy. So to rise to supremacy, there is a definite way, but to hold it there are different principles.[23]

This passage contains many essential concepts that would be later developed by Han Fei: the Way (*Dao*), different from particular principles (*lì*), and the conception of the circumstances of a certain time 勢 *shì*. The incentive 'to not imitate the past or the present' appears in the *Shangjunshu* many times.[24] Consequently, employing history as a manual for ethics and politics is aimless, especially in the case of the *Songs* and the *Documents*.[25]

However, the above arguments do not mean that Shang Yang was not interested in any theorizing about history. On the contrary, the seventh chapter of the *Shangjunshu* presents a theory of human history and an origin of the state that is unique in all Chinese thought.[26] Shang Yang distinguishes there three major historical epochs. The first is the matriarchate, in which people were close to their relatives and feared strangers. It was a primitive state, though not a state of war. In the second epoch, population growth resulted in chaos. Disputes arose and people sought to subjugate with violence. At that time, sapient individuals created rules of impartiality and justice, established public order different from private, and taught people the principles of morality (*rèn*). In lieu of favouring relatives was promotion of the virtuous. The population, however, continued to increase, which again led to chaos. Enlightened people who held power established private property: they demarcated territories and determined which wealth belonged to whom. There was also division of female and male spheres of activity. Because of the new arrangements, a number of prohibitions were also set up, along with officials to guard them, and finally a duke who would unite and control the clerks. Then, in place of virtue they began to promote honour.[27]

Epoch	Power of the...	Principle of the system	Innovations
former 上世 shàngshì	family (mothers)	kinship	─ ─
middle 中世 zhōngshì	judges	virtue	principles of justice, morality, public order
late 下世 xiàshì	prince and officials	honour	private ownership, division of labour as per gender, interdicts, offices

Figure 3 Three epochs in the history of humanity according to Shang Yang.

The eighteenth chapter presents a slightly different typology, perhaps created by another thinker, but in the spirit of the *Shangjunshu*.[28] There are four epochs associated with specific legendary rulers. In the days of Hao Ying (literally the 'Great Hero'), the animals dominated people, who killed them to survive. In the era of Rendi ('Human Emperor') people were vegans with simple customs. In the days of Shennong ('Divine Farmer'), farming began, and women's duties began to differ from men's, and there were no penalties or troops. After Shennong's death, a few strong people began to oppress the weaker majority, when Huangdi ('Yellow Emperor') established the authority of princes and rituals, and called up a mercenary army. Common features of both theories are the recognition that the primitive state was a state of harmony, and most importantly, the characteristics of history in terms of social evolution. Both theories are astoundingly empirical, and the first shows the continuous modification of variable factors in response to the growth of a constant background factor (population). It is not surprising, therefore, that this vision resembles the ideas of nineteenth-century Western social evolutionists.[29] But then the following question arises: does it assume the idea of progress?

The belief that Shang Yang was a proponent of progress was shared by many Chinese intellectuals, even Hu Shi, as well as the Chinese Communists.[30] In fact, Shang Yang was very temperate in talking about the future. He pessimistically and helplessly stated that the Three Dynasties had not yet been joined by the Fourth.[31] It is certain that Shang Yang wanted another dynasty (probably the Qin, which he served), to be guided by impartial law and strict punishment, and to base the government on the army and agriculture. Yet he did not give a direct form to this vision as any kind of description of an epoch analogous to the above. Pines speculates that it would be an era in which punishment brings righteousness and *ren* around the world.[32] However, the passage to which he refers[33] only reads that the penalties support virtue, and by making use of them one can (*néng*) promote morality in the world. The term 'epoch' and other concepts familiar to Shang Yang do not appear here, and cannot appear, because the principles of *ren* had already been introduced in the second epoch (or in the Hunagdi era, in the second view). Zhang Linxiang validly concludes that Shang Yang's philosophy of history is incompatible with the Western vision of progress.[34] This vision presupposes the existence of historical laws or any principles enabling prediction of the future, from which Shang Yang resigns in the name of desubstantialization of the philosophy of history, advising us to vigilantly adjust to the changing circumstances of the time.

Han Fei's philosophy of history

Han Fei develops and complements the main themes of Shang Yang's philosophy of history. Compared to Shang Yang, Han Fei is even more willing to refer to ancient times and legends of Yao and Shun. As Eirik Harris emphasizes, Han Fei is selective in this respect and supports the rulers for having reacted appropriately to the needs of their time, by assigning them the views he himself supports.[35] For example, he states that the ancients rejected self-interest and were guided by public law, while Yao, Shun and the first kings are said to extend institutions, always treated at any time as extravagance and prodigality.[36] Han Fei does so within a consciously applied rhetoric tool. He openly criticizes Confucians and Mohists for attributing their own views to former kings,[37] and argues against the use of history as a source of moral guidance from epistemological positions:

> Both Confucius and Mozi referred to the ways of Yao and Shun, but they differed in what they accepted or rejected, yet each claimed this is true Yao and Shun. But if Yao and Shun cannot rise from the dead, who is going to determine the justness of Confucians and Mohists? From the times of the Shang and Zhou it has been upwards of seven hundred years, from the times of Yu and the Xia – more than two thousand years; hence, one cannot determine whether Confucians or Mohists are right. Now, if anybody wants to investigate the ways of Yao and Shun who lived three thousand years ago, it is even hard to imagine! To be sure of anything that has no evidence, is stupid; to adhere to anything one cannot be sure of, is fraudulent. Hence, those who openly quote the early kings and dogmatically determine Yao and Shun, must be mendacious, if not stupid.[38]

Han Fei was a disciple of Xunzi, who for a similar reason considered talking about former kings improper, yet did not give up his faith in the unity of history. Han Fei radicalizes this criticism in the spirit of Legalism. Within the framework of the specific 'rhetorical war' with the Confucians, Han Fei portrays Yao, Shun and the ancient kings as criminals who punished officials whose crimes were innumerable, who as ministers murdered or expelled their rulers, and who acting against the rules of righteousness at every turn caused the gradual decline of the principles that are nowadays promoted by the scholars.[39]

In the area of political philosophy, Han Fei describes the ideal ruler similarly to the Daoists ('doing nothing', with unbiased laws acting for him),[40] but in the philosophy of history his understanding of Dao is distinctive. In contrast to Daoism, Han Fei treats Dao primarily as a principle of political order in existing (not utopian or primitive) states.[41] At the same time, Dao is always contrary to the prevailing views of a given era.[42] Individuals who are ready to promote it opposing the people of their times are called 'martyrs' 烈士 *lièshì*.[43]

As a result, Han Fei follows Shang Yang, criticizing the business of modelling things on the standards of the past as not only ineffective, but even irrational:

> If anyone had tried to open channels for the water during the Shang or Zhou dynasties, Tang and Wu would have laughed at him. This being so, if people in the present age go about exalting the ways of Yao, Shun, Yu, Tang, and Wu, the sages of today are bound to laugh at them. For the sage does not try to practice the ways of antiquity or to abide by a fixed standard, but examines the affairs of the age and takes what precautions are necessary.[44]

In another place, Han Fei writes that 'if one does not look for the proper means for the matters of the state, but takes advice from the former kings, is like a man returning home from the market to take a measure of his feet'.[45] However, Han Fei does not fall into the extreme of a 'cult of change' – the sage does not think at all in terms of change, but of what is useful. Where changes are not necessary, old solutions can be maintained.[46]

Just like Shang Yang, Han Fei also deals with the origins of the state and typology of historical epochs. But as Li Yucheng notes, *Hanfeizi* is not consistent in classifying epochs, sometimes distinguishing three (former-mean-present), sometimes four (former-middle-near-present).[47] According to Han Fei, in the age of remote antiquity, animals dominated people in number, thus the latter ate only plants. Then there appeared a man who created nests to protect people so the people made him their ruler. At that time they ate fruits, grains and oysters, which hurt their stomachs and caused illness. Then another sage appeared, inventing fire, and he also received the dignity of being a ruler. In the epoch of middle antiquity, there was a flood that Gun and Yu restrained through the invention of canals. The time of the near past began with the defeat of Jie, that is, the establishment of the Shang dynasty. As Han Fei observes, mankind had gone from a state of self-sufficiency in terms of goods, to a state in which it had to compete for fewer goods. The reason for this is reproduction: if everyone has five children, a grandfather will have twenty-five grandchildren, and so on. This will lead to poverty.[48] In this respect, Han Fei was by no means an advocate of the idea of progress. What is more, Han Fei's analysis anticipated the ideas of Malthus and Lewis Morgan, a nineteenth-century social evolutionarist.[49]

Characterizing the age of the middle antiquity, Han Fei argues that the first known rulers did not want power, because they did not see any benefit in it. In the 'modern' age, the opposite is true: people are fighting for office because the positions they vie for bring significant benefits.[50] Pines believes that this point connects Han Fei's thought with the famous Marx's dictum that 'social existence determines consciousness',[51] but this implicit idea is not developed further in a systematic way. This should be treated instead as an ethical statement – people desire power not for moral reasons, but for profit. Another interpretation by Pines is that the driving force of history in Han Fei's philosophy is technological development,[52] which seems to be more justified, although epochs of the near past and the present are distinguished on the basis of political criterion. Unlike Shang Yang, who elaborated on the social genesis of institutions, Han Fei stresses the role of a single eminent individual in each historical age.

Following the political criterion, Han Fei depicts his own utopia:

> If the arrow hits the target, and the rewards and penalties match the merits, Yao can rise from the dead and Yi will appear once again. At that time, the superiors do not encounter disasters that the Xia and Shang dynasties met, inferiors do not suffer from calamities like Bi Gan, sovereign sleeps peacefully, and ministers rejoice in daily work, Dao spreads across Heaven and Earth, and virtue lasts for ten thousand generations.[53]

This passage is one of the few in which Han Fei speaks of the future. As Pines emphasizes, it is characterized in the same way as the present epoch and is not radically different from the present.[54] Nick Mithen believes that the vision of Dao unchanging throughout the rest of history clearly contrasts with Han Fei's theses on the variability and uniqueness of historical epochs. For this reason, he attributes to Han Fei the idea of the 'end of history'.[55] Of course, as in the case of earlier analogies, there is no question of a systematic concept. Nevertheless, this explication seems somewhat convincing in light of the impossibility of attributing Han Fei with any idea of progress: if social evolution does not continue, it must finally stop, and this will be after the government fully relies on strict, effective laws. But then, from the very heart of Legalism, one can pose the question of how do we know that the circumstances of the future will not differ from those of the present? This leads us to the concept of *shi*.

According to François Jullien, the notion of *shi* 勢 underlies the most important philosophical ideas in China.[56] The character *shi* denotes 'power' (both physical and political), 'propensity', 'circumstances' and 'opportunity', and originally meant 'energy'. The *Art of War* devotes a separate chapter to the concept of *shi*, interpreted as 'energy',[57] the 'physical disposition' of troops, and at the same time an 'advantage' resulting, for example, from terrain.[58] This consists in the broader notion of favourable, objective circumstances that a ruler can make use of. In another sense, *shi* is found in the *Shenzi* by Shen Dao, who is often credited with creating the very notion of *shi*. Shen Dao identifies *shi* with authority 權 *quán*. Using the example of virtuous rulers who have influenced the world only once they have gained power, one can see that 'morality is not enough to subordinate the wicked, but *shi* is enough to subjugate the virtuous'.[59] Both meanings of *shi*, as well as three others which are very important in later Chinese philosophy of history, also appear in the *Shangjunshu* (though not so much explained as simply used):

1. *Shi* as political power;[60]
2. *Shi* as the specific circumstances of a certain time, in which context Shang Yang creates the notion of the '*shi* of time' 時勢 *shíshì*;[61]
3. *Shi* as the general conditions for something;[62]
4. *Shi* as a propensity towards order or chaos that cannot be overcome;[63]
5. *Shi* as the internal, natural energy of things.[64]

Han Fei, being aware of those meanings, explicated the notion of *shi*. In his opinion, *shi* is a generic term that occurs in two basic senses:

> *Shi* is one name, but it covers countless changes. If *shi* always came out of nature, it would not make sense to discuss it. That is why the *shi* I am writing about is the *shi* that a man can create (...) That natural *shi* man cannot create.[65]

Hence, Han Fei divides *shi* into the *shi* of nature 自然之勢 *zìrán zhī shì*, which is independent of human will, and the *shi* that could be controlled by humans. But if, just as in the case of the *shi* of nature, the fate of the states depends on the *shi* controlled by people, one cannot at the same time think that human fate is determined by morality. Between these theses, there is an unmovable contradiction 矛楯 *máodùn*.[66] This means that for Han Fei not only politics, but also history, is characterized in a realistic way. The idea of the objective trend of historical development will have a great impact upon the later Chinese philosophy of history.

Conclusion

Both Shang Yang and Han Fei opposed to a philosophy of history that recognizes morality as the driving force of history and consistently believes in the almost unlimited and decisive influence of man on history. From the viewpoint of Legalism, the considerations are rather focused on adapting to the times and their circumstances (*shi*), which consistently excludes any form of imitation of allegedly universal, historical models. Both thinkers employed the notion of *shi*, and Han Fei distinguished the *shi* of nature from the *shi* that can be controlled by human. This distinction gives expression to the fact that the Legalists interpreted history through the prism of structural transformations, and thereby gravitated towards historical realism. For Shang Yang, conditions of history could be explained through social transformations of power, while for Han Fei history is mainly driven by subsequent breakthroughs in the technological development. Accordingly, it was Han Fei who tended to walk away from theoretical focus on superindividual mechanisms, due to his interest in the historical role of sage-inventors and other eminent individuals, who because of their conflict with the beliefs of their times usually ended up as 'martyrs' (*lieshi*). Neither Shang Yang nor Han Fei, however, attempted to predict the future based on the knowledge of the trend of history. Instead, they were much closer to the belief in the 'end of history'.

The philosophy of history in Mohism, Daoism and the Yin-Yang School

This part of the chapter discusses philosophies of history of the Warring States Period created outside of Confucianism and Legalism. At first glance, they may appear not as systematic as the above-described approaches to history, but due to the variety and uniqueness of these ideas, most of them are taken up in the following development of the Chinese philosophy of history, even at the price of subsuming them into the (Neo-) Confucian views of history. Our discussion includes the Mohist philosophy of history, the elements of the philosophy of history present in the classical Daoism, the philosophy of history of the *Book of Changes* and the Yin-Yang School, and, finally, various eclecticisms and syncretisms, which show that right before the emergence of a new paradigm of understanding history, Chinese philosophy of history in the Warring States Period reached its theoretical limits.

The Mohist philosophy of history

Mohism is in many respects a unique philosophical school, distinguished by the revolt over prevailing rituals, the belief in a personal God, and the interest in epistemology and logic which is unparalleled in Chinese thought. This is all the more surprising since after the Warring States Period the school of Mozi, although familiar to the later philosophers (the names of a dozen Mohists are known), was almost completely ignored. Interestingly enough, Mencius himself confirms that in his day it was even a dominant school.[67] Finally, assuming that at least part of the work entitled *Mozi*, which is attributed to Mo Di (墨翟, 470–390 BC), were the work of his hand, he would be the first Chinese philosopher who wrote treatises. At the same time, this contrasts with the fact that *Mozi* is in fact the only surviving text from the school of Mohists. Taking into account that it was created over a period of two hundred years, it should be treated as an 'evolving text' that reflects, as the experts point out, the ideas of the particular sub-schools.[68]

Despite these controversies, the Mohist thinkers created a consistent philosophy of history, although it should be stressed that there is nothing to suggest that this was their purpose. Rather, it has to be reconstructed and explicated on the basis of the entire *Mozi*. This philosophy is similar in its structure to the Confucian. Not without reason did the Legalists criticize both the Confucians and the Mohists for their frequent references to legendary emperors and kings: historical anecdotes can be found in every chapter outside the canons and the military section. But as befits thinkers interested in epistemology, their philosophy is methodologically justified. To distinguish what is right/true 是 *shì* from what is wrong/false 非 *fēi*, one has to use the following three criteria 三表 *sān biǎo*:

1. The criterion of the basis 本 *běn*, i.e. whether the former rulers acted in a certain way;
2. The criterion of source 原 *yuán*, i.e. whether it is consistent with perception (literally 'the eyes and ears of ordinary people');
3. The criterion of application 用 *yòng*, i.e. whether it benefits the people of the state.[69]

Admittedly, it is impossible to follow all the ancient rulers, therefore – since these criteria are in force altogether – one can only model oneself on those rulers whose government benefited all of their subjects.[70] From the perspective of the Mohists, the basis criterion did not differ from the other descriptive criteria – it was an empirical criterion, for 'knowing the past one knows the future' 以往知來 *yǐ wǎng zhī lái*.[71]

Nevertheless, although the pattern of historical thinking of the Mohists was similar to Confucian thought, it differed in the fulfilment of the general form through its specific content. Former kings are said to have elevated only the worthiest, but this also means that they did not heed the blood ties.[72] In other words, they all show 'impartial care' 兼愛 *jiān'ài* (also translated as 'universal love'), in which relatives are not loved more than strangers. If everyone loved without differences, Mozi argues, there would be no war in the world, for war comes from taking care of the people of one's own state over people from others.[73] Consequently, Mohists believed that the former kings did not practise offensive warfare, although they did allow defensive war. But how can the annexation of neighbouring states in the past be explained? Mozi says these were cases of 'punishment' and not 'conquest', which are two different classes of terms.[74] The criterion for distinguishing between the two cases would again be utilitarian: punishment ultimately brings benefits to both parties.

So does this mean that the Mohists, like the authors of the *datong* concept, believed that a utopian state of universal love existed at the beginning of history? On the contrary:

Master Mo said: 'If we look back to the past, when people first came into being, from the vantage point of the present, it was a time when there were not yet any government leaders. In fact, there was the saying, "The people of the world all differed in their principles." This meant that for one person there was one principle, for ten people ten principles, and for a hundred people a hundred principles; the more people there were, the more so-called principles there were. This also meant that each person took his own principle to be right and the principles of others to be wrong. As a result, there was mutual disagreement (…) It became clear to people that not having leaders of government who could unify the principles of the world brought disorder to the world. This was the reason for choosing the world's most worthy, sagacious, wise, discriminating and clever man, and establishing him as the Son of Heaven, giving him the task of bringing unity to the principles of the world.[75]

The Mohist vision of ancient times is also a concept of the genesis of the state, not to say a social contract. Unlike the vision of Great Unity or even Legalism, it recognizes that the primitive state was a state of war. Interestingly, Mozi examines this state of war on the epistemological level, as a conflict between the principles that govern the individual. People give up their own principles not because they agree with another general principle, but because such a solution guarantees social stability. In this sense, the Mohists might be called consistent political consequentialists.

Mozi states that the utility of the actions of the ancient rulers was mostly manifested in the fact that they created such things as houses, clothes and vehicles, or in short, everything that was different from nature.[76] According to Michael Puett, unlike Confucians, the Mohists stressed the actual creation of new social institutions.[77] The rulers contemporary to Mo Di were, unfortunately, quite different from the ancients, and thus the world fell into a chaos.[78] The full picture of history therefore begins with the original state of chaos, which was succeeded by the state of universal love during the reign of the sage kings, and culminates in the present state of war. The reintroduction of the state of universal love is desirable – as it is evident from the appeals contained in the *Mozi* – as another historical epoch. And while in no passage of the *Mozi* can we find the idea of historical cycles, it does at least give us the 'sinusoid' of historical epochs, if we only assume that the second epoch of universal love will eventually end history by preventing any further conflicts from happening.

The structural similarity between the Mohist and the Confucian philosophy of history is also manifested in the question of Heaven. Mohists believed that the commandment of impartial care must find a deeper, metaphysical justification. Such a justification can be found in the actions of Heaven, which takes care of all people equally, since it feeds them (sending, for instance, good crops) without making any distinctions. Heaven should be imitated in this respect, as the ancient rulers whom Tian bestowed with good fortune did – unlike the cruel rulers to whom the catastrophes were sent.[79] Just as in Confucianism, virtue precedes the actions undertaken by Heaven: the great kings were 'firstly' characterized by an indifferent concern for the people, and were then rewarded by Heaven. The punishment for not following Heaven is not, however, external to the purely ethical imperatives. As the

Mozi informs us, if people do not do what Heaven desires, Heaven delivers what people do not want: misery, disease and catastrophe.[80] This explains the presence of Tian in history.

But the similarities with Confucianism end there. Mozi treats Heaven as a personal being who acts with a certain intention and has its own wishes,[81] which resulted in the title of one of the *Mozi*'s triads, the 'Will of Heaven' 天志 *Tiānzhi*. Heaven wants and loves (or does not want or love), which cannot be said of the Confucian Tian. Moreover, the *Mozi* contains a passage unique on the scale of ancient Chinese philosophy, in which Heaven speaks in independent speech, using the first-person pronoun: 'Heaven said in its mind: "All whom I love, love with universal love; all whom I benefit, benefit without an exception."'[82] It is possible that Heaven was to a certain extent understood as a creator, as evidenced by the passage which reads that Heaven's love manifests above all in the fact that it 'has done' (為 *wéi*) the sun, the moon and the stars,[83] albeit it does not mean that they are created *ex nihilo*.

Accordingly, since history is ultimately an area of actions of free persons – namely Heaven and people – there is no such thing as fate. Lu Yihan validly concludes that in Mozi's philosophy of history, it is the people themselves who determine their own destiny.[84] Erica F. Brindley even considers *Mozi* one of the roots of individualism in early China, arguing that the Mohists 'believe strongly in the fundamental agency of each individual to choose his or her own destiny according to the constraints of Heaven's judiciary control'.[85] Accordingly, the Mohists do not use the phrase *Tianming* and they do not claim that Heaven preordain who will be granted power. Heaven does not offer or withdraw the throne in the *Mozi*, but only sends down auspicious signs or disasters that can make it easier or more difficult. It is up to the free decision of prominent individuals whether they want to model their conduct upon Heaven's impartiality. By applying the 'three criteria' (basis, source, application), Mohists criticize the Confucian idea of *ming*. First, fate cannot be perceived by the senses. Second, former kings did not believe in *ming*, so they took matters into their own hands, creating government and bringing order. Third, if there was such a thing as fate, there would be no sense of doing good, and this would be bad for society.[86] The Mohists would also have objected to the Legalists and the concept of *shi*, because the history of mankind is wholly a result of the actions of persons. However, the question of how history unfolds when the three criteria are not taken into account goes beyond the scope of the *Mozi*.

Classical Daoism and the philosophy of history

Despite all the controversies over the authorship and dating of the earliest texts of Daoism, the *Laozi*, the *Zhuangzi* and the *Liezi*,[87] it turns out that Daoist writings, including the statements ascribed to Yang Zhu, did represent consistent views of history. This is because the Daoists, who in many places opposed the Confucians, rejected the speculative philosophy of history.

The Daoists believe that Heaven does not intervene in history,[88] that no one can know *ming* (fate or Mandate),[89] and even that history itself cannot be the subject of knowledge:

Memory of the ancient times passed away, who could have remembered it? The history of the Three Emperors is neither preserved nor forgotten. The history of the Five Kings is like a dream and like a reality. The history of the kings of the Three Dynasties is sometimes hidden, sometimes visible, we do not even know one in a hundred million events. The history of our own times we sometimes know indirectly, sometimes directly, we do not even know one in a ten thousand events. Current events sometimes we remember, sometimes we forget, we do not even know one in a thousand events. It is impossible to count the years that have passed since antiquity until today.[90]

The Six Classics, a source of Confucian wisdom, are merely 'the old worn-out paths of the former kings'.[91] Masters from the past cannot be understood, and even if they could, they were not a model of conduct, for they rather stultified the people and acted contrary to the Confucian ethos.[92] Moreover, Zhuangzi often portrays the kings of Zhou as wrongdoers, deriding the legends of Yao and Shun, depicting them as incapable of ruling, and frequently pictures Confucius as a Daoist, ascribing objections to the references to antiquity to him.[93] It seems that like the Legalists, Zhuangzi deliberately 'abuses' these figures, yet he does so not from a perspective of open criticism, but rather of ironically questioning the meaning of such tools: whereas the Legalists mocked Confucian legends to reject their morality and make room for their own 'empirical' genesis of the state, Zhuangzi is poised to compromise any 'theory' of history: 'instead of praising Yao and condemning Jie, it would be better to forget both of them and transform oneself with the Way'.[94]

Leung pertinently observes that the Daoists invite us to 'transcend history', although the rest of his argument, which states that they do so in order to make room for the 'deep past' of 'cosmogonic history', is less convincing.[95] The very term 'cosmogonic history' is quite problematic, not only because early Daoist cosmogony relates to essentially pre-human times and is devoid of references to particular historical events, but also because there arises a more fundamental question of whether it deals with 'the times' at all. Franklin Perkins convincingly shows that the 'common point in these cosmogonies is that the ultimate source remains immanent in the world (. . .) That is, the progressions they describe may be ontological rather than chronological'.[96] This scepticism regarding chronological approach to cosmogony is echoed in the well-known passage of the *Zhuangzi*:

If there is a beginning, there is also something that was before the beginning and also something that existed before something before the beginning. If there is being, then there is also non-being and something that was before the non-being as well as something that existed before something that existed before the non-being. Then it turns out that non-being exists, and nobody knows what exists and what not.[97]

In other words, the Daoists opt for an agnosticism with regard to history. Note that the Daoists give a negative answer to all of Wichrowski's questions that were addressed in Chapter 1: history cannot be the subject of knowledge (1); there is no definite pattern of history (2); this scheme is not known (3); the direction of variation is not reversible[98] (4); changes must not be objectively valued (5); and particularly the direction of change does not coincide with an increase of desired values (6). The question is: were the Daoists consistent in this regard?

Some scholars, such as Fang Litian, attribute a utopian philosophy of history to Laozi.[99] The only excerpt to which he refers comes from the penultimate chapter of the *Daodejing*, which describes a small state with a small group of unarmed residents using knots in place of script, and not in contact with the surrounding states. However, the specificity of the language of this fragment allows it to be translated: '*let* the state be small ... let the arms be' etc., that is, as a vision of an ideal political community, not a vision of a 'lost paradise'.[100] Much better examples are provided by the *Zhuangzi*, which describes a primitive state that is very similar to Shang Yang's vision: animals dominated people, who lived in nests, 'knowing their mothers, but did not know the fathers', living in a matriarchy.[101] Another passage describes the old days full of peace, when people 'used the knots' and did not visit each other – this wording is identical to that of the *Laozi*, but this time it has an undoubtedly historical character. Furthermore, the passage mentions the names of kings ruling before Yao and Shun, including Rongcheng, whom we met when discussing the *Rongchengshi*.[102]

In another place this state is called the Supreme Unity 至一 *Zhìyī*, and is described as the epoch in which *yin* and *yang* were in perfect harmony, and people died of old age, having never made use of knowledge. The same passage claims that after that time virtue declined: concurrence replaced unity, and then mere sedateness took the place of concurrence. The real crisis arose with the reign of Yao and Yu:

> Virtue continued to dwindle and decline, and then Yao and Yu stepped forward to take charge of the world. They set about in various fashions to order and transform the world and in doing so, defiled purity and shattered simplicity. The Way was pulled apart for the sake of goodness; Virtue was imperilled for the sake of conduct. After this, inborn nature was abandoned, and minds were set free to roam, mind joining with mind in understanding; there was knowledge, but it could not bring stability to the world. After this, 'culture' was added, and 'breadth' was piled on top. 'Culture' destroyed the substantial; 'breadth' drowned the mind; and after this, the people began to be confused and disordered. They had no way to revert to the true form of their inborn nature or to return once more to the Beginning. From this we may see that the world has lost the Way and the Way has lost the world; the world and the Way have lost each other.[103]

The primordial state of the Supreme Unity was thus a state of total harmony between people and the harmony of people with nature. This state lasted until 'great sages came, stubborn in their benevolence'.[104] However, because this was a time preceding any conflict, even contact with other municipalities could be described as being in a 'prehistoric' state. A return to this state would require moving away from (if not entirely abandoning) history, which is marked by the governments of successive rulers, and 'transforming oneself with Dao'. In this sense, the classical Daoist approach to history may to some extent be treated as a debarment of philosophizing about history, although it does raise the question of the consistency of such historical agnosticism. This, in turn, could have reflected the diversity of Daoist circles, or, looking from a diachronic perspective, the development of Daoism, since a similar vision is also found in the *Lüshi Chunqiu*,[105] which will be analysed in the following subsection.

The philosophy of history in the Yin-Yang School and Eclecticism

The philosophy of the Yin-Yang School developed and systematized earlier ideas that could be found in, among others places, the *Hongfan* chapter of the *Book of Documents* and in many passages in the *Book of Rites*, but mainly in the *Book of Changes* 易經 *Yìjīng*.[106] The *Yijing* is derived from a practice of the oracles based on cracks in shells and bones, symbolically represented as hexagrams. But very soon the book was conceived theoretically as a collection of veiled teachings, or even as a source of true wisdom and knowledge of the world. As early as the Warring States Period, the *Zhouyi* was already being treated as a Classic, and at that time also received its final shape.[107] The enigmatic and ambiguous records of the *Yijing* received numerous comments attributed to – who else – Confucius, which were codified during the reign of Han Wudi (156–87 BC) as the *Ten Wings* 十翼 *Shíyì*. The most important of these is the *Great Commentary* 大傳 *Dàzhuàn*, or more precisely 繫辭傳 *Xìcízhuàn*. It informs us that former sages created *bāguà* 八卦, the eight basic trigrams that reflect the relationship between *yin* and *yang*, which determine all the changes in the world.[108] These transformations are simply the endless cycles of *yin* and *yang*.[109] Both forces – active, bright masculine *yang* and passive, dark, female *yin* – are therefore interdependent and fluidly melt into one another. The structure of historical change to be determined by transformations of *yin* and *yang* has received numerous interpretations.

According to Liu Shu-hsien, the principle of the unity of opposites certainly resembles the dialectics of Hegel and Marx, albeit with one fundamental difference: it is a dialectics devoid of a definitive end, which Liu puts down to the lack of a Christian influence. Secondly, the philosophy of time and history in the *Yijing* is characterized by its treatment of space and time as a single continuum, and a specific holism that refuses 'to separate fact and value, immanence and transcendence, subjectivity and objectivity',[110] Chung-Ying Cheng agrees with this statement, arguing that descriptive patterns of *bagua* lead to prescriptive norms.[111] There are scholars who believe that the second principle of dialectics, the transformation of quantity into quality, is also reflected in the *Yijing*. As Zheng Wangeng argues, each change in the *Book of Changes* is based on the gradual increase/infill or decrease/dis-quantifying of *yin* or *yang*'s potential.[112]

These statements of the contemporary interpreters of the *Yijing* are, however, abstract without citing the original Chinese expressions, mainly from the *Xici shang* commentary. This text provides us with a list of features all the changes are equipped with, which had its direct impact on many Chinese philosophers of history, who built upon these categories even in the seventeenth century. In *Xici shang* we find the following statements[113]:

1. Changes are distinguished by constant 常 *cháng* regularities;
2. Changes and transformations are perceptible (變化見 *biànhuà jiàn*);

3. Changes are long-standing 久 *jiǔ* and incremental 大 *dà*;
4. Regularities are knowable 知 *zhī*, precisely reasonable 理 *lǐ*, and could be followed 從 *cóng*;
5. Observing the reasonable pattern 理 *lǐ* of changes one can find out the causes of what is hidden and manifest (知幽明之故 *zhī yōu-míng zhī gù*);
6. Things consist of subtle essence and matter-energy, *qi* (精氣為物 *jīng-qì wèi wù*), that is why the spirits are neither different in their substance from other things nor opposed to them; spirit is, in other words, an unfathomable part of the changes of *yin* and *yang*;
7. The succession of *yin* and *yang* forces is called Dao (一陰一陽之謂道 *yī yīn yī yáng zhī wèi dào*); this order is good and is expressed in human nature;
8. Events are continuous changes (通變之謂事 *tōngbiàn zhī wèi shì*), being in toto an infinite continuity of the past and the future (往來不窮謂之通 *wǎnglái bu qióng wèi zhī tong*);
9. Changes have their ultimate limit 太極 *tàijí*; what exists beyond the visible form is Dao, all the rest are concrete things (形而上者謂之道，形而下者謂之器 *xíngérshàng zhě wèi zhī dào, xíngérxià zhě wèi zhī qì*);
10. Changes could be used based on the knowledge of their laws and by means of reasoning from their continuity.

Hence, as Tian Chenshan points out, it is the idea of *tongbian* that may be considered a native, Chinese equivalent of dialectics, with the proviso that it is rather a dialectic of complementary correlatives than opposites, which does not refer to any transcendent basis, including God,[114] being self-sufficient, i.e. natural, rational and good, and at the same time infinite in time and covering spirituality, entirety of all transformations.

In addition to the *Book of Changes* and its classical commentaries, other recently discovered texts closely associated with the circle of the *Yijing* commentators, such as *Héng Xiān* 恆先, essentially complement this thought. One of the main categories in the *Heng Xian* is 'return' 復 *fù*. The text claims that there is nothing that does not return to its beginning,[115] which in an almost formal way defines the cyclical nature of the described changes. However, it is only a philosophy of time; due to the lack of any mention of extending these ideas to the history of the Chinese dynasties, it is impossible to talk about the philosophy of history here. Xie Xuanjun tries to defend the thesis on 'the philosophy of history of the *Yijing*', although the paragraph in which he argues for the 'theory of renewable history' in the *Yijing* is entitled 'The *Zhouyi* as a foreword to the philosophy of history' (*Zhōuyì lìshǐ zhéxué dǎoyán*),[116] which is quite emblematic. The philosophies of both time and history within this paradigm of reflecting upon the nature of historical change were created only by the Yin-Yang School.

Unfortunately, we know very little about the Yin-Yang School.[117] The school itself also had very discordant opinions. Sima Tan stated that the *yin-yang* doctrine caused fear among the people.[118] Sima Qian attributed the knowledge of magic techniques to Zou Yan,[119] while Han sources claimed that he possessed knowledge of alchemy and life extension techniques.[120] In contrast, Joseph Needham describes the *yin-yang* experts as 'the Naturalists' and the founders of Chinese scientific thinking. The correctness of these interpretations could be partially decided by means of an analysis of Zou Yan's philosophy of history, which can be reconstructed on the basis of the two passages: Sima Qian's record and the fragments of the *Zouzi* from the *Yuhan Shanfang ji yishu* collectaneum by Ma Guohan (1794–1857).

This is how Zou Yan's thought is portrayed in the *Shiji*:

> He examined deeply into the phenomena of the increase and decrease of the Yin and the Yang, and wrote essays totalling more than 100,000 words about their strange permutations, and about the cycles of the great sages from beginning to end.[121] His sayings were vast and far-reaching and not in accord with the accepted beliefs of the classics. First he had to examine small objects, and from these he drew conclusions about large ones, until he reached what was without limit. First he spoke about modem times, and from this went back to the time of Huang Ti. The scholars all studied his arts. Moreover, he followed the great events in the rise and fall of ages, and by means of their omens and (an examination into their) systems, extended his survey (still further) backwards to the time when the heavens and the earth had yet to be born, (in fact) to what was profound and abstruse and impossible to investigate (...) Then starting from the time of the separation of the heavens and the earth, and coming down, he made citations of the revolutions and transmutations of the Five Powers (Virtues), arranging them until each found its proper place and was confined (by history).[122]

This fragment is interesting not only because it attributes to Zou Yan a distinctive view of history, namely considerations regarding the origins of the world, humanity and the cycles of 'great sages', but also because it characterizes its method. Zou Yan's system was holistic in its content: it encompassed both nature and the history of the dynasty, contemporary things and the most ancient past of both humanity and the cosmos. His method, however, was not holistic at first sight, since he starts from small and nearby things to create an image of all the transformations of *yin* and *yang* based on inference 推 *tuī*. On the other hand, after reaching the beginning of history, on the basis of the theory of 'five phases' 五行 *wŭxíng*, Zou Yan made a proper reconstruction of history, selectively picking out examples so that he could confirm the scheme he established. This practice and the fact that Zou Yan spoke about things 'impossible to investigate' 不可考 *bùkěkǎo* with such freedom contradicts Needham's opinion. Zou Yan was not a naturalist (at least not in the Western sense of this term), but rather a full-blooded speculative metaphysician, reaching 'what is without limit'. For this reason, two methods recorded by Sima Qian can testify to the existence of a method of persuading opponents, which was different from the actual method of investigation.

The fragment from the *Yuhan Shanfang ji yishu* collectaneum illustrates the former method, presenting Zou Yan's scheme of history:

> The Five Elements dominate alternately. (Successive emperors choose the colour of their) official vestments following the directions (...) Each of the Five Virtues (Elements) is followed by the one it cannot conquer. The dynasty of Shun ruled by the virtue of Earth, the Hsia dynasty ruled by the virtue of Wood, the Shang dynasty ruled by the virtue of Metal, and the Chou dynasty ruled by the virtue of

Fire. When some new dynasty is going to arise, Heaven exhibits auspicious signs to the people. During the rise of Huang Ti (the Yellow Emperor) large earth-worms and large ants appeared. He said, 'This indicates that the element Earth is in the ascendant, so our colour must be yellow, and our affairs must be placed under the sign of Earth.' (...) Then the colour will have to be black, and affairs will have to be placed under the sign of Water. And that dispensation will in turn come to an end, and at the appointed time, all will return once again to Earth. But when that time will be we do not know.[123]

Zou Yan's scheme synchronizes the laws of nature, history, customs and politics, which has to be governed by specific rules if it wants to be effective. As Needham observes, it was a subsumption of human affairs and history under the same law, to which the phenomena of non-human nature were subjected. 'All changes in human history were thus considered manifestations of the same changes which could be observed at the lower, "inorganic" levels.'[124] In this sense – but only this – it was an instance of naturalism.

Indeed, the key idea of this passage stands in stark contrast to all of the currents of the philosophy of history in China that have been discussed so far, but not because of its naturalism. The distinctiveness of Zou Yan's approach lies in the fact that he gives a very detailed picture of the future, without knowing when the moment of change of the dominant element comes. Hence, his certainty is founded on his speculative model, not quasi-scientific thinking. Furthermore, the only rationale for recognizing a given epoch as being dominated by one or another element are omens, not to mention that the very concept of an element ruling in a particular time over others has a metaphysical character. The idea of foreseeing the future on the basis of a speculative historical pattern appears in the chapter 'Foreknowledge' 先識 *Xiānshí* of the contemporaneous *Lüshi Chunqiu*: 'Generally, when a state is about to perish, those who possess the Dao are sure to depart before it happens – in this, antiquity and the present are the same.'[125] Elsewhere *Lüshi Chunqiu* informs us that 'a sage surpasses ordinary men because he uses foreknowledge (...) Ordinary people lack the Dao to achieve foreknowledge, and since they do, they attribute it to magic or to luck.'[126] *Yin-yang* practitioners believed therefore that they conveyed accurate and verifiable knowledge, which proves that they were already refuting the allegation of magical thinking.

The work to which we owe this information is the *Spring and Autumns of Mr. Lü* 呂氏春秋 *Lǚshì Chūnqiū*, one of the largest and most well-preserved works of Chinese antiquity. It is a monumental encyclopaedia of contemporary knowledge and a compilation of sources, written in 239 BC under the auspices of Lü Buwei 呂不韋 (291–235 BC), the chancellor of the Qins. According to Sima Qian, at the gate of the Qin capital there was a sign announcing that every scholar who added anything to the *Spring and Autumns* would receive a thousand pieces of gold, and so 'in this work, all matters concerning Heaven and earth, all creatures and history, were put in order'.[127] The *Lüshi Chunqiu* is thus a monument to Chinese eclecticism: the free compilation of various currents, which should be distinguished from syncretism, namely the theoretical attempt to not so much combine as to reconcile contradictory standpoints. As Chen Qiyou estimates, 1/4 of the text represents the Yin-Yang School, 1/5 the

Militarists, 1/8 Legalism, 1/8 Mohism and 1/4 other schools: Confucianism, Daoism, the School of Agriculture, Hedonism and the School of Music.[128]

With regard to the philosophy of history, the following ideas can be found therein:

1. from the Yin-Yang School: former rulers followed the principles of *yin-yang*, modelling themselves on Heaven and Earth and using their *qi*; *yin-yang* forces are responsible for the cycles of the rise and fall of the dynasties, according to the Five Phases scheme, which is foreseeable;[129]
2. from the School of Militarists: the right strategy always brought the old kings victory, they never changed their methods according to the circumstances; thanks to their knowledge, the disposition of the people, and the proper use of weapons, they became heroes;[130]
3. from Legalism: one cannot adapt the old rules (the Militarists differ from the Legalists in believing in the existence of strategy that is effective at all times);[131]
4. from Mohism: former rulers were impartial and promoted only the virtuous; if good cannot be clearly distinguished from evil, the state will fall;[132]
5. from Confucianism: former rulers were guided by loyalty and filial piety, and treated the people according to the norms of righteousness;[133]
6. from Daoism: former kings ruled in secret, 'they did not act', so the people knew nothing of them, and the world lived in a state of primordial community without any rituals;[134]
7. from the School of Agriculture: former rulers focused only on agriculture, living in harmony with the seasons and did not take the opportunity to initiate wars;[135]
8. from Hedonism: former rulers cared only for themselves and their bodies, while the ancient dynasties were concerned only with their own people;[136]
9. from the School of Music: former rulers created music that reflects the Original Unity, the Dao, and the harmony of *yin* and *yang*; in a fallen epoch, there are fallen musical forms.[137]

As for the schools of Militarists, Agriculture, Hedonism and Music, *Lüshi Chunqiu* is practically the only source of our knowledge about the elements of their own philosophies of history. The *Lüshi Chunqiu* also shows that the philosophy of history in other schools was fully formed at that time. For instance, the following passage expresses the basic principle hidden behind the Confucian philosophy of history:

> The relationship between the present and the past is the same as the relationship between the past and later ages. The relationship between the present and later ages is the same as that between the present and the past. Thus, one who knows the present well can know the past, and one who knows the past can know later ages. Past and present, before and after, have one and the same principle.[138]

Interestingly, these words, which were written before the end of the third century BC, directly contradict Koselleck's thesis that the conceptual recognition of the three times of history appeared only with the European Enlightenment. Koselleck's thesis remains valid only regarding the modern notion of history.

Another example of eclecticism is the *Master Guan* 管子 *Guǎnzǐ*, created probably in the third century BC, but attributed to Guan Zhong (725–645 BC). The theme specific to the *Guanzi*, which will return in the Han dynasty, is a belief that historical success is gained by those who care about the living conditions of the people, and even form 'one body' with the people by virtue of knowing their hearts.[139] Apart from that, we find in the *Guanzi* a typically Confucian belief in the historical role of Heaven,[140] a Mohist idea of modelling on the will of Tian,[141] a Daoist vision of unity with Dao through mind control,[142] a Militarist view on the decisive character of the troops,[143] a Legalist stress put on the historical efficiency of the law,[144] and a Naturalist conception of gaining power by those who used the *yin* and *yang*.[145]

The *Master Yin Wen* 尹文子 *Yīnwénzǐ* could be considered an example of syncretism in the philosophy of history. In contrast to the syncretists, all of the schools distinguished only one way of gaining and maintaining power. According to the *Yinwenzi*, in turn, there are many causes which can (simultaneously) contribute to the fall of the state, and in order to gain power one usually has to go so far as to break the law and commit murder. Elsewhere, benevolence, names, penalties and law are listed together among the eight equivalent 'arts' used by the ancient kings.[146] In addition to the Legalist and Confucian motifs, there are also Daoist themes. In fact, it is even said that the government following the Great Dao, as described in the teachings of Laozi, is superior to the teachings of the Schools of Names, Legalists, Confucians and Mohists.[147] This declaration notwithstanding, the *Yinwenzi* aims at reconciling all views of history created within classical Chinese schools of philosophy.

Another instance of syncretism in the Chinese philosophy of history of that time is *The Pheasant Cap Master* 鶡冠子 *Héguānzǐ*, a text which, according to Carine Defoort, was created probably under the Qin, and certainly before the Han.[148] One of the key concepts of the text is destiny (*ming*), which extends from one day to a human life, being omnipresent and unavoidable.[149] As Marnix Wells shows, the *Heguanzi* interprets Dao as a necessity expressed in law and virtue, combining the idea of destiny with human will by situating both factors within a great tendency 大勢 *dàshì*. Moreover, the knowledge of *dashi* is attributed to 'nine augustans' 九皇 *jiǔhuáng*, who are equipped with foreknowledge, including the knowledge of the imminent end of the world.[150] In this way the *Heguanzi* synthesizes ideas coming from Daoism, Confucianism, Legalism and the Yin-Yang School, although it is distinctive in its explicit idea of the end of history, which also contains some messianic threads. The authors of the *Heguanzi* believe that in last days the 'Complete Ninth' 成鳩 *Chéng Jiū* will appear. Cheng Jiu is supposed to use his royal axe in order to bring peace and universal law to the world, so that people will not need walls in their dwellings, all barbarians will pay homage to him and there will be no alien ideas in the affluent empire.[151] It is undoubtedly an individualist view of history and the *Heguanzi* does not hide this:

Pangzi said: Is there, accordingly, a difference between ancient and modern ways? Heguanzi said: Antiquity is indeed past due to individuals; masses are formed as masses also due to individuals – this is what is different about them! If some model is good, it cannot be forgotten even after ten thousand ages [– this is what is constant].[152]

The person hidden behind this mysterious figure of the messiah is undoubtedly no one other than the First Emperor of China. In this manner the *Heguanzi* constitutes a bridge between the syncretist philosophy of history of the late Warring States Period and the new hopes of the philosophers of history living in the unified empire, first Qin and then Han.

Conclusion

Chinese philosophy of history in the Warring States Period covers a considerable variety of standpoints, which offered an alternative to both Confucian and Legalist solutions. While the Daoists dismissed and derided any speculation about the meaning of history, the Mohists attempted to defend it based on their methodological criteria, and the proponents of the Yin-Yang School believed in almost unlimited cognitive abilities to grasp the most distant past and the upcoming future. This notwithstanding, the Daoists tended towards the view that history is ultimately all about the fall of the primordial state of natural harmony. The Mohists shared some of the Confucian schemes, although carefully filled them with the distinctive content: impartial care instead of benevolence, personal Heaven in place of impersonal Tian, and accordingly rejected all the fatalism connected with the doctrine of *Tianming*. Unlike Daoism and Confucianism, Mohism defended the thesis that the primitive state of history was a state of war, and not of harmony. Both Mohism and Daoism, however, appear to represent linear views of history, in contrast to, for instance, the philosophy of history from the commentaries to the *Yijing*. The systematic and coherent cyclical view of history contained therein is rooted in almost formal (and according to many scholars, dialectical) 'changeology', which presents the historical world as a rational and natural totality of complementary and continuous events, devoid of God or any other transcendent basis. This theoretical innovation was already manifested in the philosophy of history in the Yin-Yang School, which aimed at speculative inference of the sequence of particular historical cycles, which all depend upon the transformations of natural elements, and thereby allow for predicting the future. The idea of 'foreknowledge' was particularly developed in the eclectic *Lüshi Chunqiu*, which along with such texts as *Guanzi* collected numerous approaches to history represented at the end of the Warring States Period. Other texts of that time, such as the *Yinwenzi*, went even further, actively combining various views of history, whereas such texts as the *Heguanzi* foresaw the upcoming end of history and the emergence of the messianic figure of great governor, which responded to the hopes that gave rise to the Qin and Han empires.

Nature, People and History

The Philosophy of History in the Han Dynasty

Introduction

In the times of the Han dynasty, both the Western (206 BC–9 BC) and Eastern (25–220 BC) Chinese philosophy of history entered its systematic and mature phase. This would not have been possible without the historical events that separate the Han dynasty from the Warring States Period and define its internal division, i.e. the short yet tumultuous reigns of the Qin (221–206 BC) and Xin (9–23 BC) dynasties. Their influence on the interpretations of history made by contemporaneous Chinese philosophers is invaluable, which only confirms the thesis about the impact of historical conditioning on the philosophy of history. Since the significance of the Xin dynasty will become clear in the light of the events and concepts that preceded it, I shall return to this point later in this chapter, now moving on to the role that the Qin dynasty played in the reorientation of the Chinese philosophy of history. The conquest of various Chinese states and the creation of the first empire in Chinese history carried out by Yin Zheng, the later First Emperor of China 秦始皇帝 *Qín Shǐ Huángdì* (259–210 BC), brought unification to many spheres of social life. First of all, it meant the birth of a centralized and absolutist monarchy that was to exist in China for over 2,000 years. At the same time, ancestral property was abolished, private property was established and the aristocracy was resettled, which was a blow to the power of the old elites. It was a time of the unification and standardization of the monetary system, measures and weights, wheelbase and, most importantly, Chinese script. In the spirit of the Legalists, among whom were Qin Shi Huang's chief adviser, Li Si, consistent and strict state laws were also passed. The Qin reign had an exceptional spirit of novelty. The conviction of break up with history and opening up to an entirely new future was reflected in the numerous inscriptions on the steles spread across China. The stela of the mountain Yi informs us that 'blood was shed in the open countryside—This had begun in highest antiquity (...) Now today, the August Thearch has unified All-under-Heaven into one family—Warfare will not arise again!'[1] Sima Qian attributed to Qin Shi Huangdi the following words: 'we are the First Emperor. The generations that will follow us will take the numbers of the Second, the Third, and so forth to the thousand and ten thousand generations let their power go on endlessly.'[2] In such a way, he justified the fact that, instead of an epithet, he had a number in his title. It is therefore possible to say that he opted for a linear vision of the historical process, close to what Pines and Mithen referred to as the 'end of history'. On the other hand, Sima Qian states in the same place, 'The First Emperor established the order of succession of virtues. Recognizing that the virtue of the Zhou dynasty was fire, and that the Qin dynasty came after the Zhou, he adopted as the virtue of the Qin dynasty a virtue the Zhou dynasty cannot overcome. Thus, the [reign of the] virtue of water began.'[3] Thus, he was no less sympathetic to the theory of the Yin-Yang School, which assumed, however, the cyclical nature of historical change and the future overthrow of the Qin. As Wang Gaoxin notes, the use of the philosophy of history of the Yin-Yang School was selective and served mainly to legitimize the takeover of power, albeit at the same time it was an expression of the outstanding historical consciousness of Qin Shi Huang.[4]

Indisputable historical consequences resulted from the cooperation of the emperor with Li Si, who openly opposed the Confucian vision of imitating the ancient rulers. Sima Qian recounts the memorial of this philosopher, which led Qin Shi Huangdi to the infamous burning of the Confucian books:

> Five Emperors did not repeat anything after their predecessors. The Three Dynasties did not imitate one another. Each of them ruled in their own way, yet did not do so because they opposed each other, but rather because the times had changed. (...) Meanwhile, scholars do not want to take the example of the present times, but imitate antiquity instead in order to disaffirm the present times. They raise doubts and confusion among the black-haired people. Your Chancellor Li Si, risking the death sentence dares to say: In the old days, the world was divided and lived in chaos. And there was no one who could have succeeded in unifying it (...) Now, when the Emperor himself conquered the whole world, clearly separated white from black and established unity, they still praise private studies and coalesce with each another (...) Your servant suggests that all the histories except the records of the Qin kingdom should be burned. Apart from those who hold the office of the Learned Scholars, all who have dared to keep the *Book of Songs*, the *Book of Documents*, and the discourses of all schools around the world, should take them to local authorities to burn these books. Whoever dares to talk about the *Book of Songs* and the *Book of Documents* should be killed, and his body will be exposed on the market. Whoever will refer to the past to criticize the present should be killed with all his family.[5]

As can be seen, at the centre of Li Si's arguments was the Legalist philosophy of history. Ironically, in the long run, the burning of books put an end to the non-Confucian schools.

The real scale of the 'burning of books and burying of scholars' is hard to measure. We have lost most of the chronicles of individual Chinese states. The treatises of the philosophical schools such as the Yin-Yang School, the School of Music and the School of Agriculture have been lost; for the next two thousand years, the history of Chinese thought did not have any significant representative from the School of Names and Mohism. Although most of these works could have been kept by the 'learned scholars', the burning of the imperial library in 206 BC by the Han army only intensified the effects of the edict of Qin Shi Huangdi. The Han dynasty intellectuals were faced with a radical discontinuity between history and the times they lived in. In opposition to the First Emperor, however, they sought to bridge this gap and to create a unified and comprehensive vision of Chinese history, both in the field of philosophy (Dong Zhongshu) and historiography (Sima Qian), and, as a result, laid the foundations for the official ideology of the Chinese Empire.

On the other hand, scholars of the early Han dynasty often cited writings that since then will be known and venerated as 'the Classics'. Undoubtedly, the part of the Confucian writings has survived the edict, which became the seedbed of a famous dispute. Thinkers of the so-called New Text School wrote down the allegedly memorized works using the new, clerical script. This school centred around Dong Zhongshu and interpreted the Classics in light of the *Gongyang Commentary* 公羊傳 *Gōngyángzhuàn*, a commentary on the *Spring and Autumn Annals* 春秋 *Chūnqiū*, which portrayed Confucius as a kind of prophet. However, in the second century BC, the allegedly pre-Qin Classics, written in the old script, were found in the wall of Confucius' house in Qufu. This event gave rise to the Old Text School, which concentrated later around Liu Xin 劉歆 (50 BC–23 CE). He catalogued and edited (and for some historians rather falsified) the *Zuo Commentary* 左傳 *Zuǒzhuàn* and the *Zhou Rituals* 周禮 *Zhōulǐ*. The dispute proper was thus initiated during the Eastern Han Dynasty. This philological debate was connected (although, as I will show, not identical) with a fundamental philosophical dispute that will be covered in this chapter.

The idea of correlation between nature and humanity

The tumultuous historical changes, the reinterpretation of pre-imperial Chinese philosophy and the efforts of the emperors of the Han dynasty to theorize the legitimacy of their power, mainly by inserting a new reign in the schema of the previous rulers: all this lies at the root of a unique, blooming period of the Chinese philosophy of history between the second century BC and the second century CE. History itself seemed to confirm the philosophical theories: the Qin, Xin and Han dynasties fell (at least partly) as a result of peasant uprisings, even the first Han dynasty emperor was a peasant; the uprising against the only emperor of the ephemeral Xin dynasty was a reaction to a natural disaster – a giant Yellow River flood; finally, the Qin dynasty almost became punished for the condemnation and destruction of the work of the sages. This does not mean, however, that all thinkers agreed on the interpretation of these historical events: on the contrary, from the perspective of time one could distinguish a particular dispute that aroused the minds of the philosophers. On the one hand, it was not an institutionalized dispute; on the other hand, it is impossible to overlook it on the basis of the ideas and polemics of that time. The point of the dispute was the answer to the question: do we observe in history a relationship between nature and humanity? In the context of one of the concrete forms of this problem, in which Heaven acts as a mediator between mankind and nature, i.e. in the famous concept of the correlation between Heaven and humanity 天人感應 *Tiān-rén gǎnyìng*, the question is: do people influence Heaven with their behaviour, so that Heaven reacts and 'responds' to people through transformations of nature, in this way shaping history? The positive answer to this question leads to a specific holistic synthesis of ethics, metaphysics, the philosophy of nature and the philosophy of history.

Among the followers of the idea of the correlation between nature and humanity there are both those who assumed the mediation of Tian, namely Dong Zhongshu and the authors of the *Chunqiu Fanlu*, He Xiu from the New Text School, Liu Xin from the Old Text School, and the eclectics: Ban Gu and Wang Fu, as well as those who understood this idea in another way, like Lu Jia and the authors of the *Huainanzi*. In this way the idea of correlation between nature and people transcended Confucianism, which over time, at least in the field of the philosophy of history, merged with Legalism and the Yin-Yang School.

The philosophy of history of Dong Zhongshu and the *Chunqiu fanlu*

The central position of Dong Zhongshu 董仲舒 (179–104 BC) in the New Text faction was connected with his reputation for being an expert on the *Gongyang zhuan*. Hence, I shall firstly have a brief look at the historiosophy of this commentary on the *Chunqiu*.

The *Gongyangzhuan* espoused a common interpretation at that time, according to which the *Spring and Autumn Annals* are meant to express moral judgements about past figures and events. If a person 'deserves' censure, disapproval must be expressed in the chronicle, but this should be done with a homogeneous narrative style.[6] Moreover, the *Gongyang zhuan* connects the philosophy of history with metaphysics. Great individuals are said to have a close relation to Heaven; a key role is played by the ruler who 'is of one body with his state'.[7] The very first piece of the work argues that the purpose of the *Chunqiu* was to praise the 'great unity' 大一統 *dà yītǒng* of the ruler and the state.[8] The commentary claims that states deprived of a sovereign fell into chaos, as evidenced by historical events.[9] If such importance is attributed to the ruler, then how to explain the historical role of Confucius, who was never enthroned? The *Gongyang zhuan* reinterprets (not to say 'perverts') history to create the image of Confucius as a 'king without a crown'. On the one hand, it is claimed that he had a real influence on individual rulers. On the other hand, it is stated that the *Chunqiu* 'brought order in times of chaos and restored what was right', by promoting the ways of the legendary Yao and Shun, and proclaiming the imminent arrival of a 'future sage' 後聖 *hòushèng*.[10] In this way, the *Gongyang* authors referred to the Mencian legend of the *Chunqiu*, which implied the vision of historical cycles, determined by the comings of the sages. Dong Zhongshu developed this cyclic approach, at the same time combining all the threads loosely connected in the *Gongyang zhuan* into a new and coherent whole.

The main problem facing an investigator of Dong Zhonghsu's philosophy of history is the reliability of the sources of his thought. The work usually treated as his magnum opus, the *Luxuriant Gems of the Spring and Autumn Annals* 春秋繁露 *Chūnqiū fánlù*, is mentioned for the first time only in the sixth century, and none of the works attributed to Dong Zhongshu in the Han literature has survived to our times. The *Chunqiu fanlu* is, besides, a patchy literary work, and many of the ideas contained there are mutually exclusive.[11] This unfortunately includes chapters devoted to the philosophy of history.[12] Hence, the main reliable source of information about Dong Zhongshu's ideas are his three replies to the instructions of Emperor Han Wudi concerning the relation between Heaven and man 天人三策 *Tiān-rén sāncè*, included in the *Book of Han* 漢書 *Hànshū*. There are at least three main theories about the relationship of the *Tian-ren sance* to the *Chunqiu fanlu*. The radical version, represented by Michael Loewe, separates both works, stating that the *Chunqiu fanlu* is not a source of knowledge about Dong Zhongshu.[13] In the 'moderate' version, defended by e.g. Sarah Queen, it is claimed that some of the *Chunqiu fanlu* chapters convey the original ideas of Dong Zhongshu, and perhaps some of his original writings.[14] In another version, Gary Arbuckle states that the *Chunqiu fanlu* is a work whose subsequent chapters correspond to the evolution of the New Text School, including part of the original ideas of Dong Zhongshu; that the *Chunqiu fanlu* develops themes only indicated in the *Hanshu*, and that elements of the philosophy of history from the *Luxuriant Gems* could be found in the text entitled *Shangshu dazhuan* from the end of the Qin dynasty.[15] I agree with Queen that some parts of the *Chunqiu fanlu* reflect Dong Zhongshu's thought and with Arbuckle that this text is an important source for concepts that develop the ideas of this philosopher. Revision of the legend of Dong Zhongshu does not mean his importance is reduced: granted, he did not make historical use of the *wuxing* theory, but he did apply the *yin-yang* theory; he did not single-handedly contribute to the triumph of Confucianism, yet he referred to Confucius more often than anyone in those times; it was owing to him that the worship of Heaven replaced for good the past cults (particularly the cult of 五帝 *wǔdì*), and it was he who first presented a systematic conception of the correlation between Heaven and humanity, which interests us most.

The *Tian-ren sance* informs us that the *Chunqiu* describes past events by means of showing an interaction between Heaven and humans, precisely because Heaven sends various signs to the rulers and when they do not respond with their conduct, it causes catastrophes that contribute to their defeat and the collapse of their states. To be exact, the bad conduct creates a bad kind of *qi*, which disturbs the rhythm of the *yin-yang* forces, which in turn causes natural disasters. However, this is not being done by human acts alone, but through Heaven, which directly affects the *yin* and *yang*. On the other hand, human actions have a decisive influence on this state of affairs; as Dong Zhongshu argues, when the ruler of Qin, whose tyranny and cruelty is unequalled throughout history, ceased moral education, his dynasty collapsed. The king who will cultivate the five great virtues (benevolence, righteousness, ritual propriety, wisdom and trust) will receive the support of Heaven and the spirits, and his virtue will reach all living beings.[16] The ruler receives from Heaven the Mandate in exchange for his actions, which allows him to accomplish things impossible from the perspective of an ordinary man, also the hearts of the people turn to him; all the omens that accompany this are the response of Tian to his virtue.[17] On the basis of this vision, Dong Zhongshu reinterprets at the beginning of the second memorial the history of China from the times of Yao to the Xia, Shang and Zhou dynasties, concluding that despite various times they form a single thread.[18] Moreover, the correlation between Heaven and humanity is not limited only to the past, but also extends to the future:

The depth of [a relations between] Heaven and humanity forms the Dao of history (...) [Confucius] recorded the faults of various states and clans, linking them with disasters and extraordinary changes to show that human conduct, no matter how good or evil, reaches and penetrates Heaven and earth, so the past and the future correspond to each other. This is the highest principle of Heaven.[19]

It is clear from this passage that people and Heaven, conduct and nature, the past and the future, form one whole in Dong Zhongshu's philosophy of history.

The essential unalterableness (or rather the unalterableness of the essence) of history raises the question that the emperor himself asked Dong Zhongshu: how is it possible that the ways of ancient kings differed so much from one another?[20] In other words: are there other rules specific to particular epochs apart from the principle of history, i.e. the relation between Heaven and humanity? Dong Zhongshu admits that Dao does not change and lasts for tens of thousands of years,[21] however individual dynasties differ in their regulations and ways of responding to the mandate of Heaven, establishing the first month of a new era and the colour of official robes. The general nature of these regulations and governance can be reduced to the rules specific for the dynasties: the principle of the Xia dynasty was loyalty 忠 *zhōng*; the principle of the Shang dynasty – respect 敬 *jing*; and the principle of the Zhou dynasty – refinement 文 *wén*. Most importantly, this list exhausts the spectrum of rules, so the Han dynasty must return to loyalty and abandon the lavishness of the Zhou.[22] This will complete one historical cycle. Second, although the world of antiquity is the same world as the one we live in, in the old days there was a harmony and order that will never be achieved again – 'by comparing the past and the present, how far is the present from the past!'[23] An implicit linearity is thus entered into historical cycles: people will no longer have such moral qualities as their ancestors and former rulers, so responding to Heaven through conduct will only be more difficult. The Han Dynasty will not return completely to the paradigm of the former Xia Dynasty. It is also clear from the schema that the Han reign will be replaced by a government based on respect. Therefore, as Arbuckle observes, Dong Zhongshu's philosophy of history could not have become the ideology of the Han dynasty without any alterations.[24]

Let me now confront this very rich material with the content of the several hundred pages of the *Chunqiu fanlu*. It will be seen that this work develops the ideas outlined above and adds the concepts absent in the *Hanshu*, which, if they had not fall into contradiction, could have originated from Dong Zhongshu and/or his circle of disciples.

The basic frame of reference for the construction of Dong Zhongshu's philosophy of history is his exegesis of the *Chunqiu*, as evidenced by the title and the content of the *Chunqiu fanlu*. Dong refers to the alleged Confucius quote, which states that 'explaining things with abstract theories is not as good as the breadth and depth of past events for parsing and illuminating things'.[25] It is difficult to find a better description of the significance of historiography for Chinese philosophy, and thus the importance of the philosophy of history. From the perspective of Dong Zhongshu, the function of the *Spring and Autumn Annals* was not limited to the collection of moral teachings, although this dimension was not subject to discussion.[26] First of all, the *Chunqiu* would in itself present a certain philosophy of history: 'By studying the *Chunqiu*, I observe successes and failures, cover the various causes of the rise and fall of the past epochs'.[27]

However, since in Dong Zhongshu's eyes the rise and the fall of states depends upon the interaction between Heaven and man, this truth is also to be found in the *Chunqiu*. Indeed, in the memorial from the *Hanshu* Dong seeks to convince us that the first sentence of the *Annals* (analogous to each sentence beginning the entries), 'the first year, spring, the king's first month' 元年, 春, 王正月 *yuǎnnián, chūn, wáng zhèngyuè* means that the king establishes his first month according to the season established by Heaven, and just as the word 'king' occurs after the word 'spring,' so the ruler imitates Heaven.[28] In other words, in his esoteric exegesis, Dong Zhongshu wishes to demonstrate that the *Chunqiu* explained history through the prism of the mutual correlation between Heaven and humanity. It might be said that this part of his reflection transcends the division of philosophy of history into the philosophy of historiography and the speculative philosophy of history, creating something that may be called a 'speculative philosophy of historiography'.

The above considerations do not exhaust his speculative philosophy of historical writing. Unlike the previous exegetists of the *Chunqiu*, who claimed that the chronicle is a collection of moral teachings, Dong Zhongshu asks about the conditions of this state. Judging historical figures requires at least three conditions: on the part of the subject, the ability of the people to make judgements; further, the object of this judgement, that what is properly judged (intention, result or the character of historical figures); finally, the criteria for judging the past and the present are assumed to be common, otherwise the past is so different from the present that it cannot be judged. Each of these conditions can be traced back to Dong Zhongshu. As for the 'power of judgement', Dong's opinion was that it is given by Heaven: 'To praise good and to condemn evil, to rejoice in honor and to repudiate dishonor – these are not things that man alone can produce, man is rather endowed with them by Heaven.'[29] Second, when evaluating historical figures, one should evaluate intentions, not actions:

An *Ode* declares: 'What other human beings possess in their hearts, I can measure by reflection.' This indicates that all events have their counterparts. By observing the external fact of an event, one can see what lies within. Now if we look into the actions of Dun to observe his heart, [we will find that] his original intention was not criminal (...) If his heart were not sincere, then how was he be able to act in that way? Therefore, if we follow [his intentions] from beginning to end, we will find that he did not intend to commit regicide.[30]

A key role is played by deduction: 'in discussing the case, the *Chunqiu* always go by the facts to get through to the intentions; when the intention is evil, it does not wait for committing an act [in order to judge it].'[31] It is notable that the importance of reconstructing the intentions of actors on the basis of historical records was emphasized in the West only by Dilthey and Colingwood. In their case, however, this was a distinctive method for the historical sciences, while for Dong Zhongshu this was the basis for speculative philosophy.

The third condition of judgements on historical figures was already quoted: it is the assumption of the unity of the past and the present, called in the *Hanshu* the 'single thread' or Dao of history. Moreover, it is possible not only to make judgements of the past, but also past events themselves can constitute sources of knowledge about the present and the future:[32]

> I have not heard that there are two Daos in the world, thus although the ways in which the sages ruled were different, their principle was common. The past and the future are intertwined and penetrate each other.[33]

In this way, Dong Zhongshu accepts the thesis that distinguishes the Confucian philosophy of history: history is the realization of one principle, and from this perspective the past and the present are one, allowing us to learn moral lessons from history. This certainly implies some sort of essentialism. As Liu Jiahe notes, if one combines this idea with the vision of the correlation between Heaven and humanity, it turns out that in the historical process, as Dong Zhongshu understands it, three layers can be distinguished. The first layer is the immutable Dao of history; the next, variable layer, is the transformation of nature, which – mediated by Heaven – is reflected in the changes taking place in the third layer, namely in the social and political world, that is the history in the strict sense.[34] This concept can be represented as follows:

Layer	Description	Dynamics	Status
third	human world	variable	real: social
second	nature	variable	real: natural
first	Dao	constant	ideal

Figure 4 The basic structure of historical process for Dong Zhongshu.

Between nature and the human world, there is a relationship of mutual correlation: the order or chaos in a given epoch depends on the transformation of nature, of the *yin* and *yang* forces.[35] On the other hand, if the ruler does not handle the government properly, people are affected by disease; there are disasters (such as drought) that even involve animals.[36] This interaction is not direct: Heaven mediates between human behaviour and the changes of nature. The virtues of those who become rulers reach Heaven, which treats them just like its own sons. It must be stressed that Heaven does not give the Mandate to actual kings and emperors, but 'the king must first receive the Mandate and only then be the king.'[37] In order to maintain the Mandate, the king must not only be virtuous, but also practise rituals that 'unite Heaven and earth and embody the *yin* and *yang*'.[38] After receiving the Mandate, the ruler of the new dynasty changes the calendar by establishing the new first day of the year, accepts a new name and changes the colour of the robes.[39] The ruler's feelings correspond to Heaven, and as such he is said to participate in Tian; he is observing Heaven, therefore he strives for harmony with it. This means, however, that Heaven takes on many features of a personal being. Dong writes that by studying the intentions of Heaven we see that it is infinitely good, bestowing that goodness on all people.[40] As Joachim Gentz observes, such a vision of Heaven is not so much of Confucian, but rather of Mohist origin.[41] Taking this into consideration, it has to be admitted that the theories of Dong Zhongshu initiated the development of Confucianism towards the theistic direction. Sarah Queen adds:

> In contrast to the Judeo-Christian tradition, for example, which posits an ontological gap between God and humanity and thereby understands humanity to be fundamentally different from God, early Confucians maintained that there was an essential ontological unity between Heaven and humanity. (...) The concept of unity illuminates not only the spiritual dimensions of the Confucian tradition in general, but also the religious quality of Tung Chung-shu's thinking in particular.[42]

Dong Zhongshu himself emphasized the holistic and religious nature of his own system when, in the chapter under the notable title *Heaven's Way is not Dualistic*, he argues that the actions of Heaven are not manifested in a dualistic way, but rather a 'unifying' one; the chapter concludes with a significant quotation from the *Book of Songs*: 'God (*Shangdi*) is close, in a heart that is not split.'[43]

To show that Heaven is a mediator between human deeds and transformations of nature, one has to demonstrate not only the unity of Heaven with humanity, but also with nature. Accordingly, Dong Zhongshu states that 'the will of Heaven constantly puts *yin* in empty places and takes them to accompany *yang*';[44] Heaven manages the changes of *qi* in a gradual manner, so that nothing becomes suddenly hot or cold.[45] Furthermore, these changes are characterized by a set order, in which the similar transforms into the similar: '*yang* increases *yang*, *yin* increases *yin* (...) when [Tian] wants to bring rain, it activates *yin*, causing *yin* to rise; When it is going to stop the rain, it activates *yang*, causing *yang* to rise.'[46] Hence, Heaven intervenes in history: 'the rise and fall are determined by Heaven, the sage knows this and also knows that there are situations when he cannot save himself, which are the destiny.'[47] Of course, there is the question of where the fatalistic implications of Dong's theory come from,[48] since people are provoking Heaven to particular decisions. It turns out that in the spirit of the monarchism typical for the *Gongyangzhuan*, Dong Zhongshu concludes that only the ruler influences Heaven with his conduct, while the rest of the people, including the sages, are helpless in the face of Tian's decision to condemn the ruler and to bring about natural disasters. For this reason, the Dong Zhongshu's detailed vision of history, to which we now proceed, reflects China's political history.

As we know from the *Hanshu*, the general vision of the correlation between Heaven and human beings served Dong Zhongshu to present a detailed typology of history: the cycles of the Xia, Shang and Zhou dynasties, which respectively corresponded to the principles of loyalty, respect and style. However, the typology of virtues does not appear in the *Chunqiu fanlu*. In fact, there are quite different typologies that could be reconciled with difficulty, presenting a very inconsistent vision of history. It is possible to assume that the typologies contained in Chapter 23 of the *Chunqiu fanlu* do not come from Dong Zhongshu and also are not the work of one author. This does not mean, however, that those typologies should not be analysed; on the contrary, they express a keen interest in the philosophy of history among (probably) the successors of Dong.

In place of the virtues, these dynasties are associated with colours, which refer to the whole ritual system that each dynasty should preserve: the Three Standards 三統

Sāntǒng of the white, red and black. This corresponds respectively to the Shang, the Zhou and the Spring and Autumn period. The last was treated there as a royal dynasty,[49] the ruler of which would probably be Confucius. From the view that the Three Standards start with black and the cyclical nature of the *Santong*, it may be indirectly concluded that black was also the standard of the Xia dynasty, preceding Shang. Moreover, each of the standards is combined with the reign of one of the rulers preceding the Xia: the Spring and Autumn period with Yu, the Zhou with Shun, and the Shang with Yao. With the help of favourable interpretation, it can be assumed that the 'black-white-red' cycle started with Yao. Yet, the chapter is silent on the issue of the stages of the cycle. Naturally, the Qin should accept white, and the Han red. But this is not the end of interpretative complications. The chapter reads that black and white are the standards of the simple 質 *zhì* rituals, while red of refined ones 文 *wén*. The Zhou dynasty would be, again, the dynasty of the virtue of *wen*. This leads to the conception of the cycle of the repetitive principles of simplicity and refinement, reflected in the Shang and Xia dynasties.[50] In the next part of the chapter, simplicity, refinement, Shang and Xia are treated as four separate models 四法 *sìfǎ*, which not only interprets Shang and Xia as common names, but also implies paradoxical consequences when the Shang rulers have not adopted 'Shang' as their model. I agree with Arbuckle and Wang Gaoxin that these are basically two, not four, stages of the cycle.[51] It is also worth mentioning that these divisions concern only the Chinese inhabitants of the Central States 中國 *zhōngguó*; the barbarians and the inhabitants of other lands who do not know the rituals lie 'outside' the Three Standards. At the same time, it is claimed that the Three Dynasties ruled the whole world,[52] which means that non-Chinese nations are not so much explicable by some other pattern as irrelevant to the course of history as such. To sum up, Dong Zhongshu's 'cohered' philosophy of history as described in both the *Hanshu* and the *Chunqiu fanlu* could be presented in the following form.[53] (Omission of the Qin is deliberate[54]):

Period	Color	Virtue	Style	
Yao	*black*	*loyalty*	*simple*	
Shun	*white*	*respect*	*refined*	
Yu	*red*	*refinement*	*simple*	
Xia	black	loyalty	refined	
Shang	white	respect	simple	
Zhou	red	refinement	refined	
Chunqiu	*black*	*loyalty*	*simple*	

Figure 5 Cohered and complemented scheme of history according to the *Chunqiu fanlu* and *Hanshu* 56 (deduced elements in italics).

Although this detailed vision of historical cycles was not very popular, the basic idea of the correlation between Heaven and humanity later found a large number of followers.

The idea of the correlation between Heaven and humanity in the Eastern Han dynasty

The belief in the mutual influence between Heaven and humanity in history was in some ways the dominant philosophical view of the Eastern Han dynasty. Interestingly, this idea was accepted not only by the direct followers of Dong Zhongshu (the New Text School), but also by the main representative of the Old Text School, Liu Xin, and independent thinkers like Wang Fu 王符 (82–167 CE). In the case of Liu Xin, it was connected with his endorsement of Wang Mang 王莽 (45 BC–23 CE), a magnate who, after years of his guardianship over underage puppet rulers, finally decided to proclaim himself emperor of a new dynasty, in fact called the 'New Dynasty' 新朝 *Xīn cháo*. Wang Mang was probably the first emperor who openly voted himself the Mandate of Heaven from the beginning of his reign; what is more, according to the *Hanshu* account (which deserves credibility especially because it is very unfavourable to Wang Mang), he was to combine this idea with the forgotten theory of the Five Phases, claiming that the time of the virtue of fire, namely the Han dynasty, had already passed.[55] These efforts were, of course, aimed at legitimizing violence against the power of the Han, although the idea of returning to antiquity which was hidden behind his social reforms indicated that they might have been the result of Wang Mang's authentic beliefs.[56] Long-lasting drought, followed by a great flood resulting from the change of the mouth of the Yellow River led to the rebellion of the peasantry that was 'properly' directed by the house of Liu, thereby restoring the Han dynasty. Significantly, the theory of the Five Phases and the interaction of Heaven and humanity perfectly explained the fall of Wang Mang. As the first emperor of the Eastern Han Dynasty, Guangwu decided that apocryphal texts on divination 讖緯 *chènwěi* should have lectures devoted to them at the Imperial Academy, and as a result of the conference in the White Tiger Hall in 79 CE the theory of the correlation between Heaven and humanity combined with the *yin-yang* and *wuxing* concepts became the official doctrine of the empire. It was the triumph of the New Text School.

The debate of 79 CE resulted in the *Comprehensive [Discussions] from the White Tiger Hall* 白虎通 *Bóhǔtōng* compiled by Ban Gu 班固 (32–92 CE). *Bohutong* is a peculiar repository of knowledge about the culture and thought of this period, covering matters of worship, rituals, music, law, education, management, commerce and even clothing. Not without reason in the titles of later works on philosophy of history does the character 通 *tōng* appear, which emphasizes the holistic nature of the discussions. As Ren Jiyu stresses, from the perspective of that time, the synthesis of knowledge in the spirit of the correlation between Heaven and humanity and the forces of *yin* and *yang* that was performed in the *Bohutong* could only be compared with Hegel's synthesis, bearing in mind the fundamental difference in the logical nature of the latter.[57] At the same time, as every encyclopaedia, the *Bohutong* owes the originality of its approach to its systematic nature. It is argued, for example, that disasters and strange events are the way Heaven cares for the ruler, encouraging him to think about his actions and cultivate virtue.[58] The change of the ruler is conducted through a cycle determined by the mutual transposition of the five forces: water, metal, earth, fire and wood.[59] But most importantly, the *Bohutong* does not make strictly historiosophical use of these ideas; there is no 'pattern' of history to be found in the whole work.

He Xiu 何休 (129–182 CE), one of the leading representatives of the New Text School, was more interesting in this respect. He Xiu commented on the *Gongyang zhuan*, reinterpreting literally every disaster as a warning from Heaven to humans. His concept of interaction between the two classes of being 二类 *èrlèi*: human affairs 人事 *rénshì* and natural disasters 災異 *zāiyì*,[60] was rooted in the interpretation of particular history and not in theoretical discourse, which transferred to frequent manipulations of the sources, like 'adding' disasters that both the *Chunqiu* and the *Gongyang zhuan* do not mention.[61] However, unlike Dong Zhongshu, who on the basis of his exegesis defended the cyclical and regressive view of history, He Xiu assumed a linear and progressive idea of history, distinguishing the epochs of chaos 衰亂 *shuāiluàn*, rise 升平 *shéngpíng* and supreme peace 太平 *tàipíng*, which correspond to, respectively, what Confucius had known from the transmission, what he heard and what he saw.[62] But since He Xiu did not use this typology outside the Spring and Autumn Period, it is difficult to treat it as a universal scheme.[63]

Despite significant differences in philology, in the philosophy of history the main thinkers of the Old Text School, Liu Xiang 劉向 (79–8 BC) and his son, Liu Xin, did not diverge from the line established by Dong Zhongshu and continued by He Xiu. In a work known as *New Arrangements* 新序 *Xīnxù*, Liu Xiang selected and edited existing historical anecdotes to illustrate certain moral attitudes, in which he went without the *wuxing* theory (special emphasis was placed on the historical dimension of the virtues of filial piety 孝 *xiào* and its extension, the virtue of a good minister[64]). But we also know from the *Hanshu* that Liu Xiang wrote a work devoted entirely to the *wuxing* theory, *Hongfan wuxing zhuanlun*, which has not survived to our times, and whose subject was the analysis of 'records of catastrophes from the earliest antiquity to the Qin and Han dynasties'.[65] One of the recorded statements of Liu Xiang spells out his project:

> The result of harmonious *qi* are good omens, and of irregular *qi* – miraculous events. Many good omens means peace of a state, may miraculous events – its crisis. This is the constant thread that connects Heaven and Earth and the holistic meaning of history.[66]

Unlike his father, for whom each disaster was linked to politics, Liu Xin created a selective schematization of history.[67] His scheme can be represented as follows:

Phase	Rulers: first cycle	Rulers: second cycle	Dynasties: third cycle
wood	Fuxi	Ku	Zhou
saltus to: water	Gonggong	Zhi	Qin
fire	Shennong	Yao	Han
earth	Huangdi	Shun	Xin
metal	Shaohao	Yu (Xia dynasty)	(?)
water	Zhuanxu	Tang (Shang dynasty)	(?)

Figure 6 Historical cycles according to the *Classic of Epochs* by Liu Xin.[68]

This theory differs in several important points from the view of Zou Yan, who also explained the dynastic changes in reference to the Five Phases. First, Liu Xin's scheme goes back much earlier, and as a result the Xin dynasty is the middle stage of the third cycle, while for Zou Yan it would be the beginning of the first new one. Second, the elements of nature do not abandon themselves 相胜 *xiāngshèng*, but rather produce each other 相生 *xiāngshēng*. Third, the order of elements is different than that for Zou Yan. Fourth, Liu Xin found a way to incorporate in his scheme the rulers and dynasties (mainly the Qin), which ruled in a manner devoid of legitimacy. Based on the fact that Qin Shi Huang recognized his dynasty as the rule of water, Liu Xin created a scheme in which this declaration made a too hasty 'leap' in the proper and seemingly rigid order of elements. His belief in the continuity of power also has an additional, unexpected justification: the *Classic of epochs* reads that the next rulers were their own descendants in a direct line. The falsity of this assertion is indisputable from the perspective of historical sources. Less obvious is the philosophical meaning of this thesis: is this how Liu Xin wanted to show that the rulers – like the elements – literally 'produce each other'? And if so, is there not an act of patricide at the source of the new dynasty? The *Classic of Epochs* is silent on this issue.

The fact that both the cyclical vision of Liu Xin and the linear vision of He Xiu fall within the ambit of the same paradigm shows both the diversity of the epoch and its basic limitation. Independent Han thinkers, such as Xun Yue 荀悦 (148–209 CE) and Wang Fu, shared the view of the epoch, but with reservations. The *Annals of the Han* 漢記 *Hànjì* of Xun Yue assert that 'human affairs change considerably also when large scale events do not change', although explicit support for the theory of the mutual influence of Heaven and humanity is visible in other places of the *Hanji*.[69] Wang Fu also describes the transformation of the five elements in history.[70] The way of associating individual rulers with elements is not different from that of Liu Xin.[71] However, while Xun Yue limited the influence of Heaven on people, Wang Fu had doubts about the limits of people's influence on Heaven:

> A man can control his good or bad fate, but it is ultimately determined by destiny. Behavior is a substance of humans, and destiny is the system of Heaven. The man can control what depends on him, but he cannot know anything that depends on Heaven.[72]

This shows the exhaustion of a certain model and the pressure of critical voices, which without such clauses openly rejected the idea of the correlation between Heaven and humanity.

Lu Jia's philosophy of history

The concept of the mutual influence of Heaven and humanity was not the only form of the idea of a correlation between nature and humanity in history, which was developed in the Han dynasty. In the period preceding Dong Zhongshu, on the threshold of the Han rule, this idea found a follower in Lu Jia 陸賈 (d. 170 BC), to whom the *Records of the Historian* ascribe the peculiar 'conversion' of Liu Bang, the founder of the Han dynasty, to Confucianism. Liu Bang was supposed to have said that he did not need either the *Book of Documents* or the *Book of Songs* because he had conquered China on horseback; Lu Jia asked him if he was still able to govern China without dismounting from the horse, and then using the example of the Qin argued that governments devoid of benevolence and righteousness collapse. The frightened emperor asked Lu Jia for an explanation of the cause of the rise and fall of states in history;[73] and that is why – at least according to this legend – Lu Jia created the *New Words* 新語 *Xīnyǔ*, the work explicitly devoted in its part to the philosophy of history.

As Lu Jia believes, the *yin* and *yang* forces are responsible for natural phenomena, notably the four seasons, and disturbances in their rhythm result in disasters. People are born from the *qi* of Heaven and earth, thus the ancient sages studied the Heavenly and earthly phenomena.[74] All the great rulers and ministers acted in accord with the transformations of *yin* and *yang* and observations of Heaven.[75] And since Lu Jia emphasizes the observability and measurability of those changes,[76] it is more about (proto-)astronomy than a vague idea of imitating nature. The consequence of this rationality is the belief that Heaven does not make decisions about particular matters, but directs the course of concrete things with the help of general principles; the ruler who, imitating Heaven, is guided by matters of great importance, guarantees peace.[77] Lu Jia believes not only in rationality, but also in the constancy of the Way of Heaven. Tian does not affect human history:

> Therefore the essence of peace and crisis, signs of luck and misfortune, all depend on man. Dao of saving the states and their vanishing, the matters of victory and defeat, all of this results only from good conduct. The sun and the moon did not change under Yao and Shun, who mark rise, and the stars did not change under Jie and Zhou, who mark fall. The Way of Heaven does not alter, only the Way of people changes.[78]

However, the way in which according to Lu Jia human conduct really shapes history has little to do with rational humanism, which seems to be suggested by the previous quote:

> The decline of the epoch and the loss of the Dao are not the result of Heaven's action, but the result of the actions of the ruler. Bad policy gives rise to bad *qi*, bad *qi* gives birth to catastrophes. Along with this bad *qi* different species of snakes and vermin are born; due to the politics there could be seen a [bad omen like] rainbow. When the Dao of governance is lost at the bottom, celestial signs change at the top. When bad politics spreads among the people, vermin proliferate in the fields and the rainbow appears.[79]

This fragment expresses a clear idea of the correlation between nature and history without the intermediary role of Heaven, which, as a being that operates with a set of general and constant rules, has nothing to do with changeable history. Human governance alone generates the bad or good type of *qi* that directly influences nature. The course of history is determined by the people, whose conduct affects nature, so that natural disasters eventually lead to the collapse of states. The possibility of omitting the middle link of natural transformations allows Lu Jia to focus on the right type of historically effective morality. This middle link, however, cannot be totally neglected. The declarations of even such interpreters of Chinese philosophy as Xu Fuguan, who recognized Lu Jia as an 'enlightened thinker',[80] or Ren Jiyu, who considered Lu Jia a 'progressive thinker',[81] can hardly be reconciled with the idea of the direct influence of human acts upon catastrophes and the proliferation of insects.

The relation between morality and nature is also taken by Lu Jia from a different angle: only morality fully develops the potential of the forces of *yin* and *yang*.[82] Neither strength nor wealth have, in this respect, as great a significance as morality, although position and power are required to promote virtue.[83] Because people imitate the ruler, his virtue transforms the people as the river carves a riverbed.[84] In the spirit of Mencius, Lu Jia states that countries deprived of benevolence and righteousness are falling.[85] That the abandonment of virtue results in the fall of the state is 'the unchanging law of ten thousand generations, the universal principle of history'.[86] One and the same principle explains the rise of Yao and the fall of Qin, and because the actions of the ancients are no different from those of the people of today, one does not need to refer to ancient times.[87] In other words, antiquity is not a moral example per se, for it is full of vile rulers, and the present times do not deserve total condemnation. Lu Jia regrets the tendency of his contemporaries to respect everything that is ancient and to despise the latest works.[88] Everyone who puts Dao in practice could become Yao and Shun.[89] Good rulers did not perform any superhuman acts; on the contrary, they ruled by doing nothing and hid themselves in the age of chaos.[90]

The conviction of the unity and continuity of history led Lu Jia to the linear concept of history. Lu Jia divides history into a period of former, 'middle' and later sages. In the time of the ancient sages, people studied astronomical and geographic phenomena, created trigrams and already knew the differences between genders, the duties of son to father and minister towards the ruler, which contributed to the establishment of offices and, finally, the monarchy. Successive monarchs taught the people new technological and administrative solutions: Shennong taught cereal harvesting, Huangdi – building houses, Houji set boundaries for fields and countries, Yu tamed the flood, Xi Zhong constructed vehicles and Minister Gao Yao introduced a system of rewards and punishments. In the 'middle age', men like Wen Wang and Zhou Gong created rituals and moral principles, establishing social hierarchy. When the Zhou dynasty collapsed, Confucius wrote the Classics that examine and exhaust the principles connecting Heaven, earth and people, and explain the causes of the fall of states.[91] In his discussion of Lu Jia's attitude towards the past, Leung rightly observes:

> The classics themselves are the product of a historical process, the very end of a teleological movement, but as soon as they come into existence, their comprehensive quality, incorporating all necessary principles into a synchronic whole, renders that entire history that led to their own creation irrelevant.[92]

Accordingly, just as the emergence of the universal meaning of the Classics crowns historical development, so is political history (primarily changes of dynasties) universally dependent on the ruler's conduct, despite the empirical factors Lu Jia used to explain the genesis of social institutions. In fact, the message of the Classics encapsulates in this relation of dependence.

The philosophy of history in the *Huainanzi*

The modification of the Confucian philosophy of history by Lu Jia was not the only version of the idea of the mutual relation between nature and the social world in the early Han dynasty preceding the development of the *Tian-ren ganying* concept. Another vision, this time growing out of the spirit of Daoism, was presented in the *Huainanzi* 淮南子, which is a collection of essays by many thinkers who gathered around 139 BC at the court of Liu An, King of Huinan. The main subject of this large work is the portrayal of the ideal ruler, and the idea of *ganying* is, as Charles Le Blanc points out, one of the main themes of this vision.[93]

By Daoism I mean its special form, that is the so-called Huang-Lao School, which was the dominant current of philosophy at the beginning of the Han dynasty, especially during the reign of Empress Lü (195–180 BC). Thanks to the discovery of the probable corpus of the Huang-Lao School in the Mawangdui grottoes in 1973, the *Four Canons of the Yellow Emperor* 黃帝四經 *Huángdì sìjīng*, these theories, which combine classical Daoism, Yin-Yang School and Legalism, saw the light of day. Dao is treated there as the source of *fǎ* and the principle of the right time. The sage follows Dao, therefore he understands the causes of success and failure. The way of Heaven, earth and the seasons is constant, and only departure from this way causes calamities; harmony and unity with nature brings peace, as evidenced by history.[94] With the exception of the few fragments that assume the possibility of intervention from Heaven,[95] basically the *Huangdi sijing* treats correlation as a natural process, and rewards and punishments as spontaneous results of the very essence of things. This concept is developed in the *Huainanzi* and related to the philosophy of history.[96] As Feng Youlan aptly observes, the *Huainanzi* transforms the formal concepts of Daoism (being beyond time and space) into positive concepts (within time and space).[97]

The transformation of Daoism is primarily due to the extension of the idea of original utopia. According to the authors of the *Huainanzi*, in ancient times Fuxi and Nüwa remained in unity with Dao, their spirit agreed with the changes of nature and 'there was no event to which they did not answer' 事無不應 *shì wú bùyìng* with their conduct. Thus, by not acting, they kept the whole world in harmony, in accordance with the changes of Heaven and earth, *yin* and *yang*, the seasons, and *wuxing*. Due to their 'answers', each being lived in harmony with its own nature, and there was peace and happiness in the world.[98] The ancestors matched their *qi* with the *qi* of Heaven and earth, and that is why they lived in an age of unity. Benevolence and rituals were not known at the time, yet it was a time of great order.[99] The departure from the state of unity and harmony took place during the reign of Fuxi, when people abandoned original ignorance for self-awareness and thus they excluded themselves from oneness with nature. The fall continued in the days of the Divine Farmer and the Yellow Emperor, the first dynasties of Xia and Shang, and reached its peak after Zhou, when Confucians 'stepped in' with the norms of *ren*, rituals and the Classics. This era was so corrupt that the individual efforts of the people were not able to resist it.[100] As Roger Ames observes, the dominant theme of the philosophy of history in the *Huainanzi* is fall.[101] The only exception is the nineteenth chapter, which deals with technological progress that took place thanks to the first rulers,[102] but as Michael Puett justifiably points out, 'the progressive inventions of the sages seem also to have broken the harmony that existed in distant antiquity (...) The result is a history that is both progressive (involving an accumulation of inventions) and degenerative (based on the loss of what existed before).'[103] The numerous narratives of the fall differ in details, which is a consequence of the heterogeneous nature of the *Huainanzi*, but they all agree that the ideas of benevolence and righteousness came exactly when the original virtue collapsed. According to one of the views, virtue itself was a sign of the fall of the original Dao, which leads to the division of history into three epochs: ancient (of Dao), middle (of virtue) and late (of benevolence and righteousness).[104] In the background there is constantly an idea of the correlation of the human world and nature: the sixth chapter reads that as a result of abandoning the primordial virtue and political chaos associated with it, natural disasters occurred and the animals started to behave in an unprecedented way.[105]

According to the *Huainanzi*, it is possible to return to the state of harmony and order, although it will not be identical to the prehistoric natural state, in which people were deprived of knowledge and were no different from animals. One fragment even suggests that this state actually returned in the times of emperor Han Wudi, but it is difficult to treat this declaration honestly.[106] Le Blanc thinks that although the idea of a gradual fall implies a 'defeatist' vision of history, the possibility of return introduces a 'wave' pattern of history: the scheme of the *Huainanzi* resembles in this way, in Le Blanc's eyes, the Christian vision of Eden, fall and paradise or the Hegelian 'triad' of thesis–antithesis–synthesis.[107] The resemblance, if any, is only of a structural nature. It is even questionable as to whether the *Huainanzi* interprets the future as a regression. Puett reminds that the *Huainanzi* does not call for a return to the earlier state of harmony, but for the creation of a new harmony in the existing world, which includes the innovations brought about by the sages.[108]

In fact, the *Huainanzi* quite often employs 'anti-regressivist' argumentation. It is postulated that one should not emulate the ancient heroes, for it is impracticable, or study the *Chunqiu*, because it is an expression of a degenerate era, nor imitate old times at all, since 'the unchanging past cannot be followed'.[109] No such models in fact exist, they change depending on the times and the era; also the standards of what is true and false are different at different times.[110] However, this does not lead to relativism, because the *Huainanzi* assumes that individual circumstances as a whole belong to the natural tendency, *shì*. This trend should be used for one's own benefit, for attempts to oppose *shi* are doomed to failure.[111] One of the basic expressions of the tendency-*shi* is the right time, giving victory or enabling meeting the right person. Not morality, as Confucians and Mohists believe, but the right time determines the success of the rulers.[112] Compliance with time is just another type of compliance 因 *yīn* with nature, since true correlation includes compatibility with one's own time, people, spirits, and Heaven and earth.[113]

The philosophy of history in the *Huainanzi* aims at combining the Daoist utopia, Confucian vision of the fall and the Legalist ideas. Yet it is not an incoherent amalgam of Daoism, Confucianism and Legalism, but an attempt to approach historical reality from all points of view, or – as Le Blanc puts it – a holistic integration of the individual and the world, the cosmos and the community, spontaneity and structure.[114] This is confirmed by the last sentence of the work: 'expand this book to the [dimensions] of the whole world, and it will not leave free places.' Certainly, the creator of such an idea of holism has a quasi-Hegelian confidence in his own abilities to grasp the totality of historical process, which in connection with the 'wave' pattern of history, results in a specific idea of the end of history:

> The striking move in the *Huainanzi*, however, is that the authors want to claim that this progressive/degenerative history is now coming to an end – or, more specifically, that the *Huainanzi* itself is bringing it to an end. By building upon all previous sagely inventions and bringing them together into a unified system, the *Huainanzi* thus re-creates the unity that existed before (…) The authors of the *Huainanzi* took a position very similar to Hegel's. They too claim to have achieved a final summation of knowledge (…) The authors, living at a late stage of human history, understanding the workings of the larger cosmos, and understanding how a text can serve as the Great One, are bringing harmony to all that exists. They are thus able to build upon all that was created by the previous sages and to reach a final summation.[115]

In a way, it is the postulate of exhausting the totality of history that leads to the idea of the end of history, because only finished history could be phrased as a system. This holistic and at the same time linear way of viewing history will be later followed by the Neo-Daoists.

Conclusion

The philosophy of history under the Han was dominated by the idea of a mutual relationship between nature and humanity. This concept was reflected in the holistic philosophy of history of Dong Zhongshu, who even aimed at combining his speculation on the nature of history with his speculative philosophy of historiography. Dong believed that the past and present are intertwined and penetrated by the 'Dao of history', the very essence of historical process, which due to the intercessory role of Heaven determines the transformations of the natural world, and is thereby reflected in the historical changes of the social world. The latter are performed in the cyclical manner, marked by the repetitive alterations in the field of ritual and, generally, culture. However, some of the later proponents of the idea of correlation, such as He Xiu, defended the linear and progressive view of (Chinese) history; others, like Liu Xin, tried to combine it with the theory of 'self-produced' Five Phases. At the threshold of the Han, the idea of correlation between nature and humanity, although devoid of the intermediary role of Heaven, was supported by Confucian Lu Jia and Daoist authors of the *Huainanzi*. While Lu Jia believed that the practice of benevolence guarantees effective employment of nature, Daoist authors yearned for the lost state of perfect, spontaneous relationship between people and nature, which was broken up along with the invention of Confucian virtues. Interestingly, both Lu Jia and the authors of the *Huainanzi* employed the anti-regressivist argumentation: Lu Jia assumed the linear and progressive view of history, whereas the *Huainanzi* combined Daoism with the Legalist philosophy of history, calling for a 'renewal' of the state of nature.

Han philosophy of history beyond the idea of correlation

The popularity of the idea of correlation notwithstanding, many philosophers of the Han period rejected and criticized the synthesis of cosmology and the philosophy of history. Some of them saw the only driving force of history in humanity, either in the individual sense, as in the elitism of Yang Xiong, or the collective one, as in the historical populism of Jia Yi and Zhong Changtong. The others separated the natural and social laws of history, finding the causes of historical changes in positive laws, as in the case of the Neo-Legalists Cui Shi and Huan Tan, or the natural ones, as in the historical fatalism of Wang Chong. The discussions between proponents and opponents of the idea of correlation also had a significant impact on Sima Qian and Ban Gu, the fathers of official Chinese historiography, whose historiosophy will be discussed at the end of this chapter.

Yang Xiong's philosophy of history

Yang Xiong 揚雄 (53 BC–18 CE) is an interesting case of a philosopher who rejected the idea of the correlation between the natural and human world in the philosophy of history, but not in the other spheres of philosophy. His *Canon of the Supreme Mystery* 太玄經 *Tàixuánjīng*, being a speculative commentary on the *Yijing*, contains a holistic and correlative metaphysics, which is the first metaphysics of this kind created within Confucianism (though not without the inspiration of Daoism). This is clearly illustrated by the following excerpt:

> The Supremely Profound Principle deeply permeates all species of things but its physical form cannot be seen. It takes nourishment from vacuity and nothingness and derives its life from Nature. It correlates matters of spiritual intelligence and determines the natural course of events. It penetrates the past and present and originates the various species. It operates *yin* and *yang* and sets material force in motion. As *yin* and *yang* unite, all things are complete in Heaven and earth.[116]

Yang Xiong's metaphysics is also holistic in the basic sense of the word: as Brook Ziporyn observes, for Yang Xiong the meaning of the part is a function of its relation to the whole and the whole is present in every part. This is related to the ontological theory of time–space cycles that repeat into infinity,[117] which remain, nonetheless, the cycles of nature as such.

The *Taixuanjing*, however, cannot be used to reconstruct the philosophy of history. This can be done on the basis of another work by Yang Xiong, *Model sayings* 法言 *Fǎyán*, which are a representative for the Old Text School. The philosophy of history presented in the *Fayan* is orthodoxically Confucian, devoid of references to the theory of *yin-yang* and *wuxing* and focused in an unprecedented way on the person of Confucius and the Five Classics.[118] As Yang Xiong himself admits, he wrote the *Fayan* because the principles restored by Confucius have been abandoned again. He therefore compares himself to Confucius, and in another place also to Mencius.[119] Yang Xiong firmly believes that Confucius' teachings exhaust Dao, to the extent that the Dao of Heaven 'was present' in Confucius.[120] Also Confucius, although dead, is present in his teachings.[121] When the sage is gone, the book must be consulted, because the principle of the sage's life and of the book are the same.[122] This implies respect for the Classics. Works inconsistent with the Classics are not worth the attention, says Yang Xiong.[123] Unfortunately, some of the Classics have disappeared or have been damaged, which leads to many practical problems, of which Yang Xiong, as a representative of the Old Text School, was especially aware.[124] Of course, one may ask: why create any works after the Classics? The author of *Fayan* responds that although his work is new in terms of its form, its content is no different from the Classics; it is transmitted and not created, only clarifying benevolence and righteousness.[125]

The conservative approach to Confucian writings is inevitably associated with faith in the moral function of historiography. Yang Xiong writes that history is a mirror 鑒 *jiàn* in which people of the present times can view themselves. Not every tradition, however, is worth imitating: only the Way of the ancient kings could serve as a model.[126] The ways of Yao, Shun and Wu penetrate the whole of history, including the present. The ways of other schools: Daoism, Legalism and Yin-Yang School are thus criticized.[127] It is not true, however, that the ancient kings did not make any changes. It was they who created the rituals in response to the original chaos;[128] in addition to technological innovations there were also changes in the style of government. And although the Dao of emperors and dynasties was identical, Yao and Shun actualized it through abdication, the Xia through good deeds, and the Shang and Zhou through humanitarian punitive expeditions.[129] In a manner typical for the Confucian philosophy of history, Yang Xiong distinguishes the unchanging essence of history from phenomenal changes. In the spirit of the Confucian tradition, he also elaborates on the Mandate of Heaven as endowed upon ancient kings, although it is emphasized that not all dynasties received it, for instance the Qin opposed the eternal Dao, therefore Heaven rejected the Qin, leading to their collapse.[130] After that, the Mandate was given to the Han dynasty, as evidenced by its prosperity, including the establishment of the Imperial Academy.[131] The Mandate, or destiny, means what cannot be avoided and what comes from Heaven. Because the sage knows the principles of Heaven, he is not afraid of *ming*.[132]

By learning the Dao of Heaven, the sage is not limited to the standards that are appropriate for the family, or even for the state, but he examines reality and himself with the help of universal standards appropriate for the entire world.[133] Such were also the sages and rulers of antiquity who 'meet their destiny halfway'. Only in an epistemological context – not ontological – should one understand the sentence stating that 'sage harmonizes everything that is between Heaven and people'.[134] Elsewhere, Yang Xiong writes that just like 史 *shǐ* (astrologer, later a historian) foretells the affairs of people from Heaven's movements, so the sage discourses on Heaven on the basis of people's behaviour,[135] discovering Tian's influence on history. Xu Fuguan thinks that such a vision is a result of Yang's interest in philosophical speculation,[136] which is true as long as it concerns the cognitive powers of the sages.

This is because the vision of a sage, who due to the extraordinary abilities is able to embrace in one cognitive scheme Heaven and people, is in line with those parts of the *Fayan* in which Yang Xiong rejects the metaphysics of history. Despite his esteem of Mencius, he rejects the view according to which a sage appears every 500 years. As Yang Xiong notes, Yao, Shun and Yu, as well as Wen, Wu and Zhougong lived at the same time, while Tang and Confucius appeared several centuries after the last sage. It is impossible to predict whether a sage will appear in a year or in a thousand years.[137] When asked whether Qin's fall and Han's rise were caused by Tian or man, Yang Xiong answers: both this and that. The choice of the right people and time depended on people; the rest depended on Tian. In practice the description of these events in the *Fayan* is focused on administrative reforms and individual errors.[138] In this way, Yang Xiong's philosophy of history is eventually elitist: history is an arena of the activities of the sages (with Confucius on top) – activities based on speculative cognition that ultimately does not have any predictable pattern, at least from the viewpoint of the common people.

Historical populism: Jia Yi and Zhong Changtong

Another view of history that did not assume the idea of a correlation between nature and humanity, at the same time avoiding Yang Xiong's elitism, was proposed by Jia Yi 賈誼 (200–169 BC). His philosophy of history is reconstructed on the basis of the *New Book* 新書 *Xīnshū*, which was written probably by his disciples.[139]

Jia Yi shared the Confucian idea according to which one should draw lessons from the mirror of history and tells us a great deal particularly concerning the causes of the fall.[140] Jia Yi, however, does not mean literally imitating the past. What needs to be investigated and imitated in history is its general principle, explaining the causes of order and chaos, rise and fall.[141] Jia Yi proposes therefore a speculative philosophy of history that will seek this principle. Importantly, it will not be Heaven, because all the important events occurring in history do not result from actions of Tian, but from people.[142] There are no reasons to believe in historical cycles. First, the same dynasty can retake power,[143] a possibility which was rejected by the classical concept of the Mandate of Heaven and the dynastic cycles in the *Shangshu*. Second, particular dynasties are not separated by any regular time intervals: from the Shang to the Zhou there were twenty generations, from the Zhou to the Qin – thirty, while the Qin ruled for only two generations.[144] The only cyclicality that Jia Yi does not reject is the sequence of periods of order and chaos that cannot be predicted in advance.[145]

The question then arises: what if not Heaven is the principle of history and how does it shape the course of history? Jia Yi gives a decisive answer: the principle of history, standing behind periods of order and chaos, is people 民 *mín*. It is worth quoting a longer passage from the central part of the *Xinshu*, the chapter *On Great Politics I*:

> It is said that in government, the people are in every way the root (base). For the state, the ruler, and the officials, the people constitute the root. Thus the security of the state or its endangerment depends on them (...) If victory is won, it is because

the people want to be victorious; if an attack succeeds, it is because the people want it so; if defense succeeds, it is because the people want to survive (...) Disaster and fortune, as we see, are determined not in Heaven but by the officers and the people (...) Good deeds will in the end bring good fortune, and bad deeds will inevitably bring misfortune. Those who are blessed by Heaven need not thank Heaven, and those who suffer from natural disasters need not blame Heaven, for it is all one's own doing (...) Even the lowest of the people should not be slighted, and the most foolish among them should not be taken advantage of. Thus, throughout history, those who oppose the people sooner or later are defeated by the people (...) Thus the people are the root of [dynastic] longevity (...) Oh, be warned, in any opposition to the people, the people will win.[146]

This view may be called 'populism' in the fontal sense of this term (not associated only with demagogy), which primarily means ideology recognizing the will of the people as the only source of legitimization of the system, and treating the people, usually common people and often the rural population, as a simple and homogeneous social body.[147] With regard to the philosophy of history, as distinct from political philosophy that focuses solely on the abstract problem of the legitimization of power, the descriptive and explanatory consequences are drawn: the people, thus understood, are the main force of history, and thereby should be respected as such. This definition of 'historical populism' fits perfectly with Jia Yi's thoughts, with all the implications.

The historical role of the people can be seen in two ways. On the one hand, in order to understand the causes of order and chaos it is enough to know the nature of the people.[148] On the other hand, one can refer to history itself, namely to the example of former rulers, who achieved success thanks to their caring for the people; one of them, Yu the Great, is said to have worked together with the people.[149] The best illustration of the opposite pattern was the Qin dynasty. In the famous essay *On the faults of the Qin*, which is a systematic attempt to answer the question of the cause of the fall of the first imperial dynasty, Jia Yi not only accepts the thesis identical to that put forward by Lu Jia, i.e. that the Qins wrongly governed the state with the same techniques as they used to conquer and unify China, but he also emphasizes that in their politics there was no *ren*, which is nothing more than a concern for the people and the appeasement of the internal and foreign situation. As a result, the peasants led by Chen She started an uprising that ultimately led to the collapse of the Qin. As Jia Yi writes, 'Chen She did not measure up in the talents even to the people of the middle class, nor did he have the talents of Confucius and Mozi' and yet he unified the people who 'filled the world, gathered like clouds and sounded like thunder'.[150] The first Han dynasty emperor, peasant by birth, is also said to have reacted to the events of his time.[151] Hence, there is no doubt that Jia Yi's populism was inspired by these events, to which he was an eyewitness. This confirms the thesis that historical events have the greatest influence on the emergence of new philosophies of history.

The concern for the well-being of the people is the highest form of *ren*.[152] And although the ruler must use his position and power (*shi*) to be able to implement benevolent policy, he should not build his governments on punishment, but rather on the respect and trust of the people, 'as evidenced by the whole history'.[153] Also, rituals are needed only insofar as they help rulers to not lose the support of the people. A sovereign is for the people what parents are for their children. As Jia Yi has repeatedly pointed out, the people reciprocate the attitude of the ruler. The people are afraid and love such rulers, thanks to which harmony prevails.[154] To Machiavelli's question of whether it is better to arouse fear or love, Jia Yi would answer that these are not mutually exclusive. However, this entails a specific, 'populist' understanding of the people.

Although there are fragments claiming that caring for the people means caring for each of its members individually,[155] the people are mainly treated as a homogeneous body with very specific characteristics and positions. The people can only deal with agriculture; any striving for something else will only lead to their misfortune. They should not go beyond the direct exchange of goods, for money should not be used by people. Otherwise, there will be a catastrophe, precisely 'when money spreads over the lower class, there will be many false coins, using it will cease to be reliable and the stupid people will question it.'[156] Elsewhere it is directly said that the people are stupid, which means that they have to be guided. This fact also implies that the people cannot choose officials; instead, the wise ruler chooses them for the people. The main task of these officials is to care for the people and get the support of as many people as possible.[157] This fragment is very ambivalent. As Fang Litian emphasizes, there is a progressive element in it, connected with the firm imperative to strive for people's support, but on the other hand it shows the limitations of Jia Yi's era and it would be an anachronism to judge it from today's perspective.[158] This point, however, weakens the overtone of Jia Yi's main thesis: if the people can be controlled, then the officials and the sovereign who designates them to an office are ultimately responsible for order or chaos in history, to which Jia Yi openly admits.[159] The ruler can be compared to the throne, ministers and officials to the steps, and the people to the ground, the floor.[160] Jia Yi's philosophy of history is therefore situated between Confucianism and Legalism: on the one hand, he talks about lessons drawn from history and *ren* understood as caring for the people; on the other – the people are objectified and the whole burden of a historic initiative rests upon the officials who are able to control it.

The thinker who witnessed the fall of the Han, Zhong Changtong 仲長統 (179–220 CE), returned to these ideas. According to Zhong, the Qin collapsed because it oppressed the people. The virtues of benevolence and righteousness could be reduced to a concern for the well-being of the people with the help of the skilful use of law and institutions.[161] However, Zhong Changtong distances himself from Legalism, stressing that one should imitate the solutions of the ancients, for nowadays the people and the officials live in a very difficult situation.[162] Former kings treated the people, especially the poor, just like their relatives, which changed the social hierarchy and the execution of law turned into chaos.[163] Essentially, the pessimistic assessment of history is deepened by the observation that the times of order are short and periods of chaos are long.[164] Zhong Changtong even presents the exact structure of the historical process justifying this state of affairs. At the first stage there is a war, the winner of which establishes a new dynasty. As Zhong writes, people 'mistakenly take it for a message from Heaven'.[165] The second stage is a consolidation of power, 'the people are calming down', and at this time there is a period of order. In the third stage, power degenerates, the 'upper and lower layers' of society begin to hate each other, the hierarchy breaks down and chaos is born. This state is being used by a new dynasty, and so – as Zhong Changtong himself points out – the process starts again.[166] This belief in the existence of political cycles proceeds without Heaven, which would initiate and conclude these cycles. Zhong criticizes not only the 'wrong' recognition of historical changes as being the result of the will of Heaven, but also strongly and explicitly rejects the idea of the correlation between Heaven and humanity in the form that dominated in his time:

> That those two rulers [Gaozu and Guangwudi] and a number of their servants conquered the world, revealed their virtue to the simple people, achieved success by making a great work and established their fame for a hundred generations – all this is the result of human action, no doctrine about Heaven is needed here. On the contrary, those who took over the world and became great ministers did not wait to know the way of Heaven. The only thing they appreciate in the way of Heaven is concern for the affairs of the people in accordance with the stars and following the four seasons in managing public works. What can one know about good or bad omens? If one studies the way of Heaven, but there is no plan for people, one lands in the company of shamans, doctors, fortune-tellers and ghost-makers, a stupid people without any knowledge. Entering the way of Heaven and turning away from human affairs: this is how the lost rulers behave in the times of chaos and ministers in the times of the fall of the state.[167]

The above fragment is one of the clearest declarations of opposition to the idea of *Tian-ren ganying* formulated during the Han dynasty. It grows out of Zhong Changtong's specific humanism, which is reflected even in the language he uses. Instead of folk (*min*), Zhong writes about people (*ren*). The reason for this is not so much the empowerment of the people as the recognition of the rulers as an equal causative factor: not only the people, but both *min* and rulers, i.e. people as opposed to Heaven, are the source of historical changes. He Zhaowu validly situates Zhong in the intellectual climate of decay of the Han dynasty and doubts the idea of the Mandate of Heaven together with Cui Shi,[168] to whom we will now move on.

The Neo-Legalist philosophy of history: Huan Tan and Cui Shi

The defeat of the Qin dynasty, which was partially caused by social resistance to reforms and the strict law introduced in the manner of Legalism, did not ultimately contribute to the fall, or to the fiasco, of Legalism. The first emperor of the Han continued the Qin policy with a significant correction in the form of decentralization of power and granting fiefs to members of his family, but at the same time throughout the reign maintained Li Si's edict on burning books. Thanks to the Legalist advisor of the emperors Wen and Jing, Chao Cuo 晁错 (200–154 BC), the idea of centralizing the government returned. He left a book, reconstructed and known as the *Chaoshi Xinshu*, in which one of the determinants of Han Legalism appears, namely, the centralized rule of law is placed in the ancient days, specifically: in the times of the legendary Five Emperors.

At the turn of the Han dynasties and the times of the Xin Dynasty, Huan Tan 桓譚 (43 BC–28 AC), who belonged to the Old Text School, contributed to the revival of Legalist ideas. Huan Tan is the probable author of the *New essays* 新論 *Xīnlùn*. Probable, because in the whole work there are threads that are mutually exclusive, and the *Xinlun* itself is a collection of quotes attributed to Huan Tan as reconstructed by Yan Kejun. The purpose for which Huan Tan wrote the *Xinlun* was – as he admits – 'discussing history'.[169] This discussion partly takes the form of a specific case study of the reasons for the fall of Wang Mang, whom Huan Tan served. First, Wang Mang relied solely on himself, unlike Liu Bang, who relied on the opinion of other people, just like Yao, who exalted his minister, Shun. So there was nobody who would have dared criticize Wang Mang.[170] Huan Tan emphasizes that 'the rise and fall of states depends on political issues', and more specifically on advisers, as is evidenced by the examples of both their heyday and fall.[171] In this respect, one can learn from the past.[172] Second, Wang Mang gazed at patterns from antiquity, unlike Liu Bang, who did not ignore the ideas of his time.[173] And although Huan Tan believes that a real sage appears once in a thousand years, he points out that every sage proclaims new ideas.[174] Third, Wang Mang fell because he consulted the oracles too often and awaited extraordinary signs.[175]

New fragments of the *Xinlun* collected by Timotheus Pokora also show the historical role of objective and not necessarily strict laws in the thought of Huan Tan. The way of law and bureaucracy is called there 'the way of hegemons',[176] which in the historical scheme of Huan Tan follows on the way of the divine rulers (*huáng*), emperors (*dì*) and kings (*wáng*), continuing until today. Accordingly, *huang* ruled using Dao, emperors – by means of virtue, kings – through *ren* and *yi*.[177]

The most prominent Legalist of the late Han period was Cui Shi 崔寔 (d. 170 CE), the author of the *Treatise on Politics* 政論 *Zhènglùn*. Cui Shi emphasizes in the spirit of classical Legalists that the Three Dynasties differed in terms of the laws they introduced and although the ideals of Confucius and Mencius were quite right, they were only right for their times, and not even completely, because none of them achieved what he intended.[178] One should not, therefore, follow the way of the ancients, but rather follow the way of hegemons who arouse fear through strict laws and punishments. It is not a coincidence that since the reign of Han Yuandi (75–33 BC), imbued with Confucian patterns, the Han dynasty began to fall.[179] The order or chaos of a given era is caused by proper punishment.[180] This thesis is rooted in the belief that human nature seeks pleasures, riches and honours, and an uncontrollable expression of people's desires leads to chaos, which is why ancient kings created laws and punishments that were intended to limit the desires of the people.[181] Cui Shi believes that the inability of the Han dynasty to introduce laws in accordance with the needs of the new time contributed to its crisis and decline.[182] Another reason why the Qin and Xin dynasties collapsed – since, as Cui Shi points out, the Han policy did not differ significantly from that of the Qin – was the poor pay of officials.[183] The rewarding of officials gave peace in the old days of Yao and Shun, and the reliance on effective ministers brought order to the state.[184] Not only they, but also former rulers in general skilfully operated the system of penalties.[185] Therefore, Cui Shi is convinced that in this sense it is necessary to follow the (relevant) ancient examples.[186] As he writes, 'when it comes to the fall of the three dynasties [of Zhou, Qin and Xin], despite different times, its cause is the same; my dynasty did not learn from this lesson.'[187]

As Hsiao Kung-chuan aptly observes, the ideas of Cui Shi from the *Zhenglun* combine Confucianism and Legalism.[188] Due to this fact and the differences between the thought of Huan Tan and Cui Shi on the one hand, and Shang Yang and Han Fei on the other, one should rather use the term 'Neo-Legalism', which is used very rarely and in relation only to the Tang times.[189] In the field of the philosophy of history, both Huan Tan and Cui Shi believe that the political tools promoted by classical Legalism, namely law and effective administration, are a universal guarantee of order. What is more, they claim that this order existed in antiquity, thus these solutions should be imitated regardless of the times. This stands in opposition to the ideas of Shang Yang and Han Fei, who wrote that we should neither imitate antiquity nor follow the present, for every form of imitation omits the specificity of time and its conditions (*shi*). It is probably no coincidence that the notion of *shi* does not play any important role in the philosophy of history of either Huan Tan or Cui Shi. Their thought is therefore Legalist in its content, but Confucian in its form. In other words, it is just an 'inverted Confucianism' that promotes 'the way of hegemons' instead of 'the way of kings'. For both Confucians and the Neo-Legalists, the dynastic cycles are inscribed into one line of history, which is understood as the process of departing from ancient times, and the only difference between them lies in the fact that for Confucians these times were model because of their morality, while the Neo-Legalists esteemed the efficiency of the ancient system of laws and punishments.

Historical fatalism of Wang Chong

Our analysis of views in the field of philosophy of history that reject the idea of a correlation between Heaven and humanity moves from the ideas of an 'orthodox' Confucianism to its opposition, which found its representative in the form of Wang Chong 王充 (27–97 AD), author of the *Balance of Discussions* 論衡 *Lùnhéng*. Wang Chong proposed a comprehensive philosophy of history, in which he opposed not only the followers of the *Tian-ren ganying* vision, but also many of the thinkers mentioned in this subsection. His philosophy was the biggest attack on traditional historical thinking in China since Shang Yang and Han Fei.

Wang Chong challenges the dominant view on the historical role of Heaven. Heaven does not choose outstanding individuals to grant them power, because the rulers are mostly mediocre, unless we admit that this is the highest standard that Heaven accepts, but nobody will adopt this position.[190] Also, catastrophes do not constitute a warning for the bad behaviour of the ruler, for it would lead to an analogous thesis that diseases affecting individuals are an instrument and punishment of Heaven.[191] The premise behind each of these beliefs is the idea that human behaviour can affect Heaven. Wang Chong rejects this view:

> As for disasters, I have already expressed my doubts that Heaven uses them to warn people. It is also said that the sovereign moves Heaven with his politics, and Heaven sets the *qi* in motion (...) Heaven can move things, but how can things move Heaven? People and things depend on Heaven, Heaven is their master (...) When Heaven's *qi* changes at the top, man and other beings answer at the bottom

(...) When Heaven intends to send rain, crickets and ants run away (...) Therefore, man occupies the same place between Heaven and earth as ants and crickets in their hiding places.[192]

The above passage, however, shows that Wang Chong does not reject the influence of Heaven on people, although he emphasizes that it is one-sided, that Heaven's activity concerns only natural phenomena. Secondly, Heaven itself is understood here as a natural being:

The way of Heaven is the same as the way of man, if we want to know Heaven, we must take human matters as their starting point. We will not know the answer to the question if we do not meet a man personally and we do not ask him. Meanwhile, we want to ask Heaven, which is high, which is so far away from us. If Heaven has no ears and is devoid of a body, so it is *qi*. Being *qi*, it is like clouds and fog, so how could it edify people?[193]

Heaven is therefore only a specific complex of *qi*. All orders attributed to Heaven should therefore be treated in the spirit, as we would say today, of deflationism: according to Wang Chong, references to Heaven present in the Classics serve only to arouse fear among the ignorant and emphasize the meaning of the words as supposedly coming from Tian, though the will of Heaven is never known directly, but manifested in the intentions and deeds of the rulers.[194] It also leads to the breaking of the *Tian-ming* phrase: the destiny received by the former kings did not come from Tian, but was inscribed in their nature 性 *xing* already at birth.

At the expense of the role of Heaven, it is destiny that occupies a central place in Wang Chong's philosophy of history. Everyone who has a 'head, eyes and blood in his veins' is destined for a certain length of life, successes and failures; this applies to both kings and ordinary people.[195] In addition, 'conduct may be good or bad, but whether it will be rewarded or punished depends only on good or bad luck' 偶 *ŏu*, writes Wang Chong, and gives numerous examples from history illustrating this relation. Even if one has the ability of a sage, like Shun or Confucius, nothing can be done without luck.[196] Virtue has no effect on destiny; those who claim it does, usually also maintain that when rulers were virtuous, everyone followed them, which is false.[197] Sometimes a good person is accompanied by an evil one (e.g. a minister) and this is bad fate.[198] It happens, however, that the virtuous are happy, which strengthens – mainly due to historical books – the already common belief that Heaven sends happiness depending on one's deeds. The division into virtuous and vile does not ultimately matter, because all the actions of each individual from birth to death are the result of destiny and random factors, mainly time.[199] The thought of Wang Chong, therefore, combines two concepts that in Western philosophy are generally opposed to each other: contingency and fate/destiny. It can be assumed that while destiny is inscribed in the nature of every human being, as an internal and subjective factor, fortune is determined by external and objective factors. This relationship can be represented as shown in Figure 7.[200]

Heaven does not affect the social world, which is located between the hammer of fate and the anvil of contingency. The course of history can therefore be theoretically

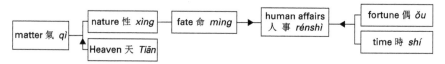

Figure 7 Wang Chong's fatalism (arrows should be read as 'influences', lines without an arrow – as 'constitutes').

known from the constellation of both. That is why 'whenever we talk about human matters, we should talk about their whole, which cannot be divided'.[201] However, it is impossible in practice to know the destiny of all people and take into account all random factors; these are things that no one can know.[202] Wang Chong does not accept the idea of the law of history that would determine the fate of particular people 'over their heads'; hence, he is not a historical determinist. As a consequence, one cannot predict the future; any attempt to forecast the future is, at the very most, reasoning by analogy, 'discussing the palace when sitting in a mud hut'.[203] Forecasting the future does not make much sense because the principles of nature are permanent:

> Ancient Heaven is the same as the Heaven of later epochs. Heaven does not change, because *qi* does not change. The people of antiquity are no different from the people of later eras, they are all filled with the same original *qi*. The original *qi* is pure and harmonious, unchangeable throughout history.[204]

Wang Chong's naturalism is thus ahistorical, like most naturalisms. Nature is permanent and, unlike social institutions, is not essentially a subject of historical change. This leads to a certain essentialism: 'tools and methods change, but nature and behavior are the same', writes Wang Chong, and then goes on to criticize Dong Zhongshu's philosophy of history, according to which certain epochs were characterized by simplicity and others by refinement: 'the rise and fall occur in every epoch (...) whether the method [of government] is refined or simple happens throughout history.' This also means that the heroes of ancient times are no different from the present ones.[205] Wang Shounan, who brings Wang Chong under the label of 'historical evolutionism', is not thus right.[206] According to Wang Chong, the rulers of the Han dynasty do not differ from the wise men of antiquity, and since only the ancient sages are credited with the establishment of the era of the highest peace (*taiping*), it should be concluded that in the Han era, the highest peace has already been established.[207] According to Puett, Wang Chong has in mind a vision of waiting for the future sage and the future era of prosperity.[208] Unfortunately, Puett does not provide any quotes that would confirm this interpretation. It seems that the chapter 'Praise of the Han' is a clear affirmation of the present, aimed at overcoming the differences separating it from the past.

The same premises in a radicalized version lead to criticism of the Confucian philosophy. As Wang Chong observes, Confucians only have eyes for antiquity and believe that all the words from ancient sages are devoid of error, and thus in practice, the views of the teacher cannot be undermined. People blindly believe in the Classics, which usually exaggerate and draw the longbow.[209] Two chapters of the *Lunheng* (twenty-five and twenty-six) are devoted to these exaggerations, such as the thesis that in the times of Yao and Shun no one was punished, despite the fact that they suppressed the Miao people.[210] One should examine what is true or false in general; following antiquity has nothing to do with it.[211] Unfortunately, people believe that everything that was written on bamboo and comes from ancient sages is flawless; hence when the true record does not comply with these old writings, they reject the former.[212] Confucians do not study the history of Qin and Han at all, focusing on the Classics, which are relatively young compared to the works of distant antiquity.[213] Their criterion of 'antiquity' is therefore arbitrary. On the other hand, it is fictitious because Confucians do not treat the Classics as historical works. The Classics were written in response to the crisis of their time, and had it not been for these events, these works would not have come to life.[214] This is evidenced by, among other things, the fact that scholars do not investigate the historical origin of the Classics or their authorship. Do they know when the *Book of Changes* was created and who its author is? Are they aware of the fact that there are three different versions of the *Book of Documents* with a different number of chapters, and if so, on what basis do they consider one of them to be reliable, and where were the allegedly saved versions supposed to have been stored? Similar questions are posed by Wang Chong regarding the *Chunqiu*, *Shangshu* and *Liji*.[215] These questions, which vividly resemble a contemporary source criticism and to a large extent dominate the current business of the Sinologists, show Wang Chong's unique awareness of the historicity of historical works themselves. Xu Fuguan has no doubt that for Wang Chong classical writings are historical works,[216] which significantly anticipates the reflection of Liu Zhiji and Zhang Xuecheng. It might be said that while on the basis of the theory of historical process Wang Chong defends essentialist and ahistorical naturalism, the works of human culture are subjected to radical historization in the spirit of rational criticism. It needs to be investigated as to what extent contemporaneous Chinese historiography was the embodiment of this spirit.

Philosophical meaning of the official Han historiography

Our study of Chinese philosophy of history would not be complete without having a brief look at the formation of official historiography in the Han dynasty, in the form created by Sima Qian and Ban Gu. This issue is important for at least two reasons. First, the chronicles of Sima Qian and Ban Gu largely shaped Chinese historiography: later chronicles imitated their style and structure, while the works on the philosophy of historiography made them the starting point of their analysis. Second, the works of Sima Qian and Ban Gu were not only the subject of reflection for philosophers, but also contained many philosophical elements, which, although often implicitly embedded in the narrative, influenced future generations of thinkers to a not lesser extent than strictly theoretical concepts. Defining the restrictive boundary between the historical discourse (which was just being born) and the philosophical discourse at that time is, to some extent, an anachronism.

At this point, the question may be asked why Sima Qian and Ban Gu are considered the first representatives of classical Chinese historiography, since there had already been such works as the *Book of Documents, Spring and Autumn Annals* or *Zuo Commentary*. First of all, it is doubtful that the original intention of these works was a faithful description of past events (rather, the transmission of certain moral and political truths); even if so, they do not reveal their method and do not pay attention to the sources; their narrative is simplified, and the style one-sided (the *Shangshu* is mainly a collection of talks, the *Chunqiu* an enigmatic record of events, the *Zuozhuan* a commentary explaining and broadening the meaning of the *Chunqiu*). The same applies to other 'historical' works of the time (e.g. the *Zhushu Jinian* or *Zhanguoce*), which are devoid of the methodological background of Sima Qian and Ban Gu. Secondly, in these works the term 史 *shǐ* does not yet mean a historian, but the hereditary office of a scribe employed on the occasion of ritual ceremonies, recording extraordinary events, being at the same time astrologer, diviner and shaman 巫 *wū*.[217] This information is also confirmed by the autobiography of Sima Qian.[218]

This autobiography is a very important source of knowledge about Sima Qian's motivation to write the chronicle, as well as information about his father Sima Tan, who began this work. Sima Tan is the author of the aforementioned division of Chinese philosophy into six major schools (of which he favoured Daoism). The problem of which parts of the *Records of the Historian* 史記 *Shǐjì* are the father's work, and which are not, is still being investigated.[219] According to the autobiography, Sima Tan did not want to neglect the historical materials he had collected and hoped that his son, like Confucius, who edited the *Chunqiu*, would write a chronicle for the new era. Sima Qian openly undertook this task, pointing out that just as five hundred years had passed since the fall of the Zhou to Confucius, a half-millennium had also passed since Confucius' death to his own times.[220] He thus referred to the Mencian conception of historical cycles, recognizing himself as a sage initiating a new cycle. Sima Qian identified himself with Confucius who, although called the supreme sage 至聖 *zhìshèng*, was also, according to his biography, rejected many times and misunderstood (Sima Qian was accused of treason and castrated).[221] Poignant expression of his sadness and frustration is found in a letter to Ren An.

The autobiography gives not only the reasons why Sima Qian decided to write the chronicle as such, but also justifies the presence of its individual parts. The work of Sima Qian, a record of 2,500 years of China's history from the Yellow Emperor to the beginnings of the Han dynasty, is not only an unprecedented universal history, but also an extremely complex work. The *Records* are divided into *Basic Annals* 本紀 *Běnjì*, *Chronological tables* 表 *Biǎo, Treatises* 書 *Shū, Hereditary houses* 世家 *Shìjiā*, and *Other biographies* 列傳 *Lièzhuàn*. The direct implication of this division was the fact that one hero usually appeared in two narratives: the chronicle and the biography, which portrayed her or him differently. The leading historical figures were even presented differently within the *Benji*, e.g. Xiang Yu is portrayed as a cruel man in the chapter dedicated to Emperor Gaozu, but in the *Xiangyu benji* his motives and tragic character are shown. This implies a specific form of perspectivism, and thus problematizes the issue of the objectivity of Sima Qian's narrative. Elsewhere, Sima Qian admits that if he cannot decide beyond any doubt which of the transmitted versions of events is credible, he writes down both.[222] This does not mean that he was utterly uncritical. He rejects, for instance, all records of history from before Huangdi, for they are contradictory, inconsistent with other records and full of later theories, mainly the *wuxing* theory.[223] As Stephen Durrant emphasizes, instead of asking if the *Shiji*'s narrative is true, one should ask where and in what form Sima Qian makes proper truth claims.[224] The more valuable research goal was for Sima Qian to create a complete narrative, and as we know today thanks to Gödel, completeness is always achieved at the expense of the consistency of the system.

The striving to grasp the whole of history is also manifested in the other parts of the *Shiji*. First of all, Sima Qian devoted separate chapters to the states coterminous with the Han empire, i.e. Xiongnu (probably the Huns), Nan Yue (a state from Canton to northern Vietnam), Dong Yue (south of China), Chaoxian (North Korea and parts of northern China), Xinanyi (Sichuan and Yunnan) and Dayuan, or 'Great Ions', an Indo-Greek state bordering with the Kushans. The inclusion of non-Chinese peoples in universal history was an unprecedented event. Secondly, in addition to historiography, Sima Qian included treatises on rituals, music, law, calendar, astronomy, ceremonies, rivers and channels, and financial administration in the *Shiji*. In explaining the decision to include these books, Sima Qian emphasized their relation with history: customs adapt to historical changes, the law illustrates these changes in the social world of the present era, etc.[225] As rightly noted by Wang Gaoxin, Sima Qian's programme is essentially holistic.[226] Returning to our typology of holisms, this opinion can be clarified, as Sima Qian definitely represents holism regarding time and space and partly regarding meaning. Does he, however, support holism regarding reason? In other words, does his historiography contain normative elements?

This issue could be called Sima Qian's own historiosophy, as expressed by either his commentaries on narratives (beginning with the phrase 太史公曰 *tàishǐgōng yuē*, 'the grand historian says'), or directly by some non-narrative parties (e.g. introductions to chronological tables). According to Sima Qian, the former rulers of the Yu and Xia dynasties ruled the people through virtue and advised Heaven before they began their reign, which resulted in their rise; the Shang and Zhou kings ruled with the help of *ren-yi*, and the Qin dynasty replaced the rule of virtue with the rule of force, which contributed to its downfall.[227] The diagnosis, according to which the cause of victories in history was the cultivation of virtue, while the fall and chaos was due to a lack of it, appears in the *Shiji* repeatedly, also in the historical narrative itself, such as when Sima Qian explains the reason for replacing the Xia by the Shang.[228] His explanation of the fall of the Qin is not different from the explanation of Jia Yi.[229] Although particular historical events are explained by empirical causes, in terms of explaining large-scale historical processes, such as the fall of one dynasty and the emergence of the other, Sima reaches for 'tried' interpretations of the Confucian philosophy of history. What is more, he also refers to the theory of Dong Zhongshu, connecting the dynasties of Xia, Shang and Zhou with the specific virtues of loyalty, respect and refinement, and adds that 'the way of the three royal dynasties is like a cycle, ends and starts again', thus the rise of the Han implies a return to the rules of the Xia dynasty.[230] In other words, Sima Qian openly supports a certain cyclical metaphysics of history. This aspect is often overlooked by Western scholars who read the *Shiji* from the perspective of literary-centric narrativism, or from the perspective of the scientific standards in this work. Interestingly, many Chinese scholars (such as the quoted Wang Gaoxin) fall into the other extreme, arguing that Sima Qian completely agrees with Dong Zhongshu and the idea of a correlation of Heaven and humanity.

Both the philosophical and (proto-)scientific nature of Sima Qian's project becomes clear in the light of his own declaration from the letter to Ren An:

> I spread a web over neglected and lost records of the past, examined [past] deeds and events, analyzing the reasons for success and failure, growth and decline. In one hundred and thirty chapters, I tried to exhaust everything that lies within the boundaries of Heaven and the people, holistically describe historical changes and create an original theory.[231]

In this way, Sima Qian openly credited himself with holistic aspirations.

Therefore, for the full picture of Sima Qian's historiosophy, it is necessary to look at the role that Heaven plays in his statements and – indirectly – the narrative. Basically, Sima Qian avoids references to Heaven as often as possible and recognizes that man is the main, if not the only, historical actor. A causal and rational explanation is inserted, devoid of references to the will of Heaven, and put in the mouth of Chen She, who is responsible for the collapse of the Qin dynasty.[232] Another hero of this time, Xiang Yu, says that a lost battle was not his fault, but rather a decree of Heaven, which is explicitly criticized by Sima Qian in his commentary.[233] In turn, the tragic fate of Boyi and Shuqi, who were distinguished by morality, led Sima Qian to openly doubt Heaven's reaction to the virtuous behaviour of people, and even the existence of Tian.[234] An exception to this type of narrative, however, is significant, since it concerns Liu Bang, the founder of the dynasty, who is not only credited with special support and the choice of Heaven, but it is also said that the real father of Liu Bang was a dragon.[235] 'Scientific' standards were thus used selectively, which exposed the problematic situation of the historian himself, who in the face of a conflict with the Han ruler had to show loyalty and involve historiography in the task of political legitimacy, which is more vividly demonstrated by the example of Ban Gu and his *Book of Han* 漢書 *Hànshū*.

The main difference between the *Hanshu* and the *Shiji* is that the former is a chronicle of the Western Han dynasty, not a universal one. This model will be imitated by most of the later works of Chinese historiography, at the cost of universal histories. As for the structure, the *Hanshu* imitates the *Shiji*, sharing the division into 'annals', 'tables', 'treatises' and 'biographies'. Treatises (called 志 *zhì*) concerned measures and calendar, punishments, music and rituals, offerings, food and goods, rivers and canals, geography and administration, astronomy, as well as the *wuxing* theory and literature (the last treatise, 藝文志 *Yìwénzhì*, is the oldest preserved Chinese bibliography). Separate *zhuan* were also devoted to the Huns, the southwestern people and the lands of the Far West (Central Asia). Ban Gu maintained Sima Qian's holistic programme with regard to its form, and crystallized history as a discipline having a broader meaning than its contemporary European form. However, his evaluation of Sima Qian's historiography was complicated. On the one hand, he appreciated the temporal scale of the *Shiji* and believed that Sima Qian had 'the talent of a good historian, properly organized the sequence of events, discussed without coloration, [wrote] straight but not vulgar, his style was direct, and described facts – important. He did not despise beauty and hide evil, which is why his work can be called a "true record".[236] On the other hand, the same rigidity and objectivity provoked the criticism of Ban Gu, who explained the lack of the Confucian vision of history in the *Shiji* with the Daoist provenance of Sima Qian. As Wang and Ng emphasize, 'Ban Gu had one paramount goal: to legitimize the position of the Han dynasty in history. To this end he unequivocally supported Dong Zhongshu's theory of "Heaven-humanity resonance" and employed it time and again to promote Han legitimacy'.[237]

Ban Gu, who, like Sima Qian, continued the work of his father, Ban Biao 班彪 (3–54 CE),[238] included in the *Hanshu* his *Essay on the kingly mandate* 王命論 *Wángmìnglùn*, which, in the spirit of Confucianism, credited the dynasty founders with receiving the Mandate of Heaven. In addition, this essay favours Liu Xin's *wuxing* theory, recognizing Liu Bang as the equivalent of Emperor Yao, and the Han dynasty as a period of the virtue of fire. Ban Biao combines this metaphysics with his own methodology: when describing periods of growth and decline in history, one cannot omit the role of the *Tianming*, and at the same time should not embellish the record, 'describing and not creating'.[239] The conflict between the two layers is ostensible, because it is history as a meaningful whole which 'happened' in the eyes of a historian, regardless of the fact that from our perspective this sense is rather constructed. The collapse of Wang Mang resulted therefore from the lack of *ren*; elsewhere the disruption of *yin-yang* harmony is the cause of the fall, while harmony in the time of the sages is called the way of Heaven.[240] Ban Gu's model, connected with the legitimization of power, was popular during political chaos, while the historians of the Song times often returned to Sima Qian.

Conclusion

To sum up, in the philosophy of history of the Han period, a view prevailed that history is explained through the prism of correlation between human behaviour and changes in nature, drawing near to what Adorno called the 'natural-history'.[241] Many philosophers of history of the Han times, however, rejected the idea of a mutual relationship between nature and history, separating the laws describing the human world, including the world of history, from the laws of nature. All of these thinkers excepting Wang Chong, the creators of official historiography included, assumed that each of the given factors coincides with what is desirable. In other words, the actions of outstanding individuals (Yang Xiong), the people (Jia Yi and Zhong Changtong) or the positive laws (Huan Tan and Cui Shi) played a crucial historical role in the times of prosperity. It is therefore not surprising that the Neo-Legalist belief in the historical function of positive laws that have to be used by skilful ministers ultimately approaches the elitist view of Yang Xiong (with the difference that the sages are equipped with supernatural cognitive abilities) and historical populism of Jia Yi and Zhong Changtong, since the people – declaratively brought to the forefront of history – have to be controlled and moulded by rulers and ministers. It is only Wang Chong for whom neither the people (both in the individual and the collective dimension) nor their social products (particularly the law) have an impact upon the course of history. Wang Chong also ridiculed and undermined the uncritical faith in the Classics and historiography at the very same time that official historiography emerged on the horizon of Chinese culture. And although he shared the critical attitude towards historical sources with the author of *Shiji*, Sima Qian's belief that man is the main historical actor had no place in his thought. All these discussions regarding the conditions and limits of human impact on history directly influenced the philosophy of history in the later epoch.

The Basis of History

The Philosophy of History from the Eighth to the Twelfth Century

Introduction

This chapter discusses the philosophy of history that was created during the millennium that is often called the 'Chinese Middle Ages'.[1] In the 'Early Middle Ages', so to speak, that is from the third to seventh centuries, Chinese philosophy of history was centred around the departure from the holistic and speculative views of history rooted in the Confucian understanding of the idea of correlation between Heaven and humanity. This was expressed in the blooming of the Neo-Daoist conceptions of history that stressed the historical role of either individuals or community (as in the case of the *Taipingjing*), as well as in the inception of the philosophy of historiography. However, the period from the eighth to the twelfth century was marked by a return to the systematic Confucian visions of history, which absorbed the preceding criticism and brought the ideas formulated by the Han thinkers to another level. This resulted in the rise of a 'Neo-Confucian' philosophy of history, which was, in itself, unprecedentedly diversified and mature. Neo-Confucian philosophers of history – from Liu Zongyuan and Shao Yong to Zhu Xi and Chen Liang – held sophisticated yet clear views regarding the basic substance of historical process, which might be interpreted in terms of historical realism and idealism, as it will be shown based on their works.

Early medieval philosophy of history

In the field of the Chinese philosophy of history, the 'medieval' sense of intermediateness and, consistently, breakup with the ancient ideas was initially expressed in the fact that in the face of political disintegration and war, the Confucian ideas of the Mandate of Heaven, correlation between Heaven and humanity, and other historical views used to legitimize the power of particular dynasties, were in crisis. From the perspective of time, it could be seen that the rejection of the metanarratives typical of the Han dynasty took place in three ways. First, counter-metanarratives came to life, this time not Confucian and focused on the past, but, instead, Daoist and future-oriented. Second, as a result of the abandonment of any systematic conception of history, reflection centred on outstanding individuals and their influence on history. Third, the speculative philosophy of history in general was phased out in favour of the philosophy of historiography, as especially represented by the *Shitong*.

This lack of interest in the systematic views of history coincided with the increasing importance of Buddhism within Chinese culture. As indicated in Introduction, because of the Indian origin of Buddhism, the religious nature of its view of history and the lack of direct influence on the later Chinese philosophy of history, the Buddhist vision of history is omitted here. First, Buddhist thinkers were not so much interested in the philosophical theories of history. The human world is only one of the many worlds, in addition temporary and – in some perspectives – illusionary, and this led to a lack of interest in political history. What are the dynasties in the face of the *kalpas* distinguished by Buddhists – epochs lasting 4.3 billion years? Second, although due to its cultural function Buddhism had an undeniable influence on the content and partly the form of Chinese historiography,[2] criticism of Buddhism had an even greater impact.[3] The concept that Buddhist devotion helps the emperor to receive Heaven's support did not find widespread espousal.[4] In addition, it reduces Buddhism to a tool to achieve a Confucian goal. As for the Buddhist historiography itself, it should be emphasized that it was, to a large extent, once again of a religious character, whether in the form of the hagiographies of the eminent monks, such as the *Gaoseng zhuan* and the *Xu gaoseng zhuan*, or the so-called Dharma transmission lineages. As Robert Sharf aptly points out, this transmission ultimately transcends human history.[5] In fact, it was Daoism, and not Buddhism, that largely shaped the philosophy of history of that time.

Historical heroes: the philosophy of history in the third and fourth centuries

In the light of constant changes of the dynasties, convictions about the central influence of individuals on the course of history and the accompanying doubt in the existence of impersonal 'mechanisms' of history, was natural. This trend is visible in so-called Neo-Daoism, or more precisely 'mysterious learning' 玄學 *xuánxué*, which in its social philosophy approaches the Confucian position. For example, in the *Laozi weizhi lüeli* Wang Bi 王弼 (226–249) claims that antiquity and the present are interconnected, so that one can take lessons from the past,[6] while in the *Commentary to Zhuangzi* Guo Xiang (郭象, d. 312) uses the Emperor Yao as an example of someone who, following the principle of *wuwei*, achieved political success.[7] Wang Bi claims that order in a state is made possible because the ruler is deprived of knowledge, and that such a ruler gains the world, for only he is a guarantee of continuity of Dao from antiquity until today.[8] Ge Hong 葛洪 (283–343) in the *Baopuzi waipian* states that 'only a sage unites virtue with Heaven'. One example of this is that the sages Yao and Confucius, responding to Heaven and changing the mandate, behaved in new and not always humane ways.[9] Puett comments on this as follows:

> For Ge Hong, these sages are the crucial figures in human history (…) Without sages, humans would have continued to live throughout their history as they initially did: in caves, without clothing, without agriculture, without a state. The

reason that human history has gone differently than that of any other earthly creature is because sages, born with a bit of Heavenly clarity, have invented successive pieces of artifice to lift humanity to higher levels (...) The shift of the dynasties, therefore, was not a result of a benevolent ruler replacing a non-benevolent one. It was an example of sages, acting out of heavenly clarity, acting in non-benevolent ways. And they were right to do so.[10]

On the other hand, as Puett points out, although the sages are key to human history, Ge Hong does not attribute any extraordinary abilities to them,[11] in contrast with the immortals 神仙 *shénxiān*, to which he dedicated a separate hagiography, the *Shenxian zhuan*. As Robert Campany shows, Ge Hong makes a specific re-contextualization of the past, so that Mozi, Dong Zhongshu and Kong Anguo turn out to be alchemists seeking immortality.[12] The *Shenxian zhuan* is one example of a biography of eminent figures created in those times.

The turn to the abilities and talents of individual historical figures is also noticeable in the historiography of that time. The best example of this is the *Records of the Three Kingdoms* 三國志 *Sānguózhì*, which unlike the *Shiji* and *Hanshu*, is essentially a collection of biographies (involving over 500 people). The depiction of the main characters of the chronicle of Chen Shou 陳壽 (233–297), such as Cao Cao, Liu Bei, Sun Quan, Zhuge Liang, Guan Yu and Zhang Fei, focuses on their specific talents. Thanks to this, it was possible for the *Sanguozhi* to become the basis of the fourteenth-century novel *The Romance of the Three Kingdoms* 三國演義 *Sānguó yǎnyì* – the novel that begins with the sentence summarizing the historical thinking of the age of chaos: 'the tendency of the world is that what has been divided for a long time will unite, and what has been united for a long time will fall apart.' As noted by Pang Tianyou, the style of the *Sanguzhi* influenced the later medieval chronicles:

> Penchant in assessing the character and talent of persons reflected a social trend of the search for individual emotions. This trend had an overwhelming influence on historians of the Northern and Southern Dynasties. Fan Ye's *Hou Hanshu*, Shen Yue's *Songshu*, Wei Shou's *Weishu*, Xiao Zixian's *Nan-Qishu*, etc. in their biographical part were increasingly evaluating personality and temperament of the character.[13]

In line with Pang Tianyou, Charles Holcombe speaks of the 'discovery of the individual' that took place at that time.[14]

This trend has also resulted in the theoretical concept of the historical hero, which can be found, among others, in the *Description of characters* 人物志 *Rénwùzhì* by Liu Shao 劉邵 (182–245 CE). Although the *Renwuzhi* is the first Chinese work in the field of psychology (in the sense in which the term is used while discussing Theophrastus' *Characters*), it emphasizes the historical role of the sages.[15] In the eighth chapter devoted to the heroes, it is claimed that the hero is a combination of a wise 英 *yīng* and a strong 雄 *xióng* person. An example of such a rare combination, *yingxiong* (which also means 'hero' in modern Chinese), is, for instance, the founder of the Han dynasty. Without strength one cannot bring any intentions into effect, and without wisdom there are no plans that are worth carrying out. Each of the two elements defining the hero is divided into the next two elements, so that the hero is eventually a person who has the wisdom to devise plans, the intelligence to implement those plans, the force to subordinate the people and the courage to overcome difficulties.[16] Thanks to this, the characteristics of the hero are integrated into the overall characterology of Liu Shao; it is said elsewhere that *yang* stands behind wisdom, and *yin* gives rise to force.[17] Because the phenomenon of the heroes is explained almost 'scientifically', while the extraordinary abilities of the sages exceed the possibilities of understanding[18] – as Fang Litian emphasizes – in Liu Shao's philosophy of history the sage has a higher status than the hero.[19]

Neo-Daoist philosophy of history: the millenarism of the *Taipingjing*

Internally diversified Neo-Daoism did not stop at reflecting on individuals in history, but also developed an original and systematic interpretation of history which was intertwined with the very history of China. The Yellow Turban Rebellion, which broke out in 184 CE and was ultimately suppressed twenty-one years later, indirectly contributed to the fall of the Han dynasty. Its standard-bearer was Zhang Jue, the leader of the Daoist sect of Supreme Peace 太平道 *Tàipíngdào*, who proclaimed the advent of an era of peace, equality and community of goods. The *taiping* ideal returned a long time after the fall of the uprising, in the first half of the fifth century, when two kings (of Wei in the north and Liu-Song in the south), aspiring to the unification of China, described themselves as the 'rulers of the supreme peace'.[20] There are many indications that Zhang Jue relied on a work entitled *The Classic of the Supreme Peace* 太平經 *Tàipíngjīng*. As early as the Han dynasty, though, there were two versions of the text, of which the longer version became part of the Daoist canon. What we know today as the *Taipingjing* took its final shape at the end of the sixth century. The writings included in *The Classic*, undoubtedly of many authors, were in circulation during the entire period of political disorder, responding to the needs of time and competing with other apocalyptic trends, as evidenced by numerous criticisms of 'false prophets' in the *Taipingjing*.[21]

The connection between the *Taipingjing* and Han thought is testified to by the idea of a correlation between nature and humanity. As Barbara Hendrischke argues, the *Taipingjing* radicalizes the holistic idea of a mutual relationship between people and nature, but shifts the emphasis towards human influence on nature.[22] This compliance is explicitly recognized as an answer 応 *yìng*, which extends not only to Heaven, but also to the transformation of *yin-yang* in general, including astronomical phenomena.[23] Since nature is 'moved' by human behaviour, it is to some extent deprived of agency. No natural phenomena have an independent effect on the history of people: 'if the cyclical revolutions of the spheres are natural and regular, what benefit can they bring to people who do good?'[24] However, this does not imply naturalism, for significant and extraordinary historical events are explained by a completely new factor, specific to the *Taipingjing*: 'ancient and newer texts often proclaim that [something happens] because of the conjunction of Heaven and earth, *yin* and *yang*, whereas it is not so – all misfortunes result from inherited guilt.'[25] Therefore, the analysis of the philosophy of history in the *Taipingjing* requires examining the idea of 'inherited guilt' 承負 *chéngfù*.

This concept implies a historical narrative according to which former rulers acted in harmony with Heaven and earth, and ruled with the help of Dao, living in harmony with the will of Heaven, without punishments and rituals.[26] At some point, though, evil was committed. This moment is indefinite: in one place it is said that it happened hundreds of thousands of generations ago, in another that the fault is as old as Heaven and earth itself.[27] It seems that the time of the ancient rulers who embodied Dao and lived in harmony with Heaven was not a utopia, but had features of evil from the very beginning. However, it is emphasized that in times of the most distant past, when everyone knew Dao, there was only little evil.[28] Each successive generation caused, by its deeds, that evil to increase, as is confirmed by history from the earliest antiquity through the middle ages up to the latest times.[29] What is more, each generation passes to the next generation not only their own faults, but also everything that has been passed on to them, so the sin grows heavier from generation to generation.[30] The word 'generations' is used here, because in contrast to the idea of karma, or the biological concept of inheritance, this is not passed from person to person, but to all humanity. (However, as opposed to the idea of original sin, the inherited guilt progressively increases.) As a result, all humanity suffers from the faults of individual emperors and kings, and people experience the effects of actions they did not commit.[31] As Michael Puett notes, this leads to paradoxical consequences. If the ancients were able to understand the world and act properly, and yet they committed evil and passed it on to future generations, then they are ultimately responsible for the chaos of the present; people who only inherited the guilt are innocent, and not responsible for what is happening in their time.[32] Even if the ruler has the virtue of ten thousand people, he will not be able to improve the situation or reduce the corruption of humanity. Chaos and corruption are not the only disasters affecting humanity because of inherited guilt. These include all catastrophes, miraculous events and anomalies.[33] Hence, the idea of correlation takes the form of a pessimistic idea of disasters caused by inherited conduct. The *Taipingjing* radicalizes the Daoist idea of decline expressed in the *Huainanzi*. The distinctive feature of this second vision was to go without the mediation of Heaven, while in such a heterogeneous text as the *Taipingjing* one can find fragments in which Heaven acts as a specific enforcer of the consequences of inherited guilt. It is even claimed that when people blame Heaven for unhappiness caused by inherited guilt, Heaven is angry and starts to fight them, ultimately striving to exterminate the whole human race.[34] In this context, Tian acquires theistic features, which is even closer to the *Tian-ren ganying* idea.

As one might guess, a constant and gradual increase of evil leads to further escalation of cataclysms, and eventually to apocalypse. In a result of drought and epidemics, humanity will be completely extinct: no human being will survive this ultimate 'annihilation' 滅盡 *mièjìn*. The unity of Heaven, earth and humanity will be broken, Heaven and earth will be destroyed, and with them all beings will cease to exist.[35] There are many passages that speak of the imminent arrival of this time.[36] For this reason, the philosophy of history in the *Taipingjing* can be described as a millenarian one. However, Stephen Bokenkamp polemicizes with the thesis that there actually was Millenarianism in China, for he believes that chiliastic visions are related to the linear view of history, whereas the Chinese were preoccupied with the cyclical view, so that the concepts of Millenarianism and 'apocalypse' can only be used metaphorically in these cases.[37] It is surprising, though, that the *Taipingjing* is not listed among the many Daoist writings to which Bokenkamp refers – all the more, this work implies a linear conception of history, to which the concept of millenarianism may be referred even under Bokenkamp's assumptions. It is true that the *Taipingjing* mentions cycles such as the lifecycle, the seasons or the cycle of traditional chronology, but the concept of the cycle is not used in the 'macro' scale to refer to the consequences of guilt, and is even criticized in this context.[38]

But apocalypse is not the only possible scenario for the end of history. The main message of the *Taipingjing*, i.e. that an era of supreme peace is coming, is fundamentally optimistic. The Taiping era is depicted by a series of images. The text reads that people will be deprived of basic needs, including procreation, and will work only in a manner adjusted to their abilities, in this way earning their living. Furthermore, they will not destroy nature, as this would have – on the basis of correlation – an effect on nature; instead, it will become regular and will yield only healthy crops.[39] There will be peace in the state, wars and chaos will disappear, the people will be happy and misfortunes will not occur anymore.[40] Violence against women will also cease.[41] In the state of supreme peace slaves, bondswomen and barbarians will be equally recognized.[42] This concept only confirms the linear interpretation of history in the *Taipingjing*. As Jens Petersen notes,

> The Heavenly Master[43] seems willing to concede that history will stop; if the *qi* of Great Peace is given a chance to assert this influence, then from now on, and presumable for ever, peace will reign. The Heavenly Master does not discuss the possibility of a future decline in the state of the world; the present moment thud seems to present man with a chance to jump out of history and create a world where no change occurs and no change is needed.[44]

If we agree with this interpretation, we will see how different from the Confucian vision of history the Neo-Daoist vision was. It was oriented towards the future, not the past, ultimately conveying an optimistic, not pessimistic, envoi. It also allowed the possibility of the 'exhaustion' of history and transcendence of it, in this way situating itself between the 'inner-wordly' Confucian philosophy of history and the Buddhist eschatology. But how is it possible that chaos and violence will stop in the face of increasing sin? The effects of inherited guilt would have to be eliminated. But then how to do it? What should one do on the crossroads of history to go towards utopia rather than apocalypse?

The solution is certainly not the advent of any messiah, a 'future sage' 後聖人 *hòushèngrén*, because he will not add anything to what has been passed on in the *Taipingjing*. Departing from the true message of the *Classic of the Supreme Peace* will lead to an even greater anger of Heaven and will exacerbate the bad condition to the point that there will no longer be any salvage.[45] This stems from the idea that inherited guilt is perpetuated by wrong teachings, which – imitated and practised by people – lead to the escalation of disasters, and who are then unable to prevent them in any way, as history shows.[46] Each of these teachings subsumes nature and history only partially, doing so in its own way, which leads to the emergence of different teachings.[47] If one person teaches ten, and these ten teach ten more, then in time there will be doctrines so dominant that, although mostly false, will not be criticized.[48] At the same time, each of these doctrines carries the seeds of truth and is not completely false, because the sages are ultimately sent by Heaven.[49] History, then, brings hope for liberation, although this is not a messianic hope. For this reason, Petersen calls it 'anti-Messianic Millenarianism'.[50]

Importantly, each doctrine contains a seed of truth that complements the others, together creating a total Truth. Therefore, all these fragments from all eras (ancient, middle and late) should be collected to form a single scripture.[51] This solution is given only by the Heavenly Master, who *de facto* acts as a messiah, stating that he is not proclaiming anything new but communicating the truth revealed to him by Heaven,[52] a view which, unlike previous ones, is predicated not on reality but on other doctrines (and thereby should not be treated as yet another doctrine). All humanity must take part in the compilation process: old and young, women and men, slaves and barbarians. With the dissemination of the scripture and its bringing into effect by all people, evil will give way and the highest peace will occur.[53] This sort of holism concerns not only time, space and causality, but also meaning, reifying the idea of the whole of history in the form of the ultimate scripture. It might be said that in this way the *Taipingjing* somehow mediates between the speculative philosophy of history of the Han period and the early medieval philosophy of historiography, which will be now discussed.

The birth of the philosophy of historiography: Liu Xie i Liu Zhiji

The early Chinese Middle Ages, that is the Wei and Jin dynasties (220–420) and the Period of the Southern and Northern Dynasties (420–589), was a time of exceptional flourishing of literary criticism, or as expressed by the most eminent modern Chinese writer Lu Xun (1881–1936), 'the era of literary self-awareness'.[54] This reflection was largely inspired not so much by Confucianism, but by the then-dominant Neo-Daoism.[55] In spite of the political break-up, this time abounded in historical works that preserved the continuity of historiography. What is more, it was precisely the continuity of dynastic legitimacy 正統 *zhèngtǒng*, that became the main theme, if not the obsession, of the chroniclers.[56] Each dynasty identified itself as the legitimate successor of the Han, recognizing its predecessors and competitors as deprived of this legitimacy, and even – as in the case of the *Wei History* – as barbarians (which, incidentally, came from the 'barbaric' nation of Tuoba).[57] With the establishment of the Tang Dynasty and the reign of Emperor Taizong (626–649), China entered its golden age of economic and military expansion. Taizong, whose reign is commemorated by a collection of historical anecdotes recognized as a compendium of statecraft, *Essentials of politics from the Zhenguan reign* 貞觀政要 *Zhēnguàn zhèngyào*, sought not only to memorialize himself, but also to improve the work of historians. He did this by establishing the Historical Bureau 史官 *Shǐguǎn*, whose task was to draw up a state history of the ruling dynasty 國史 *guóshǐ*, as well as chronicles of the previous dynasties. Their work was to be guided not so much by political interest as the credibility of the records. According to the founding act of 629, 'the historiographers are responsible for the compilation of the National History. They may not give false praise, or conceal evil, but must write a straight account of events.'[58] The process of compiling *guoshi* could be summarized as follows:

> *The Diary of the Emperor's Activity and Leisure* was prepared every day; during the Tang period the tradition was still preserved that the emperor had no right to see the text, then, during the Song dynasty emperors, this valuable custom was abandoned. Materials from *The Diary* along with reports from the ministries were then combined for the compilation of *Daily Raports*, which in turn served as the basis for writing the *Veritable Records* of each reign, actually constituting the current history of the dynasty. The next dynasty used these *Veritable Records* for the compilation of the official history of its predecessor.[59]

In practice, due to the increasing control over this process and the re-writing of records by the dynasty, which gained power in overcoming its predecessor, the Bureau was moving away from its mission, which was noted as soon as in the century after its establishment.

Another pattern of history writing, closer to the *Shiji* rather than the *Hanshu*, was the *Comprehensive [Exposition] of Institutions* 通典 *Tōngdiǎn* by Du You (杜佑, 735–812) – a 200-chapter long encyclopaedia and institutional history of food and goods, examinations, offices, rituals, music, the army, criminal law, and the territory of the state and its borders. One hundred chapters alone were dedicated to rituals. Du You links rituals with every stage of historical development,[60] calling them the principle of the order of the ancient rulers, although practising rituals, and generally culture, requires a proper material 'base'.[61] However, for many other thinkers it was rather literature that occupied a distinguished position in culture.

One of the most eminent instances of such interest was the work entitled the *Literary Mind and the Carving of Dragons* 文心雕龍 *Wénxīn diāolóng* by Liu Xie 劉勰 (465–522). In this treatise, Liu Xie examines the sources of literature, various literary genres, stylistic means (such as metaphor, hyperbole) and ways of creating a literary work. And although Liu Xie was a secular Buddhist, his work was much inspired by Confucianism.[62] Liu believed that the works of Confucius, namely the Classics, express and convey Dao in the most perfect way, thus constituting an imperishable model of literary creativity.[63] Consequently, Liu Xie was influenced by the 'common notion of "historical regression" in literature, the assumption that present works are necessarily inferior to those of the past'.[64] However, this prevented him from taking a purely descriptive approach to literature: a good literary work, including a historical one, must meet certain criteria and requires specific abilities, including the 'talent of a historian' 史才 *shǐcái*.[65] Liu Xie treated historiography as a part of literature: specific, but subject to the same general principles, as expressed in the chapter *On Historical Writings*.

First of all, the chronicle must have a sufficient empirical base and rational justification: 'to take into account the sources collected by hundreds of authors, withstand the test of thousands of years, show the sources of rise and decline, and give reasons for successes and failures.'[66] Secondly, it is not enough to collect as many sources as possible: when the chronological scale of the chronicle is too big, it is difficult to determine the sequence of events. When there are too many events, it is difficult for their synoptic and synthetic image to emerge.[67] It is therefore necessary to select plentiful material, rejecting what is unreliable, and to determine the correct sequence of events and concepts that best match the facts; all of this should be guided by the general principle 大綱 *dàgāng*.[68] Importantly, the idea of a general principle lying behind events will return in the later, speculative philosophy of history. But in the present case, it is merely a principle of arranging historical records to form a coherent and meaningful historical narrative: something that Hayden White referred to as 'the transformation of the chronicle into history'.[69] Since for Liu Xie historiography is a part of literature, this standard applies to literary work in general: every work needs an ordering principle, in both its language and content, which guarantees the consistency of the work from beginning to end.[70] This especially applies to philosophical works that are supposed to include as many matters as possible.[71] In relation to historiography, Liu Xie seems to have no doubt that this principle should be the rule of praise and blame, present in the Classics and formulated by Confucius. This leads to the third criterion: the historian should be honest, i.e. should not: exaggerate facts, focus on extraordinary events, describe in detail the distant and unexplored past, give theses without justification, and most notably should not record doubtful events. Only when he avoids these vices can he create a reliable history 信史 *xìnshǐ* (literally, 'a history one can trust').[72] A historian must also beware of political prejudices, and maintain an objective pure mind 素心 *sùxīn*. This is required by the historian's responsibility 史之為任 *shǐ zhī wèi rèn*, for each historian is responsible to everyone for the moral judgements he makes.[73] The reference of strictly ethical concepts to the profession of a historian anticipates the later idea of the 'virtue of a historian'.

Liu Zhiji 劉知幾 (661–721), the author of the world's first treatise on historical criticism, *Comprehensive [Inquiry into] Histories* 史通 *Shǐtōng*, essentially agreed with these assumptions.[74] At first glance the *Shitong* is a series of countless, detailed comments on the entire corpus of Chinese historiography, which in part contributed to the still-recent overlooking of this work by historians and philosophers, and even Sinologists (the *Shitong* has not yet been translated into any Western language). As Hsu Kwan-san emphasizes, one should be patient enough to bring out the 'innermost idea of the whole structure of his philosophy of history', and more precisely 'the philosophy of historiography'.[75]

A significant part of the *Shitong* is also a history of historiography, which is justified by theoretical premises: particular species of historical writing change with time,[76] while the greatest differences can be seen from the perspective of time, between antiquity and modern times.[77] Liu Zhiji even believes that these genres should adapt to their times,[78] which is why the mannerist use of classical phrases in the newer chronicles is criticized as an anachronism, and opposed to the recording of actual statements in the colloquial language of a given time.[79] The criticism of the latest historical works, however, makes Liu seem bewitched by the conviction of the gradual fall of historiography.[80] Paradoxically, the main premise of this criticism is an excessive inclination to antiquity among his contemporaries, and the tendency to look for unusual and miraculous events,[81] for which there is no place in chronicles. The belief in the limitations of the historiography of this time is innovatively connected with the thesis on the temporal variability of historiography: all historians are limited by the times in which they live, and therefore are unable to fully express themselves.[82] In this way Liu Zhiji not only anticipates the later historization of the Classics, but also historizes historical knowledge itself and demonstrates the basic limits of historical cognition, while also showing the apparentness of the then-popular ideal of self-expression.

A historical review of Chinese historiography led Liu Zhiji to create several typologies. In the first chapter, he lists six schools of historiography (perhaps by analogy to the Six Schools of philosophy), paradigmatically established by six seminal works: *Shangshu, Chunqiu, Zuo zhuan, Guoyu, Shiji* and *Hanshu*. Elsewhere, a more general classification of four types of narrative 敘事 *xùshì* appears, dividing narratives into those: 1) directly describing characters and conduct; 2) focusing on events; 3) based on the statements of the characters; and 4) using a separate author's commentary.[83] These types are assigned to particular chronicles, so as Niu Runzhen notes, Liu Zhiji (re-) constructs the genres of history writing by reinterpreting works of the past using his own conceptual apparatus.[84] Moreover, Liu Zhiji distinguished ten types of private historiography: records of eyewitnesses; private biographies; anecdotes; collected sayings; local chronicles; family genealogies; chronicles of social groups (women, children, etc.); stories about strange and wonderful events, and descriptions of urban architecture.[85] Because these genres complement the official ones, the *Shitong* truly deserves its title of 'comprehensive inquiry into historiography'.

The basic criterion for distinguishing types of historical writing are stylistic differences. All chronicles should, however, employ a simple and substantive language,[86] as this is enough to praise and blame historical figures or to examine customs. If the language of a chronicle is too sophisticated and redundant, it will not be history, but rather literature.[87] For writing history, one needs the specific talent of a historian (*shicai*), which is not only very rare, but also fundamentally different from literary talent.[88] Unlike Liu Xie, Liu Zhiji sees a clear difference between history and literature, which does not mean that history can dispense with literature – without literary means, it would not spread and would not affect people.[89] A historian should also not beware of metaphors, even though their meaning is open.[90] The order of the narrative is also important, as the beginning must consort with the end, creating a coherent sequence. According to Liu Zhiji, it is better to use anticipation than retrospection for this purpose.[91] Liu is aware of the active role of language: the narrative cannot be internally contradictory in both its language and sequence of events, as this makes a real, consistent order of events incoherent.[92] Even the best writer cannot be a historian if he never worked in archives – a spare, accurate narrative is not enough, because the task of the chronicle is to explain events.[93]

The relation of narrative to reality is no less an important aspect of the philosophy of Liu Zhiji. In the first stage of explanation, a selection of the material must be made: narrative cannot coherently cover all events.[94] In ordering events, one should keep in mind the final intention of the work, which is that the reader 閱之者 *yuèzhīzhě* has to follow the sequence of events.[95] Only the correct combination of events and their placement in relation to each other gives them final meaning.[96] Hence, Liu Zhiji would accept the thesis of semantic holism (which in this book is referred to as 'holism regarding meaning'). This does not mean that historians have to approach events selectively. On the contrary, he cannot omit any – positive or negative – aspects of the described reality.[97] His room for manoeuvring is restricted to means of expression and the proportions of the sources used. A historian should be marked by a rarely seen impartiality, and the pursuit of truth;[98] he should be like clean air and a transparent mirror that shows both the good and the bad aspects of things. Only such an objective work can be called a 'veritable record' 實錄 *shílù*.[99] Interestingly, unlike the vast majority of Chinese philosophers and historians, Liu Zhiji uses the mirror metaphor in the same context as European thought, speaking of a mirror reflecting reality rather than one's own countenance, thus placing the accent on its transparency.[100]

Unfortunately, these standards are rarely implemented. Historians often follow a given philosophical school, which deforms their records.[101] Most often, however, it is political interests that answer for those deformations, as in the case of the *Wei Chronicle* criticized by Liu Zhiji, which constantly exalts this non-Chinese state, comparing it to the Han Empire and considering its competitors barbarians.[102] This also applies to the newly-established History Bureau – if the stories of the dynasties preceding the Tang had begun to be written down by the grandsons of the persons involved in the events, they would not have corresponded to reality, as evidenced by the comparison of these records with eyewitness accounts of the events.[103] Not without significance is the fact that outsiders, without a historical education, also work in the History Bureau, so that '1/10 or 1/5 of them have no idea what the historian's job is about'.[104] Above all, however, it is an emperor who interferes in the process of writing chronicles, whose main task is to commemorate great deeds. As Liu Zhiji writes ironically, 'I have heard of those who died because of faithful records, but I have not heard of those who have been condemned for making the false ones'.[105] Liu was therefore fully aware of the historical as well as political determinants of historiography. This conviction lay behind the detailed criticism of many 'myths' repeated by Chinese historiography, such as the thesis of abdication of Yao and Shun, or the belief that in the old days no crime was committed.[106] Criticism does not bypass works imitating the Classics, which as they were 'discovered' only later are largely unreliable,[107] nor the Classics themselves, in which there are not a few unbelievable or even impossible passages, especially in the celebrated *Spring and Autumn Annals*.[108] Such criticism must have caused considerable indignation among his contemporaries, especially in the face of the renascence of Confucianism.

If one of the principles of good historiography is the careful selection of materials, the question arises of what key sources should be selected. For Liu Zhiji, this principle lay, paradoxically, in the giving of moral examples through the praise and blame of given attitudes (*baobian*).[109] This principle does not conflict with the norm of faithful records of the past, since only credible records could be the basis of moral teachings.[110] The historian is principally responsible for the commemoration of virtuous figures. What is more, good examples should be recorded rather than bad ones, which are already surplus, and in this way the reader will not focus on them.[111] This also concerns social values: traditional meanings of names and titles along with the associated social hierarchy should be kept in the chronicle, which is why Sima Qian made a 'mistake' by placing Prince Xiang Yu in the royal annals.[112]

The complicated relation between the various layers of Liu Zhiji's philosophy of history is put in order in the *Old Book of the Tang*, according to which Liu Zhiji was to distinguish three conditions of being a historian: talent 才 *cái*, knowledge 學 *xué* and insight 識 *shì*.[113] Today, Liu would say that history is a mixture of literature, science and philosophy. The order of these conditions is, nonetheless, stated: the root of Liu Zhiji's approach is the study of the sources and narrative of events (*xue*); events must then be cleverly transmitted in simple language (*cai*), and eventually, one must be aware of the moral function of a historical work (*shi*). It seems, though, that the conflict between realism and moralism is ultimately inevitable. Perhaps Liu Zhiji did not see it, or maybe – as he noted himself – as a historian he was limited by the times in which he lived.

Conclusion

During the period from the third to seventh centuries, there emerged hitherto unknown spheres of philosophical reflection. The belief in the crucial historical role of the sages and 'heroes', as exemplified by such works as *Baopuzi* and *Renwuzhi*, was accompanied by a view that current historical situation stems from crimes of all previous human generations, and thereby only the whole humanity is capable of preventing the apocalypse and creating the future era of 'supreme peace', as instanced by the *Taipingjing*. At the opposite end of the scale there were thinkers who did not show any interest in speculation on the nature of history, but instead focused on the nature and function of writing about history. It was particularly Liu Zhiji, who followed up Liu Xie's idea that ordering the events in simple language should be guided by some general principle. Accordingly, Liu Zhiji tried to balance the principle of praise and blame not only with the criteria of 'veritable records', but also with actual form of historical narratives and political determinants of historiography in contemporaneous China. In comparison with Han views of history, the *Taipingjing* went even further in speaking of the most distant past and the end of history, as a matter of fact transcending human history based on religious premises, whereas the philosophy of historiography got rid of any references to the metaphysics of history, in contrast to the philosophy of history in the subsequent epoch.

The Neo-Confucian philosophy of history

The renascence of Confucianism, which took place during the Tang and Song, also entailed the development of the philosophy of history. Despite the temporal distance and the break in the continuity of Confucian vision of history, key issues have returned in a more mature and profound form. For this reason, when referring to the period from the ninth to twelfth centuries I will talk about a 'neo-Confucian' philosophy of history. The main problem of this philosophy of history was of a general nature and reflected ontological findings, as it turned out to be a debate over the ultimate 'substratum' of history. This meant an answer to the question of whether any form of a timeless being is realized in history. This led, as in the Han times, to a dispute between two groups of thinkers. Of course, only in light of the accepted criteria and from the perspective of time can one distinguish the representatives of the parties, as they were not particularly organized factions. On the other hand, in the final phase this debate became an open confrontation, in the form of a correspondence between Zhu Xi and Chen Liang, the culmination of which (famous statement of Zhu Xi that Chen Liang is 'corrupted by history') shows the validity of the distinction made here. This dispute overlaps with the dichotomy of historical thinking in the Song era observed by Thomas H.C. Lee, about the difference between thinkers acknowledging history as subordinated to the Classics, and those defending the independence of history as a discipline and subject of reflection.[114]

The philosophers who assumed that history is the implementation of timeless and non-empirical principle are framed here in terms of historical idealism. If they recognized that the role of this principle is fulfilled by the spirit, be it personal (Wang Anshi) or supersonal (Shao Yong), I attribute to them the position of historical spiritualism. The fact that the Chinese term *shen*, meaning spirit, never assumes such a radical dualism as in Western philosophy, but accepts that spirit is part of the same universe as visible forms (*xing*), does not change the fact that when it is considered the cause of history, it is imperceptible within history itself. It should also be remembered that in the case of Wang Anshi and Shao Yong, thinkers deeply rooted in Buddhist philosophy, the concept of *shen* is given a new meaning, unprecedented in the classical Confucianism. In both cases, a speculative philosophy of history is developed, either cyclical or linear, which prefers regressivism and individualism, namely explanation of historical processes by referring to the actions of individuals, usually sages (and specifically, their minds). In addition to these historical spiritualists, historical idealists in the strict sense, such as the Cheng brothers and Zhu Xi, should also be distinguished, for they saw the principium of history in the generally conceived, metaphysical (and ultimately timeless) principle, *li*.

Their opponents will be called historical realists. A historical realist is one who thinks that insight into history itself is sufficient to explain the nature of history. The opposition realism-idealism in the philosophy of history corresponds therefore with the opposition realism-idealism in political philosophy. Among historical realists there are both agnostics, who believe that knowledge of what is timeless is not needed to understand history (Ouyang Xiu), as well as those who actively reject the idealist solution. Among them, then, there are both thinkers for whom the point of reference are dependencies resulting from the totality of historical changes (Su Xun), as well as those who attribute decisive historical role to one of the material factors determining the course of history, and who consider that the transformation of the social world is dependent on material changes, whom I will call historical materialists. In this place two things should be emphasized. First, historical materialism as such is a general position, even though it is contemporarily treated as a byword for Marx's view. Materialism, however, allows for the whole range of concepts and definitions of 'matter', from natural matter to the matter of social relations. The appropriation of the attractive and general notion of historical materialism by Marxism, which in fact should be referred to as 'economic determinism', is probably the greatest obstacle in recognizing the convention adopted here. Nevertheless, due to Chinese philosophers of history it is possible and even it should be attempted to 'disenchant' this notion. This all the more excludes the 'good guys-bad guys' attitude as represented in the ideologized narratives in the PRC.

Second, historical materialism cannot be identified with ontological materialism: these are theoretically independent positions, however often they go hand in hand. Even then, Chinese philosophers give the concept of *qi* a new, broader and philosophical meaning, comparable to the views of matter in the Stoic philosophy (the idea of *pneuma*) or contemporary new materialism, which include animate and mental phenomena. However, the controversy over the applicability of *qi* as matter does not affect the category of historical materialism. Matter means here observable factors determining history. It may be a matter of nature, namely geographical conditions and climate, as well as character fluids (Chen Liang); social material, that is produced artefacts and relations of their distribution (Liu Zongyuan), as well as economic matter: goods and landed property (Li Gou). The last sense includes Marx's view, which turns out to be only one among possible historical materialisms.

Idealist and spiritualist currents

The revival of Confucianism was largely due to Han Yu 韩愈 (768–824). Although his views contain elements of social evolutionism, the main idea of Han Yu's philosophy of history, namely that there exists the Dao of history which is transmitted and saved by the sages, has established the horizon of idealist philosophers of history during the Song.

According to Han Yu, at the dawn of human history there was chaos and people were exposed to many dangers: wild animals, hunger, disease, frost, murder and theft. They lived naked in caves or on trees, not differing significantly from animals. Everything changed thanks to the sages, who remedied these ills: they invented clothes, houses, medicine and tools, created rituals and a government (monarchy), defined a system of punishments and organized an army. Had it not been for the sages, concludes Han Yu, the human species – devoid of wings, claws and scales – would have completely extinguished.[115] Han Yu's theory of social development paradoxically closes on Legalism, albeit its amplification leaves no doubt about the Confucian origin of this philosophy of history. First of all, the sages were not only extraordinarily talented, but above all extraordinarily righteous; they were the standard of conduct for all subsequent generations.[116] Secondly, these are concrete sages. The only real Dao, different from the Way of Daoism and Buddhism, was passed from sage to sage; from Yao, through Shun, Yu, Tang, Wenwang, Wuwang and Prince Zhou to Confucius and Mencius. No sage has appeared since then. To restore Dao, it is necessary to return to the ancient teachings (this was the 'return to antiquity' 復古 *fùgǔ* movement); the Daoist and Buddhist books should be burned, and the monks forced to return to a secular state.[117] The thought of Han Yu continues the philosophy of Yang Xiong and takes up the Mencian strands, although this is a linear vision. The rise of society is the result of a culture created by virtuous, outstanding individuals.[118]

The idea of *shengren* was developed in the spirit of idealism at the beginning of the Song dynasty by Tian Xi 田錫 (940–1003). In the *Essay on Heaven's works* 天機論 *Tiānjīlùn*, he claims that the sages model themselves on Heaven, and apply its mechanism: just like Heaven sends favours or catastrophes, so the sage rewards or punishes his people.[119]

Shao Yong

The idea of the relation of Heaven to humanity, along with the *yin-yang* and *wuxing* theories, was close to another Neo-Confucian philosopher, Shao Yong 邵雍 (1011– 1077). In his *Book on the highest principles governing the world* 皇極經世書 *Huángjí jīngshì shū*, Shao Yong points out that in order to understand human matters, one must first have an insight into the nature of Heaven.[120] This does not mean 'insight' with the help of actual sight or even the mind, but with the principle 理 *lǐ*, which is to be found in all beings.[121] In other words, this is a programme of philosophical speculation: a purportedly unmediated and intuitive knowledge of reality. This type of inquiry is often connected with spiritualism, and this was also the case of Shao Yong. As Don Wyatt demonstrates, for Shao Yong, spirit 神 *shén* precedes the genesis of the cosmos, and even numbers.[122] All changes have their beginnings in the spirit, and come back to the spirit in the end.[123] The spirit is understood as indivisible and different from matter, as not present in any particular place, yet omnipresent.[124] People are different from the spirit: they are only things among things (the sages are also only people),[125] although they differ from other things having a soul 靈 *líng*.[126] As with Han Yu, for Shao Yong too the sages are the greatest of people, although this thesis receives additional metaphysical justification in the philosophy of the latter: the sages are one with Heaven.[127] In addition, there is also an epistemological justification: the knowledge of the sages reaches to the furthest points, which is why it is the most spiritual,[128] and in certain interpretations even transcends the dualism of the subject and the object, for the sage looks at things from the perspective of the things themselves.[129]

The sages therefore serve as a model for speculative cognition. This knowledge extends to the all-being, including – which is most important here – all of history. As Shao Yong notes, knowledge of the section of time will always depend on the subject:

> The present is called the present when it is seen from the perspective of the present. When the present is observed from the perspective of time, it is called the past. The past is called the past when it is seen from the perspective of the present. When the past is seen from the perspective of this past, it is called the present. Let it be known that the past is never necessarily a past, and the present is never necessarily the present. All this has its source in that it is observed by us. Is it not that people from a thousand years ago and people for ten thousand generations will observe the times from their own perspective?[130]

Shao Yong's argument brings to mind the well-known reasoning of J.E. McTaggart,[131] and to a large extent it also resembles (and perhaps was inspired by) the reasoning of the Buddhist Seng Zhao 僧肇 (384–414).[132] Unlike the two philosophers, Shao Yong used this reasoning not to declare the unreality of time, but to make room for a speculative philosophy of history that grasps history from the viewpoint of 'the whole', beyond the perspective of the subject.

The first three chapters of the *Huangji jingshi* divide the history of the universe in an openly cyclical way. According to Shao Yong, thirty years make up one 'generation' 世 *shì*; twelve generations constitute a 'revolution' 運 *yùn*, just as a day consists of twelve hours; thirty revolutions make up one 'epoch' 會 *huì*, just as a month consists of thirty days; twelve epochs form one 'era' 元 *yuǎn*, just as a year consists of twelve months. Thus, one era covers 129,600 years. At the end of an era, the cycle begins again, and so without end.[133] This means that it has been a hundred generations since Yao, while Shao Yong lived at the beginning of the tenth epoch of his era.[134] At the same time, in the era of Yao and Shun, *yang* reached its maximum, and in the era of Shao Yong it began to decrease at the expense of *yin*, which meant a coming collapse.[135] What is more, since the cycles are repeated endlessly, generations, revolutions and epochs of eras are distinguished, with the 'era of eras' on top, which covers 16,796,160,000 years, after which the world will be destroyed and re-created.[136] Chan Wing-tsit thinks that 'the whole scheme is as arbitrary as it is superficial. The idea that one world succeeds another is evidently Buddhist-influenced, for Buddhism conceives existence in terms of an infinite series of worlds, whereas the Chinese idea of cycles means a rise and fall within the history of this world.'[137] Chan's opinion is, however, unfair in three ways. First, there is nothing wrong in being inspired by Buddhism. Second, Shao Yong's chronology is not entirely arbitrary, as it is based on an analogy to the calendar year and its numerology. Third, his view does not reject political history. On the contrary, it integrates it into the history of the universe.

The time from Yao to the end of the Zhou Dynasty is divided (as in the case of, among others, Huan Tan) into the period of divine rulers (*huang*), emperors (*di*), kings (*wang*) and hegemons (*ba*).[138] These periods correspond in turn to the spring, summer, autumn and winter of human civilization.[139] They are also linked with four different types of mandate received from Heaven, and four different kinds of statecraft.[140] This means, again, that due to the considerable time lag that has elapsed even from the royal period, humanity witnesses a fundamental downfall of the original law.[141] However, since in the interim there were also temporary periods of flowering (the Han and Tang dynasties),[142] in the field of reflection on political history, Shao Yong maintains a cyclical view, although with a slightly linear flavour. Interestingly, as Martin Dösch observes, Shao Yong did not believe that the last period of the cycle is followed by the first one, but rather by the penultimate phase, and so to the beginning. In other words, after period of hegemons, there will be a period of kings, and then of emperors, and only then of divine rulers. This does not mean, however, as Dösch states,[143] that such approach is a linear one. First, the change concerns only the sequence of phases of the cycle, while its number and order are still fixed. Second, the new sequence is no more 'linear' than the previous one, as far as the inner structure of cycles is concerned. Third, the sequence 'ABCD-DCB' is ultimately followed by just the same structure, in a manner typical for Shao Yong, with greater cycles including the smaller ones. This shows that the cycles of political history are carefully inscribed into cosmic history, which, in itself, is a priori known, at least from the viewpoint of those who are able to grasp history from the perspective of its source – the spirit.

Wang Anshi

Although such historical idealists as the Cheng brothers opposed the reforms of minister Wang Anshi 王安石 (1021–1086), and these reforms implemented some of the ideas of the historical materialist Li Gou, Wang Anshi's philosophy of history was much closer to idealist positions. This is one of the cases of a similar political philosophy being combined with different philosophies of history.[144]

Wang Anshi agrees with the main theses of the philosophy of history of Mencius and Han Yu. In line with Mencius, he claims that order or chaos depends on whether the ruler is or is not *ren* (moral, humane), on whether he is noble (*junzi*), or petty (*xiaoren*).[145] Or even more explicitly: 'a state that entrusts responsibility to virtuous people, flourishes, and the one that turns away from them, falls down – these two truths are a necessary tendency of reality, the overall meaning of history and common knowledge conveyed through rituals.'[146] As Wang Mingsun accurately observes, Wang Anshi interprets history through the prism of the relations of two groups, picked out not by class, but by moral ability.[147] As a result, Wang Anshi distinguishes three periods in history: the first, when the virtuous were dominant; the second, when the wicked were predominant, and the present, when the proportions of both groups became even.[148]

The motif of the historical role of the sages has been taken from Han Yu, albeit with a specific, spiritualistic complement. Sages are not only responsible for civilizing humanity, for they are also the epitome of Dao and virtue, agreeing their actions with Heaven and ghosts.[149] Wang believes that although Heavenly Dao differs from the Dao of people, it is essentially consistent with it. Former kings used both 'ways', because they understood that in order to gain the support of Heaven, one must gain the support of the people.[150] Analogically, the basic definition of sages is that they are wise and moral people, who introduced rituals, although the rituals as such are grounded transcendentally, having their source in Heaven.[151] As Fang Litian states, this is one of the crucial arguments for attributing historical idealism to Wang Anshi.[152] There are, however, many more such arguments. Wang Anshi writes that the sages acted in accordance with Heaven's will.[153] The exclusive relation between the sages and the spiritual entities implies a kind of escapism: the sages do not pay attention to the world; their desires are in general contradiction with the intentions of the 'world'. Wang goes even further, claiming that from a certain perspective, sages are simply spirits acting in the world,[154] and adds that:

> What the spirit does, even in the highest stage, is not visible in the world. It becomes visible only when it manifests itself in morality and when it is expressed in use. In this way, the sages purify their mind, closing themselves back in their mystery.[155]

For this reason, his escapism is, in contrast to Daoist, only partial. Wang Anshi criticises Laozi, writing that Dao requires 'incorporation' into the deeds and words of people.[156] The study of history, therefore, comes down to guessing and understanding the intentions of the sages.[157] Also in this sense it is an idealistic programme, following in the footsteps of Dong Zhongshu. In addition, these are not sages' intentions that can be fully realized, because the cognition available to the sages is speculative, intuitive and spiritual:

> All beings have their ultimate principle, which only the sages can know. The way to knowing the principle consists in achieving unity with it, and nothing more. If this

unity is achieved, all beings can be known without any reflection (...) One who is able to do so can enter the spiritual stage. This stadium is the epitome of Dao. At this stage [one gets to know] without thought or action, in a state of perfect silence.[158]

Hence, recognition of Wang Anshi as a historical materialist in the PRC is not justified.[159]

However, Wang Anshi combines this idea with a concept foreign to most idealists of his time. Dao, starting from the time of Fuxi, through the era of Yao and Shun, the Xia, Shang and Zhou, was constantly changing; the sages, on the other hand, adapted to these changes by establishing laws.[160] What is more, the Shang laws were better than the Xia laws, and the Zhou laws were better than the Shang ones.[161] The dynasties themselves knew about this, since each of them considered themselves more civilized than their predecessors.[162] The principles of the sages cannot be thus implemented without regard to changes in time and power.[163] If one follows the exact steps of the sages, without taking into account the role of the passage of time, it will be another Dao, although in the same form. Wang Anshi believes that the desire to return to the earliest antiquity is 'stupid', mainly because it was a time when people did not differ significantly from animals.[164] In no way, however, was Wang Anshi an advocate of progress, nor, as Wm. Theodore de Bary aptly points out, was he a revolutionist.[165] In the famous memorial to Emperor Renzong, Wang Anshi describes his own programme:

> Now our age is far removed from that of the ancient kings, and the changes and circumstances with which we are confronted are not the same. Even the most ignorant can see that it would be difficult to put into practice every single item in the government of the ancient kings. But when your servant says that our present failures arise from the fact that we do not adopt the governmental system of the ancient kings, he is merely suggesting that we should follow their general intent.[166]

As James Liu claims, Wang Anshi's 'ultimate goal was still the Confucian ideal of a moral society in which ethical values would be fully realised. In this sense he was an institutional reformer, but still within the Confucian tradition.'[167] This remark applies in no less a degree to Wang Anshi's philosophy of history. What Confucians could not accept was the fact that Wang Anshi tried to reconcile his linear spiritualism, which otherwise complies with traditional Confucian view, with a reformist attitude that bears significant practical implications.

The Cheng brothers

The founders of the 'school of principle' 理學 *lǐxué*, namely the Cheng brothers, Cheng Hao 程顥 (1032–1085) and Cheng Yi 程頤 (1033–1077), are known mainly for their metaphysics and moral philosophy, but in their writings one can also find a consistent philosophy of history, which – as in the case of metaphysics and ethics – was taken up and developed by Zhu Xi 朱熹 (1130–1200), the most eminent Neo-Confucian philosopher.

The Cheng brothers transfer their metaphysical concepts to the ground of philosophy of history. Cheng Yi believes that there is one common principle (*li*) lying behind various phenomena, all changes included.[168] As Yao Xinzhong observes, 'according to Cheng Yi, principle exists eternally and is unchanging through time and space; thus, understanding principle is the first step in one's spiritual cultivation, something which can be done only through investigating things thoroughly and extending one's knowledge to its utmost.'[169] Among the various ways of investigating the principle 窮理 *qiónglǐ*, in second place, just after actual study of the Classics, the study of history 考古今 *kǎo gǔjīn* is mentioned.[170] The principle is a mechanism responsible for periods of order and chaos, therefore it should be investigated when the chronicles are studied.[171] Cheng Yi claims that 'essentially, in the study of history, one cannot merely record an event, but also has to be aware of the principle of order and chaos, peace and crisis, prosperity and decline, preservation and extinction'.[172] The principle is therefore not only a metaphysical *principium*, that is, the imperceptible essence of the historical process, but also a criterion for interpreting and evaluating historical events. Because these events are evaluated from a transcendent perspective (though still immanently present in the universe), history is not a 'judgement over the world'. As Cheng Yi writes, 'contemporaries believe that the victors acted rightly, and the defeated – no, not knowing that there was a lot of iniquity among the victors and a lot of justice among the defeated.'[173]

The idea that there were periods of decline in the times of the 'victors', just like there was no deficit of prosperity in the times of 'defeated' was developed by the Cheng brothers to form a specific, speculative concept. Highs and lows happen in history in general, but also in the scale of one epoch, one month and even one day.[174] The inspiration here from the cyclical view of Shao Yong is unquestionable. On the other hand, it merges with the linear approach:

The cycle of rise and fall is hard to understand. In terms of generations, [the age of] the Two Emperors and Three Kings was [the time] of rise, and the later ages that of decline. In terms of a single age, Kings Wu, Wen, Cheng, and Kang [of the Zhou] were [the time of] rise, Yu, Li, Ping, and Huan that of decline. In terms of a single sovereign, the Kaiyuan reign period (713–741) was [the time of] rise and the Tianbao reign period (742–756) that of decline. In terms of a year, spring and summer are [the time of] rise, fall and winter that of decline. In a month the first ten-day period is rise and the last is decline. In a day the hours *yin* (3–5 a.m.) and *mao* (5–7 a.m.) are rise, *xu* (7–9 p.m.) and *hai* (9–11 p.m.) decline. The same holds for an hour. But in, for example, the hundred years of a human life those before fifty are rise, those after that, decline. Thus there are cases of decline and revival and cases of decline without return. If we discuss this in terms of the great cycle, the [period of] the Three Royal Houses [Xia, Shang, and Zhou] did not rise to the height of the Five Emperors; the two Han dynasties did not rise to the height of the Three Royal Houses, and, again, those who came later did not rise to the height of Han.[175]

Individual cycles complement each other and form a part of larger cycles, each subsequent cycle is a fall, a 'smaller' rise in relation to what was before, and thus the only non-relative change is the fall.

The Dao of people fulfilled itself in antiquity and turned the full 'cycle of Heaven'; since then no sage has appeared and no sage will appear, thus imitating ancient times is practically impossible.[176] While the Three Dynasties followed the principle, the efforts of the Hans were focused only on maintaining power.[177] The way of the ancient dynasties was the way of Heaven, incidental to receiving the Mandate of Heaven, while the subsequent dynasties represent the way of hegemons (*badao*), employing either knowledge or strength to maintain power.[178] The power of the first was received, the power of the second was maintained. On the one hand, the main and immediate cause of both order and chaos is man.[179] On the other hand, one of the passages criticizing the *Tian-ren ganying* theory reads that human affairs always follow the principle of Heaven, while the principle of Heaven never adapts to human affairs.[180] As Wu Huaiqi points out, in the case of the Cheng brothers 'the principle of Tian is the ultimate foundation for socio-historical change',[181] which confirms the idealist dimension of their philosophy of history.

Zhu Xi

The philosophy of history of the Cheng brothers was developed by Zhu Xi, as evidenced by numerous references in the *Close Reflections* 近思錄 *Jìnsīlù*.[182] As Conrad Schirokauer emphasizes, Zhu Xi 'did not develop a fully articulated "philosophy of history"' and his vision of history must be extracted from the entire philosophical system.[183] Zhu Xi's philosophy of history is to a large extent an application of his metaphysics of the principle to the field of reflection upon history. As Zhu Xi writes, it is necessary to read historical books and judge historical figures so that one will see the principle 'existing' in them.[184] This does not mean, however, that history is entirely an embodiment of the principle. Only the Classics, as directly transmitting the thoughts of the sages, contain the principle in its entirety, while histories describe only an 'outer skin', the phenomena of things.[185] This implies that the chronicles, as describing the changing reality, should be interpreted only in the light of the Classics transmitting eternal principles.[186] Hence, Zhu Xi's metaphysical dualism of the principle and phenomena, however complementary, translates into an analogous dualism in the philosophy of history, ultimately resulting in the subordination of historicity in a strict sense to the universal essence of history.

Wu Huaiqi argues that in this way 'historical research can hardly come to a new conclusion, because historiography does not go beyond the eternity of the principle, rules and system of ranks and customs.' In effect, Zhu Xi's philosophy of history is idealistic and conservative.[187] Wang and Ng believe, however, that in contrast to the *Observations from Studying History* 讀史管見 *Dúshǐ guǎnjiàn* of Hu Yin 胡寅 (1098–1156), Zhu Xi's thought is not a type of eternalism,[188] as it implies a specific philosophical-historical scheme of the blooming of Dao, and its gradual decline and recovery by Neo-Confucians in the Song times.[189] On the other hand, this pattern does not in any way stem from the nature of Dao, which is ahistorical, but comes from the discontinuity or disturbance of its transmission:

> People are just these people, and Dao is just this Dao – how could it differ with respect to the Three Dynasties, Han, and Tang dynasties? However, when the

teachings of the scholars are not passed on, and since the times of Yao, Shun, Yu, Tang, Wena and Wu, there are no minds to be endowed with it, although the individual Han and Tang rulers may coincidentally agree with the principle, they essentially focus on their profit and desires (...) If we now want to break the border and the wall dividing the old times from those present, we have nothing else but to explore the way of thought of Yao and Shun.[190]

Hence, Zhu Xi's epistemology of history is also idealistic: it is all about investigating the way the minds of the sages grasped Dao. But how can one know thoughts from thousands of years ago? Commenting on Zhu Xi's philosophy of historiography, Huang Chun-Chieh states that according to the idea that 'the principle is one but its manifestations many' 理一分殊 *lǐyī fēnshū*, Zhu Xi argues that the principle of good is shared by both the sages and common people, and the differences arise only from the material constitution of people.[191]

In fact, the concept of the material constitution of people plays an important role in Zhu Xi's philosophy of history. The times of following righteousness and the principle are called by Zhu Xi the kingly era, while the era of focusing on profit and desires – the era of hegemons. As Fang Litian notes, 'Zhu Xi believes that from the time of the Three Dynasties, the principle gradually falls, and the role of human desires is significantly increasing'.[192] The 'fall of the principle' is obviously a brachylogy: the principle as eternal cannot fall. On the other hand, it is matter (*qi*) that degenerates: 'since the days of Qin and Han, both types of *qi* [*yin* and *yang*] and Five Elements are gradually obscured, not fitting the brightness and purity of *qi* in ancient times (...) From Qin and Han there is only a constant fall'.[193] Additionally, the natural ability to create culture 文氣 *wénqì* has fallen up to the present state, in which one cannot revoke it anymore.[194] Zhu Xi's regressivism embraces therefore not only the process of transmitting the principle in histories and the presence of the principle in the rulers' minds, but also changes of matter. Matter is (paradoxically) historized, which shows that there are some ideas in the philosophy of history Zhu Xi shared with his main opponent, Chen Liang.

As in the case of the Cheng brothers, Zhu Xi inscribes the cycles 循環 *xúnhuán* of rise and fall in the general trajectory of collapse.[195] The general rule, according to which after growth follows crisis and vice versa, results from the essence of nature, the transformations of *yin* and *yang* in the scale of days, life and history.[196] These strands are drawn from the exegesis of the *Book of Changes*, which is a concrete example of the search for the principle presented in the classic scriptures in history itself. As Wu Huaiqi reminds us, this does not lead to a new vision of history: inscribing cycles into the line of a fall is a motif that has been present in the Confucian philosophy of history since the time of Mencius. One of the most eminent modern Chinese historians, Qian Mu, is right in saying that in this sense 'Zhu Xi maintains a pure, traditional Confucian view of history'.[197]

The idea of the eternal principle lying behind history and the irreversible degeneration of *qi* leads to the question of whether Zhu Xi was a fatalist. Interestingly, the opinions of scholars are quite consistent on this matter. Huang Chun-chieh believes that Zhu Xi strongly emphasized the role of the subject in shaping history, and would not accept historical determinism.[198] Yongsun Back thinks that although Zhu Xi assumes that 'two aspects of *ming*, moral command and command of one's given lot, share the same attribute: they are commanded by Tian and no one can avoid or change them as they please', Zhu Xi was not a fatalist, and 'even if he believed that one's innate qualities and external conditions are basically predetermined, one can still exercise control over one's own life'.[199] So *ming* is not so much a factor determining action, as what sets its limits. An additional argument is the fact that Zhu Xi criticizes philosophy of history that he considers fatalistic, including the view of Shao Yong:

> For Zhu Xi, the major weakness in Shao Yong's cyclical view of history is that it was too mechanistic to allow any room for human influence. The impersonal pattern of Shao Yong's huge cycles of cosmic time took the greater directions of historical development completely out of the hands of man. In this sense, Zhu Xi saw Shao Yong's cyclical theory of history as tantamount to fatalism.[200]

The reason Zhu Xi does not fall into fatalism in the philosophy of history is the difference brought by the epistemic dimension: the principle must first be known through 'examination of things' (including the study of histories). Then, there is still the need for the power of 'measuring' 權 *quán*, which is the ability to relate eternal principles to changing circumstances, compared by Schirokauer to Aristotle's *phronesis*.[201] As Zhu Xi writes,

> The classic standard is a principle that must be put into practice. The ability to measure is a principle that penetrates changes, which is used when a permanent principle cannot be introduced and when there is no other way out.[202]

The ability to measure requires a responsible human decision and assumes the risk of departing from the principle. Zhu Xi was therefore not a fatalist, primarily because his philosophy of history is not built on the idea of the deterioration of *qi*, but on the principle that is inscribed in the essentially good nature of man.[203] Understanding and implementation of this is not necessary, but it is something that needs moral effort and which enables achievement of the status of sage, thus allowing one to 'run against the flow' of the progressive fall.

It should be added that the idea of irreversibility of historical change was not unknown to Zhu Xi. He believed that a complete return to antiquity is not possible: 'to wish to apply the ancient system and the laws of the Three Dynasties today is very far from the [nature] of Heaven and earth.'[204] Although the principle is common to all ages, a return to specific political phenomena can only bring damage: 'to live in the present era and agree to get rid of current laws, applying the ancient political solutions: I see no use in it.'[205] This is particularly true of the feudal system of the Zhou period:

> Feudalism cannot be implemented in reality. If we talk about the era of the Three Dynasties, then there were favourable conditions for feudalism, that is, the nature of the ruler and the people were coordinated, [in this way] peace could last long and there were no calamities. It does not resemble the centralised prefectural system of the next era, for because of the yearly changes even the righteous man

were not able to implement the good policy (...) That is why I say: 'feudalism is only a remnant of old times, and the conditions are no longer beneficial. This what Liu Zongyuan is right about.'[206]

Paradoxically, in his assessment of feudalism Zhu Xi approaches Liu Zongyuan (see below); this is because for both of them feudalism is a transient social institution, a product of history. The difference between them lies in the fact that Zhu Xi accepts the existence of a 'deep layer' of history, from the perspective of which some of the changes are only superficial.

Finally, it should not be forgotten that for Zhu Xi, *li* is the moral principle. This means, as de Bary notes, that 'one could not accept as true principle what did not lead to Confucian ethical practice'.[207] This implies a specific kind of holism:

> For Zhu Xi, a genuine holism could only mean the simultaneous realization of the 'whole substance and great functioning' of human nature because the humanness which forms 'one body with heaven, earth and all things' cannot be simply a subjective experience of undifferentiated unity – it must also express itself in loving actions of a particular sort.[208]

The principle of reality, including history, is also the principle of conduct by which one should live. This transcends the division into the normative and descriptive order, which, as applied to the field of the philosophy of history, is called in this book a 'holism regarding reason'. It is also a 'holism regarding causality', since, as de Bary continues, 'holism may be seen as implicit in the Confucian sense of individuality',[209] because the moral development of an individual is based on the implementation of a supra-personal and existing principle.

These assumptions imply the idea of the moral dimension of history and the didactic function of historiography. Providing moral examples is, as Ng and Wang observe, the main function of historiography for Zhu Xi.[210] However, it does not exhaust the topic of 'uses of the past' in Zhu Xi's philosophy, which also covers the social and political implications of histories. According to Robert Hartwell, moral didacticism, in which moral lessons are taken up by individuals, has to be distinguished from what he calls 'historical analogism', in which history is said to provide the tools for assessment of social and political institutions.[211] This seems to be confirmed by Zhu Xi:

> The *Book of Songs* and the *Book of Documents* are vehicles of Dao, and the *Spring and Autumn Annals* are their application made by the sage. The *Songs* and the *Documents* are like a recipe, and the *Annals* like a cure for disease (...) The place of the *Annals* among the Classics is of the verdict in the legal sphere. The law only gives norms of conduct, it is only in the judgment that the application of the law becomes visible.[212]

Furthermore, Zhu Xi does not limit himself to pointing out the practical function of classical historical records, but also takes on the task of conveying principle through historical narrative. This resulted in Zhu Xi's *Outline of the 'Comprehensive Mirror'* 通鑑綱目 *Tōngjiàn gāngmù*, which is the first Chinese chronicle translated into a European language (the French *Histoire générale de la Chine*, translated by Joseph-Anne-Marie de Moyriac de Mailla). The *Tongjian gangmu* summarizes and restructures the *Comprehensive Mirror to Aid in Government* 資治通鑑 *Zīzhì tōngjiàn* of Sima Guang 司馬光 (1019–1086) in a manner consistent with the didactic function of historiography, and the idea of legitimization (*zhengtong*) in the version supported by Zhu Xi. The preface to the *Tongjian gangmu* reads that the work is intended to accord with Heaven, to brighten the Dao of people by indicating legitimate dynasties and to pass on examples and counter-examples in the light of the principle.[213] As Qiu Hansheng comments, in this sense history is the result of the study of the principle,[214] which confirms the idealist character of Zhu Xi's philosophy of history and the primacy of metaphysics over the history expressed in it.

Realistic and materialist currents

This section discusses realist and materialist tendencies in the philosophy of history in the Song period. However, in order to present the full context of the era, we should first look at the realistic tendencies in the historiography of that time.

As Thomas Lee notes, although causal explanation was very rare in the historiography of the Song period, there are exceptions to this rule, with Zheng Qiao 鄭樵 (1104–1162) on top.[215] Zheng Qiao is the author of a 200-volume encyclopaedia entitled *Comprehensive Tretises* 通志 *Tōngzhì*, which deals with history, genealogy, philology, astronomy, geography, urban planning, customs, music, offices, law, economics, archaeology, zoology and botany. Thus, history is integrated into the whole of knowledge. As Lee continues, Zheng Qiao 'believes that knowledge of history is the key to other knowledge, but the true understanding of history can be achieved only if one comprehends the "general history", by which he means a history that covers the entirety of human past.'[216] This holistic approach finds its expression in the preface to the *Tongzhi*, where Zheng Qiao describes the ideal of 'continuity and whole' 會通 *huìtōng*, compared to the ocean in which all rivers converge.[217] In a similar spirit, Lü Zuqian 呂祖謙 (1137–1181) claimed that one should seek to grasp the 'whole of the relations' 統體 *tǒngtǐ* of a given epoch.[218] This requires not only a collection of facts, but also finding their causes by putting oneself in the place of the participants of events.[219]

Zheng Qiao's incorporation of history into the knowledge of nature resulted in a peculiar evolutionism. Humans are essentially beings of the same type (同物 *tóngwù*) as animals. As a result of the transformations of nature, immobile plants came to life, followed by moving animals, from which people isolated themselves over time. This was due to their uncommon intellect and upright posture, allowing them not to focus their eyes in other directions than just downward, to the ground. Thanks to outstanding individuals (sages), people living in caves learned to protect themselves from animals, grow plants and use fire. The sages became rulers in this way, establishing trade and other social institutions.[220] The thinkers analysed below will understand the history of humanity in a similar way.

Liu Zongyuan

The most important representative of the 'materialising' current of Confucian thought in the Tang Dynasty was Liu Zongyuan 柳宗元 (773–819). It should be noted that despite the many points differing Liu Zongyuan from other Neo-Confucian thinkers, his philosophical affiliation is not open to doubt. Liu states that in his philosophy he primarily intends to search for the Way of Yao, Shun and Confucius, which is incomparable to that of the later dynasties and is deservedly praised by historians.[221] Liu accepts the moral function of history and encourages his friend, Han Yu, to not lack the courage to take on the responsible task of writing history for future generations.[222] The responsibility of the historian comes from the fact that the Dao of the ancient sages is public, not private, which emphasizes the importance of history for society.[223]

However, acceptance of these premises of Confucian philosophy of history does not stop Liu Zongyuan from criticizing almost all other components of the Confucian philosophy of history. Liu openly refuses Dong Zhongshu's philosophy of history, considering it to be incompatible with the former Confucianism and responsible for the errors of successive generations of philosophers, even comparing it to the words of 'fortune-tellers and blind shamans'.[224] A separate work was devoted to criticizing the fortune-telling in the *Guoyu* chronicle.[225] Above all, the classical theory of the Mandate of Heaven is criticized, for Dong Zhongshu's philosophy of history is treated as only one of its versions. As Liu Zongyuan writes, only a fool awaits the compassion and humanness of impersonal Heaven: neither virtue nor anger is a feature of Heaven, but only of human beings. For this reason, the theory of *Tianming* is self-contradictory, and only people are responsible for order or chaos. The mandate – that is, empowerment to govern – is obtained from people, not from Heaven.[226] Why, then, did the ancients talk about 'Heaven'? Liu Zongyuan replies that in this way, they adapted to the asininity of the people.[227] What is more, the idea of Heaven appeared at a certain time, being the product of history itself: both Yao and Shun did not invoke the will of Tian until the Shang dynasty, when Heaven replaced Shangdi as a deity.[228]

Criticism of the traditional vision of Heaven is also rooted in the materialist ontology of Liu Zongyuan. The *Discourse on Heaven* 天說 *Tiānshuō* reads that diseases are not sent by Heaven, but come from the *qi* contained in blood, because man is simply a compound of the matter-*qi*.[229] In contrast to later philosophers of nature, such as Shao Yong, Liu Zongyuan thinks that there was no spirit at the beginning of the universe, only primitive *qi*, uncreated and infinite, with no centre and no borders. Consistently, there is no other way to conceptualize Heaven than to take Tian as a material being: Heaven is simply a name for the azure sky over our heads.[230] Liu Zongyuan refers to Zhuangzi, treating Heaven as a byword of nature.[231] In light of this concept, it becomes clear that Heaven, i.e. the sky, can in no way intervene in human history. This raises the question of what, if not Heaven, is responsible for events and changes that are classically attributed to Tian? Liu's answer quite surprisingly dusts off the notion from Legalism and the School of Militarists: the development of beings and their historical changes is caused by the tendency of reality, *shi*.[232] This does not mean, however, as Liu stipulates, that everything happens spontaneously by itself (as in the thought of the Daoists or Wang Chong); the course of things and the course of history depends on the cooperation 合 *hé* of people with nature. This cooperation is determined by the rational principle of reality 理 *lǐ*.[233] In this way, Liu Zongyuan not only provides a metaphysical and natural justification for the belief that only people are ultimately responsible for history, but also lays the foundations for Neo-Confucian metaphysics of the principle, putting it from the beginning in an unspecified relation to the propensity of reality. The cooperation of man with nature is understood as the prolongation of the operation of the laws of nature: just as nature makes the growth of plants, so man creates laws and social institutions.[234]

Liu Zongyuan's positive philosophy of history stems from this motive to prolong the action of nature. Liu thinks that at the beginning of history, humanity lived in a warless and childlike stage of simplicity. So as to protect against atmospheric phenomena, people lived in trees and caves, taking care of their clothing. After people began living with each other, their numbers gradually increased; famine became a problem, but was solved by hunting animals. The rise of families and clans led to conflicts, and the escalation of these conflicts to chaos. The victors imposed order by force, and in order to preserve this new state of affairs and guarantee the effectiveness of their order, they established administration and sanctioned it legally.[235] The causes of conflict and a detailed path from the state of nature to the full state of administration is shown in the celebrated *Treatise on Feudalism* 封建論 *Fēngjiànlùn*. Explaining the beginnings of society, Liu Zongyuan refers to the natural weakness of people: as they did not have fur, claws or wings, they were forced to compensate for these inborn deficiencies with 'artificial things' 假物 *jiǎwù*. Artefacts satisfy human needs, but at the same time are not entitled to anyone by nature, which is why the fight broke out. Originally, in cases of opposition to the established order, rebel units were only instructed later, when their original instructions ceased to be effective, that punishment was necessary. This involved not only the establishment of an administrator, but also the consolidation of a group of people in the form of a tribe. As a result, the conflicts moved to a higher level, becoming a war between tribes. This required the recruitment of soldiers, and commanders to lead and control the soldiers. But with time, rivalry grew between these commanders until the point the barons decided to institute an emperor. As Liu Zongyuan concludes, 'hence, feudalism is not [the result of] the sages' intentions, but of the tendency of things (*shi*)'.[236] Feudalism is treated as a result of structural and unintentional changes, an effect of impersonal historical tendency.[237] Jo-Shui Chen rightly attributes social evolutionism to Liu Zongyuan, although he refuses to label him a 'materialist'.[238] However, the philosophy of history of Liu Zongyuan gets close to historical materialism, who frequently declares that the way of the sages has nothing to do with the spirit (*shen*).[239] Although Liu does not use the terminology of nineteenth-century philosophy, he undoubtedly sees the sources of social and historical changes in the transformations of artefacts and relations of authority and servitude, which – as in the case of Marx – are considered necessary and independent of human will. Consistently, Liu Zongyuan is also a 'historical realist' in our sense of this term, for material factors explaining history are immanently present in history itself.

It is noteworthy that although our understanding of historical materialism is integrally linked to the Song debate over substratum of history, Liu's philosophy of history also meets external criteria of historical materialism. Elaborating on 'non-Marxian historical materialism' introduced in 1981 by Polish 'revisionist' philosopher, Leszek Nowak, Krzysztof Brzechczyn identifies three basic ideas that are constitutive for historical materialism. First, belief in the dependence of culture upon the material fundaments of social life. Second, interpretation of history through the prism of structural transformations, and not in relation to human intentions. Third, social, political and economic relations are understood in terms of antagonism between social classes (groups).[240] Liu's concepts of artefacts and *shi* testify the presence of the first two points, but what about the third?

Interestingly, Liu Zongyuan brings up the idea of conflict between members of various social classes, although this is not a class struggle but a conflict between members of the same social class. Liu does not believe that history is 'fuelled' by the conflict between feudal lords and peasants, but he does not overlook the place of the peasant's station in history, or the conflict between peasants and feudal lords. Liu does not agree with the opinion that since land is property of feudal lords, people are treated kindly by them, like children. On the contrary, landlords are arrogant, greedy and devoted to fighting, as evidenced by the history of Zhou. This fact did not result from any particular political solution 政 *zhèng*, but from the entire system 制 *zhì*. However, oppression under the Qin monarchy took place only because of the ruler and his disposition, while the system itself avoided the defects of the feudal system of Zhou. After the Han dynasty, which returned to feudalism in a form partially rooted in Qin centralism, the Tang rulers restored the prefectural system, which is essentially characterized by peace.[241] Nevertheless, the people were still in a bad situation, because they were encumbered with high taxes and obliged to perform military service at the borders.[242] Description of the oppression of peasants appears often in the literary works of Liu Zongyuan (for example, in the 'Story of the Snake Catcher'), while the former sages Yao, Shun and Yu, are credited with constant concern for the people.[243] Liu thinks that the aristocrats rob the people, and their titles have become empty names, since it is not virtue but only their origin that stands behind them.[244] Liu compares members of society to the figures on a chessboard: although they are made of the same wood, they get different status as a result of being painted different colours.[245] As Jo-Shui Chen emphasizes, although this is not a vision of the abolition of classes, it directly expresses the idea of the equality of people and the 'artificiality' of social differences.[246] In other words, the social system built upon artefacts is in itself artificial. This notwithstanding, it has to be remembered that nowhere did Liu Zongyuan call for a 'revolution', but rather yearned for a restoration of the most beneficial, that is ancient, form of the existing social system, which constitutes an important difference between medieval form of historical materialism in China and its Western modern counterpart.

Li Gou

One of the most important continuators of the 'materialistic' trend in the philosophy of history under the Song was Li Gou 李覯 (1009–1059). In Li Gou's opinion, the problem of the relationship between the sphere of culture and material conditions, including the economic ones, is clearly and openly formulated. The term, which in his philosophical dictionary most closely approaches the meaning of the concept of culture is 'customs' 禮 *li*, taken in the most general sense possible. As Li Gou writes, *li* is the standard of humanity, basis of the development of individuals and the statecraft. *Li* include all customs associated with nutrition, clothing, housing, burial, sacrifices, principles of kinship, marriage, parenthood, seniority and power. In addition, morality (*ren-yi*), politics, system of punishments and music are also included in this concept. All customs were created by ancient kings in response to human needs, mainly related to hunger and climatic conditions.[247] By ancient kings Li Gou means, following Xunzi, primarily the later kings, with Prince of Zhou as an exception.[248] In this sense the Confucian provenance of his thought is unquestionable. However, as the customs were to arise in response to physical needs, Li Gou emphasizes that when these needs are not satisfied, when peasants are hungry and poor, educating the people with the help of *li* becomes almost impossible.[249] Like Liu Zongyuan, Li Gou thinks that the 'Mandate of Heaven' is identical to the will and support of the people,[250] which means that the destiny of the state and the world depends on such matters as gathering grain,[251] and finally the food in possession of the peasants. This idea was expressed in the philosophy of history already a century earlier, in the *Book of Transformations* 化書 *Huàshū* by Tan Qiao 谭峭 (tenth century), who claimed that both animal and human development is determined by only one factor: food. The times of famine are times of rebellion, and the times of peasants' prosperity are times of peace.[252] Li Gou agrees with Tan Qiao that only deceitful ways refers to ghosts,[253] but he was not inclined towards naturalism, because it takes into account also the role of the social matter: of goods, money and landed property.

Li Gou believes that the issue of food is a derivative of property relations. Former kings, especially Shun, were aware of the fact that without regulating the question of land ownership by peasants, it was impossible to teach and spread customs. Hence, during the Zhou Dynasty, an ideal economic well-field system was created: moving away from this system means only that the rich will be richer, and the poor will become poorer from day to day.[254] Ancient rulers, especially the later ones, provided for the peasants so that they were not overworked.[255] Li Gou notes that the abandonment of the well-field system resulted from the increase in population, which was followed by fiscal pressure, but not by peasants' nutritional standards. Self-sufficient fields with 100 mu (c. 5 ha) per farmer over time began to be replaced with latifundia.[256] Li Gou's analysis requires us to take a brief look at China's economic history of that time. At the beginning of the Tang Dynasty, 100 mu of unpopulated land was leased to every peasant; by paying taxes, working forcibly and serving in the army, they maintained the feudal aristocracy, which was totally exempt from taxes. With time, the peasants who were unable to pay taxes fell into debt and sold land, so that at the end of the eighth century only 5 per cent of the peasants owned the land. The situation improved slightly in the times of Li Gou, but the rent was still 50–70 per cent of the harvest.[257] Li refers to this situation by saying that the aristocrats, unlike the people, can afford to eat meat, but they are not strong enough to start sowing fields themselves: 'they eat, not working', and their only profession is oppression of the people. And just as the poor have strength, but no land to feed, so the rich need the strength of another man, although he has a field. As a result, the only thing a lord cannot afford is to become independent from the vassal, says Li Gou,[258] concluding the reasoning that is somewhat reminiscent of the intersection of Marx's theory of class struggle with the Hegelian dialectics of master and slave.

For such a diagnosis Li Gou responds with an utopia of the state in which 'there are no kings outside, and the world is one family, each foot of land is a field, and each of the people is treated like a son, the whole country is full of goods and money, like a money bag, while taxes and rentals flow equally from everyone.'[259] At the same time, he claims that this state does not differ from the situation of the former rulers, as they did not have private finances. Li Gou's project is therefore a retro-utopia: a plan for the future mediated by the past. At the same time, as Shan-Yüan Hsieh emphasizes, this utopia is in itself a result of materialistically understood evolution of civilization.[260]

The description of the utopia contains the notions of goods and money that are crucial for Li Gou's thought. Not only do food and land ownership relations shape the customs, but also, if not above all, the 'usable goods' 財用 *cáiyòng*, that is 'commodities' 貨 *huò*, the most important of which is 'money' 金 *jīn*.[261] As Li Gou writes, 'stupid Confucians' argue that politics is impossible without morality and education, despite the fact that the *Hongfan*, i.e. the canonical fragment of the *Book of Documents*, reads that the first condition of politics is food and the second is goods. The basis and 'reality' of the statecraft are precisely the usable goods. Without the goods there can be no customs relevant to living, food, clothing, army, offices, sacrifices (religion), along with customs related to marriage and kinship and the division into civilization and barbarism.[262] Accordingly, such principal good as money has to play an even more important role. Li Gou regrets that unfortunately the aristocracy banished the original function of money. For the ancients, money was primarily a means of exchange, which is why peasants used it; for the feudal lands of the present, money is a treasure, thus the only way to multiply it is to increase the fiscal oppression of the people, the same people who are doomed to poverty without money.[263] The tendency to go beyond this stalemate situation made Li Gou rehabilitate tradespeople, traditionally placed at the lowest level of the social ladder, even below farmers and craftsmen. Li argues against Mencius that the pursuit of profit is not evil, because it is an inseparable element of human nature, without which no work of the ancients would have taken place.[264] The diagnosis of the current crisis results, again, from the (re-)construction of China's ancient history.

Li Gou's philosophy fulfils the criteria of historical materialism even more than the thought of Liu Zongyuan. First of all, Li explicitly accepts that the basis (or 'root') of historical process is of a material nature: it is food, which depends on the possession of land, which in turn depends on the disposal of goods, especially money. The goods are said to be the necessary condition for the implementation of *li*, that is customs, which cover here the entire sphere of culture. Second, Li Gou reconstructs the history of China through the prism of changes in means and relations of production; historical censures are set by changes in the systems of land and money management. Third, Li Gou sees and describes the antagonism of the class of owners and peasants. All these similarities with Marx's version of historical materialism notwithstanding, it must be remembered that Li Gou combines it with a quasi-idealistic retro-utopia that ultimately resembles capitalism rather than communism.

Ouyang Xiu

Ouyang Xiu 歐陽脩 (1007–1072), the Song dynasty polymath, was not a materialist in the sense of Liu Zongyuan and Li Gou. However, his criticism of all references to transcendence, especially in historiography, and the orientation of the philosophy of history to the immanent sphere of human behaviour, makes him an apologist for historical realism, as it is broadly understood in this book.

Ouyang Xiu strongly criticized the Han theory of the correlation between Heaven and humanity. In his opinion, it was no coincidence that this theory arose after the death of Confucius in the era of fighting kingdoms, when the way of ancient kings ceased to be understandable.[265] One cannot know anything certain about the relationship between Heaven and humanity, and what can be ascertained are only things concerning man alone. Heaven is knowable only insofar as we can observe the traces of Tian in things, and the intention of Heaven can be revealed only in human behaviour.[266] As Douglas Skonicki aptly observes, Ouyang Xiu's agnosticism here means that the correlation between Heaven and humanity is irrelevant from the perspective of political philosophy and the philosophy of history.[267] Ouyang Xiu resigns from any speculation about the disasters that have occurred in history.[268] Knowledge of the causes of order and chaos in history does not depend on knowledge of the will of Heaven, but on conversance with the people – more precisely, their feelings.[269] Ouyang Xiu's philosophy therefore focuses not so much on social or economic changes, but on mental ones. The questioning of everything that would transcend this sphere results from the reinterpretation of Confucian orthodoxy. Ouyang Xiu claims that everything that a human can know has already been expressed by Confucius. The wisdom of Confucius rested upon the rejection of everything that was unnecessary, that is, 'distant and difficult to understand', as it does not affect a person being noble.[270] The history of humanity is therefore secular, immanent and self-sufficient. The only transcendence that gets a word in edgewise in interpreting history stems from the necessity of 'reaching' the intentions of Confucius,[271] intentions which were best expressed in his *Annals* and which not only indicate what is good and bad, but also distinguish truth from falsehood.[272] The choice of the *Annals* is not coincidental, since *Chunqiu* put aside a significant part of the epistemological investigations.[273]

The key to understanding history, or rather historiography, is to examine the intentions of Confucius and the sages of that time.[274] Ouyang Xiu justifies this view by the fact that we no longer have access to the teachers of the past, but we do have books that convey their intentions.[275] However, he is aware that this activity is exposed to the same objections he made against the speculative doctrines:

> But when it comes to the intentions of the sages and the righteous people of antiquity, do not those who claim and apprehend them for tens of thousands of generations, do so through the transmission of words? How is it possible that the intentions of the sages are not preserved in the scriptures? Therefore, although the books are not able to exhaust every nuance of words, they grasp their essence; and although the word does not exhaust every subtlety of intent, it grasps its principle.[276]

Hence, the point here is not 'what the author had in mind', but an understanding of the general intent and nature of the message. Consequently, incorporating the principles of the past into life, one has to not so much graft the direct content of these events, as their structure, i.e. the order in which the sages dealt with the matters of their time.[277] As Peter K. Bol points out, a total return to the past is impossible for Ouyang Xiu, for the very fact of creation of various schools of exegesis shows that it is not known what the Classics meant then. In contrast to naïve conservatism, the old intentions were to adopt new forms.[278] This puts people at risk of making many mistakes, but this also happened to the sages.[279]

Nevertheless, Ouyang Xiu's philosophy of the history is not reduced to doubts and limitations on the scope of investigation. In place of theories explaining the beginnings of history and subsequent historical changes through appeals to the decisions of Heaven, Ouyang proposes his own approach, consistent with the programme of classical Chinese historiography. The problem of the succession of the dynasty is, for Ouyang Xiu, in the first place a question of legitimizing (正统 *zhèngtǒng*) these dynasties. It is in this context that the theories of the Mandate of Heaven and the Five Phases were used. In Ouyang Xiu's opinion, two conditions are sufficient for historical legitimacy: first, the unification of the state; second, the adherence to standards of Confucian morals in the public sphere. The descent from a legitimate nation, state or dynasty – almost the only mode of understanding the category of *zhengtong* in the time of the breakdown between the third and seventh century – does not make a dynasty legal.[280] Interestingly, the Qin dynasty was deemed legal. The conviction about the illegality of the Qin is described by Ouyang Xiu as being the 'private view of the Han family', although his defence of the Qin is unconvincing, since he also mentions that the fall of virtue began with Qin Shi Huangdi, and that the Qin emperor did not follow the ancient way.[281] Eventually, legitimacy means belonging to Chinese culture, thus barbaric dynasties are simply excluded from the succession.

Despite his interest in the normative criteria of evaluating political history, Ouyang Xiu did not neglect the evidential side of history. Contrarily, he stated that history must be based on evidence.[282] He was also interested in archaeology, collecting stele inscriptions. What is more, his theory of the origin of Chinese history treats history as a 'response to the material conditions and emotional requirements of the populace', devoid of any 'previously existent external standard'.[283] *Treatise on the Root* 本論 *Běnlùn* states that the golden age of antiquity came about through use of the well-field system, in which everyone had land and was educated by customs during their leisure time. The needs and feelings of the people were then met by the system (*zhi*); in part because the same needs gave rise to customs concerning everything from marriage to burial rites, hunting and sports, etc. The crisis arose when the needs and feelings of the people ceased to be met. First, the well-field system was rejected, which in turn led to the fall of customs (and not vice-versa).[284] From then, rituals became 'empty names', ceremonies detached from human needs.[285] Also for this reason, one cannot return to antiquity. In this way, Ouyang Xiu drew near to the materialist postulates of Li Gou.

Su Xun

A realist philosophy of history was also developed by Su Xun 蘇洵 (1009–1066), the father of Su Shi. To a higher degree than other Neo-Confucians, Su Xun follows the thought of the Legalists and Militarists. The primary fact that philosophy has to face is, in his opinion, the lack of timeless and unchangeable standards:

> The ancient law was simple, and the current law is complicated. Simplicity does not match the current [conditions], and complicacy would not fit into antiquity. Not because the law of antiquity does not match current law, but because current times are different from ancient times.[286]

The idea that although ancient law is not inferior to the present, it cannot be applied to the present means that each of these laws was/is appropriate for its time, and this implies a certain kind of relativism that finds deeper justification in the concept of *shi*. According to George Hatch, *shi* here means not so much a necessary tendency of history as contingent historical conditions; he even calls Su Xun a 'philosopher of historical contingency'.[287] However, a better translation of the term *shi* in Su Xun would be the notion of 'historical situation', since it refers to the category of *shi* in the thought of the Militarists, where *shi* primarily meant the advantageous position of the commander and the advantage of his army. As François Jullien validly observes, even from this perspective 'anything that appears as a result of circumstance in the course of history acts as a force and is endowed with efficacy'.[288] Just as the position of a general is a force giving direction to history, so *shi* cannot be treated as merely historical contingency, in the same sense as contingence – for example, in Wang Chong's philosophy of history. According to Su Xun, historical situations can be divided into two types: favourable and unfavourable. The sage examines *shi* and responds to it with his measuring 權 *quán*. The collapse of the Zhou and Qin resulted, for example, from the failure to recognize the historical situation: the Zhou made concessions and political fragmentation followed a weak *shi*, while the Qins unnecessarily strengthened an already-strong *shi*.[289] As Peter K. Bol writes, for Su Xun 'there was nothing mysterious or esoteric about a Dao that could be seen as the path taken by men who used political power for the common good'.[290] On the other hand, many passages of Su Xun's writings show that such an opinion is precipitant.[291]

Another feature that distinguishes the historical situation from just an occasional condition is its durability. As Su Xun writes,

> When the power of the sage is used in a given era, the changes of customs become deeper, so that they cannot be undone. If happily there appears again a sage who takes over these changes and continues them, the world will be able to return to order. If not, the changes will be exhausted and there will be no more progress until they die out.[292]

The permanence of *shi* entails, therefore, the irreversibility of certain historical changes. In this sense, Jullien is right in saying that there is no way to separate *shi* from directivity.

In Su Xun's language, it even bears the name 'progress' 入 *rù*, although without human help this progress will not be made. *Shi* itself, as an impersonal tendency, tends towards expiry, not progress. This also means that if a historical situation is beneficial, one should not potentiate it, but measure (*quan*) it. For this reason, the old dynasties ruled for seven or eight centuries; theoretically, if the people have been united, and the power was stable, the situation could remain unchanged for 'ten million years', or until a new sage appears.[293] The idea of the unchanging present echoes the convictions of the First Emperor of China; in fact, as Hatch shows, 'Su places Song firmly in the context of the centralised prefectural (*junxian*) system laid down in Qin, and (...) asserts that the basic structure of the Song state could not be altered at all.'[294] Return to the well-field system is impossible, because it would mean transfers of land, and population migrations that would be almost impossible to perform. First of all, the well-field system itself was not created in one day, but started in the times of Yu, grew during the Shang times and matured in the times of Zhou.[295] It was therefore a process that lasted a millennium; historical situations should be considered on the same scale. Similarly to Ouyang Xiu, social institutions are also for Su Xun not *a priori* models, but the result of the social practices of a systemic and adaptive character.[296]

Chen Liang

The notion of the tendency *shi* also occupied a central place in the philosophy of history of Chen Liang 陳亮 (1143–1194), a thinker who openly adopted a realist and materialist position in a bitter dispute with Zhu Xi. Most of Chen Liang's works were lost at the beginning of the seventeenth century and were not recovered until 1974. Thus, he could not have influenced such thinkers as Wang Fuzhi.

In contrast to Su Xun, *shi* definitely meant for Chen Liang a directed and supra-personal historical trend, the tendency of history. As Chen Liang writes, *shi* covers a period longer than the one dynasty;[297] apart from the *shi* of a state 國家之勢 *guójiā zhī shì*, including the *shi* of China 中國之勢 *Zhōngguó zhī shì*, there also exists the *shi* of the whole world 天下之勢 *Tiānxià zhī shì*, which is essentially unique, succumbing to increases and decreases 消長 *xiāo-zhǎng*.[298] 'Increases and decreases' are a descriptive and quantitative term, in opposition to the qualitative and axiological traditional phrase 'rise and fall' 盛衰 *shèngshuāi*. What's more, Chen Liang believes that the trend of growth or decline changes to the opposite every 60 years.[299] Fang Litian claims that this is an idealistic element of Chen Liang's philosophy of history,[300] although from the text it is clear that the direct reason for its use is the reference to the traditional Chinese calendar (the system of celestial trunks and earthly branches), and thus to the cycle of nature. The immanence and objectivity of *shi* is often emphasized by Chen Liang: 'the tendency of events is obvious and visible in phenomena', although at the same time 'no human power can induce the world's tendency in a desirable direction.'[301] *Shi* is a necessary force, as it was when the fact that the Emperor Zhou could not control the barons must have led to fights between them.[302] The idea that *shi* 'necessarily had led to' 必至於 *bìzhìyú* some historical incidents appears many times in the writings of Chen Liang.[303]

In general, Chen Liang opts for a structural explanation of historical processes: '[historical] characters are like a forest: it is not enough to refer to their intentions to explain their [behaviour]'.[304] This does not mean that people are helpless in the face of the tendency of history: they can use it for their own benefit.[305] Chen Liang gives the example of Liu Bang, who took advantage of the *shi* of *levée en masse*, even though he could not rely on it after assuming the mantle of power.[306] Therefore, the objective and necessary *shi* is irreversible: there is no possibility of returning to the prevalent conditions of the time of the Three Dynasties, nor any other.[307] One can and should, however, examine characters such as the founder of the Han dynasty, who recognized the *shi* of their time and used it for the benefit of the people. Chen Liang calls such people 'heroes' 英雄 *yīngxióng*, adding that their actions cannot be explained in reference to a timeless, permanent principle 常理 *chánglǐ*.[308] Their uniqueness is not due to spirit or anything mysterious: they are simply people whose wisdom transcends the ability of an ordinary man.[309] In the *Treatise on History* 酌古論 *Zhuógǔlùn* Chen Liang analyses the cases of nineteen different historical heroes from the Han dynasty to Tang, concluding – as Zheng Jixiong observes – that the reason for their success or failure was ultimately an increase or decrease in objective *shi*.[310]

However, the uncontrollability of *shi* raises questions about its knowability. On the one hand, the complexity of changes is inexhaustible, and historical debates infinite.[311] On the other hand, everything that concerns the usefulness of these changes could be known based on the assumption of common human nature, which is a necessary cause of these changes.[312] For this reason, Chen Liang ventures to indicate the direction of the tendency of history, which in his opinion leads inevitably to the emergence of law:

> The direction of the great tendency of the world cannot be changed by Heaven and earth, ghosts and spirits, but only by man (...) Once the Way of the people is established, it is impossible not to have laws. And although the hearts of people are mostly selfish, laws can guide them to what is public. That is why the tendency of the world is inevitably moving towards laws on a daily basis (...) If the trend of the world moves towards laws, and we try to redirect it in order to rely solely on people, then not only Heaven and earth, spirits and ghosts, but also man will certainly not be able to change its course.[313]

In this sense, Chen Liang seems to be an advocate of the theory of necessary, irreversible and linear progress, but analysis of the context in which this quote appears restricts identification of his proposal with its Western counterparts. Just as the tendency develops through growth and decrease, so the linearity of the necessary pursuit of developed laws is subjected to consecutive transformations. As the essay *On People and Laws* 人法 *Rénfǎ* states, the perfect application of laws in line with human needs has already taken place, in the time of the Three Dynasties. After subsequent times of the unilateral support of governments, either on laws or on human power, the tendency of history again leads to a state of equilibrium.[314]

The phrase 'tendency of history' finally leads to the question about the substrate of *shi*, and thus the 'substratum' of history. According to Chen Liang, historical transformations are ultimately transformations of matter (*qi*), with the proviso that matter takes on different forms depending on its time and place. Chen Liang thinks, for instance, that the south of China is filled with a 'biased *qi*' 偏氣 *piānqì*, cyclically increasing and exhausting, which involves changes of a political nature. As he points out, it is the South, namely the state of Chu, which withstood the unification of China for the longest time; it was the South where Liu Xiu (later Guangwudi) renewed the Han dynasty; the South was also a place of Zhuge Liang's activity during the Three Kingdoms. However, since the collapse of the southern Jin dynasty, there was a period of five or six centuries of extinction of the southern *qi*, which resulted either in political dispersion (in the *Nanbeichao* and *Wudai* periods), or subordination of the central authority (Sui, Tang). Chen Liang believes that in the times of the Southern Song dynasty, the southern *qi* is re-entering a phase of growth, thus rulers have to 'vent it and use it', and in this way overthrow the barbarians from the North.[315]

Similar changes took place at the beginning of the history of mankind when, thanks to the sages, the 'human race' separated itself from the animals: the sages quelled the people's struggles by means of a system of punishments that gave them the right to have other people's lives at their command; the same system, though built on violence, became the basis of positive law. As Chen Liang points out, both the system of penalties and the related social hierarchy existed 'from the division of human *qi*'. They are not just names that serve to distinguish things, but things themselves, observable 'cultural entities' 文物 *wénwù*.[316] Chen Liang not only uses materialism to explain social and historical processes, but also a specific 'materialization' of history. As Zheng Jixiong writes, for Chen Liang 'the rise of a state, historiography, historical culture – all these are things [物 *wù*] (...) He also believes that individual human morality is a natural product of historical development of culture.'[317] Chen Liang simply states: 'Dao lies in the world, manifesting itself through daily usability, taking the form of human nature and feelings.'[318] In his opinion, both rituals and classical writings, including the *Chunqiu*, are not the result of the sages' intentions, but a response to the particular conditions in which they arose, in the form of the explanation of practical and perceptible phenomena 事 *shì*.[319] Tillman nicely sums it up:

> Chen Liang viewed the Dao as a complex concept combining awareness of historical context and the notion of immanence. His exposition of the Dao ran counter to Zhu Xi's trans-historical perception of the Dao (...) The crux of the debate about the Dao centred on the nature of values, particularly the impact of historical change on values. Chen Liang utilised the Dao to undermine the credibility of the notion of absolute or unchanging Confucian values (...) To Chen Liang, the continuity of the Dao meant an immanent Dao, defined by people's actions in particular times (...) Dao, as Chen Liang perceived it, might be summarised as the standard of order immanent in, and evolving with, things.[320]

As Tillman continues, this did not entail total historism for Chen Liang. Chen Liang's main concern was to run the Khitans out of China and restore the power of the Song in the North, and so he assumed the difference between Chinese and 'barbarians' as absolute. They consist of another, bad kind of *qi*, and also have their own Dao, different and lesser than the Chinese. The old dynasties had a 'constant Way' of dealing with the barbarians, which was abandoned, but, as Chen Liang felt, should be revived in his times. Chen Liang's ethnocentrism was thus an obstacle to consistent historism.[321] It implied relativism, including its cultural form: in various periods of time and places, different Dao(s) were employed. This was, of course, a thesis that Zhu Xi could not agree with.[322] According to Zhu Xi, although one, Dao was characterized in great detail: (1) as the Dao of antiquity, i.e. the times of the Three Dynasties; (2) as the Dao of kings; and (3) as the Dao based on morality. In opposition to this vision, Chen Liang rejected the view that Dao (1) was lost from the Han up to the Tang. He asked how it was possible that something that had not existed could be miraculously recovered, and how these dynasties could have flourished without Dao. He also claimed that the Dao of hegemons does not interfere with the Dao of kings (2) and can be utilized simultaneously, just as morality (3) does not stand in conflict with interests.[323] Hence, it is not surprising that Zhu Xi concluded his correspondence with Chen Liang with a statement that Chen Liang 'became corrupted by history',[324] thereby confirming that the difference between their philosophies of history was in fact the difference between historical idealism and realism.

In a way, Chen Liang's philosophy of history, though inconsistent in its historism, was the culmination of a trend in the Song philosophy of history that opted for immanence of principles governing human history. The last representative of realist historical thinking under the Song (coming after Chen Liang) was Ye Shi 葉適 (1150–1223), who explained historical changes in terms of cyclical political and administrative transformations, centred around legal and bureaucratic institutions 法度 *fǎdù*. However, since Ye Shi believed in the existence of a 'life-principle' of the rise and fall of dynasties, his standpoint should not be labelled as a materialist one. On the other hand, Ye Shi was far more 'realist' in his treatment of Chinese history than Chen Liang was. For Ye Shi, 'there are no more intrinsic distinctions between China and the barbarians', the Dao was nothing but a general name for standards of conduct, and even Confucius himself was merely an author of few commentaries to the *Yijing*, whose main claim to fame was preserving the existing texts.[325]

Conclusion

The diversity of positions held by the Neo-Confucian philosophers of history was exceptional in the scale of all Chinese thought. It is even more compelling that all these standpoints fall under two basic types of responses to the question regarding the nature of history. This means that the Neo-Confucian philosophy of history is highly intertextual, as reviving the ancient ideas, referring to the similar views of the epoch, and criticizing the opponents.

Historical idealists shared the belief in the timeless principle of history, which in the case of Zhu Xi was rooted in the most complex philosophical system that this epoch produced, being integrated with his anthropology and the theory of historiography. Cohesion cannot be denied to the spiritualist variants of historical idealism of this time either, which unlike Zhu Xi's view of history, were neither regressive (Wang Anshi), nor linear (Shao Yong). While Wang Anshi understood history as a result of subversive actions of the eminent, 'embodied' spirits, Shao Yong treated it as a manifestation of the cyclical transformations of the superindividual spirit. In fact, Shao Yong's case is probably the most consistent cyclical and speculative (almost mathematical) philosophy of history created in classical Chinese culture.

Historical realists, in turn, argued for the self-sufficiency of history, as well as for a need for structural explanations devoid of referring to the intentionality of particular individuals. Most of them believed in a tendency of history, the necessity, irreversibility and linearity of which were emphasized by Liu Zongyuan, Su Xun and Chen Liang. However, due to the rejection of any *a priori* standards, they identified the role of social response to this trend and recognized the place of opressed social groups in history. These premises were common to the materialist version of historical realism, with the proviso that the category of historical materialism is interpreted in a broad and internally diversified manner. For instance, by 'matter', Chen Liang understood both the objective (nature, environment) and subjective (the material constitution of persons) substrates of history. For comparison, to Liu Zongyuan it was rather a matter of artefacts and social relations, while to Li Gou, a matter of money and the relations of production and ownership.

The thinkers of the later times had to live in the shadow of the holistic syntheses created under the Song, a direct reaction to what was the Ming individualism. The division of the Neo-Confucian philosophy of history into realist and idealist trends also posed the task of integrating these two theories of the 'substratum' of history – a task that was undertaken at the beginning of the Qing dynasty. For these reasons, the Neo-Confucian views of history are of central importance to our interpretation of the classical Chinese philosophy of history.

Individual and History

The Philosophy of History from the Thirteenth to the Eighteenth Century

Introduction

This chapter discusses the philosophy of history that was produced between the thirteenth century and the end of the eighteenth century, in other words from the formulation of the orthodox form of Neo-Confucianism 道學 *Dàoxué* until the adaptation of ideas expressed in the Western philosophy of history and historiography. By analogy, the philosophy of history under the Ming and Qing dynasties could be described as an 'early modern' Chinese philosophy of history, with the proviso that this term serves only the internal periodization.[1] This analogy is justified since the Ming era was a time of unprecedented individualism, while in the initial phase of the Qing dynasty, the 'scholastic' philosophy of the Song period was criticized, if not rejected, by the representatives of the *kaozheng* movement.

The century of Mongol rule between the times of the Song and the Ming surprisingly did not break the continuity of the Chinese philosophy of history. The Mongol conquest of China and the associated changes in historical consciousness were the result of a long process of contact between the Chinese population and people living in the areas from Korea to Altai. From the tenth century, these territories were inhabited by the Khitan people, who founded the Liao dynasty, which was overthrown in 1125 by the Jurchens, who founded the Jin ('Golden') dynasty. The Khitans lived rather on the periphery of China, sinicized very slowly, and preferred Buddhism, and all this resulted in little interest in historical thought.[2]

The Jurchens, on the other hand, underwent significant sinicization. As Hoyt Tillman shows, contemporary discussions on the thought of Zhu Xi, Sima Guang and Su Shi were a direct continuation of the Song debates.[3] The example of Wang Ruoxu 王若虛 (1174–1243) shows that historical criticism was combined with the privileging of the didactic function of historiography, mediated by a particularly emotivist idea that 'the words of past sages expressed only human feelings'.[4] The philosophy of history of that time was dominated by idealism: Yuan Haowen 元好問 (1190–1257) adhered to the classic concept of the Mandate of Heaven, and even partly to the vision of the correlation between Heaven and humanity, whereas Liu Qi 劉祁 (1203–1259)

developed the idea of dynastic cycles, which were to depend on the state of the 'spirit of scholars' 士風 *shìfēng* at a certain time.[5] A cyclical view of history was also adopted by Zhao Bingwen 趙秉文 (1159–1232). In his opinion, cycles of growth and decline are determined on the one hand by the 'principle of nature' 自然之理 *zìránzhīlǐ* manifested in the Five Phases; on the other hand, they are also determined by compliance with Confucian morality. In turn, social institutions, such as feudalism, are explained by the conditions/tendency of a given time (*shi*).[6]

Interestingly, while the philosophy of history of the scholars living in the Jurchen state was rather idealist, the philosophers of history of the Yuan Dynasty were closer to realist positions. One of them was Ma Duanlin 馬端臨 (1245–1322), the author of the *Comprehensive Investigations into Literature and Documents* 文獻通考 *Wénxiàn tōngkǎo*. As the introduction reads, Ma intends to comprehend (*huitong*) Dao as a whole, but he is not interested in the principle (*li*) of the decline and fall of the states, but in the description of social institutions. What is more, these institutions are much more durable than single dynasties, therefore in order to examine the causes 故 *gù* of these institutions, one should first know their whole, from the beginning to the end; only then can one understand each of them.[7] Therefore, it was a holism concerning time, causality and meaning (in the sense distinguished in the first chapter of this book). Simultaneously, this holism was marked by a certain dualism, dividing institutional history into two stages: first, when everything was public 公 *gōng*, that is, the times of the Three Dynasties and the prevailing feudal system; and second, the times when the state became the private property 私 *sī* of the emperor, from the Qin onwards and the prefectural system; finally, moments when the 'public' approach was coming back.[8] However, it was not so much an effect of the attitude of the minds of the sages as of the tendencies and conditions (*shi*) of a given time.[9] This echoes Liu Zongyuan's theory, although Ma Duanlin went even further than Liu, because – as Hok-Lam Chan emphasizes – he criticized not only the application of cosmological schemes to history, but also rejected the moral function of historiography.[10] Ma Duanlin was not therefore a Confucian philosopher of history, getting closer to Legalism: commenting on Shang Yang's reforms, Ma wrote that the solutions appropriate for antiquity could not work in his day due to different causes.[11] Chan thinks that Ma Duanlin even adopted a 'somewhat fatalistic conviction about the inevitability of certain historical changes'.[12] If it is so, Ma Duanlin was not alone in his fatalism.

Another eminent thinker of that time, Xu Heng 許衡 (1209–1281), openly states that there is nothing that is not destiny (*ming*). *Ming* could be recognized in the course of time and the tendency of history (*shi*) that cannot be overborne by people. The way people adopt to the *shi* determines their progress or regress.[13] Also the tendency itself goes through the periods of order and chaos: as it is seen in the history of the world, both order and chaos cannot last in perpetuity. Already during the period of order there are indications of later chaos and vice versa; after reaching its extreme point, order turns into chaos and chaos turns into order.[14] However, people can penetrate 通 *tōng* the nature of historical changes 變 *biàn*, just like the sages did, and thereby comply with internal necessity of nature 自然之數 *zìrán zhī shù* and use it.[15] In this way Xu Heng provided foundations for the thought of Ming theorists of *shi*, which will culminate in the philosophy of Wang Fuzhi.

Philosophy of history in the Ming dynasty

The philosophy of the Ming Dynasty, often accused by later historians of Chinese philosophy of 'introvertism' and Buddhism-inspired 'empty' considerations, was in fact an attempt to resist the Song metanarratives, which was expressed in more intense than ever individualism and criticism.[16] In the field of historical writing, this was connected with the rise of private historiography, the vast majority of which was devoted not to ancient events, but to current political ones.[17] In the thought of Song Lian 宋濂 (1310–1381), the head of the Ming Historical Office and the chief editor of the *History of the Yuan*, this privacy had even grown to the rank of the principle of historiography. Song Lian believed that the development of matter (*qi*), including history and the achievements of the sages, can only be explained by the creative action of mind (*xin*). As Xiang Yannan notes, Song Lian's philosophy of history was thus based on subjective idealism.[18] However, in the philosophy of historiography of Wang Shizhen and Hu Yinglin, individualist tendencies led to historical criticism, which implied a certain degree of historism, thereby meeting prospectivism in the theory of historical process, as represented by Wang Tingxiang and Zhang Juzheng. The denouement of individualism in the philosophy of the history of that time was the thought of Li Zhi. Significantly, each of the views described in the following sections was deemed to lie outside the Confucian orthodoxy.

The Ming individualism cannot be fully understood without an insight into the philosophy of Wang Yangming 王陽明 (1472–1529). Wang Yangming, though undeniably focused on epistemology and ethics, was only apparently not interested in history. In essence, his thought reflected the tension between partly ahistorical individualism and the historization of the inherited canon, which was typical of this epoch.

Wang Yangming believes that the principle (*li*) is identical to mind (*xin*). For Zhu Xi *li*, however, was also a principle 'standing behind' history, thus for Wang Yangming it is mind which plays such a role. Like Song Lian, Wang Yangming bases his understanding of history on subjective idealism, additionally strengthened by his idea of innate moral knowledge. In other words, in Wang Yangming's eyes, there is no barrier between the individual and history, and as a result, the whole of history can be experienced immediately. As Wang Yangming writes, 'in one day man experiences the whole world of history, but he does not realize it (...) If a student trusts in his innate knowledge and does not allow to be disturbed by matter, he can still live [in the world] of Fu Xi, if not formerly.'[19] As Wang adds, from the perspective of a mind deprived of contact with matter, there is no difference between one day and the 129,600-year era described by Shao Yong.[20] In other words, if mind is the principle of history, the only way to know history is through self-awareness, which requires reaching the purified 'root of mind' and its innate knowledge. However, if events are a manifestation of mind and its content at the same time, and the difference between events and the principle disappears, then the boundary between the Classics, which are supposed to convey universal truths, and historical works becomes no less blurred. As Wang Yangming states,

> It is said that histories deal with events, and the Classics with the principle. However, with events there is also Dao, and with Dao – events. [Hence] the *Spring*

and Autumn Annals is also a Classic, while Five Classics are histories (...) In fact, Five Classics are just histories. The function of history is to distinguish between good and evil and give instructions and warnings.[21]

Understandably, this translates into scepticism regarding the Classics, especially the *Book of Songs*, which, according to Wang, should even be removed from the Confucian canon. But also with regard to historical books themselves, no less important questions concerning their credibility are posed. Wang Yangming claims that the history before the reign of Yao should not be discussed, and because of the constant changes and differences between successive ages, it is impossible to return to all the customs of the Three Dynasties.[22] However, this did not prevent Wang Yangming from perceiving the Three Dynasties era as a golden age, followed by the collapse of Confucianism.[23] In addition, by reaching the principle present in the mind, identical to the mind of the sages, one can become a sage like, for instance, Yao and Shun.[24] Hence, the thesis that the Classics are only histories, although anticipating the later view of Zhang Xuecheng, was not a manifesto of historism. It rather expressed the idea that from the perspective of a purified mind, the division into what is historical and unhistorical does not take place. Accordingly, the difference between the past and the present becomes equally irrelevant. In this way Wang's individualism has, paradoxically, a holistic character.

Prospectivism of Wang Tingxiang and Zhang Juzheng

The most influential interpretation of history during the Ming dynasty was still Zhu Xi's philosophy of history, though the critical concepts, necessarily closer to materialist and progressive positions, also came to the fore. This trend may be seen in the philosophy of history of Wang Tingxiang 王廷相 (1474–1544) and Zhang Juzheng 張居正 (1525–1582).

Wang Tingxiang's philosophy of history cannot be understood without his ontology. For Wang, there is nothing beyond matter (*qi*), although matter itself can be either formed or formless; considered from the perspective of phenomena it is a being, and from the perspective of changes – nonbeing.[25] One *qi*, 'sometimes constant, and sometimes changeable', has many manifestations. Reversing the basic assumption of Zhu Xi, Wang Tingxiang writes that matter is one, while principles are many.[26] As Youngmin Kim observes, 'Wang did not believe that there existed an overarching unified structure to the universe';[27] Chang Woei Ong adds that 'in Wang's cosmology, diversity, not unity, is the norm'.[28] In a sense, the unifying role is played by matter. It is the source of all changes, thus as a result of being determined 定 *ding* by a given type of matter certain states of affairs may remain unchanged for thousands of epochs. On the other hand, such a situation is hypothetical, for matter, endowed with time, is constantly changing and nothing is permanent.[29] As Wang Tingxiang argues, 'Dao has no established place, which is why the sages follow the times.'[30] However, the question arises of whether this time has a specific direction after all.

C.W. Ong believes that 'Wang Tingxiang in particular rejected the idea of imposing a universal and rigid standard of moral values on history and instead argued that more attention should be paid to the particularity of each historical moment.'[31] Wang, however, refers to the notion of the tendency (*shi*), which – though devoid of a normative dimension – gives historical moments a general and orderly character. *Shi* has, first of all, a linear character. In contrast to, for example, Chen Liang, Wang Tingxiang does not mention any cycles to be the stages of the tendency of history. Second, *shi* changes continuously and gradually. After a long time, all institutions and laws degenerate, which causes change, the essence of which is its gradation 漸 *jiàn*.[32] Third, 'changes caused by the tendency of the world cannot be undone.'[33] Therefore, if certain particular laws are considered universal, the degeneration that accompanies the changes will also corrupt the government that still follows these ill-assorted laws. For this reason, ancient institutions cannot be used at present and even a sage is not able to counteract the tendency tied to the passage of time.[34] There is no way to return to, for instance, feudalism, because *shi* is no longer conducive to this system.[35] From the perspective of the evolution of *shi*, morality also turns out to be something historical and contingent. Wang Tingxiang writes not only about the transition from the state in which the throne was obtained by the virtuous to the rule of succession, which started with the establishment of the Xia Dynasty, but he also believes that Mencius' ethics did not correspond to the conditions of the Warring States Period, and that the Qi and Liang states that renounced the virtue of *ren* in favour of strength did the right thing because they reacted to the growing power of the Qin, which was the result of the 'irreversible' historical trend.[36]

Wang Tingxiang does not think, though, that changes resulting from *shi* are always good: they can bring both improvement and deterioration.[37] For this reason, his specific position will be called 'prospectivism', in order to distinguish it from progressivism. Wang's prospectivism shares with the theory of progress a belief in the existence of a linear, gradual and irreversible trend of history, but it does not unequivocally evaluate the nature or aim of this trend, particularly the tendency of history is neither considered good per se nor treated as inevitably leading to the better state of affairs. In fact, although Wang Tingxiang's philosophy of history is built on the idea of a change that comes from the future, Wang nowhere sought to sketch the future era. His characterization of *shi* is done *post factum* and draws only upon examples from the past, which strikingly differs from progressivist portrayals of future utopia. Another difference between prospectivism and progressivism is the distancing of the former from absolute principles and norms. While the unfolding of the 'line of progress' ties in with an increase of desired values and/or realization of universal norms, for prospectivists, such as Wang, the tendency of history is nothing but a structure of contingent and ambiguous factors.

Wang's attack on the unity of the historical and the normative undermines the foundations of Confucian historical thinking. From the times of Zhu Xi, history was mainly treated as an implementation of the absolute principle (the objective perspective), and at least from the times of Mencius, the norms introduced by the sages were considered universally valid (the subjective perspective), which under the Neo-Confucian interpretation proved to accord with the objective principle. Wang Tingxiang, for whom the sages only followed the *shi* of the time, rejected both assumptions. As Y. Kim notes, 'for Wang, the world lacks unity and a normative dimension. Reality, as it is, is devoid of value, which has to be imposed from the outside. Wang's sage represents a governing authority who imposes value on reality.[38] Morality, laws and customs did not exist until they were established (*ding*) in an arbitrary way by the sages, albeit over the course of time they became stable institutions.[39] His view of history undoubtedly falls within an ambit of historical realism, if not historical materialism, since Wang interprets history through the prism of transforming material relations, such as changes in methods of taxation or the transformation of systems of land ownership.[40] He also assigned particular importance to the transformations of the institution of marriage.[41] None of these forms of change of social matter was considered essential or important, since 'Wang believed that the principles guiding the evolution of history and politics, just like the principles guiding the natural order, [are] many.'[42] The only place where Wang directly speaks of one Dao is literature, especially the Classics, which are said to be the 'vehicle' of Dao.[43] Therefore, it might be concluded that by criticizing Neo-Confucian historical idealism at the level of theory of historical process, Wang Tingxiang transfers Confucian belief in one Dao level 'down', to the field of historiography. The unity and good cannot be found in history itself, but rather in our thinking (and writing) about history.

Zhang Juzheng's philosophy of history could be also treated as a form of prospectivism. As Robert Crawford observes, 'if specific dynastic problems called forth these legalistic solutions, Zhang found the source of the problems themselves and justification for his solutions in a philosophy of history based on the principle of constant change in time and circumstances.'[44] Zhang Juzheng believes that the principle of events is not constant, it is rather the need to follow the times which is constant; as a result, what used to be a good thing could be considered immoral today.[45] This also applies to the law: laws and institutions are not invariable, because *shi* changes throughout history. What is more, since the law has to accord with the time, old-fashionedness or newness is not even a criterion of assessment of laws. By practising the rituals and political solutions formerly regarded as degenerated, one can attain wealth and strength in one's own times. There are no absolutely valid laws, customs, moral principles and institutions.[46] All this results from the slow and gradual transformation of *shi*; *shi* takes the form of a tendency towards order or chaos, and even a sage cannot counteract it.[47] Interestingly, this trend of history changes direction by itself.

Zhang Juzheng believes that after reaching a certain extreme stage, historical changes 'naturally' reverse their course and return to the beginning. In every age simplicity prevails at first (*zhi*), transforming with time into increasing complexity and sublimation (*wen*), and then – along with the advent of a new era – the process starts again.[48] As Crawford emphasizes, these cycles do not mean a return to the previous stage, but – as inscribed in the linearity of history – describe the structure of each epoch, which, taken in itself, is unique, meaning that each of them has a specific system of laws and governments.[49] Using this theory, Zhang interprets all Chinese history, from Yao to the Ming dynasty, locating the moments of 'solstice' and indicating the novelties brought by each of the ages.[50] His prospectivism, unlike Wang Tingxiang's thought, absorbed cyclical themes, by means of distinguishing the phases of the unfolding of *shi*, having none of them judged from a normative perspective.

Philosophy of historiography under the Ming

The development of the philosophy of historiography during the Ming dynasty resulted from the transformation of historiography itself. The foundation of the philosophy of historiography in terms of subjective idealism advanced by Song Lian was just one of many theoretical proposals of that time. Wang Yi 王祎 (1322–1373), who was closer to the objective idealism of Zhu Xi's school, postulated a closer connection between historiography and political philosophy. In his opinion, the way of the sages shown in the chronicles relied upon searching for what is useful in given times, therefore governing consists in learning from the past and, at the same time, following the specificity of time; without knowledge of history, one should not engage in politics.[51] Wang Yi also believed that the judgements made by a historian are public and that (good) historians are responsible for passing them on to future generations and thus maintaining the 'public discussion' 公議 *gōngyì*.[52] However, such a talent of a good historian is rare, because in writing history (precisely, the history of a given dynasty) one should not only study facts and craft the right words, but also base one's work on standards and find examples to follow. In order to examine the whole of a given period of history, a language is needed that distinguishes the subtleties of discourse; knowledge that is the effect of knowing even what is difficult to understand; and intellect to penetrate the principle (*li*) standing behind innumerable events.[53] The literary layer of the chronicle (*wen*) is thus treated as a visible manifestation of Dao, indistinguishable from the Way; although Dao is not identical with literariness, Dao and *wen* are not separate entities.[54]

A similar idea can be found in the thought of Xue Yingqi 薛應旂 (1499–1535), who defended the thesis that with regard to their source and nature, the Classics and histories are one 經史一也 *jīng shǐ yī yě*.[55] That equation was, of course, formulated at the expense of the status of the Classics, which, according to Zhu Xi, were subordinate to the histories; instead, the fundamental and ubiquitous significance of history was noticed, as shown in the quotation from writings of Qiu Jun 邱濬 (1421–1495): 'it is impossible for there to be one day without history and one day without historians in the world (...) It is historians who [animate] public debate that extends to countless generations.'[56]

These themes were later raised by Wang Shizhen 王世貞 (1526–1590), who stated that 'between Heaven and earth there is nothing that would not be history'.[57] As Wang writes, the Classics are just histories that are highly regarded.[58] This concerns especially the *Chunqiu*, which, although it is undoubtedly a work of the sage, contains many dubious passages that have misled subsequent generations into worshipping this work, and which should be criticized in the same way as any other historical work.[59] It is true that Wang Shizhen realized the differences between (histories that become) the Classics and (regular) histories, believing that the meaning of the *Chunqiu* and other Classics goes beyond the truths of one state and one dynasty, for the Classics are histories discoursing on the principle 言理 *yánlǐ*.[60] As Ailika Schinköthe observes, Wang Shizhen, just as Liu Zhiji once did, could have done this to protect his work against the attacks of Neo-Confucian orthodoxy, all the more so because the idea of respect for certain histories has no metaphysical or even ethical basis in his thought. Unlike the other thinkers cited here, Wang Shizhen argues that public opinion may be mistaken; what is more, the value of a history could be seen in the fact that it is underestimated and misunderstood by the masses.[61] This idea led to the programme of historical criticism of Wang, as expressed in the *Investigation of errors in historical books* 史乘考 誤 *Shǐshèng kǎowù*. As Wang Shizhen claims, due to the incompleteness of the records, the chronicles using them are unreliable, and even if the materials were complete, the desire to hide the faults of an emperor and the nation on the one hand, and the private sympathies and aversions on the other, would still render the records untrustworthy. Private historiography, however, is not a worthy alternative, because due to lack of education, private historians carry out erroneous inferences and do not verify the testimonies available to them, most of which are heard.[62] The general tone of Wang's criticism is thus pessimistic.[63]

The ideas of Wang Shizhen were developed by Hu Yinglin 胡應麟 (1551–1602). For Hu, just as for Wang, the *Shangshu* and the *Chunqiu* were merely histories, albeit since the time of these works there was a gradual collapse of historiography.[64] Like Wang Yi, also Hu Yinglin believes that the examination of facts and the choice of words, or more precisely, the three conditions of being a good historian as distinguished by Liu Zhiji, i.e. talent, knowledge and insight, are not enough, thus a historian should still be required to record events faithfully 直筆 *zhíbǐ* with a publicly oriented mind 公心 *gōngxīn*.[65] The category of *gongxin* has ethical connotations: it involves issuing moral judgements and expresses the historian's responsibility to all people. Obviously, these are hardly achievable and disjoint features. When writing a universal history, the problem is acquiring sources, but not judgement, which in turn is much more difficult in the case of a dynastic history, when there is no problem with access to eyewitness reports.[66] Moral judgement can be made both with the help of individual characters and words (as in the *Chunqiu* and the *Zuozhuan*), as well as by means of the selection of events (as in the *Shiji* and the *Hanshu*).[67]

Understanding the problem of moral judgement in the context of various literary genres and treating it as a result of 'loaded language' leads Hu Yinglin to give primacy to the linguistic dimension. As Hu writes, neither the voluminousness of history, nor the time distance is decisive for the shape of the chronicle. Good histories are those whose language is simple, while the bad ones are characterized by overly sophisticated vocabulary.[68] On the other hand, if simplicity is taken to the extreme, subtle refinement is better. In other words, simplicity should 'cooperate' with subtlety. This being the case, simplicity restricts the material, which results in the complete presentation 該 *gāi* being obtained, while subtlety yields exhausting all details of the whole 整 *zhěng*.[69] If both types of narrative are combined with objectivity, the whole as absoluteness 全 *quán* is achieved, which allows for a reasonable assessment of historical figures, taking into account what is important and fundamental, as opposed to what is secondary.[70] Hu Yinglin distinguishes, therefore, three understandings of the completeness of historical narrative, clearly striving for the most holistic approach, while avoiding the perspective advocated by Zhu Xi's school of the principle.

Thus desired objectivism is contrasted by Hu Yinglin with both the bias of the narrative itself (as in the case of Wei Shou), as well as with selectivity in presenting events (as, according to Hu Yinglin, in the case of Zheng Qiao).[71] Objectivism goes without 'being confused by the first impression, without prejudice, without willing to ingratiate, without seeking applause'.[72] The ambition to formulate the criteria of objectivity led Hu Yinglin to write a work to which he owes his greatest fame as a theorist and methodologist of history, i.e. the *Originals and Forgeries of Four Categories* 四部正訛 *Sìbù zhèng'é*. Hu Yinglin not only distinguishes various types and degrees of historical forgery,[73] but above all, he formulates the criteria for external historical criticism, strongly advising authors to search for mentions of the title of the work in bibliographies, first of all in the past and then in the contemporary works. It is also required to examine whether the expressions in the work in question were in use at a given time, whether the reported events occurred, etc. The key to external criticism is, as Hu himself admits, the identification of the author;[74] guided by this idea, Hu Yinglin showed that the *Zuo zhuan* and many other classical historical works had more than one author.

The philological denouement of Hu Yinglin's thought is not surprising. Despite striving for a holistic view of historiography, all three concepts of the whole which Hu employed are closed within the sphere of language: the first two directly, as features of historical narrative, the third one indirectly, since the *quan*-whole consisted of the objectivity and veracity of works, but their authenticity ultimately stems from references to other works and bibliographies. As Peter Bol points out, for Hu Yinglin scientific knowledge and literature are indistinguishable from each other, and scholarly knowledge develops gradually, standing in opposition to the idea of a one-time insight into the principle of history, proposed by Zhu Xi. As a result, the purpose of learning is nothing external; it is education itself.[75] The force of philologism absorbed the germs of historism present in Wang Shizhen's thought, affecting prominently the criticism of the Qing era. From the subordination of history to the Classics, through to identifying the two, Chinese thinkers reached the point where the Classics proved to be histories and histories – literature, approaching, along with the idea of a constitutive role of the language of the narrative, the narrativist philosophy of historiography.

Historical relativism of Li Zhi

Reflection on history occupied a special place in the philosophy of Li Zhi 李贽 (1527–1602), this *enfant terrible* of Confucianism. In his philosophy, Li Zhi ruthlessly criticized the Neo-Confucian metaphysical speculations, rejecting belief in the existence of one universal truth; he believed that individuals do not need authorities to acquire knowledge (it is enough to develop a 'childlike mind' 童心 *tóngxīn*), while following one's own interests and desires, including the sexual ones, is morally acceptable; finally, he believed that women should have just the same rights as men. In 1602, Li Zhi was accused of deviant views, sexual dissolution and mixing Buddhism with Confucianism; at the behest of the emperor, his books were burned and he himself was arrested, then shortly after committed suicide in prison.[76] His two main works had provocative titles that indicated that Li Zhi was aware of his iconoclasm: *The Book to Burn* 焚書 *Fénshū* from 1590 and *The Book to Hide* 藏書 *Cángshū* from 1600. Wu Congxian later used the name of Li Zhi to assign him the *Outline of history with critical remarks* 史綱評要 *Shǐgāng píngyào*, a work full of critical and sarcastic remarks about recognized historical figures, often showing the rift between Confucian ideals and their practical, historical implementation. Li Zhi himself devoted a fifth scroll of the *Fenshu* to a similar analysis of selected historical figures under the title *Reading Histories* 讀史 *Dú shǐ*, while *Cangshu* is essentially a collection of biographies of well-known officials, from Confucian scholars to servicemen, often accusing them of greed and ineptitude. The ideal of the minister was for Li Zhi someone who acts spontaneously, as if doing nothing, in accordance with his time.[77] It was, therefore, an ideal closer to the combination of Daoism and Legalism as it is represented in the *Huainanzi* than to the (Neo-)Confucian view.

The idea of adapting to times is usually associated with the concept of *shi*, and so was the case with Li Zhi. According to Li Zhi, *shi* is expressed in the cycles of order and chaos, taking place despite the lack of awareness from the participants of events. These cycles remain, similarly to Zhang Juzheng, associated with periods of simplicity (*zhi*) and subtlety (*wen*). Interestingly, for such an opponent of speculation as Li Zhi, the order is determined by the highest intensity of simplicity and uncontrolled ('wild' 野 *yě*) feelings. The apogee of subtlety and sophistication therefore leads to a state of chaos. Changes in the intensity of *zhi* or *wen* are gradual (*jian*), but the transition from order to chaos (or reversely) is discontinuous and occurs when one of the values reaches its maximum. One example of such a transition in Chinese history is the replacement of the Qin dynasty by the Han. Hence, as Li Zhi argues, the sages cannot oppose the tendency of history: one can only surrender to it without doing anything against it.[78] As Xiang Yannan justly observes, the cycles of order and chaos in Li Zhi do not result from the assumed compatibility of human action with nature, as in the case of Han thought, or the morality of the action itself, as for many philosophers of the Song period, but from the objective and dialectical (as concerning the transformation of the opposites) law of history.[79]

The axiological neutrality of the historical process fits perfectly with the historical relativism of Li Zhi: from both perspectives, good and bad figures (all the more all historical epochs) that would act as a universal model cannot be identified. As Li Zhi writes, there is no fixed standard of what is right and wrong 是非 *shì-fēi*. Only opinion is decisive; regardless of whether it is the opinion of one or a million people, it still remains merely one among various possible opinions. As Li Zhi regrets, from the Han dynasty to the Song, instead of seeking to express their own opinions, people accepted the opinion of Confucius without any discussion. What is more, opinions are not only different but also change over time:

> What was right yesterday is wrong today, and what is wrong today will be right again tomorrow. Even if Confucius were born again in our times, I would not know what things he would deem right and wrong.[80]

The historical relativism of Li Zhi, accepting the multiplicity and equivalence of time-varying opinions, leads to historism in the interpretation of the works of culture and individualism regarding the conditions of their understanding. Moral principles, which for Zhu Xi constitute the essence of history, are not even a universal cultural message, they are in fact reduced to what is known in the West as *doxa*. The above-quoted words were also referred to in the edict condemning Li Zhi.

Treating the teachings of Confucius as equivalent to private opinion also led Li Zhi to reject the traditional ideal of modelling himself on the ancient sages, and especially on Confucius. Citing Wang Yangming's dictum that 'streets are full of sages' and Buddha's [i.e. Sakyamuni's] words that each mind is identical to the Buddha, Li Zhi claims that every human being is actually a sage, so there is no reason why one should search for anything beyond oneself, in particular one does not have to 'focus on studying Confucius to become later a part of the official system'.[81] Li Zhi's historism was therefore grounded in a specific individualism, namely the faith in the role of the individual and distancing from everything that would deprecate the role of the individual. At the same time, Li Zhi did not seem to notice the conflict between such an affirmation of the individual and the thesis on the existence of the supra-personal tendency of history, which 'even the sages cannot oppose'.

Conclusion

After a period of striving with fatalist implications of great Song syntheses, the philosophy of history in the Ming dynasty opened up to an unprecedented level of individualism and historism, which was exemplified in the view of Wang Yangming, who believed that each individual 'stands in front of' the totality of history, with no cognitive obstacles whatsoever between these two spheres. This individualism was taken to the extreme by Li Zhi, who combined it with a pure-bred historical relativism. The philosophy of historiography of that time was also characterized by an open historism, namely a view that the Classics, considered to be over-historically important, are nothing but histories, while histories are in no way different from other literary writings. From the viewpoint of both Li Zhi and the philosophers of historical writing, there is no point in objective evaluation of certain historical events. This idea, in turn, tied in with the prospectivism of Wang Tingxiang and Zhang Juzheng, who by means of elaborating upon the nature of historical tendency rejected all normative elements that had been inscribed into historical process by orthodox Neo-Confucians.

Philosophy of history in the Qing Dynasty

The historical part of this book ends with an analysis of the philosophy of history created at the beginning of the Qing dynasty, namely between 1650 and 1800. Devoting separate sections to the greatest philosophers of history of that time, namely Wang Fuzhi and Zhang Xuecheng, whose views surmount the development of the classical Chinese philosophy of history, this part of the chapter also offers a discussion of the importance of the 'evidential research' (*kaozheng*) in the philosophy of history of that time, in particular in the views of such thinkers as Gu Yanwu, Huang Zongxi and Dai Zhen.

The philosophy of history in the *kaozheng* movement

The collapse of the Ming dynasty and the conquest of China by the Manchus meant for many Chinese philosophers and intellectuals at that time not only a political defeat, but also a failure of a certain project of Chinese culture built on the cult of the Classics and the belief in the universal nature of principles governing history. This movement passed into history as 'evidential research' 考證 *kǎozhèng* and was based on the application of methods of source criticism to the studies on history and the Classics. Addressing the Neo-Confucian idealism developed in the Song period, this movement was also associated with the so-called Han learning 漢學 *Hànxué*, which was marked by a return to the Han commentarial tradition. At the same time, almost all representatives of the movement remained loyal to the Ming even after its fall, refusing to accept the offices and honours offered by the emperors of the Manchu dynasty. In practice, *kaozheng* turned out to be a much broader movement, having a significant influence also on the philosophy of history. Growing from the experience of historical trauma and disappointment with the current, royal-centric and optimistic narratives, the *kaozheng* re-evaluated historical thinking and eventually led the classical philosophy of history to be curtailed to the form of philological research,[82] which happened on the eve of the meeting of Western philosophy of history.

However, the evaluation of the role of the *kaozheng* movement and its location in the comparative perspective are subject to constant disputes. As Benjamin Elman claims, the *kaozheng* movement was, from the perspective of the orthodox Neo-Confucianism, a break with the ethical values and humanist ideals of Confucianism in general, but in fact it was not so much an attack on Neo-Confucian philosophy as the deconstruction of the imperial ideology centred around it.[83] Of course, the apriorism of the *Daoxue* Neo-Confucianism fell into direct conflict with the central role of verification in the *kaozheng* methodology, opponents of which could only answer using the same methods. However, the aim of using methods of historical and philological criticism was ultimately the tendency to return to the sources preceding 'the forgeries'.[84] As a result, the *kaozheng* did not yield the complete historization and relativization of the Classics,[85] all the more it did not reject the whole classical heritage, but was a reform within it. Therefore, according to Elman, it is not possible to juxtapose the *kaozheng* with nineteenth-century German historism, although Liang Qichao and Hu Shi have defended such a thesis, even claiming that it was the birth of modern science in China; in fact, it was rather closer to the parallel Western Enlightenment.[86] A similar view is expressed by Gao Jianlong, although due to the idea of 'returning to the sources' he compares *kaozheng* with eighteenth-century Puritanism and Biblical criticism.[87] Interestingly, many representatives of this movement absorbed the achievements of Western mathematics and astronomy, and thought that the Chinese methods of criticizing sources are not as good as European ones because of the poorly developed mathematics[88] (Western philosophy, however, was either not known or not cited by the representatives of *kaozheng*). Michael Quirin points out, however, that the *kaozheng* movement was not an anti-Confucian revolution: it was not even a revolution since it expired in the nineteenth century. The comparison with the Enlightenment is no less unfounded than comparing it with historism, because it would mean that secularization took place in China due to the *kaozhengxue*, whereas this did not take place and, in a sense, could not have happened in contemporary Chinese culture:

> [I]dentifications of historicism and *kaozhengxue* do not take into account the fact that the place of history in the Christian and in the Confucian tradition is

fundamentally different. Despite the many attempts to integrate these two realms, in the Christian tradition there has always been a rather strict separation between the suprahistorical realm of god and the historical realm of humans. History was considered inferior to theology (…) The sharp dichotomy of the world of god and the world of humans so characteristic of the Christian tradition is quite alien to the Confucian tradition. Although a clear separation between an ideal sphere and a sphere of current human practice has also been made, this separation was more a distinction between two phases of history – sacred and profane – than a separation between two realms of being (…) The quasi-religious role of history and historical knowledge in the Confucian tradition provided for the high status historical studies have always enjoyed in China. Yet, whereas in the Christian tradition the historical quest was potentially disruptive of the claims of religion, it tended to work the other way around in the Confucian tradition. As long as one consented – and this was one of the basic articles of the Confucian creed – that the sacred history of Confucianism was real and full of meaning, 'going historical' was more a pious than a revolutionary act. The basic assumption was never shaken that there was more to history than just history, and instead of undermining the Confucian creed, historical studies tended to stabilize and confirm it by constantly reworking the tradition and freeing it from internal inconsistencies and interpolations from the outside.[89]

An extensive quote from Quirin's paper touches on too many issues to deal with there, thus some of them will return at the end of this book. Intentionally chosen metaphors such as 'creed', 'pious' and 'sacred', seem to suggest that the closest Western analogue to the *kaozheng* was the Reformation rather than the Enlightenment. Irrespective of these comparative controversies, their conclusions should be taken into account, because they quench any excessive enthusiasm for demonstrating the allegedly modern character of the *kaozheng* movement. It could be observed on the example of the philosophy of that time. Yan Yuan 顏元 (1635–1704), who bitterly criticized Zhu Xi's abstract learning methods, believed that learning can only be done by practising 實 *shí* a given activity (in this way Yan Yuan was compared to John Dewey), but the practice Yan Yuan had in mind were not only sports and martial arts, but above all rituals, treated in the spirit of purism and conservatism.[90]

On the other hand, the radicalism of the historiography created within *kaozhengxue* cannot be overlooked. As Qian Daxin 錢大昕 (1728–1804) emphasized, historical research must begin with facts and pass them on to successive generations without hiding what may be uncomfortable. The difference between the Classics and histories is not absolute, because it was created at a specific historical moment (in the Han dynasty).[91] A similar opinion was expressed by Wang Mingsheng 王鳴盛 (1722–1797), who criticized from this perspective the ideal of the moral evaluation of historical figures (*baobian*).[92] Yan Ruoqu 閻若璩 (1636–1704), who became famous by demonstrating that half of the Old Text of the *Book of Documents* is a forgery from the times of the Jin dynasty, wrote equally provocatively: 'my concern is only with what is true (…) If the History and Commentary are true and the Classic false, then is it impermissible to use the History and Commentary to correct the Classic?'[93] Cui Shu 崔述 (1740–1816) developed methodology of history to such an extent that he univocally distinguished sentences referring to facts from sentences expressing opinions and values, also pointing to a change in historical knowledge over time, specifically its cumulative increase, which in the scale of centuries and in the face of intermingling of traditions only renders it more difficult to reach the original sources.[94] Still, the main goal of these historians was 'to correct the Classics', not to disprove them.

The philosophy of history created within *kaozhengxue* is a kind of intersection of the main trends in the philosophy of that time, which was represented by i.a. Yan Yuan, and historiography and historical criticism built on the idea of 'evidential learning', as seen from Yan Ruoqu to Cui Shu. This sort of philosophy of history is to be found in the thought of Gu Yanwu 顧炎武 (1613–1682). On the one hand, Gu finds claims that all doctrines which are incompatible with the Classics and needs of a given epoch are useless.[95] He also believes that 'the standard of both the former and later sages is one, thus an attempt to explore Heaven without learning from the past is like intent to harvest without sowing'.[96] Note that this sentence sounds almost identical to the words of Mencius, who lived two millennia earlier. Wang Jilu also notes that Gu Yanwu in many places quite openly accepts the concept of the correlation between Heaven and humanity, even though he knew Western astronomy.[97] In this sense, he was closer to the conservative than to the revolutionary. On the other hand, Gu Yanwu was extremely critical of Neo-Confucianism, of both the Song and the Ming. In his view, if the learning of the principle 理學 *lǐxué* were deprived of its central element in the form of study of the Classics 經學 *jīngxué*, then the only thing that would remain would be the doctrine of ghosts 神學 *shénxué*.[98] Gu Yanwu did not treat the distinction between the Classics and histories as absolutely binding. As he writes, 'Mencius' words about the text that is only history concern not only the *Chunqiu*, but all Six Classics'.[99] A significant and well-known part of Gu Yanwu's scholarship is also devoted to the history of imperial administration and bureaucracy, which, in Miranda Brown's opinion, could be treated as an alternative to the popular Weberian approach.[100] This analogy could be accepted with a number of reservations, including certain utopianisms integrated into this analysis, such as the belief that life in the countryside guarantees order, and life in the town – chaos.[101]

This diagnosis is related to the more general view of Gu Yanwu, who claimed that the cause of order and chaos lies in the human psyche and customs.[102] Speaking of the psyche, Gu mainly means the importance of such attitudes as honour and shame,[103] which in the case of the ruler translate directly into the destiny of the whole state. In this sense, order and chaos, rise and fall depend on 'great people' 大人 *dàrén*.[104] The crucial role of feelings and behaviours in history is in a sense, as Gu Yanwu believes, the result of the historical process itself: referring to the passage on Great Harmony (*Datong*), Gu recalls that since the breakup of the 'world as one family' everyone has natural affection for one's own kin, which differentiates reality.[105] This does not mean, however, that the effects of individual actions are transient. As Gu writes,

> There are no unchangeable customs in the world (. . .) If [this change] harms the people, though it can be introduced from day to day, its harmful influence on the court will nonetheless last for several decades or centuries, like an inundant trend of history, which starting from this time cannot be undone.[106]

There is a continuum between the decision of an individual and the changes concerning the world. Gu Yanwu, however, discerns the role of all the intermediate steps and warns against too hastily identifying the fall of the state with the fall of the whole world, since the former is only a change of the ruling clan along with the assigned titles, while the latter manifests itself as the fall of morality and social decay.[107] In the case of the large-scale processes (something that is now called macro-history), the explanation is provided only by the tendency of history, *shi*. As Gu Yanwu states, the transition from feudalism (*fengjian*) to the prefectural system (*junxian*) is an example of the necessary and irreversible result of a long-lasting and over-personal *shi*.[108] This *shi* is a natural process, because all beings are variable and temporary in their nature.[109] Nevertheless, eventually Gu Yanwu's philosophy of history taken as a whole is quite heterogeneous, stretched between conservatism and progressivism, idealism and realism, individualism and holism, and despite his criticism of Wang Yangming's 'doctrine of mind' 心學 *xīnxué*, his explanation of historical process is also based on the reference to the psyche of individuals.

Similar tension characterizes the philosophy of history of Huang Zongxi 黃宗羲 (1610–1695). In his approach to history, Huang combined the objectivist-idealist position of Zhu Xi, the subjectivist-idealist standpoint of Wang Yangming and selected concepts of the materialists. On the one hand, the study of historical books should be subordinated to and preceded by studies of the Classics.[110] On the other hand, following Wang Yangming, Huang Zongxi claims that principle is identical with the mind of every man, so if man is one with all beings, then all is mind. This declaration appears in the introduction to his most important historical work, and the first Chinese work in the field of intellectual history, namely the *Scholarly Notes on the Confucians of the Ming era* 明儒學案 *Míngrú xué'àn*.[111] The principle encompasses only what remains unchanged throughout history, while *qi* is directly responsible for variability, that is why the evolution of beings (*wu*) up to the human forms is just as material as the transformation of small plants into trees or one season into another.[112] The common ground of both approaches is their broad perspective, which enables the discussion of the whole of history, in which political history, and even the history of the human species, is only a single episode. As Huang writes, 'states can perish, history cannot.'[113] The collapse of the dynasty is therefore not a historically significant breakthrough; Huang Zongxi does not approve of the traditional concept of dynastic cycles. It is necessary to view crises and development from a wider and non-political perspective, that is from the scale of the conditions of the people. Then it will turn out that the period of tyrant Jie, although it was the time of the fall of the dynasty (Xia), was a rise from the perspective of the people, and the coming of the Qin and Mongols into power was a period of chaos.[114] What connects Huang Zongxi with Gu Yanwu is the idea that Chinese political history no longer provides a ready-made historiosophical scheme.

The proper place where the pattern of historical change should be sought is the *Book of Changes*. Huang Zongxi believes that the *Yijing* is the work of sages, which delineates the principle of human affairs, and even more: that twenty-one official histories are only traces – that is an application – of the structure of transformations expressed by *Yijing* hexagrams.[115] By subordinating histories to the Classics, Huang thus means primarily, if not exclusively, the *Book of Changes*. As part of this 'historiosophical exegesis' of the *Yijing* Huang Zongxi also reinterprets the hexagram 革 *gé*, which in his interpretation means not only change, but also approaches the modern reading of this character, namely reform and revolution. Huang believes that *ge* refers to the transformations made by the sages in response to the crisis, which was manifested in new customs, unfortunately abandoned by later generations in favour of forceful attempts to take over the world, which essentially characterizes the wrong *ge*.[116] Earlier, in the era of the Three Dynasties, governance was based on the virtue of *ren*, as Huang reminds us in his commentary to the *Mencius*.[117] This idea may be related to the political project of Huang Zongxi, which assumed that the real power in the state is exercised not by the emperor but by the first minister, while this power is limited by the law on the one hand and public opinion from the other.[118] It was a proposed antidote resulting from a specific historical diagnosis. As Q.E. Wang and On-cho Ng rightly observe,

> What Huang saw in the long span of Chinese history was continuous oppression of the people. If peace and chaos were determined by whether the people were happy or in distress, Huang rejected the rise and fall of dynasties as a significant factor in history. What counted was the condition of the masses (. . .) The central problem throughout Chinese history had been an excessive concentration of power at the center (. . .) Throughout the march of time, China had drifted farther away from the pristine civilization of the ancient past when the sages' values had been realized in the practical world of state and society. Thus, on the whole, we may say that Huang viewed Chinese history as a prolonged process of progressive deterioration.[119]

Note that the conclusion of this accurate summary of Huang Zongxi's philosophy of history is in direct accordance with the traditional Confucian view of history.

Some ideas relevant for the philosophy of history could be also found in the thought of Dai Zhen 戴震 (1724–1777), although he is mainly known for his ethics and criticism of Neo-Confucian metaphysics from the viewpoint of naturalism. And since the basic categories of this metaphysics were of key importance to the Neo-Confucian philosophy of history, so their criticism, and precisely their reformulation, resulted in a different vision of history. As Dai Zhen claims, the principle, as the ancient sages were to teach, is present in human feelings: it is simply their ordering.[120] Hence, feelings and desires are, according to Dai Zhen, the main force creating history, and their creator is ultimately the man alone, not any impersonal force (such as, for instance, *shi*).[121] Feelings are understood as a natural constitution of man: 'spirit' or 'soul' are just the transformations of *yin-yang*. By desires, Dai Zhen understands the necessary natural needs, such as the need for food and drink, which do not change throughout history and are necessary for the survival of people.[122] The material constitution of people is in this sense as natural and spontaneous 自然 *zìrán*, as necessary 必然 *bìrán*.[123] Dao, which for Zhu Xi exists 'above [visible] form', for Dai Zhen consists in transformations of matter, especially feelings that manifest in the everyday practice of interpersonal relationships.[124] Importantly, in Dai Zhen's view language was also a part of this practice. Bringing the philosophy of history closer to the world of everyday life has also resulted, similarly to Huang Zongxi, in the idea of the key historical role of the people, namely the belief that the exploitation of the people is a phenomenon that had taken place throughout the history of China.[125] The philosophy of history has thus been absorbed by some sort of intersection of psychology and political philosophy: history became a manifestation of feelings and material needs of 'common people', standing in opposition to the traditional views of history focused on the actions of the emperor and other powerful individuals. Such a view of history had a great impact upon the philosophies of history of both Wang Fuzhi and Zhang Xuecheng.

Wang Fuzhi's philosophy of history

Wang Fuzhi 王夫之 (1619–1692), also known as Wang Chuanshan 王船山, is the author of the most comprehensive philosophy of history to emerge from the classical Chinese culture. It is all the more surprising that he worked on it being a hermit living in a mud hut at the foot of a mountain in the south of China, remaining faithful to the Ming until the end of his days, barely remembered during life and forgotten soon after death, and rediscovered only in the mid-nineteenth century. Since the publication of his writings in the 1930s, his thought has been considered one of the greatest syntheses of Chinese philosophy, which resulted in a full edition of his works being published in 1992. His philosophy of history is expounded mainly in *Discussions on the Comprehensive Mirror* [*of History*] 讀通鑑論 *Dú Tōngjiàn lùn*, covering the period from the First Emperor to the Five Dynasties, and the *Treatise on the Song* 宋論 *Sōnglùn*, which forms a continuation of these reflections.

Wang Fuzhi's philosophy of history cannot be understood in isolation from his ontology, which is central to his philosophical system. This requires an analysis of the philosophical dictionary used by Wang Fuzhi, which consists of the concepts well-known from the Chinese tradition but reinterpreted in a new and distinctive manner. The key term in the field of his philosophy of history is the notion of 勢 *shì*, the tendency of the development of reality. This tendency stands in a specific relation to the principle of reality (*li*), matter (*qi*) and Dao. In one of the most concise definitions proposed by Wang Fuzhi, *li* is defined as what enables or disables events that are, as a result, possible or not. This process is regulated by Dao, while the tendency is responsible for the temporary (and therefore also historical) realization of the principle in things.[126] Wang Fuzhi considers *li* inseparable from *qi*, treating it as some sort of internal logic of what *qi* must necessarily be. In contrast to *li*, Dao as a regulating rule has a prescriptive character and refers primarily to people. Since reality consists only of matter and of the particulars 器 *qì*, Dao is realized only in specific things and cannot exist either beyond or before them.[127] If Dao is being practised in the world, then it exists in the world;[128] consequently, Dao, as a process of regulating numerous phenomena, changes with time.[129] In this sense, the ontology of Wang Fuzhi opts for the variability, immanence and concreteness of all the principles that could guide history, which already at the starting point situates Wang Fuzhi's philosophy of history within historical realism.

The proper understanding of the ontological background of Wang Fuzhi's philosophy of history requires emphasizing that the concept of *qi* employed by Wang Fuzhi involves animated, conscious and spiritual phenomena. The spirit (*shen*) is explicitly understood as the aspect of *qi*, and more precisely as the ability of *qi* for dynamic transformation and reunification, the ability that ultimately has a mysterious character and is incomprehensible to man.[130] Even then, Wang's ontology may be called a materialistic one, for the mechanistic or physicalist understanding of matter is just one of many possible approaches, alongside Hylozoism and the Stoic idea of pneuma, extremely close to the Chinese *qi* (not to mention dialectical materialism or the so-called new materialism that incorporate animated and psychic phenomena in a typically modern and post-modern way). As Nicholas Brasovan rightly observes, Wang Fuzhi's philosophy can be described as materialistic (let us add – in the ontological sense) with the proviso that 'matter' means *qi*, while spirit, consciousness and life are not reduced to a passive, 'dead' substrate, and *qi* itself includes changes of a sublime, mysterious and 'spiritual' nature.[131] It would be most correct to characterize Wang Fuzhi's ontology as a holistic one, that in which 'the realm of Heaven (Tian) and the realm of humans are simply one unified whole. There is no transcendent realm beyond the human world, and it is the same vital energy (*qi*) and the same principle (*li*) that permeate the realm of Heaven and the realm of humans.'[132] The basis of such a holistic ontology is the *Book of Changes*:

> The *Yijing* provides a naturalistic account of the world as a coherent, dynamic, self-regulating, holistic system. As such, the philosophy of the *Yijing* does not define any given phenomenon in terms of a discrete essence (...) [I]nstead, the phenomenon is identified by the way it functions and alters in relation to other phenomena (...) Every phenomenon is *constituted* by its relationships to others. In other words, relationships are internal as opposed to external and primary as opposed to secondary (...) In terms of holism, every part comes to embody, contain, or express the whole.[133]

Building ontology upon a vision of the holistic and autonomous system of changes leads to the thesis that all changes have a temporal nature and nothing exists beyond time.[134]

Nevertheless, the ideas taken from the *Yijing* receive an additional complement. The cyclical transformations of nature described in the *Book of Changes* became inscribed in the linear tendency (*shi*), which is eventually a temporary and historical realization of the internal and necessary logic (*li*) of reality. The *shi*, responsible for the flourishing and collapse of the states, is at the same time a tendency for the development of *qi*.[135] In addition, *shi* often retains its source meaning of a favourable position (including the location of China), which thereby affects the course of history.[136] *Shi* as such is actually a collective concept that includes a number of individual *shi* unfolding and abating depending on the logic of transformations of matter at a certain place and time of history.[137] With regard to the formal structure of *shi* and the relation of *shi* to other philosophical concepts, it may be said there is one *shi*, but eventually there exist many tendencies, which are often concurrent.

Characterizing the general structure of *shi*, Wang Fuzhi emphasizes that *shi* is gradually growing,[138] namely '[particular moments] in history have definite *shi*, and when it is weak, it cannot suddenly strengthen, and when it is strong, it weakens slowly.

Therefore, even when *shi* does not necessarily determine the crisis and collapse, one can determine it by oneself, trying to rapidly strengthen *shi* in conflict with its nature.'[139] In the weak tendency there are already the seeds of a strong *shi* and necessarily in a strong *shi* there are also present seeds of a subsequent weakening.[140] After reaching the maximum value, *shi* turns in the opposite direction.[141] As Jullien observes,

> In Wang Fuzhi's opinion, the course of history is always decided by a twofold logic. On the one hand, every tendency, once born, is naturally inclined to grow; on the other hand, any tendency carried to its ultimate limit becomes exhausted and cries out for reversal. This principle is absolutely general and constitutes the justification for alternation.[142]

These requirements have a striking resemblance to the laws of dialectics: the change of quantity into quality and the unity of opposites. The naturalness and the necessity of these dependencies is constantly emphasized, which makes them unique historical laws. As Wang Fuzhi writes, 'a strong *shi* in its final phase necessarily weakens, weak *shi* also finally reverses and changes, for such is the necessity of the changes of *shi*. Compliance with the necessary *shi* is [possible due to] the principle, while the naturalness of the principle is [identical with] Heaven. A noble man adapts to the principle of things, being agile to follow *shi*, which is why it has long been known that man cannot fight Heaven.'[143] Once set in motion, *shi* cannot be stopped, which is why the ancient rulers were restraining themselves before *shi* took on an uncontrollable form.[144] *Shi* is necessary (*biran*), usually as a *shi* of fall 必亡之勢 *biwàng zhī shì*.[145] It is extremely difficult to turn back *shi* and practically impossible to fight it, while after exceeding a certain value, *shi* is irreversible.[146]

The only way to save oneself when disasters occur everywhere as a consequence of *shi* is certainly not by relying upon one's own opinion, but adjusting to the *shi* of time, even if it means hatred on the part of other people or the need to harm them. Signs of the impending fall of the state are fortunately visible, thereby forming the basis for the lesson drawn by the rulers of the next dynasty.[147] The weakening of *shi* and the general impossibility of changing the historical position is accompanied by the decline of customs. Hence, one does not have to be a sage in order to recognize *shi*.[148] One should rather expect the upcoming change, because it comes gradually, although most people are impatient to do so.[149] The tendency of history is like a current of water, which finally makes a breach in the dam in just one day, so that all the water will totally pour out.[150]

The defeatist vision of the necessity to come to terms with *shi* raises the question of whether Wang Fuzhi's philosophy of history is a form of fatalism or historical determinism. In order to answer this question, it is worth looking at the way in which Wang Fuzhi applies the concept of historical tendency to the description of concrete historical changes.

Analysing the phenomenon of the end of the feudal system (*fengjian*), Wang Fuzhi emphasizes that this was the effect of changes lasting hundreds of years, and feudalism itself fell in one day only because the *shi* had already crossed the critical threshold.[151] The prefectural system (*junxian*) that replaced feudalism was distinguished by similar durability, bringing two thousand years of lasting political stability (in contrast to continuous wars between the warring states), which was the effect of *shi* recognized by the First Emperor.[152] Feudalism cannot return, but people tried to restore it, and as a result, the transition to the new system was also gradual.[153] The reasons for attempting to revive feudalism were the short period of time from the Three Dynasties era and a strong attachment to the institutions of feudalism. However, these attempts had to come to naught, because the *shi* favourable to them had already expired.[154] Not only will feudalism not come back: 'speaking from the viewpoint of the overall tendency of history 古今之通勢 *gǔjīn zhī tōngshì*, after the times of the Three Dynasties, it is no longer possible to combine rule by army and rule by culture, nor can one return to the well-field system or to the corporal punishment system'.[155] Thus, the analysis of the fall of feudalism is focused on the factors of irreversibility and necessity of change, and their linearity, combined with the idea of rendering the ancient institutions obsolete, brings this aspect of Wang Fuzhi's thought closer to the theory of progress, since – unlike for Wang Tingxiang – new changes are valued positively, as better suited to the times.

In the analysis of the reasons for the fall of the Tang and Song dynasty, however, the factors unaccounted for in the case of feudalism come to light. Wang Fuzhi draws attention not so much to the power of *shi* as to the effect of the interaction between the tendencies of history and man. As Wang states, a subject, when faced with things, may contribute to their development or regress through 'cooperation' with them; but if, contrary to things, one wants to trigger their progress, there will be an even deeper regress.[156] Wang Fuzhi writes that the founder of the Tang Dynasty, Tang Gaozu, using his 'mystical ear', heard the 'sound' of the upcoming changes, patiently waited for them and seized the moment.[157] Shortly afterwards, however, the hire of barbarian mercenaries led the Tang to the road of decline, though this was not anyone's goal.[158] As Wang emphasizes, the fall of the state takes place as part of a given *shi*, but due to only two direct causes (in the scale of history as a whole): bad ministers and barbarians.[159] The *shi* of the fall of the Tang was already decided during the An Lushan Rebellion, but the collapse of the dynasty was delayed by the actions of general Guo Ziyi,[160] therefore the fall can be stopped even after its preordaining, if only there are people capable of doing so. In other words, the necessary character of the *shi* of growth or fall is relative, i.e. unless people contribute to the development of the embryonic growth trend or stop the flourishing tendency of collapse, the *shi* itself, by virtue of its internal logic, will unfold in the predetermined direction. According to Wang Fuzhi, during the times of Emperor Xuanzong (712–756) it was still possible to save the Tang, but people did not believe in it anymore and this attitude of people ultimately determined the fall of the dynasty. Wang stresses that even the smallest stirring of resistance can maintain or overthrow a dynasty, for which no resources 資 *zī* are required: this was the case with the Han, Sui and Tang dynasties that fell as a result of grassroots uprisings, although resistance was not as extreme as in the case of the Qin or Mongol authorities.[161] The situation of the Song dynasty was similar. During the reign of Emperor Huizong (1082–1135), the *shi* of the fall was already necessary and unstoppable, not because of the increased power of the Jurchen who defeated the Khitan, but because people were no longer hopeful; if their minds had been different, a fall would not have been necessary.[162] Hence, Wang Fuzhi not only rejects the potential allegations of total determinism, but also incorporates some idealist motifs, claiming that with the right will and the right state of mind-heart, regardless of the lack of material means, one can reverse the course of history.

As JeeLoo Liu points out, Wang Fuzhi's philosophy of history is determined only by the general pattern of development of the whole system, but not the occurrence of individual events within it. It depends on people whether the current seeds of the trend mature or will never be stopped. Thus, 'rotation does not come at fixed points in history; in particular, it is not that after one hundred years of good times, bad times will necessarily ensue.' Of course, if people 'miss' the development of a given historical tendency, a moment will come when no one will be able to prevent it. Nevertheless, even if the internal maturation of the historical tendency is necessary, the human will is not determined by it. Therefore, although we know the law of the development of *shi*, we are not able to predict the future, because it depends on the human response/reaction to *shi*. What is more, Wang Fuzhi's interpretation of past events makes it impossible to attribute to him (atomistic) historical determinism no less than the question of the uncertainty of future. As Liu continues, order is not strictly the cause of chaos. Chaos is only the final phase of the maturing tendency towards chaos that exists parallel to an exhausting tendency of order.[163]

Jullien points out a holistic dimension of the philosophy of history based on the notion of historical tendency:

> For instead of constructing a hypothetical chain of causality, the Chinese favor an interpretation in terms of 'tendencies' from which they simply deduct the 'ineluctable' (...) In consequence, when we consider events „which do not come about in a single day," it is necessary to 'return to the starting point of the whole evolution' which, through continuous change, has resulted in things as they are (Hence the traditional interest in Chinese thought in a long-term view and the 'silent transformations' of time) (...) Historical evolution must be considered as an overall proces that constitutes a system in isolation (in contrast to the causal explanation that remains open) (...) Chinese civilization is particularly suited to such an attitude. Since it takes account only of its own tradition and considers it invariably from a unitary perspective (such being the strength of its ethnocentrism), it tends to consider its history as unfolding in isolation.[164]

The main, and sometimes almost the only, example used by Jullien to illustrate these general theses about Chinese culture is the philosophy of history of Wang Fuzhi,

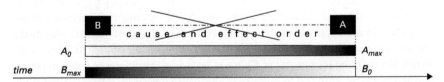

Figure 8 The development of historical tendency according to Wang Fuzhi (A – chaos, B – order).

treated (correctly) as the culmination of this tradition of interpreting history. Combining this with phenomenalism emphasized by Brosovan we get a holistic image that does not assume any essence or 'deep' layer of the historical process: from the perspective of a Western scholar, trained in such systems of ideas as occasionalism, a situation in which the opposite and parallel tendencies are compatible with each other without any external 'reconciliation' (namely God) is almost unthinkable, but from the viewpoint of Wang Fuzhi, for whom nature is a self-sufficient system of changes, not requiring any Creator or Overseer, it is a feature of history itself.

The frequency with which Wang Fuzhi reflects on the nature of historical change is not therefore surprising. In order to know and follow the principle of reality and the trend of its development, one should first recognize the specifics of a given time: different times imply different *shi*, and different *shi* also mean different *li*. Without it the world cannot be conquered.[165] One cannot practise rituals in the same way as in antiquity, because they change along with time, although a few rituals that remain unchanged throughout history might also be indicated.[166] Wang Fuzhi distinguishes two types of historical changes. The first type are the political changes, which are top-down and can be reduced to increasing or relaxing rigour. The second type are changes in customs, which are limited to simplification or refinement of the existing customs and have a bottom-up character. The people have ultimately no influence upon political changes, while power does not affect changes in culture, and even if it resists new customs, this only contributes to their even faster dissemination. Attempts to return to antiquity result only in chaos, the path of the ancients has gone forever.[167] Only the principles of reality are definitively determined, which cannot be said of positive law. Law depends on time and could be promoted or weakened, intricate or simple. Wang Fuzhi, however, does not settle with the merely formal characteristics of law, stressing – with regard to its content and at the same time its normative dimension – that law should be concerned with the people and the promotion of the virtuous.[168]

The list of what is constantly (although never supra-historically) important includes, unfortunately, many of Wang Fuzhi's prejudices. Wang argues that the hierarchy of society is universal, which also applies to the gender roles, because according to Wang, women cannot enter education, for it is a 'permanent limitation on the part of nature' 固天之所限 *gù Tiān zhī suǒxiàn*.[169] In addition to social and gender differences, the third universally important difference is, according to Wang, the one between the Chinese and barbarians. Barbarians are supposed to be composed of a different kind of matter than the Chinese, which translates into different habits and dissimilar ability to understand. The mixing of both types of *qi*: Chinese and barbarian, which started with the alliance between the Han and the Huns (Xiongnu), led to the fall of China. The classism, chauvinism and racism of Wang Fuzhi were not just a part of the cultural baggage carried by this thinker, especially considering that many philosophers of the Qing Dynasty did not share his views (particularly on the issue of women's education), but they were rather significant, ethnocentric limitations of his system. As Wang Fuzhi writes, 'the meaning [of history] of China, as regarding the difference between people and animals, is the universal meaning of the history of the world.'[170] It is true that Wang admits that the necessary laws of *shi* also apply to barbarians, not just to Chinese, since Heaven cannot prohibit their expansion, but it is so because of the Chinese and often for the sake of their admonition, as when the Tang allied with the barbarians, forgetting that since the *shi* of barbarians was then in a state of weakness, it would necessarily strengthen in the future.[171]

In such multifaceted view of history there is no room for plain and naïve idealization of the past. It is true that Wang believes that the next ages are not comparable to antiquity,[172] and that after the time of the Three Dynasties, the virtue of *ren* went by the wayside.[173] The justification for this view, however, is quite different than that in the case of the majority of orthodox Confucians referring to the vision of the degeneration of the universal model. Wang Fuzhi believes that the fall of *ren* results only from the fact that times have changed and what was moral then may turn out to be immoral in the present. One should recognize those of the ancient laws that are good, then find the reason why they were good then and reform them accordingly; in case there is no equivalent for the current situation in the past law, the reason for this state of affairs should be examined and in the light of this examination new laws should be established.[174] The idea of imitating antiquity does not make sense because remote antiquity (which should be theoretically imitated to the greatest extent) is the time when people were not different from animals, and which due to the lack of sources also disappears in the darkness of the past. Because each successive epoch meant development, including the development of manners, it cannot be said that these are worse times. This applies even to the Epoch of the Warring States, which in its own way was a development in comparison with the Spring and Autumn Epoch. Criticizing popular Chinese belief in the breakdown of values, Wang Fuzhi points out that this motif permeates even such cyclical philosophies of history as that of Shao Yong.[175] The background to this part of Wang Fuzhi's considerations is his view of the origins of humanity, from the perspective of which the striving to restore the ancient order turns out to be even more absurd. In ancient times people separated from animals,[176] and the first people, including the first Chinese, did not differ in any way from the barbarians. With time, the Chinese developed a culture (*wen*), the first element of which was farming.[177] Modern barbarians are therefore something between 'true' people and animals.

The current image of Wang Fuzhi's philosophy of history, however consistent it is with the majority of its presentations, is not complete. An important role is also played by the oldest Chinese historiosophical category – Tian. And although it is true that Tian means for Wang Fuzhi simply the totality of the natural world,[178] it is impossible to equate it only with visible nature. In the writings on the philosophy of history even within a single chapter Tian is once identified with the four seasons, and soon after personified ('sees').[179] This ostensible contradiction is explained by the fact that Wang Fuzhi distinguishes Heaven-in-itself 天之天 *Tiān zhī Tiān* from Heaven-as-it-is-known-by-men 人之天 *rén zhī Tiān*. Strictly speaking, Wang Fuzhi also distinguishes three other 'types' of Heaven, depending on whether it is grasped from the perspective of things, people or outstanding individuals;[180] *Tian zhi Tian* and *ren zhi Tian* are nonetheless the basic terms. The main consequence of this distinction in the philosophy of history is the idea that apart from the way in which the presence of Tian in history is recognized there exists an unrecognizable and incomprehensible modus of the historical activity of Heaven. As the opening of the *Songlun* states, the knowledge of Heaven is ultimately knowledge of nature, because *Tian* reveals itself by operating the course of things, determining their destiny (*ming*), so that in this role it cannot be replaced by man. At the same time, however, it is difficult to clearly predicate on Heaven, not because man cannot do it, but because Heaven does not have any permanent property.[181] Thus, Liu Liangjian mistakenly claims that Wang Fuzhi fully rationalized the category of Heaven.[182] This is only partially true, as far as it concerns Heaven-in-itself. Heaven as such is identical with the principle of things and the tendency of transformations.[183] Heaven is not conscious, hence the mandate of Heaven does not differ from the principle-*li*. In this sense, only this principle, naturally determines the course of things, in the process of its development, including the existence and passing of states, which is why it cannot be opposed.[184]

On the other hand, the same Heaven is said to give its mandate in advance, before a new ruler takes power, based on either his virtue (as in the time of the Three Dynasties) or achievements (since the Han dynasty); thus, people are not aware of it at that moment. Heaven also determines those changes that a man cannot know. The 'mind' and 'virtue' of Heaven can also be partly known in the way in which it supports the people.[185] These are all phrases regarding *ren zhi Tian*. Importantly, it is no less real than Heaven-in-itself, and it is certainly not less important in the context of investigating the laws governing human history. As Chen Ming emphasizes, the mystery and specific 'spirituality' of Heaven is manifested first of all in the way in which it engages in history itself and in how it emerges from the 'shadow' in which it usually hides.[186] Wang Fuzhi gives numerous examples of Heaven's involvement in history. We read that the ruler of the Qin unified China to satisfy his vested interest, but Heaven used his interest 私 *sī* in a rather incomprehensible and mysterious (*shen*) way in order to accomplish something general 公 *gōng* in history.[187] Tian 'used the hands' of Empress Wu Zetian in a similar vein.[188] Tian contributed to the victory of the founders of the Zhou.[189] The same Heaven also 'wanted' the extermination of the Qin, Sui and Mongol dynasties, using concrete people for this purpose.[190] The reason why Heaven used these people was to relieve the people.[191] Such an understanding of the relation between Tian and the people is similar to Hegel's *List der Vernunft*. Jullien warns, however:

> But the analogy itself makes the difference between these two concepts of history all the more striking and reveals the wide divergence between each discourse. Hegel conceives reason in history as a relation between a 'means' and an 'end': everything that comes to pass over time, including the actions of great men, is only the means through which the 'end of universe' is realized, namely, man's accession to an awareness of liberty. For Hegel, who was an heir to the Judeo-Christian tradition, universal history should be regarded as a progress, the fulfillment of which constitutes from the beginning its rightful direction (. . .) The concept of *shi*, right from its initial formation in connection with strategy, never dealt with any such relation between means and end, however natural that relation may seem to us. If Heaven can make use of the individual interests of great men within the framework of history, it is purely through the internal determination of a process that will unfailingly manifest its eminently regulatory role when conceived in its global dimensions. But no providence, or concerted plan, is involved here (. . .) It seems to have no place for any idea of a pure, abstract future. The time in which the

process unfolds is infinite. Its logic, since it is self-regulating, implies no end. An end to history is unthinkable.[192]

According to Wang Fuzhi, history is essentially an open process: both to factors that escape our understanding (the actions of Heaven) and to the unknown future.

This is related to the distinctive deficiency of the normative element, so representative of many Chinese philosophies of history, which usually requires the adoption of a universal model. Wang Fuzhi states that virtue and righteousness do not guarantee historical success, because it is more important to employ the power of developing *qi*.[193] This is confirmed by the holistic character of Wang Fuzhi's philosophy of history, which emphasizes the necessity of taking into account all historical phenomena: political, military, social and cultural.[194] Wang Fuzhi believes that a comprehensive approach to history should replace the dynastic criterion that prevails in traditional approaches. The periods of order and chaos determined by *shi* only adventitiously overlap with the establishment or overthrow of the dynasty. Particular criticism is targeted at the theory of dynastic legitimization (*zhengtong*), which sanctioned the traditional approach to Chinese history, as based on the erroneous theory of *wuxing* that tries to treat the fact of the unification of China as a specifically religious event.[195] Importantly, Wang Fuzhi does not reject the idea of drawing lessons from history, but stresses that one should not draw conclusions from a stretch of time, but from all of history, which is possible due to Heaven, which connects the past, present and future. The meaning of the whole history is different from the meaning of its individual parts.[196] This means Wang Fuzhi's holism is of both synchronic and diachronic in nature. In addition, one can learn only from histories that faithfully depict the past. Exaggerations and false praise are unacceptable.[197] Wang does not deprecate the Classics, finding in the *Chunqiu* a universal method of dealing with barbarians.[198] In contrast to our next thinker, he did not historize the Classics.

Zhang Xuecheng's philosophy of history

Just as Wang Fuzhi's philosophy of history is the culmination of the classical speculative philosophy of history in China, so the thought of Zhang Xuecheng 張學誠 (1738–1801) is a specific summa of the Chinese philosophy of historiography, and even an attempt to synthesize speculative and critical philosophy of history. As in the case of Wang Fuzhi, Zhang Xuecheng also remained virtually unknown during his life and in the years immediately following his death. His main work, *Comprehensive Meaning of Literature and Histories* 文史通義 *Wénshǐ tōngyì*, was only published in 1832.

The basic concept of Zhang Xuecheng's philosophy is Dao.[199] Dao is that by which beings are what they are 所以然 *suǒyǐrán*, and not what they ought to be according to men 所當然 *suǒdāngrán*. Dao is the very process of change, the alternation of the forces of *yin* and *yang*, and not the result of this process, which always has a form and name. Therefore, Dao does not have any direct definition. At the same time, Dao has its source in Tian-nature and cannot be separated from concrete, material things, just as shadows cannot be separated from the shapes that cast it. Dao had existed before people appeared in the world, so it is not their creation. Unlike most Chinese philosophers, however,

Zhang Xuecheng believes that Dao is changing in time and even more – in the course of human history. With the establishment of social life ('as soon as three people lived with each other'), the already present Dao adopted a form, so that with the development of human communities it begin to manifest 著 *zhù* itself in new, emerging social institutions, which were increasingly complex. As a result of population increase, a sovereign able to control the masses of the people was appointed. Then, teachers and schools were established, property and division of land appeared, including the well-field system, and – generally speaking – the feudal system. Following Liu Zongyuan, Zhang Xuecheng states that all this was the result of the necessary trend of history, *shi*, and not the intention of the sages. Although Dao does not act and cannot be seen, the sages followed Dao through living in accordance with reality (which is the manifestation of Dao), in this case the necessary trend of history. In the process of continuous development, from the beginning of the world to the time of the Zhou dynasty, it is impossible to omit the numerous traces 跡 *jì* of the presence of Dao. The constant apophaticism of the category of Dao in the thought of Zhang Xuecheng has an almost religious character:

> Zhang avoids saying what the Dao is. But it manifests itself in all aspects of social life that develop gradually (. . .): the moral code ('the concepts of benevolence and rightness, loyalty and filial piety'), laws, the division of labor, land tenure, education, political structure, culture. Zhang's Dao therefore seems to be the basic potential in human nature for living an ordered, civilized life, a potential that gradually writes itself out in history, and actualizes itself in what man must come to regard as right and true. The Dao 'comes form Heaven.' But 'Heaven' for Zhang is really the order of nature, regarded with reverence. His Dao therefore commands all the respect of a religious absolute, even though it is not supernatural. He insists that the Dao must always, in itself, be distinguished from the 'forms' it takes in history, yet one gains no idea of it except through these forms. The result is that Zhang has an essentially religious reverence for the human moral order, yet at the same time he sees it as completely evolutionary and naturalistic.[200]

As Nivison continues, Zhang's sages are only people, not the 'incarnations' of Dao, and free people who are not used in any way by Dao, as is the case with Hegel's historical heroes[201] or – let us add – the heroes of Wang Fuzhi.

However, Zhang Xuecheng does not believe that historical development runs infinitely. It had already achieved its fullness during the Zhou dynasty and nobody will ever be able to add anything to it. The Dao was practised perfectly by the Prince of Zhou, and it was exhausted by the teachings of Confucius in the field of learning.[202] Moreover, in those days there was a direct 'transmission of mind' 心傳 *xīnchuán*, which transmitted the content that cannot be said and which is most closely related to Dao.[203] Above all, governments and teaching were not discrete areas of life at that time. It was only with time (exactly from the Qin dynasty) that both areas were separated, which ruined the state of harmony in which Dao was related to everyday human affairs 人倫 日用 *rénlún rìyòng*, and all the writings in which Dao was taught dealt with current political affairs.[204] Dao, once public and common to all, began to be treated as a Dao of a specific school, the 'truth' possessed by a select group (the Mohists, Confucians, etc.), and in this way became subject to pluralization and privatization.[205] As Nivison rightly observes, such a vision raises objections concerning its compliance with the metaphysical postulates of Zhang Xuecheng. First, if Dao is significantly different from its manifestations and cannot be exhausted by them, how can it be completely manifested in the ways of Zhou? Secondly, what caused the fall of the ideal state? Zhang does not answer this question anywhere, and even considers this event to be unexplained or caused by the mysterious activity of Heaven.[206] Thus, faith in the 'completeness' of Zhou's achievements also receives a quasi-religious background.

Once the complete Dao 'relinquished' history, recording current affairs ceased to be a report of the presence of Dao in the world. From the Han dynasty onwards, the works written in the golden age and edited by Confucius began to be treated as the Classics, transmitting some universal and timeless truths. Zhang Xuecheng strongly criticizes this view. According to the famous opening sentence of the *Wenshi tongyi*, 'all Six Classics are histories. The ancients did not compose treaties, nor did they leave practical matters to discuss the principle; the Six Classics are simply current political documents of former rulers.'[207] Even the *Book of Changes*, as penetrating changes, was a kind of general history. The writings known later as classical do not, therefore, deal with anything other than the affairs of their times, and they say nothing that would correspond to later times. At the same time, this did not mean a downgrading of the status of the Classics, which in Zhang's opinion conveyed the Dao fully and effectively. In other words, wanting to reconcile the Confucian faith in the primacy of the Classics and the belief in the complete historization of Dao, Zhang Xuecheng historized the Classics that transmit the Dao. It was not an act of desacralization or an attack in the style of Straussian Biblical criticism but, on the contrary, a critical expression of reverence and devotion. Elsewhere, we read that 'the great significance of the Six Classics is as clear as the sun and moon, and the successes and failures of the Three Dynasties can be extended [as lessons] for hundreds of generations.'[208] As On-cho Ng points out, Zhang Xuecheng's historism was thus limited for other reasons: 'this note of finality issuing from Zhang's faith in antiquity meant foreclosure of the historical process. The absolute normative tradition had come into being once upon a time, and it provided the most instructive and edifying path to be followed by all ages.'[209] The normative dimension of Dao also determines the value of post-Qin history of China as a fall, which was reflected in his view of the degeneration of Dao.

In his philosophy of history, Zhang Xuecheng distinguishes three basic historical periods: the development from the beginning of humanity, the peak period of the Zhou, and finally its collapse, progressing as a sequence of cycles:

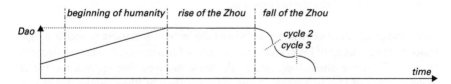

Figure 9 The general scheme of human history according to Zhang Xuecheng.

These cycles are determined by the intellectual fashions 風氣 *fēngqì* prevailing in a given era and effectively preventing the full understanding of the Dao. As Zhang writes,

> The world cannot be deprived of these intellectual fashions, and intellectual fashions cannot change other than cyclically (...) When intellectual fashion begins, it necessarily takes something as its main subject. Therefore, philology, literature and philosophy cannot avoid over- and undervaluation. When intellectual fashion matures, it already contains some defects [which are the reason for its disappearance].[210]

The order of fashions is fixed and necessary, their repetition is infinite, and what is more – this sequence is independent of man and cannot be overcome or changed by human strength.[211] The surprising lack of history among these three fashions is perfectly explained by Ivanhoe, who notes that history is the main discipline that allows the Dao to be understood in each time, and therefore does not belong to the order of erroneous fashions that should not be followed.[212] According to Zhang Xuecheng's response to the letter of Shen Zaiting, the epochs of philology, literature and philosophy correspond to (respectively): knowledge, talent and insight (among the abilities cultivated by the adults) and memory 記性 *jìxìng*, creativity 作性 *zuòxìng*, and intelligence 悟性 *wùxìng*, as far as innate abilities are concerned. The writings of philologists establish scientific achievements, literary works – beautiful expressions, while the writings of philosophers promote virtue. The times of the Han dynasty were the epoch of philology, the times of the Tang dynasty – the age of literature, and the times of the Song and Ming dynasty – of philosophy. During the Qing Dynasty, the age of philology returns. Each of these fashions is only one aspect of Dao, thus privileging one of them at the expense of others results in a deflection from the Way. This is particularly true of philosophy, which upon moving away from science, becomes merely vain speculation.[213] Dao can be fully grasped only when it is practised, and speculation makes us depart from it. For this reason, it is necessary to combine philology, literature and philosophy.[214] As another letter of Zhang reads,

> Those who place the highest priority on philology tend to be not well versed in literature. Those who pursue philosophy usually neglect empirical facts (...) This is why philosophy tends toward being vague and pointless, philology becomes nothing but a review of the dregs of former glories, and literature ends up being a mere plaything (...) [But] philology is just an empirical manifestation of philosophical principle and literature is simply a tool used to convey it. These pursuits are not fundamentally different.[215]

This passage therefore imposes an additional distinction, according to which insight concerns the meaning of history, talent is equated with language, and knowledge with events.[216] Therefore, the full picture of the three fashions that express the fall of understanding of Dao in human history since the time of Zhou can be depicted as follows:

Epoch	Cultivated ability	Innate ability	Subject of inquiry	The aim of inquiry	Devolution	Historical period
philology	knowledge	memory	events	achievements	archivalism	Han; Qing
literature	talent	creativity	language	expressions	mannerism	Tang
philosophy	insight	intelligence	meaning	virtue	speculation	Song-Ming

Figure 10 Zhang Xuecheng's view on the historical cycles of the degenerated understanding of Dao.

The closest Western counterpart to this aspect of Zhang Xuecheng's reflection is undoubtedly the philosophy of history of the almost contemporaneous Giambattista Vico (1668–1744), who also distinguished three epochs that were circling in time and returning, which were identified as being dominated by some cognitive powers and cultural forms. Interestingly, Vico also shared opinion that these cycles come after the essentially linear and universal revealed history.

The intellectual fashions distinguished by Zhang Xuecheng apply, of course, only to Chinese culture. As Nivison points out, 'Zhang's historical and cultural world is so incredibly *one* (and therefore so totally Chinese) that in it there can be only diffusion from a common source, from one Dao in the beginning of history; there is never genuine intellectual convergence.' As a result, Zhang treats all of the non-Confucian philosophical schools as developing teachings taught in one of the Classics, believing that even Buddhism – like Daoism – is originally derived from the teachings of the *Book of Changes.*[217] His essay on the original Dao 原道 *Yuán Dào* is the answer to Han Yu's essay with the same title, in which the Tang thinker showed the superiority of the Confucian Dao over the Dao of the Daoists and Buddhists. According to Zhang, Dao is basically one, and since it is also universal, the solution was a distinctive type of Confucian inclusivism.

The notions of talent, knowledge and insight, which were used in the threefold typology of epochs, are identical with the three conditions of being a good historian distinguished by Liu Zhiji. Zhang Xuecheng associates them (respectively) with the language of narrative, recorded events and the 'meaning of history'. The knowledge of a historian is based on memorization and recitation, and talent on the flowery use of words, whereas a historian's insight is expressed in the selection of events. The meaning of the history according to which this should be done comes from Heaven 史之義出 於天 *shǐ zhī yì chūyú Tiān*,[218] and since nothing is said about it, it could be assumed with a high degree of certainty that the universal meaning of history is just Dao. In this way, Zhang Xuecheng combines the speculative philosophy of the historical process and the (critical) philosophy of historiography.

Zhang, however, almost immediately adds that the three conditions highlighted by Liu Zhiji are not sufficient, for it is necessary to distinguish the fourth, which is 'the virtue of a historian' 史德 *shǐdé*. The virtue of a historian is the way in which his mind-heart functions 心術 *xīnshù*, in the sense that the one who writes a scandalous or slanderous chronicle shows that he is actually a scandalmonger or slanderer. In a broader sense, *shide* means not so much the virtue as the morality of a historian, which only sometimes may be deemed good. Never can a historian be a mere 'prisoner of events' 為事役也 *wèi shì yì yě*. It is historical events themselves that make people happy or sad, and that are right or wrong, which gives rise to some unrestrained emotions in the historian, namely the physical flow and accumulation of *qi*, resulting in such and such feelings. These feelings are translated into a work and it is them, not the style itself, that attract readers. Therefore, one cannot leave this process to take its course, but one has rather to cultivate *shide* in accordance with the principle of reality, Heaven and the meaning of history, or simply – Dao. Emphasizing the almost physiological aspect of the impact of feelings and valuation on the work of the historian (*qi* is said to flow through blood vessels directly to the historian's heart-mind), Zhang adds that historians are often unaware of the way their mind-hearts work, so it should finally be brought to light.[219] Zhang Xuecheng wants to show that focus only on the narrative language (typical for Ming philosophers of historiography) or the events alone[220] ignores the role of all the unconscious evaluations which are rooted in natural feelings and precede the recording of events, something that Western hermeneutics calls 'pre-judgements'.[221]

The hermeneutic analogies are here largely justified, for Zhang Xuecheng is vitally interested in the issue of interpreting and understanding historical works from a modern perspective. The essay *On Breadth and Conciseness* 博約 *Bóyuē* reads as follows:

> When reading books and researching the past, there are moments in which we experience original insights that will not change for the rest of our lives. In the learning process, we encounter the most subtle feelings: reading books and examining the past we have moments of joy, as well as of sadness, when we suddenly cry because of what we cannot understand (...) Today people do not study these things and do not match the ancient ones. Not because they are not equal to their abilities, but because circumstances have changed (...) This is the first difference between people today and in the past. In addition, since the functions of the official and the teacher have been separated, people rely only on written records as the source of their practice: Dao no longer manifests itself in concrete things, and its course is no longer embodied in the duties of the officials. This is the second difference (...) Heavenly time and human affairs, the present and the past cannot be reconciled by force. It is something that cannot be overcome with human strength or wisdom (...) As far as Dao is concerned, it should be grasped in its entirety. When emotions are enriched with suffering and joy, anger and pleasure, when understanding the circumstances will be extended by penetrating changes, [leading to] obtaining knowledge that is extensive, but not dispersed, succinct but not stark, such knowledge will be clean and stable, and maybe then it will be possible to approach Dao: Dao of what has passed and what will come.[222]

The starting point of Zhang Xuecheng's distinctive hermeneutics is the belief in a radical difference between the interpreter who lives in the present times and the interpreted ancient work or historical figure. The process of the degeneration of Dao certainly did not lead to a better understanding of the past. Human emotions are involved in understanding characters and words from the past, which – insofar as they are cleansed – can get closer to the original, interpreted object. In practice, however, we tend to veer between the miscomprehension and pre-judgements that we adopt for life.

The above description suggests that understanding the past is ultimately an individual matter, just as human emotions are individual. Zhang Xuecheng emphasizes, however, that 'what makes human emotions valuable is that we can understand each other by sharing joy'. In other words, emotions are common and comprehensible to all people. The problem is rather to capture them based on their expression, namely their traces (*ji*). And so it is with people in the future who will look at us in the same way as we look at those from the past.[223] Based on the understanding 解 *jiě* of common emotions, on the grounds of the existing sources-traces, the historian makes inferences 推 *tuī* that relate to the ultimately incommunicable and ineffable 不能言與數者 *bùnéng yán yǔ shù zhě* historical experience of participating in events. The participants would, paradoxically, be unable to describe their situation; for example, those who experienced the tyranny of Jie would be at a loss for words to have it recorded in full.[224] Temporal distance is therefore a condition for the interpretation of history. With time, along with the course of history, these inferences accumulate,[225] thereby creating a tradition of interpretation. Such an accumulation of interpretation can be treated as progress. In addition to the increase in knowledge, an important feature of this progress is also the correction of the previous mistakes.[226] Tradition understood in this way is obviously a burden, because every author tries – within his own abilities – not to repeat what has been said before him.[227] An even greater mistake is to stop at fragmentary analyses and refrain from conscious and comprehensive interpretation in the expectation that our descendants will accomplish this.[228] This raises the question of how to make such an interpretation.

According to Zhang Xuecheng, first of all one should be respectful 敬 *jìng* towards the interpreted figures, which manifests itself in due concentration and control of one's *qi*, and then one needs to equip oneself with empathy 恕 *shù*, which does not mean indulgence, but it is the ability to put oneself in place of the people from the past 為古人設身 *wèi gǔrén shè shēn*. Even if one understands the epoch in which the ancients lived, without understanding their own individual perspectives 身處 *shēnchù* their writings should not be discussed.[229] At the same time, one should be careful not to let empathy transform into an anachronism, resulting in imputing to the ancient the views they would not have hypothetically accepted. In this way, one does not deal as much with the people from the past as with one's own views.[230]

This raises, of course, the question, of whether we ever really deal with people from the past or rather that we only imagine that we are in their place. As Ivanhoe argues, Zhang Xuecheng believes that in an ideal situation, on the basis of shared human nature, we are able to understand people from the past. In this respect Zhang gets close to the standpoint of Collingwood, for both thinkers believe that we can understand people from the past to the same extent as they understood each other[231] (and even better in terms of the description of their experiences). Nivison reminds us, however, that Zhang Xuecheng would not accept Collingwood's idea that history is a history of thought.[232] For Zhang, history is no less real than the Dao, being a series of everyday (including academic) practices.

Conclusion

In summary, the philosophers of history active at the threshold and in the middle phase of the Qing dynasty had a lot in common, which was the result of the fact that their views grew out of or within the *kaozheng* movement. They were connected by a more or less radical historism and the conviction that the philosophy of history can no longer rely on the dynastic scheme. Particular attention was given to the *Book of Changes*, which was believed to contain a ready-made pattern of history, which culminated in the thought of Wang Fuzhi. At the same time, the importance and function of human feelings present in both everyday (Dai Zhen) and academic (Zhang Xuecheng) practice was emphasized, which was seen as a remedy for Song speculation, and in part also for Ming subjectivism.

Nevertheless, attempts were made to synthesize these (supposedly) mutually exclusive images, in a way that would transcend the Song debate between idealists and materialists (in the sense proposed in the previous chapter). In the case of Huang Zongxi, it resulted rather in a syncretic attempt to reconcile the School of Principle, the School of Mind-Heart and materialists, while Gu Yanwu mainly aimed at reconciling the vision of the developmental tendency of history (*shi*) with a specific 'historical psychology'. These two ideas were in some sense separated and taken to their developmental limits by Wang Fuzhi and Zhang Xuecheng. Wang, accepting the historical role of the mysterious Heaven, made a partial inclusion of the idealist trend, although due to ontological assumptions and belief in the absence of the supra-historical driving force of history, he was inclined towards historical realism. Zhang Xuecheng, on the other hand, approached the idealist position: although he stressed the practicality of Dao, he believed that it existed before people, understanding it as absolutely effective, standard of conduct – and research for people living in all ages – although only when it has been historically embodied.

Thus, in this way, Wang Fuzhi concluded the Ming theory of historical process based on reflection upon the structure of *shi*, while Zhang Xuecheng in his (eventually tragic) narrative about historical dissonance between Dao and human feelings made an impressive synthesis of the speculative philosophy of history and the philosophy of historiography. His thought crowns the centuries-old development of the classical Chinese philosophy of history.

Encompassing History

The Distinctiveness of the Chinese Philosophy of History

Introduction

The detailed analysis of individual Chinese philosophers of history of the classical period will be inductively generalized here, as was promised in the Introduction. At the same time, this chapter will structurally correspond to the conclusion of a syllogism, thus in this framework the major premise would be constituted by Chapter 1, which presents the accepted understanding of the philosophy of history and the idea of holism in the philosophy of history, while the minor premise consists of the other chapters that documented the presence of these categories in the works of concrete philosophers of history in pre-nineteenth century China. Therefore, in this chapter, the last chapter of the book, the following issues will be examined:

- in a *synchronic* approach: whether and to what extent the Chinese tradition of philosophical reflection on the historical process and historical writing meets the accepted definition of the philosophy of history and leads to its modification;
- in a *diachronic* approach: how the evolution of the Chinese philosophy of history has developed from its beginnings to the end of the eighteenth century, if it is considered from the perspective of the history of ideas;
- in a *critical* approach: whether and how the development of the Chinese philosophy of history was determined by various forms of the idea of holism in the philosophy of history, including the opposition to these approaches (in the sense adopted in Chapter 1).

These conclusions will therefore constitute a relatively independent part of this work, providing some general conclusions for further comparative and historical research, the perspectives of which will be outlined in the proper conclusion of this book.

The synchronic approach: the philosophy of history in classical China

The philosophy of history is identified here with any kind of philosophical reflection (that is, reflection that is sufficiently general and explicit) regarding history as such, namely the meaning (sense) of history in general, regardless of whether it is a historical process or historical writing. The last case concerns the philosophy of historiography, which from the sixth century CE onwards became an integral part of Chinese philosophical reflection. Integral, since it was closely related to historical practice, without losing its general character, as evidenced by individual concepts. The most important Chinese philosophers of historiography, namely Liu Zhiji and Zhang Xuecheng, were predominantly interested in issues such as the relation of historiography to literature, the conditions of credibility for historical works, the general types and styles of historical narrative, the model of an ideal historian, the relationship between historians and the readers of their works and, finally, the impact of emotions and political conditions on the character of historical narrative. In addition, other philosophers of historiography such as Dong Zhongshu, Liu Xie, Ouyang Xiu, Wang Yi, Wang Shizhen and Hu Yinglin also dealt with such problems as reconstructing the intentions of historical actors, social responsibility and the public dimension of a historian's work, and made important decisions in a vital debate on the relation of the chronicles to the Classics, a significant part of which consists of the canonized historical works, which ultimately came to be treated in the spirit of all-encompassing historism. These are all issues taken up by the contemporary continental and analytical philosophy of historiography, only expressed in a different language and using other concepts which were native to the Chinese soil. The fact that the philosophy of historiography had existed in China before the birth of this field of reflection in the West should not surprise anyone in the light of the scope and continuity of Chinese historiography and the social position of historians in this culture, who frequently happened to be philosophers (and often also poets and calligraphers). Hence, the Chinese philosophy of historiography was strongly associated with other fields of knowledge, which is why there was not a separate technical term for it (the nearest terms, such as *dushi* or *kaoshi*, referred to the analysis and study of historiography in general). In contrast to the analytical philosophy of history, it was also much more closely related to speculative thought, which was emblematically expressed in Zhang Xuecheng's dictum, proclaiming that 'the meaning of historiography comes from Heaven'. Surprisingly, this relationship emphasized ethical issues much more than metaphysical ones, so the philosopher of historiography was not a servant of the philosopher of history. The importance of the educational role of the chronicles, as well as the 'virtue of a historian', has led to (probably) the greatest contribution to the idea of the philosophy of historiography made by the Chinese. It was a philosophy of historiography that was not based on criticism of the speculative philosophy of history and was not embedded in scientific (or post-scientific) thinking. The main tension resulted rather from the relationship between aesthetics and the ethics of historical writing, to which the epistemological and metaphysical themes were subjected.

The personal and ideological connections between the philosophy of historiography and the historical practice itself do not mean that it merges in some way with the implicit visions of the meaning of history, called here 'historiosophies'. Through these visions, I understand the approach to the meaning of history not so much theoretically expressed as implied by historical narrative, the adopted schematization of history or poetic forms of expression of historical consciousness. Historiosophy of this type preceded the development of mature philosophical reflection (see historiosophy of the bronze inscriptions, the *Book of Songs*, the *Book of Documents* and the *Spring and Autumn Annals* with commentaries), and since the formation of official historical writing in the Han period, it also accompanied philosophical reflection. As is evident from the examples of the great Chinese historians: Sima Qian and Ban Gu, their historiosophy much more often drew upon the existing concepts of the philosophers of history than contributed to their development. In addition, in their narrative and schematization of history, Chinese historians preferred speculative concepts, referring to Heaven or the principle of historical cycles. In this way, their historiosophy was much more strongly connected with the speculative philosophy of history than the philosophy of historiography. It was historiosophy which was responsible for the diffusion and final popularization of the basic categories of the Chinese philosophy of history. A monumental example of this dependence is Zhu Xi, who realized that in order to popularize his view of history, he had to rewrite the history of China, thereby creating the *Tongjian gangmu*. The Western philosophy of history in the eighteenth and nineteenth centuries did not play such a role, for it was not a conceptual reservoir of ideas employed by historians (the later exception is, of course, Marxist historiography, which was, however, intended to be a scientific historiography).

This leads us to the speculative philosophy of history, in which the question concerning the meaning of history translates into the question about the source (basis) of the sense of historical process. In the paradigmatic form proposed by Confucius, and brought to its conclusion by Zhang Xuecheng, the ultimate source of the sense of history is Dao. Dao pervades history and at the same time is relatively independent from it. Therefore, this view led to idealistic positions. Since in most cases it is believed that Dao at some point lost its connection with human history, or rather people lost contact with Dao, which never ceases to mean a universal standard of conduct, this view (except for its Neo-Daoist variant) leads to a regressive and pessimistic view of history. The principle of the meaning of history is in this case also a moral principle. In another tradition, which was initiated by the Legalists, and sewn up by Wang Fuzhi, the source of the sense of history is the tendency of history, *shi*, which was defined as the rational yet directly invisible structure of historical transformations themselves. For this reason, this philosophical current entailed realist positions. Since *shi* can mean both a tendency of order and chaos, this approach quite often combined the cyclic and linear images of history. Unlike Dao, *shi* is only a law explaining the course of history at the descriptive level. And thus, although the theory of *shi* is essentially open to the future and does not lead to any regressive views, which otherwise would have assumed the idealization of the lost past and a return to antiquity in a rejection of new circumstances, it does not, due to its anormativity, imply the concept of progress, which is unambiguously optimistic about the future history of mankind. There are, of course, many theoretical positions located between these two types of responses to the question about the meaning of history, to which I shall return in the paragraph on the evolution of the Chinese philosophy of history. These two attitudes are nevertheless of a fundamental character, being shared by many Chinese philosophers of history.

It should also be explained what in practice it means to say that Dao or *shi* is the source of the meaning of history. It means that from the perspective of the dynamics of these principles, certain historical events receive an extraordinary historical significance, a certain value. From the perspective of the transformation of Dao's presence in history, the collapse of the Zhou dynasty, which in a strict historical sense does not differ in importance from the collapse of for instance the Han dynasty, grows into a historical breakthrough followed by a general ethical and moral fall. From the perspective of the transformation of the tendencies of history (*shi*), such an event as the fall of the Tang Dynasty turns out to be the result of a several-hundred-year, directly imperceptible trend towards chaos, initiated by hiring mercenary troops drawn from barbarians. In light of these practical consequences, the link between the Chinese philosophy of history, historiosophy and historiography in general becomes clear.

It is thus sufficient to treat the Chinese views of history as responses to the specific questions that concretize and follow the general question about the meaning of history, as argued in Chapter 1 in relation to one such list proposed by Marek Wichrowski. To the first such question suggested by Wichrowski, namely whether the nature of historical process can be the subject of knowledge, the vast majority of Chinese philosophers of history answered affirmatively. The exceptions were classical Daoists, although the only fragment arguing directly for historical agnosticism comes from the late and rather unreliable chapter of the *Liezi* devoted to Yang Zhu. The next question posed by Wichrowski, i.e. of whether there is a specific pattern of historical change, and if so, whether it is knowable, can be combined into one, since it is impossible to find a Chinese philosopher of history who would postulate the existence of a scheme of historical changes, but when asked about this scheme would answer that he does not know anything about it. In other words, the Chinese philosophers of history were further divided into those who defended the existence of a recognizable pattern of history and those who believed that such a scheme does not exist, or at least is not knowable. The supporter of the last option was partly Ouyang Xiu, who claimed – from an epistemological viewpoint – that knowledge of speculative historical schemas is not necessary for us to know history. At the same time, the knowledge of history in general is still possible for him by virtue of reference to the general intentions of the ancient sages based on their writings. One can, therefore, be a speculative philosopher of history without accepting the existence of any linear, cyclical or mixed patterns of history. Philosophers of history who openly rejected the existence of a certain pattern of the historical process were Xunzi, Yang Xiong, Jia Yi, Wang Chong, Ge Hong, Liu Shao and Dai Zhen. What is more, most of them put forward a number of arguments pointing out the inconsistency or arbitrariness of especially cyclical interpretations of history, which due to a lack of a linear scheme in their thought resulted in the absence of any speculative scheme. History is determined for them only by unschematizable activities of the sages (Xunzi, Yang Xiong, Ge Hong), heroes (Liu Shao) or the people (Jia Yi). Wang Chong is an example of a thinker who rejected the schematization of history, but who also did not believe that people are the creators of history. Hence, only one Chinese philosopher of history represented the option which was dominant within the Greco-Roman historical consciousness.

Chinese philosophers of history, who accepted the existence of a pattern of history can be then asked, after Wichrowski, whether this pattern is reversible, that is, who of them accepted the existence of historical cycles. In contrast to Wichrowski, however, we will not consider that the only alternative to the cyclical approach is a strictly linear one, as the Chinese usually combined both. Cyclical philosophies in the strict sense, i.e. those that assumed the succession of cycles to infinity without the distinguished landmarks that would otherwise orient it in a linear manner, could be found only in the philosophies of Zou Yan, Zhong Changtong and Shao Yong. The first accepted the existence of natural cycles, the second – of political ones, and the third – of metaphysical ones. Few, such as Zhang Xuecheng, accepted a linear view before a certain historical moment, and argued for a cyclical change of the subsequent period of history. In most cases, however, historical cycles are inscribed in the superior linearity of the historical process. Starting from the *Book of Documents* and the philosophy of Mencius, this synthesis acquires a classic form of the vision of dynastic cycles inscribed in the general process of the fall. This idea reached the peak of its complexity in the philosophy of the Han-era thinkers: Dong Zhongshu and Liu Xin, while its central assumption of the presence of cyclicality in any type of linear historical change was radicalized by the brothers Cheng and Zhu Xi. Independently, the synthetic view of historical cycles inscribed into one line of history was adopted by philosophers speculating on the nature of the tendencies of history, *shi*: Chen Liang, Wang Tingxiang, Zhang Juzheng, Li Zhi and Wang Fuzhi. Due to the fact that these cycles are not elements of the general tendency, but its phases, cycles themselves also reveal their internal linear structure running from the minimum intensity to the maximum saturation (or vice versa). As a result, on the 'micro' level one can notice the linear nature of changes, while on the 'medium' level the cycles emerging from these changes can be observed, which at the 'macro' level turn out to fall within the overall, linear tendency of history. The cycle only mediates linearity, since this is for these philosophers merely a technical concept, to which they devote much less attention than to the structure of *shi*.

Many strictly linear views may also be found among the Chinese philosophies of history, which is important as the Chinese philosophy of history is often identified with a cyclical image of history. These include those views that characterize the linearity of history without distinguishing its phases or periods (Su Xun, Gu Yanwu, Huang Zongxi) and those that divide the linearly unfolding historical process into a specific number of epochs. These epochs, understood as phases of the line, must not be confused with cycles, because each epoch is unique and its course is irreversible. This concept was represented by the authors of the vision of *datong*, the Mohists, the Legalists: Shang Yang and Han Fei, Lu Jia, He Xiu, Huan Tan, the authors of the *Huainanzi* and the *Taipingjing*, Han Yu, Wang Anshi, Liu Zongyuan and Li Gou. In the case of the Neo-Daoists and Li Gou, this was a three-part approach consisting of phases 'utopia-fall-return', while the Mohists opted for a four-part scheme 'original disorder-order of the sages-current disorder-future order'. The last stage – a domain of the future – was not yet determined according to both approaches.

The list of questions by Wichrowski omits the aspect regarding the number of these lines of the historical process, implicitly assuming monolinearism. Meanwhile, in the philosophy of history, Wang Fuzhi emphasizes the fact that every trend of order is accompanied by a parallel tendency of chaos, and these tendencies are potentially infinite, for each of them arises from a given historical situation at a specific time and place. Multilinearism appears in the Chinese philosophy of history also without being linked with (general) determinism, as in the *Taipingjing*, where it is claimed that humanity may be heading towards either apocalypse or liberation.

The next questions concretizing the philosophy of history concern the way of evaluating the change, that is whether changes can be evaluated and whether the direction of the changes coincides with an increase in the desired values. The prospectivists: Wang Tingxiang and Zhang Juzheng explicitly rejected the possibility of evaluating the linear historical process. Although they were both convinced of the existence of a linear, necessary and irreversible tendency of history, they also defended the thesis on the fundamental incompatibility of the moral order to history. Among the thinkers who did not reject the valuation of a specific direction of historical changes, philosophers who perceive the decline of moral values come to the fore. The paradigmatic figure was, of course, Confucius himself. After him, this belief was maintained by such philosophers as Mencius, Xunzi, the authors of the vision of *datong*, the Daoists, Mohists, Dong Zhongshu, Yang Xiong, the authors of the *Huainanzi*, the Neo-Legalists, Han Yu, Sima Guang, brothers Cheng, Zhu Xi, Li Gou and Zhang Xuecheng. For the most part, they believed that this failure, if not necessary, was certainly irreversible, which gives rise to a special nostalgia: history is like a continuous distancing from one's own home, which in time becomes barely seen on the horizon. Importantly, these thinkers were not strictly opposed to those for whom historical change is necessarily and irreversibly good, but rather to those who evaluated the historical process neutrally, stating that with the help of people and assuming that they correctly read the tendency of their times, there may be progress. The Legalists – Shang Yang and Han Fei, Liu Zongyuan, Su Xun, Chen Liang, Li Zhi and Wang Fuzhi – were of such opinion. They differed in the degree of directness and complexity in their evocation of this assumption, some of them, such as Su Xun, even openly used a separate term for progress (*ru*). None of them, however, thought that the future was definitively determined (such as the authors of the *Taipingjing*, who kept warning that the liberation of humanity had yet to be decided). Such a vision of progress was created in the West, which was under the sway of the idea of an omniscient God who mysteriously knows the future, which, since it was once revealed to the prophets, is now available to the heights scaled by the historiosophical mind. However, one cannot demonstrate on this basis that China was not familiar with the concept of progress or, as Löwith so readily does, the philosophy of history in general, for it is a misunderstanding resulting most from the ignorance of Chinese philosophy. In fact, instead of talking about the limitations of the Chinese philosophy of history in this respect, one should rather notice its caution, because the optimistic concept of necessary and pre-determined progress is something that Western thought quickly abandoned, realizing the invalid epistemological grounding of the idea of knowing the future. The Chinese philosophers did not think that progress could take place 'behind our back', let alone against us. While the fall was a tragedy that no one could do anything about, progress was a promise made to outstanding individuals capable of listening to the voice of history.

Understandably, due to the conditional nature of progress, the question about the reversibility of positively evaluated changes is answered affirmatively in the Chinese philosophy of history. However, this does not mean, as Jullien would have, that the future is unknown or uninteresting to the Chinese, but only that it was never a foregone conclusion.

The essential feature that distinguishes the speculative philosophy of history in China is the fact that it does not offer any prophetic promise, although the promise of introducing a new stage or returning to the old idyll can be made by politicians and become a political project. As an extension of political philosophy, the philosophy of history in China, however, retained much closer links to ethics than its Western counterpart. For the vast majority of philosophers looking for a pattern of history, historically represented values formed a certain structure, which made the philosophy of history something like a diachronic social philosophy. Only in this context can one understand the moral function of historiography, which is so deeply immersed in speculative thinking. The Chinese philosophy of history is therefore not susceptible to Popper's allegations. The fact that it was the other side of social philosophy did not mean that the philosophy of history was treated instrumentally as a tool for expressing the political project of the future, as it was in Europe. While a Western historiosopher was mainly focused on the end of history, the Chinese philosopher of history devoted nearly all his attention to the beginning of history. In this sense, he was a philosopher of *history* in a much stricter sense than e.g. Condorcet or Marx.

The full characterization of the distinctiveness of the Chinese philosophy of history will be possible only after presenting its underlying holism. However, first I shall summarize the basic trends in the evolution of the Chinese philosophy of history until the end of the eighteenth century.

The diachronic approach: the evolution of the classical Chinese philosophy of history

Historiosophy emerged on the horizon of Chinese culture very early, namely when the first rulers of Zhou claimed to have found a legitimization for laying violent hands on the existing power in the decision of the invisible, intervening Heaven. Interestingly, at more or less the same time and in a similar style, God was invited to history by the Israelites. The Chinese Heaven, however, did not speak, and instead conveyed its will indirectly through signs which had to be properly interpreted, which in turn fuelled historiosophical discourse at the expense of the theology of history, such as that which was developed in the Judeo-Christian tradition. Chinese thought, which could not settle for post-factum analysis, generalized the structure of the transition from the Shang Dynasty to the Zhou Dynasty to form a general historiosophical scheme, which in its mature form was already explicated in the *Book of Documents*. Indicating a number of conditions to be met by the ruler of the new dynasty and drawing up the exact structure of historical cycles determined by the act of sending and withdrawing the permission (Mandate) of Heaven, the authors of the *Book of Documents* provided the manual of (good) governance rooted in historiosophy. Against the uncompromising rationality and objectivity of the model presented there, voices of opposition were already expressed at that time, artistic evocation of which can be found in the *Book of Songs*. With time, a different way of thinking about history appeared on the horizon, the creator of which was Confucius, in whose mind the idea of dynastic cycles and the Mandate of Heaven, as understood in the *Shangshu*, are absent. For Confucius, history is first and foremost a place where Dao – an ideal model of social life and governance – had once been fully realized. And because, according to Confucius, people should follow Dao in their lives, history is for him an ethics guidebook, a collection of examples of moral and immoral conduct, implying given general moral norms, in the way which is shown in the *Spring and Autumn Annals*.

In the case of the authors of the concept of *datong*, however, history is already entirely determined by the transformation of morality, that is the transition from the state of unity to the period of Small Prosperity. The fact that the era of the Great Unity seems to contradict Confucian ideals leads rather to the opposite conclusion, for morality that does not distinguish (between kin and outsiders) turns out to be a lost paradise to which there is no return. These assumptions were radicalized by Mencius, who starts with the belief in an irreversible moral fall in history, and thus with the idealization of the past, although he considers the former rulers as the incarnation of Confucian values. It is Mencius who makes morality (precisely *ren*) the principle of history, additionally grounded in the historical activity of Heaven. The Mencian vision of cycles inscribed in the general line of collapse is a combination of Confucius' ethics of history and the historiosophy of the *Book of Documents*. Xunzi argued against such a view of history, trying to purify the philosophy of history from its references to the transcendent guarantor of the historical success of morality. Heaven becomes only a synonym for nature to Xunzi, and the philosophy of history is reduced to the description of the culture-forming role of the sages, whom Xunzi idealizes, and in this sense he is still a Confucian philosopher of history (although, being conscious of epistemic limitations, he divides them into 'early' and 'late' sages, a distinction which Mencius ignored). In this way, Mencius became the progenitor of later historical idealism, and Xunzi – of realism, in the sense adopted in this book.

A completely different historiosophical tradition was derived from the line of thinking of which Sunzi was the patron. The alleged author of the *Art of War* not only treated history in a realistic way, as the clashes of states with conflicting interests and different and time-varying powers, but he also introduced the concept of *shi* – a favourable position, and more broadly, a historical situation that gives an advantage to those who can recognize the specific conditions of their time. As Shang Yang argued later, and also Han Fei after him, these conditions change so significantly that attempting to copy antiquity does not have the slightest practical sense. Furthermore, any form of imitation and belief in timelessly important and effective principles of governance makes people escape the specifics of the objective *shi* of the times in which they actually live. In this sense, the Legalists oppose all the other currents of the Chinese philosophy of history of the Warring States Period, which searched for a transhistorically important 'key' to the success of former kings. Han Fei even subjected Dao to historical relativization (which would be radicalized by Chen Liang centuries later), stressing that due to the fact that people who recognize the specificity of Dao at a given time oppose the views that are dominant in their time, they become martyrs on the altar of history (this, in turn, will be taken up by Wang Anshi). For this reason, the vision of history in the eyes of both Shang Yang and Han Fei is completely different from the dynastic approaches, focusing on social and economic changes of a structural nature, such as population growth, political transformation and technological inventions. Liu Zongyuan will refer to these ideas, which once again shows that Legalist philosophy of history was absorbed (in time) by the broadly understood 'School of Scholars', resulting in a realistic trend within the Neo-Confucian philosophy of history.

The Mohist philosophy of history was in its structure, as has already been indicated, a mirror reflection of Confucian historiosophy, with the provisos that *ren* is replaced by *jian'ai*, morality is directly validated from the perspective of social stability, and the impersonal Heaven is replaced by the theistic Tian. This last thread, however, will be 'absorbed' by the Confucian philosophy of history of Dong Zhongshu. All the philosophies of history that are inheritors of the historiosophy of the *Shangshu*, are criticized and mocked by classical Daoism. And although the state of nature was from the perspective of Daoism a kind of 'prehistoric' state, it implied a specific historiosophy, which along with the motive of returning to this state led to a specific philosophy of history which became shaped in the Han era. Moreover, the dialectics of nature and history, which in classical Daoism is a negative dialectics of conflict, found its 'conciliation' counterpart in the commentaries to the *Book of Changes*, which provide a systematic characterization of changes that result in a vision of self-sufficient and infinite nature that is understood as a temporal continuity of complementary oppositions. This continuity has its end, beyond which the invisible begins, but this does not presume the existence of any transcendent being that would escape the described structure of changes. Mediated by the Yin-Yang school, which pioneered the recognition of the 'deep' structure of natural changes underlying transformations of the social world, the thought of the *Book of Changes* had a powerful impact on the later Chinese philosophy of history, in particular that developing during the Han dynasty. It can be said that in its entirety the later Chinese philosophy of history is to some extent deducible from the combination of its four primary sources: the historiosophy of the *Shangshu*, the 'changeology' of the *Yijing*, Confucius' ethics of history and the realism of Sunzi.

Regardless of historical assessment of the scale of the burning of books, the establishment of the empire was accompanied by a previously unknown spirit of novelty and a break with the past. This is evidenced not only by the stele inscriptions of the First Emperor, heralding the coming of the everlasting future, but also the first Messianic hopes for the coming of the warlike king who would bring peace and was glorified in the *Heguanzi*. New times required thus new syntheses. Confucian philosophers such as Lu Jia, Dong Zhongshu, He Xiu and Liu Xin adopted the Mencian view of the historical force of morality, mediating it through natural changes, which resulted in the triadic structure of the historical process: the immoral behaviour of the ruler first translates into the transformations of *yin* and *yang* (or natural disasters), so as to influence historical changes in the social world. From the time of Dong Zhongshu, this influence is further mediated by Heaven, a metaphysical guarantor of the effectiveness of morality, capable of inducing the transformations of nature. The cycles that Mencius characterized only quantitatively (as occurring every 500 years), Dong Zhongshu and Liu Xin already describe in terms of quality, linking them with ethical and aesthetic (Dong Zhongshu) or strictly natural (Liu Xin) categories. The system created in this way also allowed the relatively accurate prediction of the general features of the coming era. Importantly, the very idea of a correlation between historical nature and the social world was also associated with linear visions, as in Lu Jia and He Xiu. Moreover, the philosophy of history in the *Huainanzi* is also situated within the same current which initiated the Daoist philosophy of history in the strict sense of the word. It was a vision of the collapse of the pre-social state of harmony and unity with nature (characterized as the time of correlated conformity); this state can only be restored if new rulers correctly read the *shi* of their times, which combined Daoism with Legalism.

Against such a broadly defined synthesis, which merged the moral, natural and historical order, there were many thinkers who voiced critical views from more than one perspective. Yang Xiong defended the orthodox Confucian philosophy of history without the Han imports: he purged the theory of the historical effectiveness of morality of its mediation through natural changes. However, unlike Mengzi, he also rejected the idea of dynastic cycles initiated in fixed periods of time. The idea of dynastic cycles was also rejected by Jia Yi, who saw the only cause of historical changes as lying in the activity of the people, who were nonetheless understood quite homogeneously and instrumentally, in the spirit of historical populism. Another of the populists, Zhong Changtong, in turn defended the existence of historical cycles, which were not, however, dynastic cycles, but cyclical transformations of politics, the axis of which was the people. Han correlationism was also foreign to the Neo-Legalism of Huan Tan and Cui Shi. Legalist methods and tools, which according to Shang Yang and Han Fei were supposed to serve to adapt to the specifics of new times, were embedded by the Neo-Legalists in a concrete, idealized past and treated as a universal ideal. Wang Chong, on the other hand, occupied an entirely isolated position on the map of the Han philosophy of history. Just as Xunzi once did, Wang Chong equated Tian with nature, believing that the fate of human beings is already predestined by nature, identifying this destiny with the nature of every human being. The possibilities defined in nature are realized (or not) under the influence of contact with random factors, especially the proper time. In this naturalistic view of history as a constellation of destiny and chance, there is no room for any form of historical resonance of conduct, which placed Wang Chong in opposition to all the other philosophers of history of that time. In a sense, only the fact that Wang Chong put so much effort into criticizing different concepts allows his ahistorical naturalism to be assigned a place within the philosophy of history. Wang Chong thus saw the essence of the historical process in self-contained and immanent laws of nature, just as the Neo-Legalists found it in positive laws, whereas Yang Xiong and the populists perceived history not so much as resulting from the action of laws, but the effect of human activity: outstanding individuals (Yang Xiong) or the people (populists). The official historiography of the time ranged from supporters to opponents of the idea of correlation. Accordingly, Ban Gu was much closer to the former, while Sima Qian tried to reconcile the cyclical interpretation of history with belief in the decisive historical role of people, promoting thereby pioneering perspectivism in historical narrative.

With the collapse of the Chinese empire and the advent of the centuries-long political disintegration, the unifying metanarratives of the Han philosophers of history no longer found fertile ground. It was first contrasted with the competitive Neo-Daoist metanarrative, which is conveyed by the *Tainpingjing*, a work which can be partially traced back to the times of the Han dynasty. This work was a development of the philosophy of history of the *Huainanzi*, linking the fall of the original state of oneness with the mysterious 'inherited guilt', and placing Heaven in the role of the great avenger, thereby reactivating the theory of correlation. It would be a mistake, however, to treat the *Taipingjing* as just a footnote to the systems of the Han era, since this work covers the subjects unique throughout the Chinese philosophy of history. The introduction of a strictly religious idea (inherited guilt) to the very heart of the philosophy of the history; basically a pessimistic assessment of the entire human species, not just a selected historical period; the belief in the imminent end of the world, which will be the apocalypse and the total annihilation of all being; and at the same time the hope in the coming of the era of supreme peace, which will be the time of equality and liberation of all people – these are all threads that can be found in the *Canon of the Supreme Peace*, and which are the closest counterpart to Christian eschatology and historiosophy in Chinese culture. The only Chinese philosophy of history that allowed for history to be transcended on religious grounds and entertained the idea of liberation at the end of history was precisely the Neo-Daoist philosophy of history of the *Taipingjing*. At the same time, it should be remembered that it was programmatic anti-Messianism, assuming that liberation is only one of the possibilities, which made it a multilinear philosophy of history. In the absence of a messiah, liberation would be brought about by the effort of the whole of humanity, through the creation of a liberating scripture that gathers all the grains of truth that have been recorded throughout history. In this way, the speculative philosophy of history was bridged with the philosophy of historiography. The latter constituted, apart from various visions of prominent historical individuals culminating in the philosophy of history in the *Renwuzhi*, the only important alternative to the speculative meta-narratives.

The roots of the philosophy of historiography appeared earlier: in Dong Zhongshu, who accented the didactic function of historiography and believed that the intentions of historical actors, which have to be reconstructed by a historian on the basis of events, are subject to evaluation. Even then, however, these ideas found their opponents, such as Wang Chong, who believed that the task of a historian is to determine what is true based on the confrontation of conflicting findings regarding given events and sources. Five centuries later, Liu Xie also asked about the factors which determine the credibility of a historical work as such, linking them with the selection of material made according to the general principle, recognized by a talented but also ethically responsible historian. This idea was developed by Liu Zhiji, at a time when the Historical Office had already been established. Liu Zhiji also emphasized the necessity of selecting and sequencing events, but he insisted on impartiality, which should be an appropriate criterion for this selection, pointing out to contemporaneous historians their susceptibility to political pressure and their sacrifice of credibility for the extraordinariness sought by readers. For this reason, he clearly distinguished a historian's talent from literary talent, and ultimately, among the conditions of being a good historian, apart from talent and knowledge, he also mentioned the philosophical insight into the didactic dimension of transmitted historical truth. Recognizing, however, that historians' awareness is limited by the times in which they live, Liu Zhiji in a certain way relativized his general philosophy of historiography to the level of the theory of history, as evidenced by his lists of different styles and genres of historical narrative that were practised in particular epochs.

With the emergence of Neo-Confucianism, the speculative philosophy of history returned to favour. An old Han debate on whether morality has its natural resonance realized throughout history, which most often assumed the mediation of Heaven, rose to a higher philosophical level. The philosophers of history living under the Tang and Song dynasties, who all belong to broadly understood Confucianism (where the term 'Neo-Confucianism' is not reserved only for the School of Principle, *lixue*), were rather intrigued by the question of whether there exists any timeless principle that unfolds itself in history. Thinkers who gave a positive answer to this question were called historical idealists, their opponents historical realists. Avoiding as much as possible the metaphysical connotations of both these concepts, I drew attention to the fact that this dispute also corresponded to the tension in contemporaneous historiography, which for some was to be subordinated to the eternally important ideas conveyed in the Classics, while for others it was an independent and self-sufficient discipline. Furthermore, the idealism–realism opposition in the philosophy of history responds directly to the analogical opposition in political philosophy, in which realists, unlike idealists, reject the need to impose moral principles and all universal standards beyond the play of interests on a given political situation. Political philosophy and philosophy of history operate with a different understanding of realism and idealism than theoretical philosophy, and for this reason historical materialism is not the direct opposite of historical idealism.

The ideas that laid the foundations for later historical idealism were proposed by Han Yu, whereas Chinese historical idealism itself was rounded off by none other than Zhu Xi. Inspired (more or less openly) by Buddhism, historical idealists such as Shao Yong and Wang Anshi also identified the nature of this timeless principle of historical process with spirit, which is why I call them historical spiritualists. For Shao Yong, it was an impersonal spirit, for Wang Anshi – a personal one; Shao Yong's philosophy was cyclical, Wang Anshi's – linear. Shao Yong's philosophy of history is probably the best example of cyclical, speculative philosophy of history in general.[1] Speculative, because determined from the perspective of the spirit, as the division into three times is, according to Shao Yong, dependent on the particular cognitive subject. The spirit, although different from people and things, at the same time permeates history, and the great cycle of history, ending in a return of the spirit to oneself, can be described with strict, not only speculative but also mathematical, certainty. In this sense, Shao Yong's philosophy paradoxically embodies the closest equivalent to the methodology of Hegel's philosophy of history to emerge on Chinese soil. In a completely different context, the concept of the spirit was employed by Wang Anshi, who developed the ideas of the culture-forming role of the sages (proposed by Han Yu) in a spiritualist style. The sages are identified by him with spirits acting in the world, being specifically connected with Heaven; their cognition intuitively embraces the totality of being, while their desires, as transcending the world, are in contradiction with the intentions of 'this world'. Therefore, one should be open to accept the novelties introduced by the following epochs, imitating at most the general intentions of the sages, but not the content of their decisions, let alone striving to return to antiquity. In this sense, Wang

Anshi incorporates Han Fei's philosophy of the history along with its idea of 'martyrs'. Historical idealists in the strict sense, such as the Cheng brothers and Zhu Xi, as die-hard opponents of Wang Anshi, defended the concept of the moral universalization of particular political solutions. In their opinion, the principle (*li*) is the imperceptible essence of the historical process, the very root of the cycles of order and chaos from the perspective of which judgement can be made over history. This means history itself is not a judgement over the world, so that historical winners are not identical with moral winners, as could be seen from the perspective of the principles of history. The reaction to the moral decline of humanity, which is realized through cycles of history, are not, for both the Cheng brothers and Zhu Xi, attempts to reactivate old institutions, but rather a striving to restore the former way of exercising power. This implies precedence of the Classics over the chronicles, which describe only the 'outer skin' of things, as Zhu Xi writes. Dao, once lost, must be recovered, though it is hindered by general historical deterioration, which also encompasses the matter from which we are composed. Thanks to this, people keep their freedom, which allows them to not return to full implementation of the principle in history – Zhu Xi's philosophy of history was not therefore any form of fatalism. At the same time, the principle itself and Dao do not change, in part because they are simultaneously a metaphysical and moral principle of the universe. This is why Zhu Xi intended to 'extract' the moral meaning of recording history more accurately when he started to write the *Tongjian gangmu*.

Quite a different paradigm of historical writing was represented by Zheng Qiao, who created a chronicle of institutional and structural changes integrated into the whole of natural science, so that even the origin of man was derived from the evolution of animals. Historical realists did not think that any general principle other than history itself is needed to explain history. Thinkers such as Ouyang Xiu were quite restrained in this regard, limiting themselves to the declaration that knowledge of these principles and everything that goes beyond the sphere of human experience is not necessary, and usually is not possible, in order to know history. He conceives of the theory of dynastic legitimization (*zhengtong*) in entirely cultural terms, and historical research, unless it is an inquiry into the remains of the former material culture and economic institutions, comes down to reconstructing the intentions of the ancient sages on the basis of their writings. The historical realists in the strict sense such as Su Xun did not stop at the conclusion of the agnostics, but they believed that knowledge of the nature of history is possible in terms of the whole of history, and more precisely the overall tendency of its development (*shi*). According to Su Xun, if people seize this *shi*, historical progress will be possible. A special kind of realists were those who – by analogy with the spiritualists, narrowing the meaning of the principle to a specific being – interpreted the nature of history not so much through the prism of the whole of history, as through one particular visible being that is a part of history. These thinkers have been described as historical materialists, thus making historical materialism a general category, which ceases to be limited to Marx's position. By this history-making matter, one can understand not only economic matter, as did not only Marx in nineteenth-century Europe but also Li Gou in eleventh-century China, but also social matter, namely artefacts and relations of social dependencies that are built upon them (Liu Zongyuan), or just nature, that is a particular environment or the matter filling people (Chen Liang).

The case of Liu Zongyuan clearly shows the validity of the proposed genealogy of historical realism: the naturalistic understanding of Tian in the spirit of Xunzi is combined with the reactivation – after almost one millennium – of the category of *shi*. The necessity and structural nature of the transformations of *shi* are exemplified by the fact that the creation of artefacts that are not anyone's property by nature necessarily led to competition over those products, while the resolution of these struggles could only be achieved by the establishment of a stable social institution, namely feudalism. Consequently, this system and all differences are also 'artificial' for Liu Zongyuan (because it is superstructured over artefacts): in the absence of a universal principle that unfolds in history, there is no reason to consider any social system as a model fulfilling any prior ideal. Li Gou, who was quite critical of the aristocracy, also shared this opinion. He believed that broadly understood 'customs' (*li*), which include also morality, politics, law and art, depend on the way of solving the issue of food, which in turn derives from the relations of landed property, which ultimately stems from the disposal of goods, especially money. Therefore, economic changes ultimately determine cultural changes, which gives Li Gou the hope of restoring the state in which the peasants had money at their disposal. Another structural explanation of historical phenomena, this time referring to increases and decreases of the developmental trend of matter, whether in the local dimension, or finally in the form of a historical tendency (*shi*) of the world, was given by Chen Liang. *Shi* leads, in his opinion, from institutional forms stressing the private interest to those pursuing the public interest. That is why it is so pivotal to recognize the stage of the development of *shi*, which historical heroes were able to do, and what should also be done to expel the barbarians from China. A special role is played by the *qi* that people are made of, this basic layer of historical process over which all other 'cultural entities', as Chen Liang writes, are built up. Dao is identical with the standard of human conduct at a given time, being thereby contextualized and temporalized, in contrast to the transhistorical Dao of Zhu Xi, who described Chen Liang in his correspondence as 'corrupted by history', thus summarizing the essence of the difference between historical idealism and realism. Ideas close to the thought of Chen Liang, represented by Ye Shi, Ma Duanlin and Xu Heng, also dominated the philosophy of history in the thirteenth century.

In response to the new historiosophical metanarratives created during the Song dynasty, the philosophers of history under the Ming proposed individualism and criticism that were more intense than ever before that ultimately historized and relativized the standards of idealists like Zhu Xi. For both Song Lian and Wang Yangming, the totality of history can be grasped by means of insight into one's own mind. Identifying mind with the principle of reality, Wang Yangming blurred the boundaries between the present and the past, as well as between mind and events, and ultimately also between the Classics, which are believed to convey universally important content, and historiography. This was appreciated by the philosophy of historiography that was flourishing at that time. Recognizing the importance of historiography for public opinion (Wang Yi, Qiu Jun), it was believed that 'the Classics and histories are one' (Xue Yinqqi), and, as Wang Shizhen put it, that 'there is nothing between Heaven and earth that is not history'. If history is supposed to fulfil its public functions, it must be objective and comprehensive, as is emphasized in historical criticism of Wang

Shizhen and Hu Yinglin. The latter, however, deconstructed the ideal of objectivity, pointing out that the only way to determine the credibility of a source is to refer to other sources. In this way, the Classics turned out to be histories, and histories literature, which significantly influenced the philologism of the *kaozheng* movement at the turn of the Ming and Qing dynasties.

The speculative philosophy of history of that time developed the concept of *shi*, and its representatives – Wang Tingxiang, Zhang Juzheng and Li Zhi – were in essence outside of Confucianism. According to Zhang Juzheng, structural transformations of *shi*, which are realized through cycles of simplicity and subtlety, require new laws, customs and moral principles, for none of them are timeless. For Wang Tingxiang *shi* is not only gradual and irreversible, but also purely linear, which opens us to the future. The future, however, can be good or bad, which distinguishes Wang Tingxiang's prospectivism from Western progressivism. The division between history and morality is even deeper for him because he is not only convinced about the lack of any universal moral principles and laws but is also aware of their contingent and arbitrary foundation. These threads were radicalized by Li Zhi (who was also familiar with speculation about the nature of *shi*). Li Zhi believed that the standards of what is right and wrong are only opinions that weaken from day to day: this was the idea of historical relativism. Even the ideas of Confucius are only his private opinions, specific to his time, which over time has been made into an imperial ideology.

It was the ideologization of Confucianism that the movement of 'evidential research' (*kaozheng*) in seventeenth century China turned against. The philological search for the original Confucianism and its source did not shy away from discrediting entire sections of the classical writings as unreliable, although the only direct opponent of the thinkers of this movement was Neo-Confucian scholasticism. In the field of the philosophy of history this time was, paradoxically, a period of searching for unity. Eclectic attempts to combine the objectivist theory of *shi* with the subjectivist idea of mind as the principle of history undertaken by Gu Yanwu and Huang Zongxi were devoid of the requisite coherence. Others, such as Dai Zhen, were content with reductionism, which made history only a general form of manifesting natural human feelings and everyday life practices. The real synthesis, which was also aimed at a synthesis of historical idealism and realism, was proposed only by Wang Fuzhi. Recognizing *shi* as a diachronic form of fulfilling the principle that is inseparable from matter, Wang Fuzhi situates his philosophy of history in the perspective of the ontology of the self-sufficient (and already historical) substrate of the world, taking thereby his main inspirations from the *Yijing*. Particular moments of the 'solstice' of *shi* and the historical breakthroughs implied by them were described by Wang Fuzhi in his two strictly historiosophical works, which make a speculative interpretation of the history of China from the rise of the empire to the fall of the Song dynasty. These analyses cannot be understood through the prism of total historical determinism, because the final shape of history, including the future, depends on the behaviour of people (depending on the context of the transformations of *shi*, either their quick reaction, or resistance). Above all, these transformations of *shi* themselves do not have, due to the consistent monism of Wang Fuzhi, a cause-and-effect nature. It is also in the light of this dialectic of *shi* that one should ultimately understand his concept of Tian, which incorporates ideological themes into his essentially realistic philosophy of history. The mysterious part of nature, which is Tian, not only acts in human history and gives the rulers a mandate, but also somehow 'uses their hands' to realize the general sense of history, such as the transition from feudalism to imperial absolutism. Among the four sources of Chinese philosophy of history distinguished by us, Wang Fuzhi combines three: the ideas from the *Yijing*, Legalism and the historiosophy of the *Shangshu*. As a historical realist, however, he ignores the ethical dimension.

The synthesis derived from the fourth source, namely Confucius' ethics of history, was proposed in turn by Zhang Xuecheng. In effect, his synthesis ultimately had an idealistic character. For Zhang Xuecheng, history is simply the history of the manifestation and fall of Dao, which is both a metaphysical and moral standard preceding the existence of the world. After the initial period of human development, which was accompanied by changes within the Dao itself, the Zhou Dynasty was established, which was the peak period of following Dao in public life. From that time, Dao left everyday human life, or rather people (irreversibly) departed from Dao, thus the treatment of books created at that time, which aimed solely at reporting the realization of Dao in everyday life, as universal classical scriptures that are valid for each and every time, is the cardinal mistake of all Confucians. In this way, the historical thesis of the earlier philosophy of historiography receives its speculative justification. Furthermore, the cycles of historical collapse that follow each other since the founding of the empire, are cycles of intellectual trends (philology, literature and philosophy) of understanding culture, which correspond to specific attitudes and historical epochs. Such an account of history also had an undeniably idealistic dimension. Ming subjectivism is included in Zhang Xuecheng's idea of the 'virtue of a historian', being the belief that feelings, and generally the mind of the person recording history, directly affect the style and content of historical narrative. Many of these feelings are prejudiced, which makes it difficult for us to understand the past: only by purifying our feelings it is possible to understand the feelings of historical actors and to infer their experiences by respectfully and empathetically putting ourselves in their place. Such a synthesis of hermeneutics and the philosophy of historiography with the speculative philosophy of history, however, does not answer the question of whether such an understanding is possible in practice, and Zhang Xuecheng's pessimistic and regressive vision does not prompt optimistic conclusions. In this sense, at the expense of philosophical synthesis, the unity of the present and the past (captured as a moral ideal) that lies at the heart of the teachings of Confucius, is broken. The new impetus for the development of the philosophy of history will be later delivered from the West, but it seems that this unity, once lost, could never be regained.

A critical perspective: holism in the classical Chinese philosophy of history

The above description of the evolution of the classical Chinese philosophy of history shows that the main 'vector' of its development was the tendency to increasingly larger syntheses, allowing history and historiography to be captured in the most holistic way possible. However, the presentation of this dimension of the Chinese philosophy of history requires the use of the critical apparatus presented at the beginning of the book, which will help us with expressing the exact meaning of this idea of holism. First of all, the Chinese philosophy of history was not holistic in all possible senses of the word. Secondly, not all Chinese philosophers of history were holists, but it was the syntheses created by the holists that fuelled criticism, which was eventually tamed and absorbed by holistic syntheses.

It is worth emphasizing that the pursuit of a holistic view of history can be traced at the level of the philosophical style of Chinese philosophers of history. Already in the titles of the main works and their introductory declarations, the character 通 *tōng* is used, which means 'whole', 'comprehensive', 'penetrate', 'encompass', etc. These meanings were embodied in the works of Ban Gu, Liu Zhiji, Zheng Qiao, Sima Guang, Zhu Xi, Ma Duanlin, Wang Fuzhi and Zhang Xuecheng. With the exception of the latter two, views from the field of the philosophy of history were not presented in separate works, but rather treated essentially as an integral part of the entire philosophical system. The philosophies of history in China remained in a much closer relation to ethics and aesthetics than in the Western philosophy of history. Both, however, fostered a close relationship with political philosophy. Interestingly, also the Western philosophy of history, treated for a long time as a form of popular and therefore non-academic philosophy, was expounded in works that did not distinguish it from general historical knowledge, mixing it with historical, legendary and miracle reports, as can be seen in the examples of Vico, Voltaire and Herder. The popular image of the speculative philosophy of history, of it being elucidated in axioms and applied top-down to the historical material, is erroneous in relation to both Chinese and European traditions. An additional issue showing the striving to capture the whole of history at the level of philosophical style in China was the scale of references to historical and philosophical sources, revealing an erudition and continuity of thought unprecedented in the West. Being bound to refer to the accumulating tradition, each subsequent synthesis was somewhat necessarily broader, so it is not surprising that those who culminate the two millennia of the development of the Chinese philosophy of history do it also in the theoretical sphere. Such scale and continuity of development was not experienced in the Western philosophy of history, which was additionally marked by the dissent from the theology of history, so that after only a century of its development, after having recognized the still dominant quasi-religious structure of historical thinking, the Western world decided to dispense with the speculative philosophy of history.

This continuity also had its consequences in the objective sphere. Referring to the first sense of the concept of holism described in Chapter 1, namely holism concerning space, we see how problematic it was in relation to China. The search for a philosophical interpretation of the history of as many states or world civilizations as possible was fundamentally alien to the Chinese philosophers of history. Of course, records of non-Chinese states, including those located in the broadly understood West (up to the Roman Empire), can be found in Chinese historiography from the magisterial work of Sima Qian onwards. However, Chinese sources from the first millennium describing these countries resembled (the often exaggerated) notes typical of travel literature, recording the political system, size, population, customs, and above all, animals, crops and precious items from these lands. No philosopher of history, even after becoming acquainted with the history of India due to the Buddhists, and even after becoming acquainted with the history of Europe thanks to the Jesuits, took into account the history of non-Chinese states (including even Korea and Japan) as part of their analyses. As Wang Fuzhi put it, 'the meaning of Chinese history is the universal meaning of history'. Therefore, the failure to take the history of India or Europe into account did not occur following a demonstration that these places are 'unhistorical', but simply by ignoring them. When a Chinese philosopher wrote about the establishment of the empire, he only thought about the Chinese Empire. The only category available to non-Chinese people was that with the barbarians. Since the latter are deprived of Chinese culture, that is culture in general, they were for Chinese thinkers in the strict sense of the word 'unhistorical'. And though such philosophers as Chen Liang and Wang Fuzhi say that the *shi* of the world also includes barbarians, all the transformations of *shi* that change the history of their states are ultimately made because of China, and most often to instruct (or warn) the Chinese people. In this sense, inclusion of the history of the Mongol rulers, as the foregoers of the Chinese Yuan dynasty, is no exception to this rule. This is, of course, the reverse of the case of the Western philosophy of history, which from the very beginning embraced the histories of non-Western states. The dichotomy of universalistic and pluralist historiosophy, that is, of one universal civilization and many world civilizations that can be successfully applied to the description of Western philosophy of history, does not apply in the Chinese case, which is kind of the 'third option': the assumption of one civilization, but not that of an all-human, universal circle. In other words, traditional Sinocentrism excluded holism in the philosophy of history regarding space.

The issue of the presence in Chinese philosophy of holism regarding time has been partly established on page 178, which discussed the relationship between the theory of *shi* and the dimension of the future. By holism regarding time I understand the holistic account of history in terms of time dimensions, namely the reflection upon not only the past and the present, but also the future. Philosophers who advocated a linear approach to history did not, however, treat the future as already decided, known in advance and having thereby a (pre-)determined purpose, but rather made conditional predictions, meaning with the proviso that this and that would happen *if* people behaved in such and such a way, for instance by recognizing the *shi* of a given time and complying with it. The future was in turn described in a strict manner by philosophers defending a cyclical vision of history. In this case, however, the future is only the repetitive presentification of the past, the next cycle of 'the red' (Dong Zhongshu), water element (Zou Yan, Liu Xin) or the next 'revolution' (Shao Yong). It is not a future in the sense of something new. Even if the cycles are inscribed in a line, this is – except for theoreticians of *shi* – a line of regression: cycles are arranged linearly with regard to a beginning, but not to the future element, let alone the purpose they seek. Both theorists of *shi* who discuss novelties brought by the future in a conditional way, as well as the advocates of the cyclical views of history treating unconditionally about the future that does not imply any historical novelty, were holists regarding time only in the weak sense of the word. On the other hand, if we understand this holism as a belief in the 'deep' unity of time, such a conviction could be found in the first Confucians,

Mencius and Xunzi, who argued that 'the past and present are one', while after the *Lüshi Chunqiu* the dimension of the future also became attached to this thesis, which was epitomized by Dong Zhongshu. Certainly, for the Chinese philosophers of history the future was not something that they could not address, nor was the past for most of them an alien land that has no impact on the present and has no metaphysical union with it. Such an idea, however, was typical of the Confucian philosophy of history, which needed it as justification for its flagship belief in the didactic function of historiography. Only then are the lessons learned from the past applicable both now and in future times. As Confucian interpretation has influenced the whole course of the Chinese philosophy of history, it can be assumed that holism thus understood was an important, though often criticized, element of classical Chinese historical thinking.

The relation of Chinese philosophy to the HPH regarding causality, i.e. the belief that it is human collectives that are endowed with historical causality, is even more complex. No more than a half of the Chinese philosophers of history were holists in this sense, which seriously undermines the common thesis about the alleged 'collectivism' of Chinese culture. In the course of our analyses, we found a multitude of individualistic approaches. Ever since the *Lunyu*, history has appeared primarily as a result of the actions of individuals: be it former kings, or the people, called on to recover the Dao. Such was the thought of Xunzi, Lu Jia and Yang Xiong, as well as of the historian Sima Qian, and also of Mozi, usually a sworn enemy of the *ru*, but who in this regard agreed with the Confucians. The intensification of individualist approaches brought about the collapse of the Han dynasty, as evidenced by the views of history delineated in Neo-Daoism (Wang Bi and the *Baopuzi*), the *Renwuzhi* treatise, early medieval historiography and Buddhist hagiography. In Neo-Confucianism, individualism was reactivated by Han Yu, and rooted in spiritualism by Wang Anshi. The culmination of individualism was the philosophy of history of the Ming dynasty, which is exemplified by views of Wang Yangming and Li Zhi. Holists regarding causality in the strict sense of the word were the Legalists, historical populists, Wang Chong, Shao Yong, historical realists and prospectivists. The standpoints of the other Chinese philosophers of history escape the holism-individualism opposition, not because the opposition does not apply entirely to Chinese thought, but because Chinese thought does not treat it as an opposition in accordance with the *tertium non datur* principle. As the historiosophy of the *Book of Documents* shows, it is possible to demonstrate that there is a steady transition from the influence an individual has on history (with the person of the ruler having a decisive impact on history, according to the *Shangshu*) to the significance of structural factors, regardless of whether they are natural or moral laws resulting in the fall of a dynasty. Such continuity of thinking on historical causality can be found in Mencius, in Dong Zhongshu, in the *Huainanzi*, in Zhu Xi, and above all in Wang Fuzhi and Zhang Xuecheng. Especially Wang Fuzhi devoted a great deal of space to attempts to reconcile the existence of an objective tendency of history (*shi*) with faith in the role of human freedom, which through its reaction and cooperation with *shi* ultimately determines the course of history. In a sense, even the position of Han Fei and the realists Liu Zongyuan and Chen Liang, who similarly emphasized the historical cooperation of nature and (outstanding) individuals, cannot easily be classified as holistic, in the sense of rejecting the influence of individuals on history.

Such a view, which sides with the extreme side of the dispute, should be rather called 'collectivism'. A genuine holism in the philosophy of history regarding causality would rather consist in the belief that a holistic view of history requires acknowledging the historical role of both collectives and (outstanding) individuals, providing that such a conviction would not be only verbal, in other words, it would have to provide conceptual apparatus allowing the continuity of the transition from individual to collective historical actors to be followed. In this sense, holism regarding causality was the dominant view among Chinese philosophers of history, and also a contribution to our general understanding of these conceptual categories.

The proposed diachronic approach to the Chinese philosophy of history also showed how significant for Chinese thinkers the holism regarding substance was, namely the quest for adopting one substance of history by including (in common) both ideal and real factors within the organic, holistic vision of man and history. After the period of formation of various historiosophies during the Warring States Period, under the Han dynasty there appeared the first syntheses, created in the spirit of the idea of *Tian-ren ganying*, aimed at combining a specific type of real factors, in the form of nature, with a special form of ideal factors, i.e. morality. As a result, human action was considered to affect nature and have a direct historical effect. However, many thinkers who opposed this kind of holism rebelled against the concept of 'moral nature-history' understood in this way. A thousand years later, this dispute moved on to a higher and more general level, although it was characterized by a specific 'displacement' of philosophers emphasizing the historical role of morality in the direction of not so much holism as idealism. At the same time, however, the philosophical dispute between historical idealists and realists concerned the role of ideal or real factors as such, and in the case of spiritualists and historical materialists, by means of focus on particular types of these factors. And just as after the period of great syntheses under the Han, the Chinese philosophy of history was distinguished by the rise of individualism and the philosophy of historiography, the same happened during the Ming period. At the end of this era, the need to synthesize idealism and historical realism was expressed with redoubled strength. After a period of rather eclectic attempts to fuse the theory of *shi* with the belief in the unity of mind and history, finally a holistic synthesis of idealistic and realistic themes was made, as in Wang Fuzhi's philosophy of history, although it still gravitates towards realism, and then the philosophy of history of Zhang Xuecheng, which for the reasons described above remains essentially idealistic. This fact, however, can be treated not so much as the weakness of these philosophers – for their syntheses, which are presented in separate, extensive works devoted to the philosophy of history, were systems of thought exceeding contemporaneous Western philosophies of history in their extensiveness – but rather as a contribution to the question of to what extent it is possible to make a theoretically consistent combination of historical idealism and realism. The tendency towards synthesis itself and the strong resistance to these syntheses which can be heard in the dozens of works cited in this book testifies to the fact that the idea of holism regarding substance is an important, if not the most important, element of the classical Chinese philosophy of history.

Taking into account the role of moral factors, Chinese thinkers smoothly proceeded to what I describe as holism in the philosophy of history regarding reason, namely the idea that the proposed view of history incorporates the normative dimension, thus exceeding what we now know as the division into theoretical and practical reason. In other words, this holism means that history is no longer only what happened, but also what should happen (in the present and future), in the sense that a historical epoch embodies the moral ideal to which one should aspire. This conception of holism marks the core of the Confucian philosophy of history from Confucius to Zhang Xuecheng, implicitly implying the concept of the historical collapse of values. In a way, the philosophy of history of the *Taipingjing* also fits into this paradigm, because the future is not only what is to come, but also brings a moral imperative, in fact being the embodiment of this imperative. And although the Confucian philosophy of history does not exhaust the horizon of Chinese historiosophy in general, it was the one that determined the distinctiveness of Chinese philosophy of history, which due to its being closely intertwined with historiography on the one hand (the first task of which was of a didactic nature) and ethics on the other hand, gave no hint that it would lead to a transition to the 'science of history', devoid of any moral and didactic references. For this reason, the meeting of the classical Chinese philosophy of history with Western historical science was a collision, which most often required allegiance to only one side of the encounter, as shown by the example of Liang Qichao 梁啟超 (1873–1929). Of course, the philosophers of history anticipating or developing historical realism were the main opponents of such traditional thinking, but it would be a mistake to think that it was they who shaped the later modern philosophy of historiography. Their theory of historical process was, in the end, speculative, while the relations between 'histories' and 'history' were strongly emphasized in the 'moralizing' current. It is no coincidence that the positivist Liang Qichao reinterpreted the concept of 'the virtue of the historian'.[2] The philosophy of historiography from Liu Zhiji to Zhang Xuecheng struggled with the moral sense of history, indifferently bypassing the concept of *shi*, although this concept was used at that time in the theory of art and poetry.[3] Above all, it did not find a continuous transition from the historical process to historical writing in a way that was completely cut off from the idea of holism regarding reason.

The same philosophy of historiography insisted on its own type of holism, namely the holism regarding meaning, according to which the meaning of the whole historical narrative precedes the meaning of its parts and is more important than them. Already Liu Xie believed that the sequence of events cannot be made if the historian does not use the general rule beforehand; Liu Zhiji wrote directly that only the combination of events and placing them in relation to each other finally gives them meaning, which almost meets the definition of semantic holism. This holism manifested itself in particular remarks of a practical nature, such as in the advice to prefer anticipation instead of retrospection. The brothers Cheng and Zhu Xi continually emphasized that before one begins recording events, one should firstly grasp the general principle (*li*) that stands behind them. The ambiguity of the term *gong*, which was used by the post-Song philosophers of historiography writing about the importance of historiography for 'public debate' and the role of the 'publicly oriented mind' of a historian, should also be mentioned. The word *gong* means 'general', and the same character was also used in the philosophy of history of Wang Fuzhi, who wrote that Heaven uses the interests of individuals to realize something 'general' (and therefore public) in history. Holism in the philosophy of history regarding meaning can also be understood in the most literal way, i.e. as a striving for the most comprehensive historical narrative. And in this sense it was a distinctive feature of Chinese historical thinking, full of holistic records and encyclopaedias, the monumentality of which is unparalleled in world culture viewed as whole. Sima Qian had already allowed for a few perspectives of historical narrative, once censorious, once empathetic, sometimes neutral, in order to present history in a holistic way at the cost of its cohesion. And we know from Gödel that completeness does not go hand in hand with noncontradiction. Later philosophers of historiography, such as Hu Yinglin, even distinguished three types of completeness of historical narrative: the *synthetic*, namely a complete inclusion of everything (*gai*); the *analytic*, that is, the inclusion of everything in a complete, detailed way (*zheng*); and the *holistic* type, being a combination of both with the observance of objectivity, i.e. the semantic whole connecting reality with the chronicle (*quan*). Zhang Xuecheng was also undoubtedly a holist regarding meaning, but his holism runs beyond strictly narrativist categories, because the whole that determines the significance of specific parts of the narrative includes Dao on the one hand, and on the other – the feelings of historians, their general morality and worldview, committed to paper. Using Western categories, one can say that this understanding of narrative was not only an attack on 'narrativist atomism', but also on the 'positivist' vision of historical writing.

In its search for a holistic view of history, and thus the discursive exhaustion of its nature, the Chinese philosophy of history was holistic in more than one sense of the word. Of course, due to its Sinocentrism, it was not holistic regarding space. It was also divided on the question of holism regarding causality and represented a weak version of holism in time, but with a deeper understanding of both concepts, it exceeded the dualisms creeping into the interpretation of the category of time and causality in the philosophy of history in a highly holistic manner. The ambition to create a holistic approach regarding substance fuelled its development, holism regarding reason determined its distinctiveness, and holism regarding meaning was common to all the Chinese philosophers of historiography. Indeed, it is difficult to find a tradition of thought which would care more about taking a comprehensive approach to history.

Conclusion: The Past is Never Dead

The aim of this book was the reconstruction and philosophical analysis of the Chinese philosophy of history from its beginnings to the end of the eighteenth century. The culmination of this analysis was the demonstration that the distinctive feature of the classical Chinese philosophy of history was the striving to capture the whole of history; that it was holistic in many senses of the word.

This book, however, does not claim to have exhausted such a vast, still practically unresearched subject, so it is worth pointing out the perspectives for further research and the benefits that would accrue from this for related disciplines.

Since the proposed reading of the thought of nearly forty Chinese philosophers of history sheds new light on the each of their philosophies, it could provide a new stimulus for the discussion of the history of Chinese philosophy and for detailed Sinological scholarship. In this respect, the book would be most interesting for the scholars of Chinese political philosophy. On the other hand, it will also be fruitful to compare the Chinese philosophy of history with the development of Chinese historiography at given stages of history, which has already been partially done in this book. The most theoretically attractive, however, seems to be the perspective of comparing the classical Chinese philosophy of history with the Chinese philosophy of history in the nineteenth and twentieth centuries, following the encounter with Western historical thinking. It is only in the light of the nature of classical Chinese philosophy that it becomes clear which of the subsequent views constitute a continuation or rupture with the tradition. Was the evolutionism of Yan Fu 嚴復 (1854–1921) merely a sinicization of Spencer's evolutionism, or did it refer to classical themes, and especially – what is the relation of its concept of the destiny of history determined by the development of nature to the historical fatalism of Wang Chong? Was the speculative philosophy of history of Kang Youwei 康有為 (1858–1927), which proposed a linear and progressive view of history divided into three epochs and leading up to the era of the Great Unity, anticipated only by the idea of *datong* from the *Liji* and the *Gongyang zhuan*, or perhaps also by the Neo-Daoist philosophy of history from the *Taipingjing*, replete with similar eschatology? In what relation to historical idealism is the philosophy of history of Zhang Binglin 章炳麟 (1868–1936), usually presented as a Buddhist reaction to Hegelianism? To what extent is the thought of Liang Qichao rooted in the classical philosophy of historiography? Similarly, did the thought of Hu Shi 胡適 (1891–1962) only settle on the criticism of speculative Confucian philosophy of history with its regressivism and moralism, or did it cull inspirations from the philosophy of historical writing inspired by this type of thinking? In what relation to both historical idealism and realism does the philosophy of history of Chen Yinke 陳寅恪 (1890–1969) stay, combining objective idealism with culturalism? It will be finally particularly intriguing to examine the relation of the Chinese Marxist philosophy of history to classical historical realism and materialism, especially in its economic version (Li Gou). As Ivanhoe notes in his entry on the Chinese theories of history,

> Cruder forms of Marxist historicism became dominant and the older dynastic view came to be replaced by an equally Procrustean scheme of 'slave' and 'feudal' periods (. . .) In many respects, the Chinese Marxist view of history is both strange and familiar. Its moral temper and utopian nature are familiar features of traditional Chinese conceptions of history; and while its particular content is surely new, its general form and the trajectory it describes can be found in several of the sources and thinkers discussed above.[1]

Even the first Marxist philosopher of history in China, Li Dazhao 李大釗 (1888–1927), emphasized the activist, not determinist, themes of Marxism. As Li Dazhao writes, 'the future and the past are unlimited, so if I do not examine clearly the nature of history, to understand its tendencies, my life will be meaningless (. . .) Interpretation of history is therefore truly a standard for measuring human life.'[2] How many types of holism that have been examined in relation to the classical Chinese philosophy of history can be found in this short passage! Let me note that of all the elements of Marxism, it was its finalism, so typical of Western philosophy, and so foreign to the Chinese tradition, that was rejected by Mao Zedong 毛澤東 (1893–1976) in his idea of a 'permanent revolution'. It is not surprising, then, that one of Mao Zedong's main historiographical inspirations was the thought of Wang Fuzhi.[3] Wang Fuzhi and basically the entire Confucian philosophy of history were also the reference point of Mou Zongsan, who proposed probably the most original and most comprehensive contemporary development of classical philosophies of history. Mou Zongsan develops these ideas in dialogue with the Hegelian and Marxian dialectics of history, believing that the idea of Hegel's philosophy of history is completely convergent with the classical Chinese philosophy of history. As Ady van den Stock points out, 'Mou fully accepts and preserves the formal makeup of Hegel's logic of historical development' with the proviso that Hegel's linearism is transformed into a cyclical vision in which the Orient is not only the starting point but also the ultimate goal of the unfolding of the spirit of world history.[4] As Mou Zongsan writes,

> World history has an absolute East and a determined starting point, but the latter is also exactly its fixed endpoint. In the ideally Hegelian cycle, the development of the West will ultimately return to this point of departure through the self-awakening and development of the East. The East is the native land of the spirit of humanity and the principle of life.[5]

In view of the above references to the Western philosophy of history and the numerous comparative observations made in many places in this book, the significance of the proposed analysis of the classical Chinese philosophy of history for research on the philosophy of history in general should also be emphasized. Suffice it to say that many scholars still believe that the philosophy of history is a peculiarly Western invention. The prospects of comparing so many historiosophical conceptions with Western ideas are almost unlimited. Thanks to the Chinese philosophy of history, the horizon of possible solutions to problems widened, to which Western philosophers of history sometimes responded only in a disjunctive manner, as shown in the previous chapter. Chinese solutions are also not antiquarian in any way. The dependence of the visions of history on political projects and pressure, obvious to most Chinese philosophers, was discovered in the West only thanks to Popper and Foucault. Chinese holism regarding reason, which goes beyond the dualism of the descriptive and the normative, encounters a fertile ground in the form of Neopragmatism, rejecting the dualism of facts and values, and more broadly – the entire hermeneutic tradition. In addition, the dualism of nature and culture, criticized in our times, was something foreign to all holistically oriented thinkers, something that should be transcended and embraced by a broader, comprehensive approach. In this way, posthumanism would be close to Chinese thought, especially as Chinese philosophy takes into account the historical agency of actors other than people. As shown by the work of Stanislaus Lo Kuang, in the description of solutions to historiosophical problems one can give voice to both Chinese and Western philosophers of history.[6] The creation of an intercultural philosophy of history, which, following the Chinese traditon, will non-antagonistically include the philosophy of historiography, may result in an even deeper holism, which even Chinese philosophers did not dream about.

Notes

Introduction

1 Mou Zongsan, *Lishi zhexue* 歷史哲學 (Taibei: Lianjing, 2003).

2 Luo Guang 羅光. *Lishi zhexue* 歷史哲學 (Taibei: Taiwan xuesheng shuju, 1996).

3 Karl Löwith, *Meaning in History* (Chicago and London: The University of Chicago Press, 1949), 16–17.

4 See my interpretation of that process: Dawid Rogacz, 'The birth of enlightenment secularism from the spirit of Confucianism', *Asian Philosophy* 28, no. 1 (2018), 68–83. The paper concludes that the contact of European philosophy with Chinese thought in the second half of the seventeenth and eighteenth century paradoxically influenced the rise and development of the secular philosophy of history in the West.

5 David S. Nivison, *The Life and Thought of Chang Hsüeh-ch'eng (1738–1801)* (Stanford: Stanford University Press, 1966).

6 David S. Nivison, 'Mengzi as Philosopher of History', in *Mencius: Contexts and Interpretations*, ed. Alan Chan (Honolulu: University of Hawai'i Press, 2002).

7 'Chang Hsueh-Ch'eng and Collingwood' (1957, response to Yü Ying-shih), 'The Classics are History: A Historicist Defence of Sacred Tradition' (1975), 'Historical Reality and the State: Some Aspects of Chang Hsueh-ch'eng's Philosophy of History' (no date). I am immensely grateful to Prof. Philip J. Ivanhoe for handing me these manuscripts.

8 Unpublished manuscript from 2006, which I have also received thanks to the courtesy of Prof. Ivanhoe.

9 David S. Nivison, 'Philosophy of History', in *Encyclopedia of Chinese Philosophy*, ed. Antonio Cua (New York & London: Routledge, 2003), 540. By 'critical philosophy of history' Nivison understands the philosophy of historiography.

10 Philip. J. Ivanhoe, 'Chinese Theories of History', in *Routledge Encyclopedia of Philosophy*, ed. Edward Craig (New York & London: Routledge, 1998).

11 Q. Edward Wang and On-cho Ng, *Mirroring the Past. The Writing and Use of History in Imperial China* (Honolulu: University of Hawai'i Press, 2005).

12 Vincent S. Leung, *The Politics of the Past in Early China* (Cambridge: Cambridge University Press, 2019).

13 Huang Chun-Chieh 黄俊杰, *Rujia sixiang yu Zhongguo lishi siwei* 儒家思想与中国历史思维 (Shanghai: Huadong shifan daxue chubanshe, 2016). Huang Chun-chieh and Jörn Rüsen (eds.), *Chinese Historical Thinking: An Intercultural Discussion* (Göttingen/Taibei: V&R Unipress/National Taiwan University Press, 2015). Huang Chun-chieh and John B. Henderson (eds.), *Notions of Time in Chinese Historical Thinking* (Hongkong: The Chinese University Press, 2006). Huang Chun-chieh and Erik Zürcher (eds.), *Time and Space in Chinese Culture* (Leiden: Brill, 1997).

14 Wing-cheuk Chan, 'Time in Wang Fuzhi's Philosophy of History', In *Notions of Time in Chinese Historical Thinking*, 115.

15 Feng Youlan, *A Short History of Chinese Philosophy* (New York: The Free Press, 1948), 136–138, 199–203, 278. Feng Youlan, *A History of Chinese Philosophy* (Princeton: Princeton University Press, 1983), vol. I: 316–317, 377–778, 388–389; vol. II: 58–87.

16 Ren Jiyu 任继愈, *Zhongguo zhexue shi* 中国哲学史 (Beijing: Renmin chubanshe, 1985). Ren Jiyu 任继愈, *Zhongguo zhexue fazhan shi* 中国哲学发展史 (Beijing: Renmin chubanshe, 1998).

17 Fang Litian 方立天, *Zhongguo gudai zhexue* 中国古代哲学, vol. 1 (Beijing: Renmin daxue chubanshe, 2006), 473–542.

18 Paul W. Kroll, *A Student's Dictionary of Classical and Medieval Chinese* (Leiden/ Boston: Brill, 2017).

Chapter 1

1   As cited in: Andrzej Wawrzynowicz, *Spór o mesjanizm. Tom 1. Rozwój idei* (Warszawa: Fundacja Augusta hrabiego Cieszkowskiego, 2015a), 29.

2   Marceli Handelsman, *Historyka. Zasady metodologji i teorji poznania historycznego* (Warszawa: Piotr Pyz i S-ka, 1928), VIII.

3   Jerzy Topolski, *Metodologia historii* (Warszawa: Państwowe Wydawnictwo Naukowe, 1984), 26–29.

4   Löwith, *Meaning in History*, 20–21.

5   Hayden White, *Metahistory: The Historical Imagination in Nineteenth-century Europe* (Baltimore: Johns Hopkins University Press, 1973), 24.

6   *Historicism*, which states that history is guided by necessary laws, must be distinguished from *historism*, interpreting social and cultural phenomena in terms of the conditions of their origin and development. Historism does not have to lead to historicism, and in its radical version it is even contradictory with historicism.

7   It is still far from strictness, also in philosophy and even in Hegelianism: the 'world history', *Weltgeschichte*, is constituted by 'historical nations' (*Historisch Volk*). Probably only Heidegger was disciplined enough to distinguish between these two terms, but he also introduced the term *Geschichtligkeit*, 'historicity'.

8   Phillip Bagby, *Culture and History* (Berkeley: University of California Press, 1959), 26–27.

9   Emil Angehrn, *Geschichtsphilosophie: eine Einführung* (Basel: Schwabe reflexe, 2012).

10 Andrzej Wawrzynowicz, 'Znaczenie refleksji historiozoficznej w rozwoju polskiej myśli społeczno-politycznej XIX i XX w.' *Filo-Sofija* 28, no. 2 (2015b): 58–59.

11 The word 'historiosophy' was employed and popularized in the English-speaking world by Gerschom Scholem in his studies on the Caballah. On this topic see: Joseph Dan, *Gershom Scholem: Between History and Historiosophy* (West Lafayette: Purdue University Press, 1983).

12 Arthur C. Danto, *Analytical Philosophy of History* (London: Cambridge University Press, 1968), 1–15.

13 Aviezer Tucker (ed.), *A Companion to the Philosophy of History and Historiography* (Malden: Wiley-Blackwell, 2010).

14 Danto, *Analytical Philosophy of History*, 13.

15 Marek Wichrowski, *Spór o naturę procesu historycznego: od Hebrajczyków do śmierci Fryderyka Nietzschego* (Warszawa: Wydawnictwo Naukowe Semper, 1995), 10–12.

16 Reinhart Koselleck, *Zeitschichten: Studien zur Historik* (Frankfurt am Main: Suhrkamp, 2000), 19.

17 Richard Jenkins, 'Disenchantment, Enchantment and Re-Enchantment: Max Weber at the Millennium', *Mind and Matter* 10, no. 2 (2012).

18 Jan Christian Smuts, *Holism and Evolution* (London: MacMillan and Co. Ltd, 1926), 86

19 See August Cieszkowski, *Selected Writings of August Cieszkowski*, trans. André Liebich (Cambridge: Cambridge University Press, 1979).

20 William H. Dray, 'Holism and individualism in history and social science', in: *The encyclopedia of philosophy*. 2nd edn. vol. 4, ed. Donald M. Borchert (1975; repr., Farmington Hills, MI: Macmillan, 2006).

21 Karl R. Popper, *The Poverty of Historicism* (Boston: The Beacon Press, 1957), 19.

22 Grace E. Cairns, 'Social Progress and Holism in T.M.P. Mahadevan's Philosophy of History', *Philosophy East and West* 20, no. 1 (1970).

23 Jouni-Matti Kuukkanen, *Postnarrativist Philosophy of Historiography* (London: Palgrave Macmillan, 2015), 44–49.

Chapter 2

1 Robert Eno, *The Confucian Creation of Heaven: Philosophy and the Defense of Ritual Mastery* (Albany: State University of New York Press, 1990), 190–197. Yan Buke 閻步克. 'Yueshi yu Ru zhi wenhua qiyuan' 乐师与儒之文化起源. *Beijing daxue xuekan* 5 (1995).

2 Michael Puett, *To Become a God: Cosmology, Sacrifice, and Self-divinization in Early China* (Cambridge: Harvard University Press, 2002), 40–49.

3 Robert Eno, 'Shang state religion and the pantheon of the oracle texts'. In *Early Chinese Religion. Part One: Shang through Han (1250 BC-220 AD)*, ed. John Lagerwey and Marc Kalinowski (Leiden/Boston: Brill, 2009), 71.

4 Review of hypotheses in: Ibid., 72–77.

5 Cf. David Keightley, 'The Oracle-Bone Inscriptions of the Late Shang Dynasty'. In *Sources of Chinese Tradition. Volume One*, ed. Theodore de Bary and Irene Bloom (New York: Columbia University Press, 1999) who writes about 'Shang conceptions of time', 'the origins of historical rectitude' and even 'the origins of history'.

6 Sarah Allan, *The Shape of the Turtle: Myth, Art, and Cosmos in Early China* (New York: State University of New York Press, 1991), 63–71.

7 Sarah Allan, *The Heir and the Sage: Dynastic Legend in Early China* (Albany: State University of New York Press, 2016), 9.

8 Eno, *The Confucian Creation of Heaven*, 23–24.

9 Eno, 'Shang state religion and the pantheon of the oracle texts', 100.

10 See also Puett, *To Become a God*, 59.

11 Sarah Allan, 'On the Identity of Shang Di and the Origin of the Concept of a Celestial Mandate (*Tian Ming*)', *Early China* 31 (2007): 1–46.36. It might be also translated 'may Di will not', etc.

12 Allan even claims that Tian was a place in which Di existed, see Ibid., 42.

13 Shaughnessy, Edward (ed.), *New Sources of Early Chinese History: An Introduction to the Reading of Inscriptions and Manuscripts* (New Haven: The Society for the Study of Early China, 1997), 78.

14 Mercedes Valmisa, 'Is the ideology of the "Mandate of Heaven" already present in Western Zhou bronze inscriptions?', 2. Unpublished paper. Available at: https://www.academia.edu/11319002/Is_the_Ideology_of_the_Mandate_of_Heaven_already_present_in_Western_Zhou_Bronze_Inscriptions.

15 Ibid., 24–27.
16 Shaughnessy, *New Sources of Early Chinese History*, 113–119.
17 Valmisa, 'Is the ideology of the "Mandate of Heaven" . . ., 10.
18 Michael Loewe and Edward Shaughnessy, *The Cambridge History of Ancient China: From the origins of civilization to 221 BC* (Cambridge: Cambridge University Press, 2008), 320–322.
19 Edward Shaughnessy, 'History and Inscriptions, China.' In *The Oxford History of Historical Writing. Volume One. Beginnings to AD 600*, ed. Andrew Feldherr and Grant Hardy (Oxford: Oxford University Press, 2011), 389.
20 Valmisa, 'Is the ideology of the "Mandate of Heaven" . . ., 1, 6, 12, 15.
21 Eno, *The Confucian Creation of Heaven*, 26.
22 According to tradition, Confucius chose three hundred songs from more than three thousand, guided by the criterion of compliance with rituals. The first mention of this, however, comes only from Sima Qian in the first century BC (*Shiji* 47:1914). The *Analects* states that after Confucius had returned to the Lu, 'music was corrected, and the *ya* and *song* found their proper place' (*Lunyu* 9:118), which is insufficient confirmation of Sima Qian's thesis.
23 Nylan, *The Five 'Confucian' Classics* (New Haven: Yale University Press, 2001), 8.
24 *Lunyu*, 13:173.
25 *Maoshi*, 1:13–15.
26 *Maoshi*, 6:434.
27 *Maoshi*, 0 7:466.
28 *Maoshi*, 9:583–586.
29 *Maoshi*, 12:704.754–755.
30 *Maoshi*, 18:1184.1256–1258.
31 *Maoshi*, 12:730–731. Translation from James Legge, *The Chinese Classics. Vol. IV – Part II* (Hongkong/ London: Lane, Crawford & Co./Trübner & Co., 1871), 325–326.
32 See Chen Zhi, *The Shaping of the Book of Songs: From ritualization to secularization* (Sankt Augustin: Steyler Verlag, 2007), 99–100. Note that the notion of secularization has to be used carefully and in a more general way than usual (in reference to Christianity). The key argument against interpretations such as Chen's is that Tian was not treated as a being outside the world.
33 Unfortunately, the credibility of the *Book of Documents* is far more problematic than the credibility of the *Book of Songs*. Legends bringing Confucius under the arrangement of existing records (named *Shuzhuan*) into the *Shangshu* come, again, only from Sima Qian. None other than Mencius doubted the reliability of the *Shangshu*, saying that 'it would be better not to have the Book of Documents than to give it full credence', and adding that 'unwelcome' records were destroyed (*Mengzi* 12A:321, 14A:381). Although problems with the credibility of the *Shangshu* began before the unification of China, a serious challenge emerged with the burning of the books. The New Text version, created as a result of the writing down of all remembered pieces of the *Shangshu* in clerical script, is much shorter than the so-called Old Text version. However, as a result of deliberate distortion of the Old Text version, which took place in the fourth century CE, the text is considered to be unreliable. This does not mean that the Old Text version was completely created in the fourth century – it does contain a lot of original material. The New Text version, too, is not completely free of doubts. Hence, both versions will be considered here, with specification of which quotations are sourced from the Old Text.
34 *Shangshu*, 8:196. Old Text (further OT).

35 *Shangshu*, 4:108–110.

36 *Shangshu*, 12:297.

37 *Shangshu*, 8:200.213. OT.

38 *Shangshu*, 13:342.348.

39 *Shangshu*, 5:115, 14:360, 16:422.

40 *Shangshu*, 19:536.539.

41 *Shangshu*, 8:200. OT.

42 Wang Can 王灿, 'Shangshu lishi sixiang yanjiu' 尚书历史思想研究 (PhD diss., Shandong Daxue, Jinan 2011b), 76, 84.

43 *Shangshu*, 8:191.

44 *Shangshu*, 8:200. OT.

45 *Shangshu*, 16:439.

46 *Shangshu*, 8:216. OT.

47 *Shangshu*, 5:130. OT.

48 *Shangshu*, 9:235.

49 This enigmatic phrase might indicate that they are remembered by Heaven. If so, that would be a next step towards further personification of Tian. This would resemble the Jewish culture, in which the idea of history was created along with the myth of the archive – God preserving in his infinite memory all human sins (see Peter Sloterdijk, *Rage and Time: A psychopolitical investigation* (New York: Columbia University Press, 2012)).

50 *Shangshu*, 10:258–259, 14:373.

51 *Shangshu*, 19:542.

52 *Shangshu*, 7:173.

53 *Shangshu*, 8:203. OT.

54 *Shangshu*, 17:460–461.

55 *Shangshu*, 4:99.

56 *Shangshu*, 17:453.

57 Wang Can, 'Shangshu lishi sixiang yanjiu', 60–66. This opposition is too superficial: the Jews were sentenced to exile as a punishment for sins. On the other hand, God forgave Israel many times, which returned to him. The Xia and Shang dynasties, in turn, will never get the Mandate back. On this point Wang is right, but only providing that those dynasties will be treated as different ethnically, which is highly controversial.

58 *Shangshu*, 8:211.

59 *Shangshu*, 19:552.

60 *Shangshu*, 9:226.

61 *Shangshu*, 18:486.

62 David Schaberg, 'Foundations of Chinese Historiography: Literary Representation in *Zuo Zhuan* and *Guoyu*' (PhD diss., Harvard University, Harvard 1996), 197.

63 Allan, *The Heir and the Sage*, 37–58. For an analysis of the narrative structure of the legends of Yao and Shun from the viewpoint of H. White's narrativism see Dawid Rogacz, 'The Motif of Legendary Emperors Yao and Shun in Ancient Chinese Literature', in *Rethinking Orient. In Search of Sources and Inspirations*, ed. Adam Bednarczyk, Magdalena Kubarek, and Maciej Szatkowski (Warsaw: Peter Lang, 2017), 113–125.

64 See Wang Can, 'Shangshu lishi sixiang yanjiu', 174–182.

65 *Shangshu*, 20:572.

66 Martin Kern, 'Language and the Ideology of Kingship in the "Canon of Yao". In *Ideology of Power and Power of Ideology in Early China*, ed. Yuri Pines, Paul R. Goldin, and Martin Kern (Leiden/Boston: Brill, 2015), 131.

67 *Shangshu*, 15:396. My italics.

68 Yi Ning and Wang Xianhua, 'Historical Identity in the Shangshu', *Journal of Chinese Philosophy* 40, no. 1 (2013): 187–188.

69 *Shangshu*, 13:331–340.

70 Michael Hunter quotes twenty-two works written before the common era with a total volume of approximately 227,000 characters, which might be an equivalent source of information about Confucius; see Michael Hunter, *Confucius Beyond the* Analects (Leiden/Boston: Brill, 2017), 13.

71 Makeham demonstrates that the *Lunyu* did not exist as a book before 150–140 BC; see John Makeham, 'The Formation of *Lunyu* as a Book', *Monumenta Serica* 44, no. 1 (2016).

72 Liu Fengchun 刘凤春, *Lishi zhexue shiyu xia de Kongzi ruxue sixiang yanjiu* 历史哲学视域下的孔子儒学思想研究 (M.A. diss., Yanbian Daxue, Jilin 2009).

73 *Lunyu*, 2:19.

74 *Lunyu*, 7:84.

75 *Lunyu*, 19:261.

76 *Lunyu*, 15:214.

77 *Lunyu*, 3:33.36.

78 *Lunyu*, 15:215.

79 *Lunyu*, 8:106–109. Translation from Confucius, *Analects. With Selections from Traditional Commentaries*, trans. Edward Slingerland (Indianapolis/Cambridge: Hackett Publishing, 2003), 84.

80 Allan, *The Heir and the Sage*, 125.

81 Full list in: Tan Sor-hoon, 'Balancing Conservatism and Innovation: The Pragmatic *Analects*', In *Dao Companion to the* Analects, ed. Amy Olberding (Dordrecht: Springer, 2013), 341–342.

82 *Lunyu*, 1:10.

83 *Lunyu*, 17:239. Also *Lunyu*, 14:195.202.

84 *Lunyu*, 16:224.

85 *Lunyu*, 11:142.

86 *Lunyu*, 2:23–24.

87 Leung, *The Politics of the Past*, 74.

88 Herbert Fingarette, *Confucius: The Secular as Sacred* (Long Grove: Waveland Press, 1972), 57.

89 In his commentary to this passage, Zhu Xi writes: 'The Three Dynasties [Xia, Yin, Zhou] succeeded one another, each following its predecessor and unable to change its predecessor's ways. The only sorts of alternations made involved such [minor matters as standards for ritual emblems. . .], and all of their past traces can be fully observed today. Thus, if in the future some king arises to succeed the Zhou, the manner in which he will follow or make alterations to ritual will not exceed what we have seen in the past. This will be true even one hundred generations hence, let alone only ten generations. This is the manner in which the sage [Confucius] judged the future – unlike those students of prophetic and occult arts who arose in later generations' (Confucius, *Analects*, 16).

90 *Lunyu*, 3:44.

91 *Lunyu*, 2:15.

92 *Lunyu*, 7:93.

93 *Lunyu*, 14:199.

94 *Lunyu*, 6:82.

95   Philip J. Ivanhoe, 'Heaven as a Source for Ethical Warrant in Early Confucianism,' *Dao. A Journal of Comparative Philosophy* 6, no. 3 (2007): 215. Eno distinguishes both descriptive and prescriptive elements of the conception of Tian in the *Analects* (Eno, *The Confucian Creation of Heaven*, 82–94).

96   *Lunyu*, 17:241.

97   *Lunyu*, 5:61.

98   *Lunyu*, 12:159.

99   *Lunyu*, 3:41; 18:249.

100 *Lunyu*, 9:113.

101 *Lunyu*, 14:199.

102 Chen Ning, 'Confucius' view of fate (*ming*),' *Journal of Chinese Philosophy* 24, no. 3 (1997): 330, 343. It could also argue for the *Analects* having two authors, see Ibid., 332.

103 *Liji*, 21:658–661.

104 See Bart Dessein, 'Yearning for the Lost Paradise: The 'Great Unity' (*datong*) and Its Philosophical Interpretations,' *Asian Studies* 5, no. 1 (2017): 83–102.

105 *Liji*, 21:662.668–669.

106 Michael Ing, *The Dysfunction of Ritual in Early Confucianism* (New York: Oxford University Press, 2012), 122.

107 *Liji*, 22:690.706.709.

108 Quotation from the edition in Sarah Allan, *Buried Ideas: Legends of Abdication and Ideal Government in Recently Discovered Early Chinese Bamboo-slip Manuscripts* (New York: State University of New York Press, 2015), 119.

109 Ibid., 129. The term 'love of people' (*ài rén*) did not appear there, and what we find is a 'love of kin' (*ài qīn*), which in connection with the central position of *ren* shows, as Allan claims, that this is a Confucian, not Mohist, text (Ibid., 101).

110 Ibid., 130. On the Confucian character of the *Tang-Yu zhi dao* see Xu Wentao 徐文涛 'Xian Qin Rujia lishi zhexue yanjiu – yi Kong, Meng, Xun sixiang wei zhongxin' 先秦儒家历史哲学研究——以孔孟荀思想为中心. (PhD diss., Shandong Daxue, Jinan 2006), 60–61.

111 Quotation from the edition in Dirk Meyer, *Philosophy on Bamboo. Text and the Production of Meaning in Early China* (Leiden/Boston: Brill, 2011), 269. On the *Qiong da yi shi* historiosophy: Xu Wentao, 'Xian Qin Rujia lishi zhexue', 56–57.

112 Ibid., 57–58, 271.

113 Allan, *Buried Ideas*, 225.

114 Ibid., 234–252.

115 Yuri Pines, 'Political mythology and dynastic legitimacy in the *Rong Cheng shi* manuscript', *Bulletin of School of Oriental and African Studies* 73, no. 3 (2010).

116 Allan, *Buried Ideas*, 182.

117 The most important is David Nivison: Nivison, 'Mengzi as Philosopher of History', 2002, who distinguished Mengzi's speculative and critical philosophy of history. As for Xunzi, his philosophy of history has been omitted even in the latest companion to his thought: Eric Hutton (ed.), *Dao Companion to Xunzi* (Dordrecht: Springer, 2016). I have discussed Xunzi's philosophy of history in 'In the Shadow of the Decay. The Philosophy of History of Mencius and Xunzi', *Asian Studies* 21, no. 1 (2017): 159–171.

118 *Mengzi*, 8:233.

119 *Mengzi*, 3:97, 7:211.

120 *Mengzi*, 5:127–128.

121 *Mengzi*, 4:104. Translation from Mencius, *Mencius*, trans. Irene Bloom, ed. Philip J. Ivanhoe (New York: Columbia University Press, 2001), 39.
122 *Mengzi*, 12:341.
123 *Mengzi*, 10:291. Mencius, *Mencius*, 119.
124 Cf. *Mengzi*, 2:57; 9:254.
125 On 'writing history in accord with an ideal', see Nivison, 'Mengzi as Philosopher of History', 286.
126 *Mengzi*, 3:93.
127 *Mengzi*, 13:354.
128 *Mengzi*, 8:213.226.
129 *Mengzi*, 14:405.
130 In my sense, and that of Nivison's ('picturing of history guided by a non-empirical commitment'), Nivison, 'Mengzi as Philosopher of History', 283.
131 *Mengzi*, 4:62.
132 *Mengzi*, 3:101.
133 *Mengzi*, 2:36.55.
134 *Mengzi*, 7:194.
135 *Mengzi*, 9: 256.259.
136 *Mengzi*, 12:346. Mencius, *Mencius*, 143.
137 *Mengzi*, 4:116.125. *Tiānlì* means 'Heaven's servant' and might be treated as a structural counterpart of the Western ideas of 'providential man'.
138 *Mengzi*, 3:91. Again the figure of 'Heaven's servant'.
139 *Mengzi*, 9:256–259.
140 *Mengzi*, 5:147.
141 *Mengzi*, 14:387.
142 *Mengzi*, 7:185. Mencius, *Mencius*, 73.
143 Leung, *The Politics of the Past*, 169. Leung even argues that for Mencius 'there is no particular reason to valorize the past over the present', cf. Ibid., 176.
144 *Mengzi*, 7:191.
145 *Mengzi*, 6:176.
146 *Mengzi*, 3:69. Mencius, *Mencius*, 28.
147 *Mengzi*, 6:177–178. Mencius, *Mencius*, 69–70.
148 Xu Wentao, 'Xian Qin rujia lishi zhexue', 70, 75. As Xu claims, this objectivity is manifested in historical cycles determined by *ren*, see Ibid., 80–81.
149 *Xunzi*, 18:468. English quotations generally come from Xunzi. *Xunzi: The Complete Text*, trans. Eric Hutton (Princeton: Princeton University Press, 2016), here: Xunzi, *Xunzi*, 273, and exceptionally from Xunzi, *A Translation and Study of the Complete Works*, vol. I, II, III, trans. John Knoblock (Stanford: Stanford University Press, 1988, 1990, 1994), later: Xunzi, *A Translation*.
150 *Xunzi*, 1:2.
151 *Xunzi*, 3:98.
152 Xunzi, *A Translation* (1990): 3.
153 *Xunzi*, 1:34.
154 *Xunzi*, 2:44.
155 *Xunzi*, 4:133. Xunzi, *Xunzi*, 60.
156 *Xunzi*, 2:68.
157 *Xunzi*, 1:11. Xunzi, *Xunzi*, 5.
158 *Xunzi*, 7:209. Xunzi, *A Translation* (1990): 153–154.
159 *Xunzi*, 12:332.337–338.

160 *Xunzi*, 5:172.
161 Antonio S. Cua, *Human Nature, Ritual, and History: Studies in Xunzi and Chinese Philosophy* (Washington: Catholic University of America Press, 2005), 73–98.
162 *Xunzi*, 2:63.
163 *Xunzi*, 17:442–3.
164 *Xunzi*, 8:236.
165 *Xunzi*, 2:59. I use Knoblock's translation (Xunzi, *A Translation* (1988), 189–190), because Hutton (Xunzi, *Xunzi*, 26) translated *sāndài* as simply 'three generations'.
166 *Xunzi*, 2:48.
167 *Xunzi*, 3:81.
168 *Xunzi*, 3:82. Xunzi, *A Translation* (1988), 207).
169 Masayuki Satō, *The Confucian Quest for Order: The Origin and Formation of the Political Thought of Xun Zi* (Leiden/Boston: Brill, 2003), 315–335.
170 *Xunzi*, 3:83.94.
171 *Xunzi*, 3:82.
172 Ibid.
173 *Xunzi*, 13:369.
174 *Xunzi*, 3:80.94.
175 *Xunzi*, 4:138.
176 *Xunzi*, 11:306–307.
177 *Xunzi* ,11:311.313. Xunzi, *A Translation* (1994), 17–18.
178 *Xunzi*, 11:317. Xunzi, *Xunzi*, 180.
179 *Xunzi*, 13:373.
180 *Xunzi*, 17:438.441.
181 *Xunzi*, 17:435. Xunzi, *A Translation* (1994), 151.
182 *Xunzi*, 19:488.
183 Xu Wentao argues that while the Mencian philosophy of history is centred on morality (*dàodé*), Xunzi's philosophy of history is based on the role of (idealized) social institutions (*zhìdù*) (Xu Wentao, 'Xian Qin rujia lishi zhexue', 97–106).

Chapter 3

1 *Shiji*, 130:3288–3289.
2 The thinkers of this school advocated a classless agricultural-based state, without division of labour and with constant commodity prices, where the ruler works physically just like the people. Their ideas inspired European Physiocrats, although their writings were destroyed under the Qin (Wiebke Denecke, *The Dynamics of Masters Literature: Early Chinese Thought from Confucius to Han Feizi* (Boston: Harvard University Asia Center, 2011), 38).
3 *Hanshu*, 30:1367–1378. *Jiā* literally means 'family', including the family of thinkers, that is 'school'. It could also mean 'experts', but then it does not explain the meaning of the phrases *liùjiā* and *shíjiā* (six/ten experts?), whereas rendering *jia* as 'classes/types of experts' is almost synonymous with translating *jia* as a 'school'.
4 *Zhuangzi*, 10:1082–1091.
5 Cf. Mark Csikszentmihalyi and Michael Nylan, 'Constructing Lineages and Inventing Traditions through Exemplary Figures in Early China', *T'oung Pao* 89, no. 1 (2003).
6 Arthur C. Danto, 'Narrative Sentences', *History and Theory* 2, no. 2 (1962): 154–155.

7   Randall Collins states that 'it was in this period of "the hundred schools" that Chinese intellectual life was most similar to that of Greece'. Even under his sociological interpretation of philosophical school, Collins does not understand them as organizations but rather as (only sometimes organized) 'chains of teachers and students' that form 'circles of allies (. . .) and debaters' (Randall Collins, *The Sociology of Philosophies. A Global Theory of Intellectual Change* (Cambridge/London: The Belknap Press of Harvard University Press, 1998), 65, 145.

8   On the issue of the authorship and corruption of the text throughout Chinese history: Yuri Pines, 'Dating a Pre-Imperial Text: The Case Study of the *Book of Lord Shang*', *Early China* 39 (2016).

9   Herrlee Creel, 'Shen Pu-Hai: A Secular Philosopher of Administration', *Journal of Chinese Philosophy* 1, no. 2 (1974). Eirik L. Harris, *The Shenzi Fragments: A Philosophical Analysis and Translation* (New York: Columbia University Press, 2017).

10 See Allan, *The Heir and the Sage*, 7.

11 *Zhushu jinian*, 1:1–2.

12 *Fa* could also mean 'method', 'model', or 'standard' – the term was frequently used by the Mohists and Confucians in these senses. *Fa* in the thought of Han Fei is polysemic, meaning both law and model (concordant with Dao). *Fa* in the thought of Shang Yang means usually law, which is illustrated by the following phrases: to establish law (*lìfǎ/cuòfǎ*), to change law (*biànfǎ*), to hate law (*èfǎ*).

13 *Shangjunshu*, 2:48, 3:62.

14 *Shangjunshu*, 3:82–83.

15 The 'Six Laws' chapter, *Shangjunshu* 5:147. Translation from Shang Yang, *The Book of Lord Shang. Apologetics of State Power in Early China*, trans. Yuri Pines (New York: Columbia University Press, 2017), 249.

16 *Shangjunshu*, 4:107.

17 *Shangjunshu*, 1:4.

18 *Shangjunshu*, 2:47.

19 *Shangjunshu*, 7:100. Interestingly, similar duality of political rules was noticed by Machiavelli.

20 *Shangjunshu*, 1:8. Translation from Shang Yang, *The Book of Lord Shang*, trans. J.J.L. Duyvendak (Londres: Arthur Probsthain, 1928), 173; modified.

21 The concept of substance is usually defined in contraposition to changeable and 'accidental' properties. Hence, substantialization in the political philosophy and the philosophy of history pertains to the belief in the existence of an unchangeable, and thereby universal, way of making politics and, respectively, history.

22 Yuri Pines, 'From Historical Evolution to the End of History: Past, Present and Future from Shang Yang to the First Emperor', in *Dao Companion to the Philosophy of Han Fei*, ed. Paul R. Goldin (New York: Springer, 2013), 27–28.

23 *Shangjunshu*, 2:53. Shang Yang, *The Book of Lord Shang* (1928), 228.

24 *Shangjunshu*, 1:5, 3:62, 5:147.

25 *Shangjunshu*, 1:23–24.29–30. These are the theoretical bases for the later edict on the burning of the books.

26 *Shangjunshu*, 2:41–42.

27 Shang Yang is in this respect astonishingly similar to Montesquieu, who considered virtue the principle of the republic, and honour the principle of the monarchy.

28 *Shangjunshu*, 4:106–107.

29 Yuri Pines and Gideon Shelach. '"Using the past to serve the present': Comparative perspectives on Chinese and Western theories of the origins of the state'. In *Genesis*

and regeneration: Essays on conceptions of origins, ed. Shaul Shaked (Jerusalem: The Israel Academy of Science and Humanities, 2015), 149.

30 See Pines, 'From Historical Evolution to the End of History', 26.
31 *Shangjunshu*, 2:55.
32 Pines, 'From Historical Evolution to the End of History', 35.
33 *Shangjunshu*, 3:82.
34 Zhang Linxiang 張林祥, *Shangjunshu de chengshu yu sixiang yanjiu* 商君书的成书与思想研究 (Beijing: Renmin chubanshe, 2008), 167–186.
35 Eirik L.Harris, 'Legalism: Introducing a Concept and Analyzing Aspects of Han Fei's Political Philosophy'. *Philosophy Compass* 9, no. 3 (2014): 159–161.
36 *Hanfeizi*, 2:36, 3:71.
37 *Hanfeizi*, 19:446.
38 *Hanfeizi*, 19:457.
39 *Hanfeizi*, 5:126, 15:350, 17:407, 20:465.
40 This parallel, however, is limited and captures only one aspect of Han Fei's thought. Elsewhere, we read that 'the sovereign must be sufficiently enlightened to understand the principles of governance and strict to bring them into effect. Hence, if it requires action contrary to the will of the people, he will force them into these rules' *Hanfeizi*, 5:120.
41 *Hanfeizi*, 17:410.
42 *Hanfeizi*, 4:103.
43 *Hanfeizi*, 20:467.
44 *Hanfeizi*, 19:442. Translation from Han Fei, *Han Fei Tzu. Basic Writings*, trans. Burton Watson (New York: Columbia University Press, 1964), 96–97; modernized.
45 *Hanfeizi*, 11:263.
46 *Hanfeizi*, 5:120.
47 Li Yucheng 李玉诚, *Hanfeizi lishi sixiang yanjiu* 韩非子历史思想研究 (PhD. diss., Shandong Daxue, Jinan 2014), 80–83.
48 *Hanfeizi*, 15:442–443.
49 Pines, Schelach, 'Using the past to serve the present', 150–152.
50 *Hanfeizi*, 5:444.
51 Pines, 'From Historical Evolution to the End of History', 38.
52 Ibid., 37.
53 *Hanfeizi*, 8:207.
54 Pines, 'From Historical Evolution to the End of History', 38.
55 Nick Mithen, *History and the Han Fei Zi* (M.A. diss., Fudan Daxue, Shanghai 2014), 33–34. Pines speaks of the end of history, but regarding the Qin, see Pines 'From Historical Evolution to the End of History', 39–43.
56 François Jullien, *The Propensity of Things: Toward a History of Efficacy in China* (New York: Zone Books, 1999), 12.
57 This is how *shi* is translated in Chapter Five by Lionel Giles: Sunzi, *The Art of War: Sunzi bing fa*, trans. Lionel Giles (Berkeley: Ulysses Press, 2007), 41–48.
58 See Roger Ames, *The Art of Rulership. A Study of Ancient Chinese Political Thought* (New York: State University of New York Press, 1994), 68.
59 *Shenzi*,1:9.
60 *Shangjunshu*, 2:46.49, 5:145.
61 *Shangjunshu*, 2:54, 4:113.
62 *Shangjunshu*, 3:72.
63 *Shangjunshu*, 5:146.

64 *Shangjunshu*, 5:132–133.

65 *Hanfeizi*, 17:391.

66 *Hanfeizi*, 17:392. Han Fei tells the story of a dealer who said his halberd (*máo*) pierces every shield (*dùn*), and his shield cannot be pierced by any halberd. The tem *maodun* henceforth means 'contradiction'.

67 *Mengzi*, 6:178.

68 Carine Defoort and Nicolas Standaert (eds.), *The Mozi as an Evolving Text. Different Voices in Early Chinese Thought* (Leiden/Boston: Brill, 2013), 1–34.

69 *Mozi*, 9:265.

70 *Mozi*, 9:293–295; 12:442.453–454.

71 *Mozi*, 5:130.

72 *Mozi*, 2:44–47.68.

73 *Mozi*, 4:101.

74 *Mozi*, 5:139.146.

75 *Mozi*, 3:79. Translation from Mozi, *The Book of Master Mo*, trans. Ian Johnston (London: Penguin Books, 2013), 51–52.

76 *Mozi*, 1:30–38.

77 Michael Puett, *The ambivalence of creation: Debates concerning innovation and artifice in early China* (Stanford: Stanford University Press, 2001), 54–56.

78 *Mozi*, 3:83–85.

79 *Mozi*, 1:22–23. Leung even refers to Mozi's Heaven as 'transhistorical' set of standards exemplified in the actions of exemplary historical figures (Leung, *The Politics of the Past*, 101–105).

80 *Mozi*, 7:195.201–202.204.

81 *Mozi*, 3:81–82.

82 *Mozi*, 7:195. Standaert (Defoort and Standaert, (*The Mozi as an Evolving Text*, 257)) claims that in addition to the *Mozi* the only instance of Tian speaking in direct speech could be found in the *Book of Songs*. However, that example (帝謂文王) can be successfully interpreted in indirect speech ('told the king to'), and moreover, not Tian but Di is mentioned there. In the case of *yue* and the pronoun *wo*, there are no such doubts.

83 *Mozi*, 7:202. See Puett, *The ambivalence of creation*, 52.

84 Lu Yihan 路懿菡, *Xian Qin zhuzi lishi zhexue sixiang yanjiu* 先秦诸子历史哲学思想研究 (MA diss., Liaoning Shifan Daxue, Dalian 2009), 49.

85 Erica Fox Brindley, *Individualism in Early China. Human Agency and the Self in Thought and Politics* (Honolulu: University of Hawai'i Press, 2010), 26.

86 *Mozi*, 9: 273–274.

87 See Michael Loewe (ed.), *Early Chinese texts. A Bibliographical Guide* (Berkeley: The Society for the Study of Early China, 1993), 56–66.269–292.298–308.

88 *Laozi*, 5:22.

89 *Liezi*, 6:206.

90 *Liezi*, 7:234.

91 *Zhuangzi*, 5:517.

92 *Laozi*, 15:57–58, 65:263; *Zhuangzi*, 9:1003–1005.

93 *Zhuangzi*, 1:22, 2:143–147.187–193, 3:282–285, 5:415–416, 9:965.987–988.

94 *Zhuangzi*, 3:242. Translation from Zhuangzi, *The Complete Works of Zhuangzi*, trans. Burton Watson (New York: Columbia University Press, 2013), 44.

95 Leung, *The Politics of the Past*, 162.

96 Franklin Perkins, 'The *Laozi* and the Cosmogonic Turn in Classical Chinese Philosophy'. *Frontiers of Philosophy in China* 11, no. 2 (2016): 194.

97   *Zhuangzi*, 1:79.

98   Interestingly, the rejection of reversibility of historical changes does not lead to any positive cyclical view of history, cf. *Zhuangzi* 5: 515: 'Rituals and regulations are something that change in response to the times (…) past and present are no more alike than are a monkey and the Duke of Zhou!', Zhuangzi, *The Complete Works*, 113.

99   Fang Litian, *Zhongguo gudai zhexue*, 469.

100   *Laozi*, 80:307–309.

101   *Zhuangzi*, 9:995.

102   *Zhuangzi*, 4:357.

103   *Zhuangzi*, 6:551–552. Zhuangzi *The Complete Works*, 123; modified.

104   *Zhuangzi*, 4:336.

105   *Lüshi Chunqiu*, 20.1:1330.

106   The authorship of this work, known in China as the *Changes of the Zhou* 周易 *Zhōuyì*, is attributed to Fu Xi, Wen Wang, Duke Zhou, and in the final edition, Confucius.

107   Edward Shaughnessy, *Unearthing the Changes: Recently discovered manuscripts of the Yi Jing (I Ching) and related texts* (New York: Columbia University Press, 2014), xiii. For details on the textual history of the *Yijing*, especially in the light of the recent archaeological findings, I cross-reference the work of Shaughnessy.

108   *Zhouyi*, 351.

109   *Zhouyi*, 354.

110   Liu Shu-hsien, 'Philosophical Analysis and Hermeneutics: Reflections on Methodology via an Examination of My Understanding of Chinese Philosophy' in *Two Roads to Wisdom? Chinese and Analytic Philosophical Traditions*, ed. Bo Mou (Chicago/La Salle: Open Court, 2001), 147.

111   Cheng Chung-Ying, 'Interpreting Paradigm of Change in Chinese Philosophy', *Journal of Chinese Philosophy* 38, no. 3 (2011): 345.

112   Zheng Wangeng, 'Tracing the source of the idea of time in Yizhuan', *Frontiers of Philosophy in China* 5, no. 1 (2010): 58.

113   *Zhouyi*, 349–369.

114   Tian Chenshan, *Chinese Dialectics. From* Yijing *to Marxism* (Lanham: Lexington Books, 2005), 23–41.

115   其事無不復. Esther Klein, 'Constancy and the Changes: A Comparative Reading of *Heng Xian*', *Dao: A Journal of Comparative Philosophy* 12, no. 2 (2013): 213.

116   Xie Xuanjun 谢选骏, Zhouyi *de lishi zhexue* 周易的历史哲学 (Raleigh: Lulu, 2015), 85.

117   The writings of its creator, Zou Yan (305-240 BC), have survived only in small fragments. Sima Qian emphasizes that Zou Yan – a member of the Jixia Academy – was a very popular philosopher, and the kings of the states he was visiting gave him private audiences and privileges. Sima Qian recognizes that the cause of the collapse of the Yin-Yang School was its merging with Confucianism, see *Shiji*, 74:2344–2346.

118   *Shiji*, 130:3289.

119   *Shiji*, 28:1368–1369.9.

120   Joseph Needham, *Science and Civilisation in China. Vol. 2. History of Scientific Thought* (Cambridge: Cambridge University Press, 1956), 241.

121   This may refer to the works titled *Zhongshi* and *Dasheng*; the first is mentioned by the collectaneum.

122   *Shiji*, 74: 2344. Translation from Needham, *Science and Civilisation in China*, 232–233.

123 As cited in: Needham, *Science and Civilisation in China*, 238.

124 Ibid., 239.

125 *Lüshi Chunqiu*, 16.1:955.

126 *Lüshi Chunqiu*, 20.8:1422.

127 *Shiji* 85:2510.

128 As in: John Knoblock and Jeffrey Riegel, *The Annals of Lü Buwei. A Complete Study and Translation* (Stanford: Stanford University Press, 2000), 693–698.

129 *Lüshi Chunqiu*, 1.3:35, 2.3:86, 3.5:174–5, 8.4:457, 12.2:630, 20.3:1355–57, 23.3:1563–4.

130 *Lüshi Chunqiu*, 7.2:388–389, 8.3:445–6, 9:2484–5, 9.4:504–505.

131 *Lüshi Chunqiu*, 14.5:797–8, 15.8:944, 17.6:1120.

132 *Lüshi Chunqiu*, 1.4:45, 2.4:97, 13.4:702–3. A Mohist Tian Jiu is attributed with the idea that only proper time gives success, and that without it even virtue and wisdom yield nothing, *Lüshi Chunqiu* 14.3:773. This motif, present in the *Qiong da yi shi*, does not appear in the *Mozi* and is hardly compatible with the Mohist faith in the self-sufficiency of morality. It testifies to a mistake or an intentional attempt to compromise the Mohists.

133 *Lüshi Chunqiu*, 4.2:198–199, 14.1:736–8, 19.4–6:1280–1305.

134 *Lüshi Chunqiu*, 19.3:1264–1266, 20.1:1330–1331, 25.3–4:1659–1679.

135 *Lüshi Chunqiu*, 12.4:640–641, 26.3:1718–1720, 26.6:1790–1792.

136 *Lüshi Chunqiu*, 2.2:75–77, 18.1:1151–1153.

137 *Lüshi Chunqiu*, 5.2:258–260.

138 *Lüshi Chunqiu*, 11.5:611.

139 *Guanzi*, 1:13, 12:241, 19:379, 30:565–566.

140 *Guanzi*, 2:43–44.

141 *Guanzi*, 7:125–128.

142 *Guanzi*, 49:937.

143 *Guanzi*, 6:105.

144 *Guanzi*, 14:273–275.900–906.

145 *Guanzi*, 12:250.

146 *Yinwenzi*, 2:139.141–143.

147 *Yinwenzi*, 1:103.

148 Carine Defoort, *The Pheasant Cap Master* (He guan zi). *A Rhetorical Reading* (Albany: State University of New York Press, 1997), 28–30.

149 *Heguanzi*, 5:79.

150 Marnix Wells, *The Pheasant Cap Master and the End of History: linking religion to philosophy in early China* (St. Petersburg: Three Pines Press, 2013), 60–68.

151 *Heguanzi*, 9:167–221.

152 *Heguanzi*, 9:214.

Chapter 4

1   Martin Kern, *The Stele Inscriptions of Ch'in Shih-huang: Text and Ritual in Early Chinese Imperial Representation* (New Haven: American Oriental Society, 2000), 13–14.

2   *Shiji*, 6:236.

3   Ibid.

4   Wang Gaoxin 汪高鑫, *Zhongguo shixue sixiang tongshi. Qin-Han juan* 中国史学思想通史。 秦汉卷 (Hefei: Huangshan shushe, 2002), 59.

5   *Shiji*, 6:254–255.

6   *Gongyang zhuan*, 3:55, 10:204. See my interpretation of the narrative of the *Spring and Autumn Annals* and its commentaries from the viewpoint of a postnarrativist theory of historiography: Dawid Rogacz, "'Spring and Autumn Annals" as Narrative Explanation', in *Towards a Revival of Analytical Philosophy of History. Around Paul A. Roth's Vision of Historical Sciences*, ed. Krzysztof Brzechczyn (Leiden-Boston: Brill-Rodopi, 2018), 254–272.

7   *Gongyang zhuan*, 6:123, 11:232.

8   *Gongyang zhuan*, 1:10.

9   *Gongyang zhuan*, 10:199.

10   *Gongyang zhuan*, 26:575, 28: 628.

11   Sarah Queen, *From Chronicle to Canon. The hermeneutics of* the Spring and Autumn, *according to Tung Chung-shu* (Cambridge: Cambridge University Press, 1996), 13, 40, 76-7.

12   Michael Loewe, *Dong Zhongshu, a 'Confucian' Heritage and the* Chunqiu fanlu (Leiden/Boston: Brill, 2011), 291. Gary Arbuckle, 'Inevitable Treason: Dong Zhongshu's Theory of Historical Cycles and Early Attempts to Invalidate the Han Mandate', *Journal of the American Oriental Society* 115, no. 4 (1995): 587.

13   Loewe, *Dong Zhongshu*, 16.

14   Queen, *From Chronicle to Canon*, 67.

15   Gary Arbuckle, *Restoring Dong Zhongshu (BCE 195–115): an experiment in historical and philosophical reconstruction* (PhD diss., University of British Columbia, Vancouver 1983), 116–117, 296–297, 541.

16   *Hanshu*, 56:1901–1906.

17   *Hanshu*, 56:1902.

18   *Hanshu*, 56:1909.

19   *Hanshu*, 56:1913.

20   *Hanshu*, 56:1912.

21   *Hanshu*, 56:1915.

22   Ibid.

23   *Hanshu*, 56:1916.

24   Arbuckle, 'Inevitable Treason', 592.

25   *Chunqiu fanlu* 17:183. The translation follows Dong Zhongshu, *Luxuriant Gems of the Spring and Autumn. Attributed to Dong Zhongshu*, trans. John Major and Sarah Queen (New York: Columbia University Press, 2016), 182.

26   *Chunqiu fanlu*, 3.1:48.

27   *Chunqiu fanlu*, 5.7:99, 13.4:170.

28   *Hanshu*, 56:1904.

29   *Chunqiu fanlu*, 3.4:62.

30   *Chunqiu fanlu*, 2.7:39. Translation from: Dong, *Luxuriant Gems*, 88–89.

31   *Chunqiu fanlu*, 5.5:96.

32   *Chunqiu fanlu*, 5.7:99. *Hanshu* 56:1913.

33   *Chunqiu fanlu*, 1.4:16.

34   Liu Jiahe 刘家和, *Gudai Zhongguo yu shijie: yige gushi yanjiuzhe de sikao* 古代中国与世界: 一个古史研究者的思考 (Wuhan: Wuhan chubanshe, 1995), 449–450.

35   *Chunqiu fanlu*, 81.2:647.

36   *Chunqiu fanlu*, 60:503.511.

37   *Chunqiu fanlu*, 23.2:223.10:243, 25.1:274.

38   *Chunqiu fanlu*, 34.1:354.

39 *Chunqiu fanlu*, 1.4:19, 15.1:174.
40 *Chunqiu fanlu*, 44.1:398.421.430, 44.3:426.
41 Joachim Gentz, 'Mohist Traces in the Early Chunqiu fanlu Chapters', *Oriens Extremus* 48 (2009): 64–70.
42 Queen, *From Chronicle to Canon*, 235, 234.
43 *Chunqiu fanlu*, 51:454–455.
44 *Chunqiu fanlu*, 46:436, 80.1:641.
45 *Chunqiu fanlu*, 53.5:465.
46 *Chunqiu fanlu*, 57:481.484.
47 *Chunqiu fanlu*, 9.1:147.
48 This issue and frequent references to the *ming* 命 in the *Chunqiu fanlu* significantly restricts the hypothesis of the Mohist origin of the Dong Zhongshu's concept of Tian.
49 *Chunqiu fanlu* 23.3:226–229, 23.7:240–242. Arbuckle ('Inevitable Treason', 593) mistakenly treats the Han as the 'black' dynasty. The *Chunqiu fanlu* explicitly identifies the Spring and Autumn Period with the black.
50 *Chunqiu fanlu* 23.13:243.
51 Arbuckle, 'Inevitable Treason', 593. Wang Gaoxin 汪高鑫, *Dong Zhongshu yu Handai lishi sixiang yanjiu* 董仲舒与汉代历史思想研究 (Shanghai: Shangwu yinshuguan, 2012), 156.
52 *Chunqiu fanlu*, 23.4:236.
53 Neither in the *Chunqiu fanlu*, nor in the *Hanshu* (both *Dong Zhongshu zhuan* and *Wuxing zhi*) can we find a mention of Dong Zhongshu's use of the Five Phases theory in the philosophy of history, as did e.g. Zou Yan.
54 *Chunqiu fanlu*, 65.2:536–7 reads that the Qin did not gain the support of Tian, it was thus 'non-existent.'
55 *Hanshu*, 99:3021.
56 On Wang Mang's historiosophy as reconstructed on the basis of the *Hanshu*: Zhao Wenyu 赵文宇, 'Cong Hanshu kan Wang Mang de lishi sixiang' 从汉书看王莽的历史思想, *Jiamusi Daxue Shehui Kexue Xuebao* 30, no. 1 (2012).
57 Ren Jiyu, *Zhongguo zhexue shi*, 494.
58 *Bohutong*, 16:267.
59 *Bohutong*, 9:187.
60 He Xiu, *Gongyang jiegu*, 1, in: *Gongyangzhuan*, 1:5.
61 Wang Gaoxin, *Dong Zhongshu*, 112–121.
62 He Xiu, *Gongyang jiegu*, 1:26.
63 Cf. Feng Yu-lan who sees there a theory of 'social progress' (Feng Youlan, *A Short History of Chinese Philosophy*, 201–202). He Xiu's tripartite scheme was universalized only by Gong Zizhen (1792–1841).
64 Liu Xiang, *Xinxu* 1.1:2, 2.1:47-8, 2.11:75, 3.6:125, 4.2:154.
65 *Hanshu*, 36:1515.
66 *Hanshu*, 26:1509.
67 This scheme, as Wang Gaoxin shows, was misattributed to Liu Xiang in the *Hanshu*, 25:1049 (Wang Gaoxin, *Dong Zhongshu*, 194).
68 *Classic of Epochs* 世經 *Shìjīng* is a fragment of Liu Xin's *Santong lipu*, from the *Hanshu*, 21:869–878.
69 *Qian Hanji*, 6:165. On the the *Tian-ren ganying* idea in Xun Yue see Wang Gaoxin, *Dong Zhongshu*, 134–140, 194 and Wang Gaoxin, *Zhongguo shixue sixiang tongshi*, 312, 503–510.

70   Anne Behnke Kinney, *The Art of the Han Essay: Wang Fu's* Ch'ien-Fu Lun (Tempe: Center for Asian studies, 1990), 61.

71   See *Qianfulun*, 34:593–649.

72   *Qianfulun*, 26:452–453.

73   *Shiji*, 97:2699.

74   *Xinyu*, 1:2.7.9.

75   *Xinyu*, 6:95.

76   *Xinyu*, 1:5.

77   *Xinyu*, 3:55, 7:108.

78   *Xinyu*, 11:152. This fragment undoubtedly echoes Xunzi's *Tianlun*.

79   *Xinyu*, 11:155.

80   Xu Fuguan 徐复观, *Liang Han sixiang shi* 两汉思想史, vol. II (Shanghai: Huadong Shifan Daxue chubanshe, 2002), 55.

81   Ren Jiyu, *Zhongguo zhexue fazhan shi*, 49.

82   *Xinyu*, 1:30, 8:117.

83   *Xinyu*, 10:146, 5:180.

84   *Xinyu*, 4:173.

85   *Xinyu*, 1:34.

86   *Xinyu*, 2:43.

87   *Xinyu*, 3:65, 2:41.

88   *Xinyu*, 2:37.39.

89   *Xinyu*, 12:170–171.

90   *Xinyu*, 4:59, 6:95. These are undoubtedly Daoist strands.

91   *Xinyu*, 1:7–18.

92   Leung, *The Politics of the Past*, 147.

93   See Charles Le Blanc, *Huai nan tzu. Philosophical Synthesis in Early Han Thought: The Idea of Resonance* (Kan-ying) *With a Translation and Analysis of Chapter Six* (Hong Kong: Hong Kong University Press, 1985).

94   See fragments of the *Huangdi sijing* with commentary by Harold Roth and Sarah Queen, 'The Huang-Lao Silk Manuscripts (*Huang-Lao boshu*)', in *Sources of Chinese tradition*, vol. 1, ed. Wm. Theodore de Bary and Irene Bloom (New York: Columbia University Press, 1999), 241–256.

95   Ibid., 252.

96   The *Huangdi sijing* is quoted in the *Huainanzi* twenty-six times. The political background should also be emphasized: King of Huainan came from the south of China, which was the bastion of the Huang-Lao School.

97   Feng Youlan, *The Spirit of Chinese Philosophy* (London: Kegan Paul, 1947), 112–113.

98   *Huainanzi*, 1:1–2.

99   *Huainanzi*, 2:147, 8:819.

100 *Huainanzi*, 2:197–198.234.

101 Roger Ames, *The Art of Rulership. A Study of Ancient Chinese Political Thought* (New York: State University of New York Press, 1994), 42–53.

102 *Huainanzi*, 19:1132.

103 Michael Puett, 'Sages, Creation, and the End of History in the *Huainanzi*'. In *The Huainanzi and Textual Production in Early China*, ed. Sarah Queen and Michael Puett (Leiden/Boston: Brill, 2014), 275, 282.

104 *Huainanzi*, 10:1031.

105 *Huainanzi*, 6: 692–693.

106 *Huainanzi*, 6:710. Han Wudi accused Liu An, his nephew, of plotting; also the father of Liu An conspired against the emperor.

107 Le Blanc, *Huai nan tzu*, 178, 209. This comparison is not further developed by Le Blanc.

108 Puett, 'Sages, Creation and the End of History', 283.

109 *Huainanzi*, 11:1182, 13:1331.1350.

110 *Huainanzi*, 11:1152.1173.

111 *Huainanzi*, 9:931, 19:1950.

112 *Huainanzi*, 11:1188, 18:1915.

113 *Huainanzi*, 13:1350, 14:1484.1503, 18:1919.

114 Le Blanc, *Huai nan tzu*, 209.

115 Puett 'Sages, Creation and the End of History', 288–289.

116 *Taixuan li*, 1. Translation from Chan Wing-Tsit, *A Sourcebook in Chinese philosophy* (Princeton: Princeton University Press, 1963), 291.

117 Brook Ziporyn, 'Spatio-Temporal Order in Yang Xiong's *Taixuan jing*', *Early Medieval China* 2 (1995): 50–51, 68–69, 77, 83.

118 See Xu Fuguan, *Liang Han sixiang shi*, 312.

119 *Fayan*, 2.20:52, 14.2:426. The whole text of *Fayan* is stylistically modelled on the *Analects*.

120 *Fayan*, 1.3:3, 1.24:28.

121 *Fayan*, 7.6:174.

122 *Fayan*, 2.21:53.

123 *Fayan*, 5.17:130, 5.27:140. This does not mean Yang Xiong did not respect the works created under the Han. For instance, he admired the *Shiji*, writing that this is 'a true record [of the past]' 實錄 *shílù*, 10.30:311.

124 *Fayan*, 5.21:133.

125 *Fayan*, 5.18:130, 5.20:132.

126 *Fayan*, 2.8:40, 4.16:98, 8.22:220.

127 *Fayan*, 4.1:83, 4.24:108, 4.26:110, 9.8:237–8.

128 *Fayan*, 4.10:92.

129 *Fayan*, 13.10:393.

130 *Fayan*, 6.10:151, 7.25:195.

131 *Fayan*, 13.34:420. Yang Xiong also hoped that the Han rulers would return to the old well-field system.

132 *Fayan*, 3.3:58, 6.11:152.

133 *Fayan*, 3.21:74.

134 *Fayan*, 5.4:116.

135 *Fayan*, 8.13:213–14.

136 Xu Fuguan, *Liang Han sixiang shi*, 313.

137 *Fayan*, 8.1:198.

138 *Fayan*, 10.9–10:275.278.

139 Xu Fuguan, *Liang Han sixiang shi*, 71. The title *Xinshu* appears only after the sixth c. CE, and originally this work was known as the *Master Jia*, which is probably the result of treating the 'new edition' of the *Jiazi* by Liu Xiang as the proper name of the work.

140 *Xinshu*, 1:28, 10:340.

141 *Xinshu*, 5:160.

142 *Xinshu*, 3:78.

143 *Xinshu*, 10:320.

144 *Xinshu*, 5:152.

145 *Xinshu*, 1:24.

146 *Xinshu*, 9:275–277.282. Translation from Daniel W.Y. Kwok, 'Jia Yi: The Faults of the Qin', in *Sources of Chinese tradition*, vol. 1, ed. de Bary and Bloom, 291–292.

147 Koen Abts and Stefan Rummens, 'Populism versus Democracy', *Political Studies* 55, no. 2 (2007): 408–409.

148 *Xinshu*, 5:173.

149 *Xinshu*, 9:284.302.

150 *Xinshu*, 1:6–7.

151 *Xinshu*, 10:344.

152 *Xinshu*, 1:25.

153 *Xinshu*, 2:60, 9:285.

154 *Xinshu*, 6:181.196.204.206–207.

155 *Xinshu*, 2:55.

156 *Xinshu*, 3:86–7.93.

157 *Xinshu*, 9:289.

158 Fang Litian, *Zhongguo gudai zhexue*, 499.

159 *Xinshu*, 9:288.

160 *Xinshu*, 16:68. Th title of the chapter, *The floor and the steps* 階級 *jiējí*, means nowadays 'social class' and in this sense it is used by i.a. Chinese Marxists.

161 *Changyan*, 1.5:154, 2.7:180–181.

162 *Changyan*, 2.8:185–186, 9.2:252.

163 *Changyan*, 4:208.

164 *Changyan*, 1.4:148.

165 *Changyan*, 1.1:141.

166 *Changyan*, 1.2–3:143.145.

167 *Changyan*, 9.1:275.

168 He Zhaowu, *An Intellectual History of China* (Beijing: Foreign Languages Press, 1991), 178.

169 *Xinlun*, 1:1.

170 *Xinlun*, 3:8–9, 4:12.

171 *Hou Hanshu*, 28:957. *Xinlun*, 6:19.

172 *Xinlun*, 3:11.

173 *Xinlun*, 4:13.

174 *Xinlun*, 3:6, 9:40.

175 *Xinlun*, 5:15–16.

176 Timotheus Pokora, *Hsin-lun (New Treatise) and other writings by Huan T'an (43 BC–28 AD)* (Ann Arbor: Center for Chinese Studies, 1975), 206–208, 236–238, 240–241.

177 *Xinlun*, 2:3.

178 *Zhenglun*, 1.1:19, 1.5:24–25.

179 *Zhenglun*, 2.1:30, 2.4:38.

180 *Zhenglun*, 2.3:35.

181 *Zhenglun*, 2:44. Cui Shi writes that people 'think by day and dream at night about this only'. In 7:93 he adds that in order to raise people with rituals and righteousness, one must first feed them.

182 *Zhenglun*, 1:18.

183 *Zhenglun*, 7:102.

184 *Zhenglun*, 1:2, 6:89.

185 *Zhenglun*, 3:56.

186 *Zhenglun*, 9:117.

187 *Zhenglun*, 7.6:102.

188 Hsiao Kung-chuan, *History of Chinese Political Thought, Volume 1: From the Beginnings to the Sixth Century, A.D.* (Princeton: Princeton University Press, 1979), 535–536.

189 Edwin Pulleyblank, 'Neo-Confucianism and Neo-Legalism in T'ang Intellectual Life, 755–805,' In *The Confucian Persuasion* ed, Arthur Wright (Stanford: Stanford University Press, 1960), 77–114.

190 *Lunheng*, 18:1030–1031.

191 *Lunheng*, 14:825–826.

192 *Lunheng*, 15:849–850.

193 *Lunheng*, 18:1028–1029.

194 *Lunheng*, 14:845.

195 *Lunheng*, 1:38.

196 *Lunheng*, 2:63.72.

197 *Lunheng*, 17:1012.

198 *Lunheng*, 1:2–3.

199 *Lunheng*, 6:335.363.

200 I was inspired by Xu Fuguan's figure, cf. Xu Fuguan, *Liang Han sixiang shi*, 388.

201 *Lunheng*, 3:207.

202 *Lunheng*, 26:1502.

203 *Lunheng*, 26:1480.

204 *Lunheng*, 18:1073.

205 *Lunheng*, 18:1080.1083.

206 Wang Shounan 王寿南, *Zhongguo lidai sixiangjia: Han* 中国历代思想家： 汉 (Beijing: Jiuzhou chubanshe, 2011), 384.

207 *Lunheng*, 19:1093.

208 Michael Puett, 'Listening to Sages: Divination, Omens, and the Rhetoric of Antiquity in Wang Chong's *Lunheng*,' *Oriens Extremus* 45 (2005/06): 280–281.

209 *Lunheng*, 9:500–501, 18:1088–1089.

210 *Lunheng*, 8:458. According to Wang Chong, the tendency to exaggerate is natural, see 8:483.

211 *Lunheng*, 30:1684–1685.

212 *Lunheng*, 4:232.

213 *Lunheng*, 12:715–716. The Han dynasty is in no way inferior to Zhou, Wang says, see 19:1105–1106.

214 *Lunheng*, 29:1649–1650.

215 *Lunheng*, 12:719–724.

216 Xu Fuguan, *Liang Han sixiang shi*, 357.

217 Wang and Ng, *Mirroring the Past*, 4–8.

218 *Shiji*, 130:3295.

219 A good study of theories: Esther Klein, *The History of a Historian: Perspectives on the Authorial Roles of Sima Qian* (PhD diss., Princeton University, Princeton 2010), 386–445.

220 *Shiji*, 130:3296-7.

221 *Shiji*, 47:1905–1947.

222 *Shiji*, 13:505.

223 *Shiji*, 13:487.

224 Stephen Durrant, 'Truth Claims in *Shiji*'. In *Historical Truth, Historical Criticism and Ideology. Chinese Historiography and Historical Culture from a New Comparative Perspective*, ed. Helwig Schmidt-Glinzer, Achim Mittag, and Jörn Rüsen (Leiden/Boston: Brill, 2005).

225 *Shiji*, 130:3304.

226 Wang Gaoxin, *Zhongguo shixue sixiang tongshi*, 230, 258.

227 *Shiji*, 16:759–760.

228 *Shiji*, 2:88.

229 *Shiji*, 6:282. Sima Qian also based on Lu Jia's *Chu Han chunqiu*.

230 *Shiji*, 8:393–394.

231 *Hanshu*, 62:2068.

232 *Shiji*, 48:1949–1950.

233 *Shiji*, 7:339.

234 *Shiji*, 61:2124–2125.

235 *Shiji*, 8:341.

236 *Hanshu*, 62: 2070.

237 Wang and Ng, *Mirroring the Past*, 70.

238 Ban Gu's work was completed by his sister, Ban Zhao 班昭 (45–116), the manageress of the imperial library, astronomer, poet, and philosopher, author of the *Lessons for Women* 女誡 *Nǚjiè*. Her other works have been lost.

239 *Hanshu*, 100:3086–3090.

240 *Hanshu*, 72:2313, 88:2663, 99:3075.

241 Theodor W. Adorno, *Negative Dialectics* (New York: The Seabury Press, 1973), 359. In his approach, this idea implies seeing all nature as history and all history as nature.

Chapter 5

1 On the problematic character of applying the notion of 'medievality' to China cf. Timothy Brook, 'Medievality and the Chinese Sense of History', *The Medieval History Journal* 1, no. 1 (1998).

2 For more details on that topic see Pang Tianyou 庞天佑, *Zhongguo shixue sixiang tongshi. Wei-Jin, Nan-Beichao juan* 中国史学思想通史。 魏晋南北朝卷 (Hefei: Huangshan chushe, 2003), 85–104.

3 Buddhism was blamed for the collapse of the states, and it was pointed out that it was not known in the times of order. For an overview of such narratives see Niu Runzhen 牛润珍, *Zhongguo shixue sixiang tongshi. Sui-Tang juan shangxia* 中国史学思想通史。 隋唐卷上下 (Hefei: Huangshan chushe, 2004), 287–313.

4 Mark Strange, 'Representations of Liang Emperor Wu as a Buddhist Ruler in Sixth-and Seventh-century Texts', *Asia Major* 24, no. 2 (2011): 56–57.

5 Robert Sharf, *Coming to Terms with Chinese Buddhism. A Reading of the Treasure Store Treatise* (Honolulu: University of Hawai'i Press, 2002), 132.

6 Rudolf Wagner, *A Chinese Reading of the* Daodejing. *Wang Bi's Commentary on the Laozi with Critical Text and Translation* (New York: State University of New York Press, 2003), 85.

7 Chan Wing-tsit, *A Sourcebook*, 327, 335.

8 Wagner, *A Chinese Reading of the* Daodejing, 149, 160, 163–164.

9 *Baopuzi waipian*, 37:683–685.

10 Michael Puett, 'Humans, Spirits, and Sages in Chinese Late Antiquity: Ge Hong's *Master Who Embraces Simplicity (Baopuzi)*', *Extrême-Orient, Extrême-Occident* 29 (2007): 98–99.

11 Ibid., 103.

12 Robert Ford Campany, *To Live as Long as Heaven and Earth. A Translation and Study of Ge Hong's Traditions of Divine Transcendents* (Berkeley-Los Angeles: University of California Press, 2002), 111–117.

13 Pang Tianyou, *Zhongguo shixue sixiang tongshi*, 72.

14 Charles Holcombe, *In the Shadow of the Han: Literati Thought and Society and the Beginning of the Southern Dynasties* (Honolulu: University of Hawai'i Press, 1994), 4.

15 *Renwuzhi*, yuanxu:6.

16 *Renwuzhi*, 8:115–120.

17 *Renwuzhi*, 1:15–16.

18 *Renwuzhi*, 10:175–176.

19 Fang Litian, *Zhongguo gudai zhexue*, 513.

20 Stephen Bokenkamp, 'Time After Time: Taoist Apocalyptic History and the Founding of the T'ang Dynasty', *Asia Major* 7, no. 1 (1994): 67. The Taiping Rebellion in the nineteenth century was also explicitly guided by these ideals.

21 Barbara Hendrischke, 'The Daoist Utopia of Great Peace', *Oriens Extremus* 35 (1992): 62, 66.

22 Ibid., 67. Also Barbara Hendrischke, 'The Concept of Inherited Evil in the *Taiping jing*', *East Asian History* 2 (1991): 1–30.6.

23 *Taipingjing*, 16:44, 92:366.369.

24 *Taipingjing*, 92:374.

25 *Taipingjing*, 92:371.

26 *Taipingjing*, 37:60, 41:32.

27 Different version collected in: Hendrischke, 'The Concept of Inherited Evil', 12.

28 *Taipingjing*, 72:295.

29 *Taipingjing*, 37:61, 44:143.

30 *Taipingjing*, 36:52.

31 *Taipingjing*, 102:459.

32 Michael Puett, 'The Belatedness of the Present: Debates over Antiquity during the Han Dynasty', In *Perceptions of Antiquity in Chinese Civilization*, ed. Helga Stahl and Dieter Kuhn (Heidelberg: Würzburger Sinologische Schriften, 2008), 185.

33 *Taipingjing*, 37:56.60

34 *Taipingjing*, 92:370.375.

35 *Taipingjing*, 92:373.

36 Hendrischke, 'The Daoist Utopia of Great Peace', 66.

37 Bokenkamp, 'Time After Time', 61.

38 It is even acknowledged by Hendrischke herself, who also thinks that the *Taipingjing* represents a cyclical view of history. However, there is no citation that clearly states the conditions for starting a new cycle, especially after annihilation. The phrase *jinzhe* ('now'), to which Hendrischke refers (cf. Hendrischke, 'The Concept of Inherited Evil', 18), does not imply cyclicality in any way. Petersen demonstrates that the cycles of celestial spheres are inscribed in one great cycle of history, which is essentially unique (Jens Østergård Petersen, 'The Anti-Messianism of the *Taiping Jing*', *Studies in Central and East Asian Religions* 3 (1990): 28–29). In this sense, there is no point in talking about 'historical cycles'.

39 Images summarized in: Hendrischke, 'The Daoist Utopia of Great Peace', 71–72.

40 *Taipingjing*, 91:359.361.

41 *Taipingjing*, 35:34. Particularly the infanticide, see 35:36.

42 *Taipingjing*, 91:348.352.

43 The thought of the *Taipingjing* is exposed in the form of a dialogue with the 'Heavenly Master' 天師 *Tiānshī*.

44 Petersen, 'The Anti-Messianism of the *Taiping Jing*', 32.

45 *Taipingjing*, 91:350.

46 *Taipingjing*, 91:86.

47 *Taipingjing*, 69:270.

48 *Taipingjing*, 37:58.

49 *Taipingjing*, 91:349.

50 Petersen, 'The Anti-Messianism of the *Taiping Jing*', 1–2.

51 *Taipingjing*, 91:86.350–351.

52 *Taipingjing*, 67:255.

53 *Taipingjing*, 88:333.

54 Lu Xun 鲁迅, 'Wei-Jin fengdu ji wenzhang yu yao ji jiu zhi guanxi' 魏晋风度及文章与药及酒之关系. In *Eryi ji. Lu Xun Xuanji*, vol. 2 (Beijing: Renmin wenxue chubanshe, 1992), 377. This period was initiated by Emperor Cao Pi (187–226) with his *Discourse on Literature* 論文 *Lùnwén* and Lu Ji (261–303) with his *Poem about literature* 文賦 *Wénfù*.

55 Stephen Owen, *Readings in Chinese Literary Thought* (Cambridge: Harvard University Press, 1992), 74.

56 Wang and Ng, *Mirroring* 80–82, 90. One hundred forty chronicles were created from the fall of the Han to the founding of the Tang. The term *shǐ* begins to mean 'works', not 'a historian', while under Song Wendi (424–453) 'historiography' (*shǐxué*), with literature, Confucianism and *xuanxue*, became the part of official curricula (Ibid., 99–100).

57 Ibid., 89.

58 As in: Denis Twitchett, *The Writing of Official History Under the T'ang* (Cambridge: Cambridge University Press, 1992), 13.

59 Witold Rodziński, *Historia Chin* (Wrocław: Ossolineum, 1974), 214. This process is described in detail in the above-cited monograph of Twitchett.

60 *Tongdian*, 42:1161–1162.

61 *Tongdian*, 1:1. The topic of the relation of rituals to their material 'basis' returns in the Song.

62 The only direct reference to Buddhist terminology appears in Chapter 18, when he refers to 'wisdom' (skr. *prajñā*) in the context of speculative cognition – see *Wenxin diaolong* 18:201.

63 *Wenxin diaolong*, 1:2, 2:12, 3:18–19.

64 Kang-I Sun Chang, 'Liu Xie's Idea of Canonicity', in *A Chinese Literary Mind. Culture, Creativity, and Rhetoric in the* Wenxin Diaolong, ed. Zong-qi Cai (Stanford: Stanford University Press, 2001), 28.

65 *Wenxin diaolong*, 12:128.

66 *Wenxin diaolong*, 16:171.

67 Ibid.

68 *Wenxin diaolongi*, 16:172.

69 White, *Metahistory*, 5.

70 *Wenxin diaolong*, 43:462.

71 *Wenxin diaolong*, 17:190.

72 *Wenxin diaolong*, 16:171–172.

73 *Wenxin diaolong*, 16:172.

74 Liu Zhiji directly avows that he was inspired by the *Wenxin diaolong*: *Shitong* 36:498. For another anticipation of the *Shitong* besides the *Lunheng*, Hsu Kwan-san mentions a commentary to the *Sanguozhi* by Pei Songzhi (372–451), which proposes the criteria for the reliability of historical narrative – see Hsu Kwan-San, 'The Chinese Critical Tradition', *The Historical Journal* 26, no. 2 (1983): 434–435.

75 Ibid., 435.

76 *Shitong*, 6:67, 14:181, 33:447.

77 *Shitong*, 8:106.

78 *Shitong*, 18:226–227, 20:261, 22:303.

79 *Shitong*, 20:255. Liu Zhiji particularly condemns the substitution of the native languages of non-Chinese people with the Chinese in such chronicles as the *Zhoushu* and the *Weishu*, 20:257.

80 *Shitong*, 22:251.280. In 22:307 he writes that 'today history does not look like history'.

81 *Shitong*, 28:377.

82 *Shitong*, 31:428.

83 *Shitong*, 22:286.

84 Niu Ruzhen, *Zhongguo shixue sixiang tongshi*, 242.

85 *Shitong*, 34:456.

86 *Shitong*, 22:284. Cf. Edwin Pulleyblank, 'Chinese Historical Criticism: Liu Chih-Chi and Ssu-ma Kuang', in *Historians of China and Japan*, ed. William Beasley and Edwin Pulleyblank (London: Oxford University Press, 1961), 146.

87 *Shitong*, 16:202.211.

88 *Shitong*, 31:421.423.

89 *Shitong*, 20:247.

90 *Shitong*, 22:294.

91 *Shitong*, 28:380.384.

92 *Shitong*, 21:269–270.

93 *Shitong*, 6:68, 31:426–427.

94 *Shitong*, 12:149.

95 *Shitong*, 13:160.

96 *Shitong*, 14:176.

97 *Shitong*, 20:263.

98 *Shitong*, 22:281.

99 *Shitong waipian*, 4: 633–634.

100 In the West, this sense was reinforced by Rorty's *Philosophy and the Mirror of Nature* (1979). Liu Zhiji's inspiration may have come from Buddhism, cf. a celebrated poem of contemporaneous Shenxiu (605–706): 'body is a bodhi tree,/ mind is a bright mirror's base./ Polish it constantly and eagerly,/ and must not let dust to collect.'

101 *Shitong*, 28:368–370.

102 For a detailed study of Liu Zhiji's critique of the *Weishu* see Damien Chaussende, 'Un Historien sur le banc des accuses. Liu Zhiji juge Wei Shou', *Études chinoises* 29 (2010).

103 *Shitong*, 25:341.

104 *Shitong waipian*, 1:524.534.

105 *Shitong*, 25:342.

106 *Shitong waipian*, 3:612–614. The title of the chapter (疑古 *Yigǔ*, 'doubting antiquity') can be translated as 'historical criticism', especially considering the name of the interwar Chinese school of historical criticism, the *Yigupai*.

107 *Shitong waipian*, 3:616.

108 *Shitong waipian*, 3:626, 4:642.646.

109 *Shitong*, 21:266, 23:320.

110 *Shitong*, 21:271.

111 *Shitong*, 30:407.416.

112 *Shitong*, 14:174, 22:332.

113 *Xin Tangshu*, 132:4522.

114 Thomas H.C. Lee (ed.), *The New and the Multiple. Sung Senses of the Past* (Hong Kong: The Chinese University Press, 2004), xiv–xv.

115 *Changli Xiansheng Wenji*, 11:9–10.

116 *Changli Xiansheng Wenji*, 11: 24.54.76.

117 *Changli Xiansheng Wenji*, 11:15–16. The idea of lineage has, ironically, a Buddhist pedigree.

118 A similar idea was proposed by another Tang thinker, Lü Wen 呂溫 (722–811) in the *Essay on Transforming Human Culture* 人文化成論 *Rénwén huàchéng lùn*. On Lü Wen's philosophy of history: Fang Litian, *Zhongguo gudai zhexue*, 517–518.

119 *Quan Songwen*, 90:166. Note this is not a vision of a correlation between Heaven and humanity.

120 *Huangji jingshi*, 3:125.

121 *Huangji jingshi*, 6:295.

122 Don J. Wyatt, 'Shao Yong's Numerological-Cosmological System', in *Dao Companion to Neo-Confucian Philosophy*, ed. John Makeham (Dordrecht et al.: Springer, 2010), 22.

123 *Huangji jingshi*, 7B:358.

124 *Huangji jingshi*, 7A:314. 8B:417.

125 *Huangji jingshi*, 5:251.

126 *Huangji jingshi*, 6:281.

127 *Huangji jingshi*, 5:254.

128 *Huangji jingshi*, 6:296.

129 Don J. Wyatt, *The Recluse of Loyang. Shao Yung and the Moral Evolution of Early Sung Thought* (Honolulu: Hawai'i Press, 1996), 184–187. On the importance of the methodology of 'observing things' for Shao Yong's idealist philosophy of history see also Don J. Wyatt, 'The Transcendence of the Past. Objectivity, Relativism and Moralism in the Historical Thought of Shao Yong', *Monumenta Serica* 61, no. 1 (2013): 211–212.

130 *Huangji jingshi*, 5:262.

131 John M.E. McTaggart, *The Nature of Existence* (Cambridge: Cambdrige University Press, 1927), 9–22. The A series, precisely.

132 Cf. Richard Robinson, *Early Madhyamaka in India and China* (Wisconsin: Madison University Press, 1967), 228–234.

133 *Huangji jingshi*, 7B:333.

134 *Huangji jingshi*, 3:179, 6:286.

135 For more about the influence of *qi* on order and chaos, see *Huangji jingshi*, 8B:392.

136 See Fang Litian, *Zhongguo gudai zhexue*, 523.

137 Chan 1963: 487. The impact of Buddhism on Shao Yong is much broader, including the concept of non-dual knowledge, or the idea of 'no self' 無我 *wúwǒ*, applied to knowledge of the sages (*Huangji jingshi*, 8B:428).

138 *Huangji jingshi*, 3:152.

139 *Huangji jingshi*, 6:278.285.

140　*Huangji jingshi*, 5:262–263.

141　*Huangji jingshi*, 8B:394. These ideas of Shao Yong were openly applied in the historiography of Hu Hong 胡宏 (1105–1161); see Conrad Schirokauer, 'Hu Hong as a Historian', in *The New and the Multiple. Sung Senses of the Past*, ed. Thomas H.C. Lee (Hong Kong: The Chinese University Press, 2004), 125–127.

142　*Huangji jingshi*, 6:280.

143　Martin Dösch, 'Ordering the World. Shao Yong and the Idea of History', *Monumenta Serica* 61, no. 1 (2013): 282–283.

144　The political philosophy of Wang Anshi, which is not investigated here, could be also interpreted as much closer to historical idealism. For instance, James T.C. Liu ascribes to Wang Anshi a 'bureaucratic idealism' in political philosophy (James T.C. Liu, *Reform in Sung China. Wang An-shih (1021–1086) and his New Policies* (Cambridge: Harvard University Press, 1959), 45).

145　*Linchuan xiansheng wenji*, 62:661. 63:675.

146　*Linchuan xiansheng wenji*, 69:735.

147　Wang Mingsun 王明蓀, *Wang Anshi* 王安石 (Taibei: Dongda tushu gongsi, 1994), 106. Involving himself in the debate on the difference between the kings and hegemons, Wang stresses that their way was essentially identical, but they differed in their intentions: kings sought *ren*, while hegemons opposed *buren*, see *Linchuan xiansheng wenji*, 63:714. The difference between *ren* and *buren* is therefore more basic.

148　*Linchuan xiansheng wenji*, 70:741.

149　*Linchuan xiansheng wenji*, 63:676. By 'ghosts' 鬼 *gui* Wang Anshi understands 'beings devoid of visible form', *Linchuan xiansheng wenji*, 63:668.

150　*Linchuan xiansheng wenji*, 62:660.

151　*Linchuan xiansheng wenji*, 66:701, 67:716. Both in the *Lilun* and the *Zhougong* Wang Anshi criticizes Xunzi.

152　Fang Litian, *Zhongguo gudai zhexue*, 527.

153　*Linchuan xiansheng wenji*, 69:737. It is worth emphasizing that the phrase 'to not be afraid of changes [coming from] Heaven' 天變不足畏 comes only from the *Songshi* (work published in 1346); we will not find it in Wang Anshi's works. This quote is, in the traditional Chinese interpretation, said to confirm the materialism of Wang Anshi (however, it is not known how it would confirm it). The further part of the quotation, rejecting imitation of the ancestors, suggests that this quote may be the creation of the enemies of Wang Anshi.

154　*Linchuan xiansheng wenji*, 66:703.706.

155　*Linchuan xiansheng wenji*, 66:707.

156　*Linchuan xiansheng wenji*, 68:723.

157　*Linchuan xiansheng wenji*, 64:676 reads that one should study the minds 心 *xīn* of three sages: Yi Yin, Bo Yi and Liuxia Hui.

158　*Linchuan xiansheng wenji*, 66:707.

159　Cf. e.g. Hou Wailu 侯外庐, *Zhongguo sixiang tongshi* 中国思想通史, vol. 4, shang (Beijing: Renmin chubanshe, 2011), 449–462.

160　*Linchuan xiansheng wenji*, 67:711. As title suggests, this essay shows the moral advantage of Confucius over Yao.

161　*Linchuan xiansheng wenji*, 70:748.

162　*Linchuan xiansheng wenji*, 64:677.

163　*Linchuan xiansheng wenji*, 67:713.

164　*Linchuan xiansheng wenji*, 69:731.

165 Wm. Theodore de Bary and Irene Bloom (eds.), *Sources of Chinese tradition, volume 1, from earliest times to 1600* (New York: Columbia University Press, 1999), 609.

166 *Linchuan xiansheng wenji*, 39:410. Translation from de Bary, *Sources of Chinese tradition*, 613.

167 James T.C. Liu, *Reform in Sung China*, 33.

168 *Zhouyi Cheng shi zhuan*, 3:858. Pages according to the *Er Cheng ji*.

169 Yao Xinzhong, *An Introduction to Confucianism* (Cambridge: Cambridge University Press, 2000), 104.

170 *Cheng shi cuiyain*, 1:1191. As in *Er Cheng ji*.

171 *Cheng shi yishu*, 19:258. As in *Er Cheng ji*.

172 *Cheng shi yishu*, 18:232.

173 *Cheng shi yishu*, 19:258.

174 *Cheng shi cuiyan*, 2:1241.

175 *Cheng shi yishu*, 18:199–200. Translation from de Bary, *Sources of Chinese tradition*, 660–661.

176 *Jinsilu*, 3:59. The fragment refers to the tripartite scheme of Dong Zhongshu, said to form a 'one cycle of Heaven'. The co-author of the *Jinsilu* was Lü Zuqian.

177 *Cheng shi yishu*, 11:127.

178 *Cheng shi jingshuo*, 4:1087. As in *Er Cheng ji*.

179 *Cheng shi cuiyan*, 1:1214.

180 *Cheng shi waishu*, 5:374. As in *Er Cheng ji*.

181 Wu Huaiqi 吴怀祺, *Zhongguo shixue sixiang tongshi. Song-Liao-Jin juan* 中国史学思想通史。宋辽金卷 (Hefei: Huangshan shushe, 2002), 108.

182 Particularly in the third scroll, see *Jinsilu*, 3:59–61.

183 Conrad Schirokauer, 'Chu His's Sense of History', In *Ordering the World. Approaches to State and Society in Sung Dynasty China*, ed. Robert Hymes and Conrad Schirokauer (Berkeley: University of California Press, 1993), 193.

184 *Zhuzi yulei*, 18:391. Zhu Xi regrets that in his time in reading books no principle is being sought, see *Zhuzi yulei*, 11:181.

185 *Zhuzi yulei*, 11:189–190.

186 *Zhuzi yulei*, 122: 2950. See also 11:195.

187 Wu Huaiqi, *Zhongguo shixue sixiang tongshi*, 299, 307.

188 'Hu was a champion of constant principles at all times in all circumstances,' Wang and Ng, *Mirroring the Past*, 162. Zhu Xi would, however, agree with Hu's view from the preface to the *Dushi guanjian*: 'the sage clarifies the principle, making it a Classic, and records events, making them a history; history is based on Classics.' *Dushi guanjian*: 7.

189 Wang and Ng, *Mirroring the Past*, 159.

190 *Zhuzi wenji*, 1:114–115.

191 Huang Chun-chieh, *Rujia sixiang yu Zhongguo lishi siwei*, 114–117.

192 Fang Litian, *Zhongguo gudai zhexue*, 528.

193 *Zhuzi yulei*, 134:3208.

194 *Zhuzi yulei*, 149:3298.

195 *Zhuzi yulei*, 1:5.

196 *Zhuzi yulei*, 72:1813, 74:1896.

197 Qian Mu 錢穆, *Qian Bingsi xiansheng quanji* 錢賓四先生全集, vol. 15 (Xinbei: Lianjing chuban, 1998), 38.

198 Huang Chun-chieh, *Rujia sixiang yu Zhongguo lishi siwei*, 138.

199 Yongsun Back, 'Fate and the Good Life: Zhu Xi and Jeong Yagyong's Discourse on Ming', *Dao: A Journal of Comparative Philosophy* 14 (2015): 258–259.

200 Don J. Wyatt, 'Chu Hsi's Critique of Shao Yung: One Instance of the Stand Against Fatalism', *Harvard Journal of Asiatic Studies* 45, no. 2 (1985): 662.
201 Schirokauer, 'Chu His's Sense of History', 209.
202 *Zhuzi yulei*, 37:990.
203 See Schirokauer, 'Chu His's Sense of History', 215.
204 *Zhuzi yulei*, 111:2713.
205 *Zhuxi yulei*, 108:2682.
206 *Zhuzi yulei*, 108:2679.
207 Wm. Theodore de Bary, 'Neo-Confucian Individualism and Holism'. In *Individualism and Holism: Studies in Confucian and Taoist Values*, ed. Donald Munro (Ann Arbor: The University of Michigan, Center for Chinese Studies, 1985), 341.
208 Ibid., 344.
209 Ibid., 350.
210 Wang and Ng, *Mirroring the Past*, 161.
211 Robert Hartwell, 'Historical Analogism, Public Policy, and Social Science in Eleventh- and Twelfth-Century', *The American Historical Review* 76, no. 3 (1971): 694.
212 *Jinsilu*, 3:60.
213 *Tongjian gangmu*:10.
214 Qiu Hansheng 邱汉生, 'Lun Zhu Xi 'huigui yili' de lishi zhexue' 论朱熹 '回归一理' 的历史哲学, *Zhexue yanjiu* 6 (1982): 51.
215 Lee, *The New and the Multiple*, xii–xiv. Another exception mentioned by Lee is Yuan Shu 袁樞 (1131–1205), who opted for 'narration of events from beginning to the end' 紀事本末 *jìshì běnmò*, in place of a chronological order.
216 Lee, *The New and the Multiple*, 173. The notion of *huitong* itself comes from the *Book of Changes*.
217 *Tongzhi*, 1:14. The preface reads that *huitong* was realized by Confucius and then Sima Qian but rejected by Ban Gu with his dynastic history.
218 Wu Huaiqi, *Zhongguo shixue sixiang tongshi*, 354.
219 Lü Zuqian, 'How to Study History', trans. Burton Watson, In *Sources of Chinese tradition*, vol. 1, ed. Wm. Theodore de Bary and Irene Bloom (New York: Columbia University Press, 1999), 659–660.
220 *Tongzhi*, 1:303–305; 35:105–107.
221 *Liu Zongyuan ji*, 20:557, 25:656, 30:780; 33:850.856.
222 *Liu Zongyuan ji*, 3:88.97, 31:807–812.
223 *Liu Zongyuan ji*, 33:857, 34:872.
224 *Liu Zongyuan ji*, 1:30.
225 *Liu Zongyuan ji*, 44:1265.
226 *Liu Zongyuan ji*, 1:35.443–445.
227 *Liu Zongyuan ji*, 3:91.
228 *Liu Zongyuan ji*, 16:450.
229 *Liu Zongyuan ji*, 16:441–442.
230 *Liu Zongyuan ji*, 14:365–366, 16:442.
231 *Liu Zongyuan ji*, 3:80.
232 *Liu Zongyuan ji*, 16:447–448.
233 *Liu Zongyuan ji*, 16:449.
234 *Liu Zongyuan ji*, 31:817. William Crawford justifiably points out that eventually the main source of inspiration of Liu Zongyuan's philosophy of history is not Zhuangzi, but rather Xunzi (William Crawford, 'Philosophical and Intellectual Thought', in *Liu Tsung-yüan*, ed. William H. Nienhauser, Jr et al. (New York: Twayne Publishers, 1973), 55).

235 *Liu Zongyuan ji*, 1:31.

236 *Liu Zongyuan ji*, 3:70.

237 See Jullien, *The Propensity of Things*, 181–182.

238 Jo-Shui Chen, *Liu Tsung-yüan and Intellectual Change in T'ang China, 773–819* (Cambridge: Cambridge University Press, 1992), 97, 114.

239 *Liu Zongyuan ji*, 16:458.

240 Krzysztof Brzechczyn, 'O racjonalną postawę wobec marksizmu'. In *Marksizm. Nadzieje i rozczarowania*, ed. Jacek Hołówka, Bogdan Dziobkowski (Warszawa: Wydawnictwo Naukowe PWN), 417–418.

241 *Liu Zongyuan ji*, 1:72–73. It should be emphasized that Liu Zongyuan uses the term *fengjian* in a narrow sense, to describe the feudalism of the Zhou Dynasty type. On the other hand, in fact only the Zhou dynasty meets the strict criteria of the feudal system, whereas the Qin and Tang dynasties were centralized monarchies.

242 *Liu Zongyuan ji*, 23:616.

243 *Liu Zongyuan ji*, 20:556.

244 *Liu Zongyuan ji*, 23:616; 28:756.

245 *Liu Zongyuan ji*, 24:648–649.

246 Chen, *Liu Tsung-yüan*, 157.

247 *Li Gou ji*, 2:5–6. The division of *li* is, of course, more complex: for example, the burial rite is classified as 'trunk' (*ben*) of customs, politics as their 'branches' (*zhi*), while morality is treated as an 'another name' (*bieming*) of customs.

248 *Li Gou ji*, 14:121.

249 *Li Gou ji*, 8:89.

250 *Li Gou ji*, 18:168.

251 *Li Gou ji*, 6:75.

252 On the philosophy of history in the *Huashu*, see Fang Litian, *Zhongguo gudai zhexue*, 519–520. Tan Qiao is considered a Daoist, which is why the *Huashu* became a part of Daozang, although *Siku quanshu* classifies it under *zajialei*, 'other schools'.

253 *Li Gou ji*, 16:139.

254 *Li Gou ji*, 19:183.

255 *Li Gou ji*, 22:245.

256 *Li Gou ji*, 16:135.

257 Rodziński, *Historia Chin*, 184–185, 195–197, 236.

258 *Li Gou ji*, 16:135–136.

259 *Li Gou ji*, 6:76.

260 Shan-Yüan Hsieh, *The Life and Thought of Li Kou (1009–1059)* (San Francisco: Chinese Materials Center, 1979), 104–109.

261 *Li Gou ji*, 18:136.

262 *Li Gou ji*, 16:133.

263 *Li Gou ji*, 16:137.

264 *Li Gou ji*, 29:326.

265 *Ouyang Xiu quanji*, 16:268. The passage mentions combining the *Tianren ganying* idea with legitimization of power and the concept of *wuxing*. The *wuxing* theory is also rejected by Ouyang Xiu: *Ouyang Xiu quanji*, 16:280.

266 *Xin wudai shi*, 59:705–706.

267 Douglas Skonicki, *Cosmos, State and Society: Song Dynasty Arguments concerning the Creation of Political Order* (PhD diss., Harvard University, Cambridge 2007), 270.

268 *Xin Tangshu*, 24:872.

269 *Ouyang Xiu quanji*, 61:879.

270 *Ouyang Xiu quanji*, 41:592.

271 *Ouyang Xiu quanji*, 70:1011.

272 *Ouyang Xiu quanji*, 18:307. Also 17:299.

273 A good example of Ouyang Xiu's epistemological scepticism is the essay *Guaizhubian* (*Ouyang Xiu quanji*, 18:313–314), in which he ridicules inquiries into the definition of consciousness: if this is identical with having heart (*xin*), insects also have consciousness; if 'being conscious' means 'to move', then water is also conscious, and so on. This line of argumentation shows the naturalist interpretation of *xin* as a physical heart.

274 *Ouyang Xiu quanji*, 61:892.

275 *Ouyang Xiu quanji*, 69:1010.

276 *Ouyang Xiu quanji*, 130:1985.

277 *Ouyang Xiu quanji*, 61:891. See Skonicki, *Cosmos, State and Society*, 279, 292.

278 Peter K. Bol, 'The Sung Context: From Ou-yang Hsiu to Chu His,' In *Sung Dynasty Uses of the I Ching*, ed. Kidder Smith Jr. et al., 26–55 (Princeton: Princeton University Press, 1990), 30.

279 *Ouyang Xiu quanji*, 77:1114.

280 *Ouyang Xiu quanji*, 16:269.267–272. Applying this criterion of legitimacy to the history of China, Ouyang Xiu distinguishes four periods of legitimate authority, namely the period from emperor Yao to the Han dynasty, the Western Jin, the Sui and Tang dynasties, and the Song, along with three respective intervals, i.e. the periods of Three Kingdoms, the Northern and Southern Dynasties, and the Five Dynasties.

281 *Ouyang Xiu quanji*, 16:270–271.

282 James T.C. Liu, *Ou-Yang Hsiu: An Eleventh-Century Neo-Confucianist* (Stanford: Stanford University Press, 1967), 101.

283 Douglas Skonicki, 'The Authority of the Classics: A Comparative Analysis of the Hermeneutics of Ouyang Xiu and Ogyū Sorai', *Sungkyun Journal of East Asian Studies* 11, no. 1 (2011): 20.

284 *Ouyang Xiu quanji*, 17:289–290.

285 *Xin Tangshu*, 11:307–308. This passage is choicely commented in Bol, 'The Sung Context', 29.

286 *Jiayouji*, 5:65.

287 George Hatch, 'Su Hsun's Pragmatic Statecraft', in *Ordering the World. Approaches to State and Society in Sung Dynasty China*, ed. Robert Hymes and Conrad Schirokauer (Berkeley: University of California Press, 1993), 62–63.

288 Jullien, *The Propensity of Things*, 178.

289 *Jiayouji*, 1:13–14.

290 Bol, 'The Sung Context', 32.

291 The essay *Bianjianlun*, which is attributed to Su Xun, but was not included in the *Jiayouji*, reads that *shi*'s compliance with *li* is difficult to know even for a sage (*Shaoshi wenjian lu*, as in *Zeng Guofan jingshu baijia zamiao*, 2:522). On the other hand, the *Yilun* (*Jiayouji*, 5:81) reads that the sage must examine the spirits (*kao guishen*), and without knowing the spirits and divination, he will not be effective in politics.

292 *Jiayouji*, 6:88–89. However, later on Su Xun mentions the transition of the standard of loyalty into simplicity and elegance. Thus, he takes up a strictly idealistic typology.

293 *Jiayouji*, 1:13.

294 Hatch, 'Su Hsun's Pragmatic Statecraft', 66.

295 *Jiayouji*, 5:76.

296 See Hatch, 'Su Hsun's Pragmatic Statecraft', 74 and Bol, 'The Sung Context', 35. However, in the *Treaties on Histories* 史論 *Shǐlùn* Su Xun writes about the complementarity of the Classics and history and about moral function of the latter: *Jiayouji*, 8:117–122.

297 *Chen Liang ji*, 1:3.

298 *Chen Liang ji*, 1:5.

299 *Chen Liang ji*, 1:8.

300 Fang Litian, *Zhongguo gudai zhexue*, 531.

301 *Chen Liang ji*, 1:13–14.

302 *Chen Liang ji*, 1:10.

303 *Chen Liang ji*, 1:13; 3:39; 11:126.

304 *Chen Liang ji*, 1:9. Chen Liang criticizes Wang Anshi for having overlooked the role of *shi* and believing that only compliance with the 'intention of the sages' is important (1:6). This confirms the validity of our treatment of Wang Anshi as a historical idealist.

305 *Chen Liang ji*, 1:20.

306 *Chen Liang ji*, 3:38. Chen Liang joins the discussion about the difference between historical conditions of the war and peace, which was initiated by Lu Jia and Jia Yi on the basis of evaluating Liu Bang.

307 *Chen Liang ji*, 13:155; 22:235.

308 *Chen Liang ji*, 5:50; 6:61. See *Chen Liang ji*, 11:129 about the fact that after the Han dynasty there are no more sages, but only heroes.

309 *Chen Liang ji* 8: 82.

310 Zheng Jixiong 鄭吉雄, 'Chen Liang de shigong zhi xue' 陳亮的事功之學, *Taida Zhongwen Xuebao* 6 (1994): 263.

311 *Chen Liang ji*, 1:16.

312 *Chen Liang ji*, 3:37, 11:116.

313 *Chen Liang ji*, 11:124.

314 Tillman believes that in the face of criticism of Zhu Xi, different approaches to the law should not be treated as a manifestation of one Dao, but of different ways (Hoyt C. Tillman, *Ch'en Liang on Public Interest and the Law* (Honolulu: University of Hawai'i Press, 1994), 24). In fact, Chen Liang accepts the existence of many Daos, but 'the great tendency of the world' is one, which is overlooked by Tillman.

315 *Chen Liang ji*, 1:7–8.

316 *Chen Liang ji*, 4:43.45. In 11:119 also the virtues of *ren-yi* are treated as 'objects' (*wu*).

317 Zheng Jixiong, 'Chen Liang de shigong zhi xue', 261. See also Fang Litian, *Zhongguo gudai zhexue*, 530.

318 *Chen Liang ji*, 10:104. See 28:345–346 on the fact that Dao does not exist without people, and 28:351 about Dao being a thing in the world.

319 *Chen Liang ji*, 10:103–108. See also 12:137.

320 Hoyt Tillman, *Utilitarian Confucianism: Ch'en Liang's Challenge to Chu His* (Cambridge/London: Harvard University Press, 1982), 154–155, 157.

321 Ibid., 166–168. These are the passages: *Chen Liang ji*, 1:1; 4:48–49.

322 Hoyt C. Tillman, *Confucian Discourse and Chu His's Ascendancy* (Honolulu: University of Hawai'i Press, 1992), 178–182.

323 *Chen Liang ji*, 28:340.348.354.

324 *Zhuzi yulei*, 123:2965.

325 See Winston Wan Lo, *The Life and Thought of Yeh Shih* (Hong Kong: The Chinese University of Hong Kong and the University Presses of Florida, 1974), 79, 115, 124, 139, 141, 162, 169, 175.

Chapter 6

1 Another reason is the fact that initial response to Western philosophies of history was rooted in the categories developed during that time. However, I refrain from using the terms 'renaissance', because of its evaluative nature, its concrete cultural baggage and the fact that in China the term 'renaissance' was appropriated by the representatives of the New Culture Movement. Cf. Thomas Meisner, Barbara Mittler, *Why China did not have a Renaissance – and why that matters* (Boston/Berlin: De Gruyter Oldenbourg, 2018).

2 History of the Liao was created during the Yuan Dynasty, although it was based partly on today's missing Shilu of Yelü Yan; see Xu Elina-Qian, *Historical Development of the Pre-Dynastic Khitan* (PhD diss., University of Helsinki, Helsinki 2005), 22. On historical thought of the Khitans see Wu Huaiqi, *Zhongguo shixue sixiang tongshi*, 193–220.

3 Hoyt C. Tillman and Stephen West (eds.), *China Under Jurchen Rule: Essays on Chin Intellectual and Cultural History* (New York: State University of New York Press, 1995), 71–114.

4 Ibid., 96. See also Wang Mingsun 王明蓀, 'Wang Ruoxu zhi shixue piping' 王若虛之史學批評, *Xingda Lishi Xuebao* 2 (1992).

5 Wang Mingsun 王明蓀, 'Jindai shiren zhi lishi sixiang' 金代士人之歷史思想, *Xingda Lishi Xuebao* 11 (2000): 16–17.

6 Ibid., 5, 14–15.

7 *Wenxian tongkao zixu*, 3.

8 *Wenxian tongkao zixu*, 4. These epochs are Taihe of the Wei (227–232 CE) and Zhenguan of the Tang (627–649). Ma Duanlin associated 'the public' with Heaven and 'the private' with earth, see Hok-Lam Chan, '"Comprehensiveness" (*T'ung*) and "Change" (*Pien*) in Ma Tuan-lin's Historical Thought', in *Yüan Thought: Chinese Thought and Religion under the Mongols*, ed. Wm. Theodore de Bary and Hok-Lam Chan (New York: Columbia University Press, 1982), 52.

9 *Wenxian tongkao*, 260:2060.

10 Wu Huaiqi, *Zhongguo shixue sixiang tongshi*, 439. Hok-Lam Chan, '"Comprehensiveness" (*T'ung*) and "Change" (*Pien*)', 44–46.

11 *Wenxian tongkao zixu*, 4.

12 Hok-Lam Chan, '"Comprehensiveness" (*T'ung*) and "Change" (*Pien*)', 51.

13 *Luzhai yishu*, 9:410.

14 Ibid.

15 *Luzhai yishu*, 1:283.

16 See Wm. Theodore de Bary (ed.), *Self and Society in Ming Thought* (New York/London: Columbia University Press, 1970), 1–28.

17 Wang and Ng, *Mirroring the Past*, 204.

18 Xiang Yannan 項燕楠, *Zhongguo shixue sixiang tongshi. Ming juan* 中国史学思想通史。明卷 (Hefei: Huangshan shushe, 2002), 51–53. Note that subjective idealism is an epistemological standpoint.

19 *Wang Yangming quanji*, 3:115–116.

20 *Wang Yangming quanji*, 1:21.

21 *Wang Yangming quanji*, 1:10.

22 *Wang Yangming quanji*, 1:9–10.

23 *Wang Yangming quanji*, 2:54–55.

24 *Wang Yangming quanji*, 1:27–28.

25 *Shenyan*, 77.

26 *Yashu*, 848.

27 Youngmin Kim, 'Cosmogony as Political Philosophy', *Philosophy East and West* 58, no. 1 (2008): 116.

28 Chang Woei Ong, 'The Principles Are Many: Wang Tingxiang and Intellectual Transition in Mid-Ming China', *Harvard Journal of Asiatic Studies* 66, no. 2 (2006): 474.

29 *Shenyan*, 80–81.

30 *Shenyan*, 85.

31 Ong, 'The Principles Are Many', 476–477.

32 *Shenyan*, 98.

33 *Shenyan*, 99.

34 *Shenyan*, 101–102.

35 *Shenyan*, 98.

36 *Shenyan*, 101.110.

37 *Shenyan*, 100.

38 Kim, 'Cosmogony as Political Philosophy', 118.

39 *Shenyan*, 101.120.

40 On the details of this part of Wang's philosophy: Ong, 'The Principles Are Many', 477–479.

41 *Shenyan*, 127. See Fang Litian, *Zhongguo gudai zhexue*, 532.

42 Ong, 'The Principles Are Many', 482–483. On the other hand, it seems that monarchism was the only possible and therefore universal principle for Wang, even he was unaware of that fact.

43 See Cai Fanglu 蔡方鹿, 'Wang Tingxiang Dao yuyu Liujing de sixiang' 王廷相道寓于六经的思想, *Xiandai Zhexue* 6 (2008): 111–116. C.W. Ong (Ong, 'The Principles Are Many', 485) believes that the Dao present in *wen* is not one, but he does not provide any source justification for this belief, in fact even using the phrase 'the ultimate model'.

44 Robert Crawford, 'Chang Chü-cheng's Confucian Legalism', In *Self and Society in Ming Thought*, ed. Wm. Theodore de Bary (New York/London: Columbia University Press, 1970), 374.

45 *Zhang Wenzhong gong quanji*, 11:671.

46 *Zhang Wenzhong gong quanji*, 3:551–552. Although, as in the case of Wang Tingxiang, monarchism is not subject to relativization.

47 *Zhang Wenzhong gong quanji*, 11:673–674.

48 *Zhang Wenzhong gong quanji*, 11:673–675. 6:602. This idea comes from Dong Zhongshu, although at the same time explicitly rejecting Dong's third principle of *zhong*.

49 *Zhang Wenzhong gong quanji*, 11:553.

50 *Zhang Wenzhong gong quanji*, 3:551–552, 11:675. Summary in: Crawford, 'Chang Chü-cheng's Confucian Legalism', 372, 376. Zhang also recognizes the Yuan.

51 *Wang Zhongwen wenji*, 4:199.

52 *Wang Zhongwen wenji*, 12:575.

53 *Wang Zhongwen wenji*, 15:741.

54 *Wang Zhongwen wenji*, 16:783. Inspiration of Zhu Xi's philosophy of history is evident here.

55 Xiang Yannan, *Zhongguo shixue sixiang tongshi*, 240.

56 Ailika Schinköthe, *Liu Zhiji's Shitong and its Revival in Ming Dynasty – Pacing Historiography Anew* (PhD diss., Eberhard Karls Universität Tübingen, Tübingen 2017), 265–266.

57　*Yanzhou shanren sibu gao*, 144:6827.

58　*Gangjian huizuan xu*, as in: Xiang Yannan, *Zhongguo shixue sixiang tongshi*, 264.

59　*Yanzhou shanren sibu gao*, 111:5384.

60　See Yeung Man Shun 楊文信, *The historical writings of Wang Shizhen, 1526-1590* (PhD diss., University of Hongkong, Hongkong 1992), 80–82.

61　Schinköthe, *Liu Zhiji's* Shitong *and its Revival*, 285, 291.

62　Wolfgang Franke, 'Historical writing during the Ming,' In *The Cambridge History of China. Volume 7: The Ming Dynasty, 1368—1644, Part I*, ed. Denis Twitchett and John K. Fairbank (Cambridge: Cambridge University Pres, 1998), 731–732.

63　In the *Yanzhou shanren sibu gao*, 144:6827 Wang sketches a picture of the gradual fall of historiography, openly expressing the fear that the moment may come when the further writing of history will cease.

64　*Shaoshi shanfang bicong*, 5:216. Scroll n. 5 opens the *Profound Explanation of Historical Books* 史書占畢 *Shǐshū chānbì.*

65　*Shaoshi shanfang bicong*, 5:218.

66　*Shaoshi shanfang bicong*, 5:220.

67　*Shaoshi shanfang bicong*, 5:221.

68　*Shaoshi shanfang bicong*, 5:223.

69　*Shaoshi shanfang bicong*, 5:227.

70　*Shaoshi shanfang bicong*, 5:228.

71　*Shaoshi shanfang bicong*, 5:235.

72　*Shaoshi shanfang bicong*, 23:1022.

73　See *Shaoshi shanfang bicong*, 14:573–574.

74　The list of Hu Yinglin summarized in: Hsu Kwan-San, 'The Chinese Critical Tradition', 442.

75　Peter K. Bol, 'Looking to Wang Shizhen: Hu Yinglin (1551–1602) and Late-Ming Alternatives to Neo-Confucian Learning', *Ming Studies* 53 (2006): 116, 123, 127.

76　Full text of the judgement in: Li Zhi, *A Book to Burn and a Book to Keep (Hidden): Selected Writings of Li Zhi*, trans. Rivi Handler-Spitz, Pauline Lee and Haun Saussy (New York: Columbia University Press, 2016), 385–386.

77　*Cangshu*, 9:420.

78　*Cangshu*, 1:294.

79　Xiang Yannan, *Zhongguo shixue sixiang tongshi*, 310.

80　*Cangshu*, 1:293.

81　*Fenshu*, 1:72–73.

82　In the monograph under a meaningful title *From Philosophy to Philology*, Benjamin Elman emphasizes that the philology was not only an auxiliary tool but was necessary to 'recover and relearn past structures of Confucian culture. It was used to make the past live again' (Benjamin Elman, *From Philosophy to Philology: Intellectual and Social Aspects of Change in Late Imperial China* (Cambridge: Council on East Asian Studies, Harvard University, 1984), 28.

83　Benjamin Elman, 'Criticism as Philosophy: Conceptual Change in Ch'ing Dynasty Evidential Research', *Qinghua Xuebao* 17, no. 1–2 (1985): 166, 197.

84　Benjamin Elman, 'Philosophy (*I-li*) versus Philology (*K'ao-cheng*): The *Jen-hsin tao-hsin* Debate', *T'oung Pao* 69, no. 4/5 (1983): 207.

85　Wang and Ng, *Mirroring the Past*, 238.

86　Benjamin Elman, 'The Historicization of Classical Learning in Ming-Ch'ing China,' In *Turning Points in Historiography: A Cross-Cultural Perspective*, ed. Q. Edward Wang and Georg Iggers (Rochester: The University of Rochester Press, 2002), 103.

87   Gao Jianlong 高建龙, *Tiandao yu zhengdao: Shiqi shiji Zhongguo rujia sixiang yu Qingjiao zhuyi duibi yanjiu* 天道与政道： 十七世纪中国儒家思想与清教主义对比研究 (Beijing: Zhongguo shehui kexue chubanshe, 2014).
88   Elman, 'Criticism as Philosophy', 170.
89   Michael Quirin, 'Scholarship, Value, Method, and Hermeneutics in *Kaozheng*: Some Reflections on Cui Shu (1740–1816) and the Confucian Classics', *History and Theory* 35, no. 4 (1996): 45–47.
90   Jui-Sung Yang, *Body, Ritual and Identity: A New Interpretation of the Early Qing Confucian Yan Yuan (1635-1704)* (Leiden/Boston: Brill, 2016), 73–74, 151.
91   Wang Jilu 王记录, *Zhongguo shixue sixiang tongshi. Qingdai juan* 中国史学思想通史。 清代卷 (Hefei: Huangshan shushe, 2002), 281, 293, 307.
92   Elman, *From Philosophy to Philology*, 71.
93   As quoted in: Elman, 'Philosophy (*I-li*) versus Philology (*K'ao-cheng*), 207.
94   Quirin, 'Scholarship, Value, Method, and Hermeneutics', 44, 49.
95   *Tinglin wenji*, 4:166.
96   *Rizhilu*, 2:96–97.
97   Wang Jilu, *Zhongguo shixue sixiang tongshi*, 88.
98   *Tinglin wenji*, 3:124. The term *shenxue* denotes nowadays, nota bene, theology.
99   *Rizhilu*, 3:175. He also states that the *Chunqiu* has too many understatements and omissions to be classed as a Classic, see *Rizhilu*, 4:182.
100   Miranda Brown, 'Returning the Gaze: An Experiment in Reviving Gu Yanwu (1613–1682)', *Fragments* vol. 1 (2011): 41–77.
101   *Rizhilu*, 12:721.
102   *Tinglin wenji*, 4:170.
103   *Rizhilu*, 13:772–773.
104   *Rizhilu*, 16:936–937.
105   *Rizhilu*, 3:148.
106   *Rizhilu*, 13:758–759.
107   *Rizhilu*, 13:756.
108   *Tinglin wenji*, 1:20.
109   *Rizhilu*, 1:29.
110   *Huang Zongxi quanji*, 10:314. Page number after the volume number.
111   *Huang Zongxi quanji*, 7:3.
112   *Huang Zongxi quanji*, 7:22.
113   *Huang Zongxi quanji*, 10:300.330.
114   *Huang Zongxi quanji*, 1:5.
115   *Huang Zongxi quanji*, 10:97–98. Huang exactly mentions 384 *yao*, that is lines (six times 64 hexagrams).
116   *Huang Zongxi quanji*, 9:119.
117   *Huang Zongxi quanji*, 1:90.
118   See Wm. Theodore de Bary, *Waiting for the Dawn. A Plan for the Prince. Huang Tsung-hsi's* Ming-i tai-fang lu (New York: Columbia University Press, 1993).
119   Wang and Ng, *Mirroring the Past*, 225–226.
120   *Dai Zhen quanji*, 1:153.212.
121   See Wang Jilu, *Zhongguo shixue sixiang tongshi*, 216.
122   *Dai Zhen quanji*, 1: 156.158.
123   *Dai Zhen quanji*, 1:170.
124   *Dai Zhen quanji*, 1:172.194.
125   *Dai Zhen quanji*, 5:2672; 6:3152.3160. See Elman, 'Criticism as Philosophy', 71.

126 *Shi guangzhuan*, 3:421.
127 See JeeLoo Liu, 'Wang Fuzhi's Philosophy of Principle (*Li*) Inherent in *Qi*', in *Dao Companion to Neo-Confucian Philosophy*, ed. John Makeham (Dodrecht et al.: Springer, 2010), 358–359, 362–363. Cf. *Zhouyi waizhuan*, 5:1028.
128 *Songlun*, 8:190.
129 *Zhouyi waizhuan*, 7:1112.
130 Allison Black, *Man and Nature in the Philosophical Thought of Wang Fu-chih* (Seattle: University of Washington Press, 19890, 50, 52, 63, 72, 79. The *Du Tongjian lun* reads that the spirit (*shen*) can transform into a visible form (*xing*), for both things are inseparable as aspects of one changing *qi*, see *Du Tongjian lun*, 10:404.
131 Nicholas Brasovan, *Neo-Confucian Ecological Humanism. An Interpretative Engagement with Wang Fuzhi (1619–1692)* (New York: State University of New York Press, 2017), 65.
132 Liu, 'Wang Fuzhi's Philosophy of Principle', 355.
133 Brasovan, *Neo-Confucian Ecological Humanism*, 84.
134 *Shi guangzhuan*, 3:405.
135 *Songlun*, 4:120.
136 *Du Tongjian lun*, 13:485.
137 Concrete historical explanations use the notions of comprehending 通 *tōng* and forgetting 忘 *wàng* 'various *li*' 眾理 *zhònglǐ*, see for instance *Du Tongjian lun*, 14:527, 20:759.
138 *Songlun*, 6:171.
139 *Songlun*, 4:127.
140 *Du Tongjian lun*, 25:949.
141 *Songlun*, 8:201.
142 Jullien, *The Propensity of Things*, 194.
143 *Songlun*, 7:177.
144 *Du Tongjian lun*, 15: 582.
145 *Du Tongjian lun*, 8:315, 12:456.
146 *Songlun*, 4:105, 8:191, 9:204; *Du Tongjian lun*, 20:800.
147 *Du Tongjian lun*, 10:373, 15:578.
148 *Songlun*, 10:256. 14:325–326.
149 *Du Tongjian lun*, 2:117.
150 *Du Tongjian lun*, 5:202.
151 *Du Tongjian lun*, 3:139.
152 *Du Tongjian lun*, 1:67.
153 *Du Tongjian lun*, 2:109. Wang Fuzhi deplores that people want to return to feudalism even after Liu Zongyuan's *Fengjianlun*, see *Du Tongjian lun*, 20:772.
154 *Du Tongjian lun*, 1:108.
155 *Du Tongjian lun*, 5:190. This is one of the passages in which, apart from a series of individual historical tendencies, Wang Fuzhi distinguishes one, overall tendency of history.
156 *Songlun*, 10: 255.
157 *Du Tongjian lun*, 19:732 – 20:733–734.
158 *Du Tongjian lun*, 24:921.
159 *Du Tongjian lun*, 26:1017.
160 *Du Tongjian lun*, 22:848, 23:865–866.
161 *Du Tongjian lun*, 26:1021, 27:1032.1037.
162 *Songlun*, 8:201.

163 JeeLoo Liu, 'Is Human History Predestined in Wang Fuzhi's Cosmology?', *Journal of Chinese Philosophy* 28, no. 3 (2001): 328–334.

164 Jullien, *The Propensity of Things*, 212–213.

165 *Songlun*, 4:142. 10:248. 15:335.

166 *Songlun*, 1:37–38.43.45.

167 *Du Tongjian lun*, 3:123, 10: 388.

168 *Du Tongjian lun*, 6:232–233.

169 *Du Tongjian lun*, 10:375.

170 *Du Tongjian lun*, 15:589.

171 *Du Tongjian lun*, 20:761–762.

172 *Songlun*, 3:94, 4:110, 15:336.

173 *Du Tongjian lun* 20: 813.

174 *Du Tongjian lun*, 24:938, 28:1085.

175 *Du Tongjian lun*, 20:763–764. It is noteworthy that in the sentence 'Shao Yong divided history into four epochs: of Dao, virtue, achievement, and power' the term *gujin* undeniably plays the role of a noun, a technical term denoting history as a process.

176 *Sijie*, 486–487.

177 *Siwenlu*, 467.

178 Liu, 'Wang Fuzhi's Philosophy of Principle', 360.

179 *Du Tongjian lun*, 17:627.631.

180 Respectively: *wu zhi Tian, min zhi Tian, ji zhi Tian.*

181 *Songlun*, 1:19.

182 Liu Liangjian 刘梁剑, *Wang Chuanshan zhexue yanjiu* 王船山哲学研究 (Shanghai: Shanghai renmin chubanshe, 2016), 18.

183 *Songlun*, 7:179; *Du Tongjian lun*, 7:280.

184 *Du Tongjian lun* 24: 934.

185 *Songlun* 1:19–20.46, *Du Tongjian lun*, 16:526, 19:697.

186 Chen Ming 陈明, *Wang Chuanshan Shangshu yinyi zhi dexinglun yu zhidao sixiang: yi Shangshu yinyi wei zhongxin* 王船山尚书引义之德性论与治道思想： 以尚书引义为中心 (Beijing: Zhongguo shehui kexue chubanshe, 2016), 211, 215, 217.

187 *Du Tongjian lun*, 1:68.

188 *Du Tongjian lun*, 21:802. Heaven refused, however, to support Wu Zetian's grandson, Emperor Xuanzong (685–762), although it did not 'hate' the Tang, see 23:858–860.

189 *Du Tongjian lun*, 6:217.

190 *Du Tongjian lun*, 5:206. In *Du Tongjian lun*, 17:662 Wang Fuzhi adds the Liang to that list.

191 *Du Tongjian lun*, 10:407.

192 Jullien, *The Propensity of Things*, 210–211. Note that 'an end to history' means not only its ending, but also its purpose.

193 *Songlun*, 10:252.

194 *Du Tongjian lun mo*, 1182.

195 *Du Tongjian lun*, 16:610. Also *Du Tongjian lun mo*, 1174–1175.

196 *Du Tongjian lun*, 3:138, 14:535.

197 *Du Tongjian lun*, 7:259, 13:884. *Du Tongjian lun mo*, 1178.

198 Tang Cheng 汤城, *Wang Fuzhi shixue sixiang yanjiu* 王夫之史学思想研究 (Nanchang: Jiangxi renmin chubanshe, 2016), 118.

199 Whole paragraph is based on the essay *Yuan Dao*, included in the *Wenshi tongyi*.

200 Nivison, *The Life and Thought*, 141. Spelling of Zhang and Dao modified.

201 Ibid., 145.

202 *Wenshi tongyi*, 5A:171. '5A' means *Yuandao shang*, other essays according to their order in the *Wenshi tongyi*.

203 *Wenshi tongyi*, 20:453–454.

204 *Wenshi tongyi*, 5B:182.

205 *Wenshi tongyi*, 24:505–506.

206 Nivison, *The Life and Thought*, 164–165.

207 *Wenshi tongyi*, 1:2.

208 *Wenshi tongyi*, 6C:226.

209 On-cho Ng, 'A Tension in Ch'ing Thought: 'Historicism' in Seventeenth- and Eighteenth-Century Chinese Thought', *Journal of the History of Ideas* 54, no. 4 (1993): 578.

210 *Wenshi tongyi*, 6C:211.

211 *Wenshi tongyi*, 24:548.

212 Philip J. Ivanhoe, 'Lessons from the past: Zhang Xuecheng and the ethical dimensions of history', *Dao: A Journal of Comparative Philosophy* 8, no. 2 (2009): 194.

213 *Da Shen Zaiting lun xue*, 85, in: *Zhang Xuecheng yishu*.

214 *Wenshi tongyi*, 5C:188–189.

215 *Yu Zusun Runan lunxue shu*, 224, in: *Zhang Xuecheng yishu*. It is clear from the writings of Zhang Xuecheng that by philology he understands empirical science, and by literature – art. Translation from: Philip J. Ivanhoe, *On Ethics and History: Essays and Letters of Zhang Xuecheng* (Stanford: Stanford University Press, 2009), 113.

216 *Wenshi tongyi*, 9:310.

217 Nivison, *The Life and Thought*, 76, 118.

218 *Wenshi tongyi*, 9:310.315.

219 *Wenshi tongyi*, 9:309–323.

220 'Of the two evils', Zhang Xuecheng prefers to focus on events since the main task of chronicles is the recording of events and the sequence of events should determine the order of the records. Language always adapts to events, see *Wenshi tongyi*, 2C:84. Hence, Zhang evaluted the *Shiji* and the *Tongjian jishi benmo* highly.

221 On broader background of the idea of *shide* and its modern, positivist included, interpretations in the Chinese theory of history see Dawid Rogacz, 'The Virtue of a Historian. A Dialogue between Herman Paul and Chinese theorists of history', *History and Theory* 58, no. 2 (2019): 252–267.

222 *Wenshi tongyi*, 7B-C: 224–230.

223 *Wenshi tongyi*, 25:558.

224 *Wenshi tongyi*, 13:368.

225 *Wenshi tongyi*, 13:366.

226 *Wenshi tongyi*, 19: 444. In the same essay, namely *The Metaphor of Nature* 天喻 *Tiānyù*, Zhang Xuecheng proposes similar statements in his epistemology (and, in a sense, the philosophy of science). Progress understood as an increase in scientific knowledge is possible because the concepts applied to nature are not only the product of our reason (*li*), but they also have something 'from nature'. Otherwise there would be no effective measurements. Moreover, according to Zhang, astronomical terms are only names 'imposed by force' on nature, so that the calculations could agree. By applying the idea of interpretation to science, Zhang approached the thought of Kant and the position of contemporary anti-realists.

227 *Wenshi tongyi*, 23:499.

228 *Wenshi tongyi*, 38B:742.749.

229 *Wenshi tongyi*, 15:391–394.

230 *Wenshi tongyi*, 16:414.
231 Philip J. Ivanhoe, 'Historical Understanding in China and the West: Zhang, Collingwood and Mink', *Journal of the Philosophy of History* 8, no. 1 (2014): 81, 86.
232 Nivison, 'Chang Hsueh-Ch'eng and Collingwood', 3.

Chapter 7

1 Grace Cairns even classifies it as a multicyclical theory of history; see Grace Cairns, *Philosophies of History: Meeting of East and West in Cycle-Pattern Theories of History* (New York: Philosophical Library Inc., 1962), 186–195.
2 Liang Qichao 梁啟超, *Zhongguo lishi yanjiufa* 中國歷史研究法 (Shanghai: Shanghai guji chubanshe, 1998), 157–159. On the continuity of the reflection upon the notion of *shide* in the Chinese theory of history until the twenty-first century, see Rogacz, 'The Virtue of a Historian'.
3 Jullien, *The Propensity of Things*, 75–90.

Conclusion

1 Ivanhoe, 'Chinese Theories of History', 3582.
2 As in: Maurice Meisner, *Li Ta-Chao and the Origins of Chinese Marxism* (Cambridge: Harvard University Press, 1967), 159.
3 Stephen Platt, *Provincial Patriots: The Hunanese and Modern China* (Cambridge: Harvard University Press, 2007), 184. The philosophy of Wang Fuzhi was connected with Marxism also due to the work *Wang Fuzhi's philosophy of history* (*Wang Chuanshan de lishi zhexue*) of He Lin 賀麟 (1902–1992) from 1946.
4 Ady van den Stock, *The Horizon of Modernity. Subjectivity and Social Structure in New Confucian Philosophy* (Leiden/Boston: Brill, 2016), 329.
5 Mou Zongsan, *Lishi zhexue*, 74.
6 Luo Guang, *Lishi zhexue*, 281–523.

Bibliography

Chinese sources

Baopuzi waipian 抱朴子外篇. By Ge Hong 葛洪. Guiyang: Guizhou renmin chubanshe, 1996.

Bohutong 白虎通. By Ban Gu 班固. Beijing: Zhonghua shuju, 1994.

Cangshu 藏書. By Li Zhi 李贄. *Siku quanshu cunmu congshu, shibu* vol. 23.

Changli xiansheng wenji 昌黎先生文集. By Han Yu 韓愈. *Songben chongkan.*

Changyan 昌言. By Zhong Changtong 仲長統. In *Zhenglun. Changyan* 政论昌言. Beijing: Zhonghua shuju, 2014.

Chen Liang ji 陈亮集. By Chen Liang 陈亮. Beijing: Zhonghua shuju, 1987.

Chunqiu Fanlu 春秋繁露. Attributed to Dong Zhongshu 董仲舒. *Siku quanshu* edition. Beijing: Zhonghua shuju, 2016.

Dai Zhen quanji 戴震全集. By Dai Zhen 戴震. Beijing: Qinghua daxue chubanshe, 1991.

Dushi guanjian 讀史管見. By Hu Yin 胡寅. Beijing: Gubai jucang ben, 1714.

Du Tongjian lun 讀通鑑論. By Wang Fuzhi 王夫之. *Chuanshan quanshu* edition. Changsha: Yuelu shushe, 1996.

Gongyangzhuan 公羊傳. *Shisanjing zhushu* edition. Beijing: Beijing daxue chubanshe, 1999.

Er Cheng ji 二程集. By Cheng Hao 程顥 and Cheng Yi 程頤. Beijing: Zhonghua shuju, 1981.

Fayan 发言. By Yang Xiong 揚雄. Beijing: Zhonghua shuju, 2012.

Fenshu 焚書. By Li Zhi 李贄. In *Li Zhi quanji* 李贄全集, vol. 1–2. Beijing: Zhongguo shehui kexue wenxian chubanshe, 2010.

Guanzi 管子. *Guanzi Jiaozhu* edition. Beijing: Zhonghua shuju, 2004.

Jiaoyouji 嘉祐集. By Su Xun 蘇洵. *Sibu congkan* edition.

Hanfeizi 韓非子. By Han Fei 韓非. *Hanfeizi jijie* edition. Beijing: Zhonghua shuju, 1998.

Hanshu 漢書. By Ban Gu 班固. Beijing: Zhonghua shuju, 1999.

Heguanzi 鶡冠子. *Heguanzi huijiao jizhu* edition. Beijing: Zhonghua shuju, 2004.

Houhanshu 後漢書. By Fan Ye 范曄. Beijing: Zhonghua Shuju, 1974.

Huainanzi 淮南子. *Huainanzi jiaoshi* edition. Beijing: Beijing daxue chubanshe, 1997.

Huangji jingshi shu 皇極經世書. By Shao Yong 邵雍. *Sibu congkan* edition. Zhengzhou: Zhongzhou guji chubanshe, 1991, reprint.

Huang Zongxi quanji 黃宗羲全集. By Huang Zongxi 黃宗羲. Hangzhou: Zhejiang guji chubanshe, 1985.

Jinsilu 近思錄. By Zhu Xi 朱熹 and Lü Zuqian 呂祖謙. Shanghai: Shanghai guji chubanshe, 2000.

Laozi 老子. Attributed to Laozi 老子. *Laozi jiaoshi* edition. Beijing: Zhonghua shuju, 1984.

Liezi 列子. Attributed to Lie Yukou 列禦寇. *Liezi jishi* edition. Beijing: Zhonghua Shuju, 1979.

Li Gou ji 李覯集. By Li Gou 李覯. Beijing: Zhonghua shuju, 1981.

Liji 禮記. *Shisanjing zhushu* edition. Beijing: Beijing daxue chubanshe, 1999.

Linchuan xiansheng wenji 臨川先生文集. By Wang Anshi 王安石. Beijing: Zhonghua shuju, 1959.

Liu Zongyuan ji 柳宗元集. By Liu Zongyuan 柳宗元. Beijing: Zhonghua shuju, 1979.

Lunheng 論衡. *Lunheng zhushi* edition. Beijing: Zhonghua Shuju, 1979.

Lunyu 論語. Attributed to Kongzi 孔子. *Shisanjing zhushu* edition. Beijing: Beijing daxue chubanshe, 1999.

Luzhai yishu 魯齋遺書. By Xu Heng 許衡. *Siku quanshu* edition.

Lüshi Chunqiu. Attributed to Lü Buwei 呂不韋. *Lüshi Chunqiu xin jiaoshi* edition. Shanghai: Shanghai guji chubanshe, 2002.

Maoshi 毛詩. *Shisanjing zhushu* edition. Beijing: Beijing daxue chubanshe, 1999.

Mengzi 孟子. Attributed to Mengzi 孟子. *Shisanjing zhushu* edition. Beijing: Beijing daxue chubanshe, 1999.

Mozi 墨子. Attributed to Mo Di 墨翟. *Mozi jiangu* edition. Beijing: Zhonghua shuju, 2009.

Ouyang Xiu quanji 欧阳修全集. By Ouyang Xiu 欧阳修. Beijing: Zhonghua shuju, 2001.

Qianfulun 潛夫論. By Wang Fu 王符. Guiyang: Guizhou renmin chubanshe, 1999.

[Qian] Hanji 前漢紀. By Xun Yue 荀悅. *Sibu congkan* edition.

Quan Songwen 全宋文. Chengdu: Bashu, 1988.

Renwuzhi 人物志. Attributed to Liu Shao 劉卲. Beijing: Zhonghua shuju, 2014.

Rizhilu 日知錄. By Gu Yanwu 顧炎武. Shanghai: Shanghai guji chubanshe, 2006.

Shangjunshu 商君書. Attributed to Shang Yang 商鞅. *Shangjunshu zhuizhi* edition. Beijing: Zhonghua shuju, 1986.

Shangshu 尚書. *Shisanjing zhushu* edition. Beijing: Beijing daxue chubanshe, 1999.

Shaoshi shanfang bicong 少室山房筆叢. By Hu Yinglin 胡應麟. *Siku quanshu* edition.

Shenyan 慎言. By Wang Tingxiang 王廷相. *Siku quanshu cunmu congshu* edition.

Shenzi 慎子. Attributed to Shen Dao 慎到. *Shenzi jijiao jizhu* edition. Beijing: Zhonghua shuju, 2013.

Shi guangzhuan 詩廣傳. By Wang Fuzhi 王夫之. *Chuanshan quanshu* edition. Changsha: Yuelu shushe, 1996.

Shiji 史記. By Sima Qian 司馬遷. Beijing: Zhonghua shuju, 1963.

Shitong 史通. By Liu Zhiji 劉知幾. Beijing: Zhonghua shuju, 2014.

Sijie 俟解. By Wang Fuzhi 王夫之. *Chuanshan quanshu* edition. Changsha: Yuelu shushe, 1996.

Siwenlu 思問錄. By Wang Fuzhi 王夫之. *Chuanshan quanshu* edition. Changsha: Yuelu shushe, 1996.

Songlun 宋論. By Wang Fuzhi 王夫之. *Chuanshan quanshu* edition. Changsha: Yuelu sushe, 1996.

Taipingjing 太平經. *Taipingjing hejiao* edition. Beijing: Zhonghua shuju, 1960.

Tinglin wenji 亭林文集. By Gu Yanwu 顧炎武. Kuiji: Dongshixue guzhai, 1904.

Tongdian 通典. By Du You 杜佑. Beijing: Zhonghua Shuju, 1988.

Tongzhi 通志. By Zheng Qiao 鄭樵. *Siku quanshu* edition.

Wang Wenzhong wenji 王忠文公集. By Wang Yi 王禕. Beijing: Panshi yuanjiangjie shu, 1848.

Wang Yangming quanji 王阳明全集. By Wang Yangming 王阳明. Shanghai: Shanghai guji chubanshe, 1992.

Wenshi tongyi 文史通義. By Zhang Xuecheng 張學誠. Beijing: Zhonghua shuju, 2012.

Wenxian tongkao 文獻通考. By Ma Duanlin 馬端臨. Beijing: Zhonghua shuju, 1986.

Wenxin diaolong 文心雕龙. By Liu Xie 劉勰. Beijing: Renmin wenxue chubanshe, 1981.

Xinlun 新論. *Xinjiben Huan Tan Xinlun* edition. Attributed to Huan Tan 桓譚. Beijing: Zhonghua shuju, 2009.

Xinshu 新書. Attributed to Jia Yi 賈誼. Beijing: Zhonghua shuju, 2012.

Xin Tangshu 新唐書. By Ouyang Xiu 歐陽修. Beijing: Zhonghua shuju, 1975.

Xin Wudai shi 新五代史. By Ouyang Xiu 歐陽修. Beijing: Zhonghua shuju, 1974.

Xinxu 新序. By Liu Xiang 劉向. Beijing: Zhonghua shuju, 2014.

Xinyu 新語. By Lu Jia 陸賈. *Xinyu jiaozhu* edition. Beijing: Zhonghua shuju, 1986.

Xunzi 荀子. By Xunzi 荀子. *Xunzi jijie* edition. Beijing: Zhonghua shuju, 1988.

Yanzhou shanren sibu gao 弇州山人四部稿. By Wang Shizhen 王世貞. *Siku quanshu cunmu congshu* edition.

Yashu 雅述. By Wang Tingxiang 王廷相. *Wang Tingxiang ji* edition. Beijing: Zhonghua shuju, 1989.

Yinwenzi 尹文子. Attributed to Yin Wen 尹文. In *Shenzi, Yinwenzi, Gongsun Longzi quanyi* 慎子尹文子公孙龙子全译. Guiyang: Guizhou renmin chubanshe, 1996.

Yupi Zizhi tongjian gangmu 御批資治通鑑綱目. By Zhu Xi 朱熹. *Siku quanshu* edition.

Zeng Guofan jingshu baijia zamiao 曾国藩经史百家杂钞全译. By Zeng Guofan 曾国藩. Guiyang: Guizhou renmin chubanshe, 1994.

Zhang Wenzhong gong quanji 张文忠公全集. By Zhang Juzheng 張居正. Shanghai: Shangwu yinshuguan, 1937.

Zhang Xuecheng yishu 張學誠遺書. By Zhang Xuecheng 張學誠. Beijing: Wenwu chubanshe, 1985.

Zhenglun 政論. By Cui Shi 崔寔. In *Zhenglun. Changyan* 政论昌言. Beijing: Zhonghua shuju, 2014.

Zhouyi 周易. Guiyang: Guizhou renmin chubanshe, 1991.

Zhouyi waizhuan 周易外傳. By Wang Fuzhi 王夫之. *Chuanshan quanshu* edition. Changsha: Yuelu sushe, 1996.

Zhuangzi 莊子. Attributed to Zhuang Zhou 莊周. *Zhuangzi jishi* edition. Beijing: Zhonghua Shuju, 1961.

Zhuzhu jinian 竹書紀年. *Guben Zhushu jinian* edition. Jinan: Qi-Lu shushe.

Zhuzi yulei 朱子語類. By Zhu Xi 朱熹. Beijing: Zhonghua shuju, 1986.

Zhuzi wenji 主子文集. By Zhu Xi 朱熹. Fuzhou: Zhengyi shuyuan, 1866.

Secondary literature

Abts, Koen and Stefan Rummens 'Populism versus Democracy'. *Political Studies* 55, no. 2 (2007): 405–424.

Adorno, Theodor W. *Negative Dialectics*. New York: The Seabury Press, 1973.

Allan, Sarah. *The Shape of the Turtle: Myth, Art, and Cosmos in Early China*. New York: State University of New York Press, 1991.

Allan, Sarah. 'On the Identity of Shang Di and the Origin of the Concept of a Celestial Mandate (*Tian Ming*)'. *Early China* 31 (2007): 1–46.

Allan, Sarah. *Buried Ideas: Legends of Abdication and Ideal Government in Recently Discovered Early Chinese Bamboo-slip Manuscripts*. New York: State University of New York Press, 2015.

Allan, Sarah. *The Heir and the Sage: Dynastic Legend in Early China*. Albany: State University of New York Press, 2016.

Ames, Roger. *The Art of Rulership. A Study of Ancient Chinese Political Thought*. New York: State University of New York Press, 1994.

Angehrn, Emil. *Geschichtsphilosophie: eine Einführung*. Basel: Schwabe reflexe, 2012.

Arbuckle, Gary. *Restoring Dong Zhongshu (BCE 195–115): an experiment in historical and philosophical reconstruction.* PhD diss., University of British Columbia, Vancouver 1983.

Arbuckle, Gary. 'Inevitable Treason: Dong Zhongshu's Theory of Historical Cycles and Early Attempts to Invalidate the Han Mandate'. *Journal of the American Oriental Society* 115, no. 4 (1995): 585–597.

Back, Yongsun. 'Fate and the Good Life: Zhu Xi and Jeong Yagyong's Discourse on *Ming*'. *Dao: A Journal of Comparative Philosophy* 14 (2015): 255–274.

Bagby, Phillip. *Culture and History.* Berkeley: University of California Press, 1959.

Black, Allison. *Man and Nature in the Philosophical Thought of Wang Fu-chih.* Seattle: University of Washington Press, 1989.

Bokenkamp, Stephen. 'Time After Time: Taoist Apocalyptic History and the Founding of the T'ang Dynasty'. *Asia Major* 7, no. 1 (1994): 59–88.

Bol, Peter K. 'The Sung Context: From Ou-yang Hsiu to Chu Hsi'. In *Sung Dynasty Uses of the I Ching*, edited by Kidder Smith Jr. et al., 26–55. Princeton: Princeton University Press, 1990.

Bol, Peter K. 'Looking to Wang Shizhen: Hu Yinglin (1551–1602) and Late-Ming Alternatives to Neo-Confucian Learning'. *Ming Studies* 53 (2006): 99–137.

Brasovan, Nicholas. *Neo-Confucian Ecological Humanism. An Interpretative Engagement with Wang Fuzhi (1619–1692).* New York: State University of New York Press, 2017.

Brindley, Erica Fox. *Individualism in Early China. Human Agency and the Self in Thought and Politics.* Honolulu: University of Hawai'i Press, 2010.

Brook, Timothy. 'Medievality and the Chinese Sense of History'. *The Medieval History Journal* 1, no. 1 (1998): 146–164.

Brown, Miranda. 'Returning the Gaze: An Experiment in Reviving Gu Yanwu (1613–1682)'. *Fragments* vol. 1 (2011): 41–77.

Brzechczyn, Krzysztof. 'O racjonalną postawę wobec marksizmu'. In *Marksizm. Nadzieje i rozczarowania*, edited by Jacek Hołówka, Bogdan Dziobkowski, 309–319. Warszawa: Wydawnictwo Naukowe PWN.

Cai Fanglu 蔡方鹿. 'Wang Tingxiang Dao yuyu Liujing de sixiang' 王廷相道寓于六经的思想. *Xiandai Zhexue* 6 (2008): 111–116.

Cairns, Grace. *Philosophies of History: Meeting of East and West in Cycle-Pattern Theories of History.* New York: Philosophical Library Inc., 1962.

Cairns, Grace. 'Social Progress and Holism in T.M.P. Mahadevan's Philosophy of History'. *Philosophy East and West* 20, no. 1 (1970): 73–82.

Campany, Robert Ford. *To Live as Long as Heaven and Earth. A Translation and Study of Ge Hong's Traditions of Divine Transcendents.* Berkeley-Los Angeles: University of California Press, 2002.

Chan Wing-Tsit. *A Sourcebook in Chinese philosophy.* Princeton: Princeton University Press, 1963.

Chan, Hok-Lam. '"Comprehensiveness" (*T'ung*) and "Change" (*Pien*) in Ma Tuan-lin's Historical Thought'. In *Yüan Thought: Chinese Thought and Religion under the Mongols*, edited by Wm. Theodore de Bary and Hok-Lam Chan, 27–87. New York: Columbia University Press, 1982.

Chan, Wing-cheuk. 'Time in Wang Fuzhi's Philosophy of History'. In *Notions of Time in Chinese Historical Thinking*, ed. Huang Chun-chieh and John B. Henderson, 115–130. Hongkong: The Chinese University Press, 2006.

Chaussende, Damien. 'Un Historien sur le banc des accuses. Liu Zhiji juge Wei Shou'. *Études chinoises* 29 (2010): 141–180.

Chen Ming 陈明. *Wang Chuanshan* Shangshu yinyi *zhi dexinglun yu zhidao sixiang: yi* Shangshu yinyi *wei zhongxin* 王船山尚书引义之德性论与治道思想：以尚书引义为中心. Beijing: Zhongguo shehui kexue chubanshe, 2016.

Chen Ning. 'Confucius' view of fate (*ming*)'. *Journal of Chinese Philosophy* 24, no. 3 (1997): 323–59.

Chen Zhi. *The Shaping of the Book of Songs: From ritualization to secularization.* Sankt Augustin: Steyler Verlag, 2007.

Cheng Chung-Ying. 'Interpreting Paradigm of Change in Chinese Philosophy'. *Journal of Chinese Philosophy* 38, no. 3 (2011): 339–67.

Cieszkowski, August. *Selected Writings of August Cieszkowski*, trans. André Liebich. Cambridge: Cambridge University Press, 1979.

Confucius. *Analects. With Selections from Traditional Commentaries*, trans. Edward Slingerland. Indianapolis/Cambridge: Hackett Publishing, 2003.

Crawford, Robert. 'Chang Chü-cheng's Confucian Legalism'. In *Self and Society in Ming Thought*, edited by Wm. Theodore de Bary, 367–413. New York/London: Columbia University Press, 1970.

Crawford, William. 'Philosophical and Intellectual Thought'. In *Liu Tsung-yüan*, edited by William H. Nienhauser, Jr et al. New York: Twayne Publishers, 1973.

Creel, Herrlee. 'Shen Pu-Hai: A Secular Philosopher of Administration'. *Journal of Chinese Philosophy* 1, no. 2 (1974): 119–136.

Csikszentmihalyi, Mark and Michael Nylan. 'Constructing Lineages and Inventing Traditions through Exemplary Figures in Early China'. *T'oung Pao* 89, no. 1 (2003): 59–99.

Cua, Antonio S. *Human Nature, Ritual, and History: Studies in Xunzi and Chinese Philosophy.* Washington: Catholic University of America Press, 2005.

Dan, Joseph. *Gershom Scholem: Between History and Historiosophy.* West Lafayette: Purdue University Press, 1983.

Danto, Arthur C. 'Narrative Sentences'. *History and Theory* 2, no. 2 (1962): 146–179.

Danto, Arthur C. *Analytical Philosophy of History.* London: Cambridge University Press, 1968.

de Bary, Wm. Theodore (ed.). *Self and Society in Ming Thought.* New York/London: Columbia University Press, 1970.

de Bary, Wm. Theodore. 'Neo-Confucian Individualism and Holism'. In *Individualism and Holism: Studies in Confucian and Taoist Values*, edited by Donald Munro, 331–357. Ann Arbor: The University of Michigan, Center for Chinese Studies, 1985.

de Bary, Wm. Theodore. *Waiting for the Dawn. A Plan for the Prince. Huang Tsung-hsi's Ming-i tai-fang lu.* New York: Columbia University Press, 1993.

de Bary, Wm. Theodore and Irene Bloom (eds.). *Sources of Chinese tradition, volume 1, from earliest times to 1600.* New York: Columbia University Press, 1999.

de Bary, Wm. Theodore and Richard Lufrano (eds.). *Sources of Chinese tradition, volume 2, from 1600 through the twentieth century.* New York: Columbia University Press, 2000.

Defoort, Carine. *The Pheasant Cap Master (He guan zi). A Rhetorical Reading.* Albany: State University of New York Press, 1997.

Defoort, Carine and Nicolas Standaert (eds.), *The Mozi as an Evolving Text. Different Voices in Early Chinese Thought.* Leiden/Boston: Brill, 2013.

Denecke, Wiebke. *The Dynamics of Masters Literature: Early Chinese Thought from Confucius to Han Feizi.* Boston: Harvard University Asia Center, 2011.

Dessein, Bart. 'Yearning for the Lost Paradise: The "Great Unity" (*datong*) and Its Philosophical Interpretations'. *Asian Studies* 5, no. 1 (2017): 83–102.

Dösch, Martin. 'Ordering the World. Shao Yong and the Idea of History'. *Monumenta Serica* 61, no. 1 (2013): 269–285.

Dray, William H. 'Holism and individualism in history and social science'. In: *The encyclopedia of philosophy*. 2nd edn. vol. 4, ed. Donald M. Borchert, 441–448. 1975. Reprint, Farmington Hills: Macmillan, 2006.

Durrant Stephen. 'Truth Claims in *Shiji*'. In *Historical Truth, Historical Criticism and Ideology. Chinese Historiography and Historical Culture from a New Comparative Perspective*, edited by Helwig Schmidt-Glinzer, Achim Mittag and Jörn Rüsen, 93–114 Leiden/Boston: Brill, 2005.

Elman, Benjamin. 'Philosophy (*I-li*) versus Philology (*K'ao-cheng*): The *Jen-hsin tao-hsin* Debate'. *T'oung Pao* 69, no. 4/5 (1983): 175–222.

Elman, Benjamin. *From Philosophy to Philology: Intellectual and Social Aspects of Change in Late Imperial China*. Cambridge: Council on East Asian Studies, Harvard University, 1984.

Elman, Benjamin. 'Criticism as Philosophy: Conceptual Change in Ch'ing Dynasty Evidential Research'. *Qinghua Xuebao* 17, no. 1–2 (1985): 164–198.

Elman, Benjamin. 'The Historicization of Classical Learning in Ming-Ch'ing China'. In *Turning Points in Historiography: A Cross-Cultural Perspective*, edited by Q. Edward Wang and Georg Iggers, 101–144. Rochester: The University of Rochester Press, 2002.

Eno, Robert. *The Confucian Creation of Heaven: Philosophy and the Defense of Ritual Mastery*. Albany: State University of New York Press, 1990.

Eno, Robert. 'Shang state religion and the pantheon of the oracle texts'. In *Early Chinese Religion. Part One: Shang through Han (1250 BC–220 AD)*, edited by John Lagerwey and Marc Kalinowski, 41–102. Leiden/Boston: Brill, 2009.

Fang Litian 方立天. *Zhongguo gudai zhexue* 中国古代哲学, vol. 1. Beijing: Renmin daxue chubanshe, 2006.

Feng Youlan. *The Spirit of Chinese Philosophy*. London: Kegan Paul, 1947.

Feng Youlan. *A Short History of Chinese Philosophy*. New York: The Free Press, 1948.

Feng Youlan. *A History of Chinese Philosophy*. Princeton: Princeton University Press, 1983.

Fingarette, Herbert. *Confucius: The Secular as Sacred*. Long Grove: Waveland Press, 1972.

Franke Wolfgang. 'Historical writing during the Ming'. In *The Cambridge History of China. Volume 7: The Ming Dynasty, 1368–1644, Part I*, edited by Denis Twitchett and John K. Fairbank, 726–782. Cambridge: Cambridge University Press, 1998.

Gao Jianlong 高建龙. *Tiandao yu zhengdao: Shiqi shiji Zhongguo rujia sixiang yu Qingjiao zhuyi duibi yanjiu* 天道与政道：十七世纪中国儒家思想与清教主义对比研究. Beijing: Zhongguo shehui kexue chubanshe, 2014.

Gentz, Joachim. 'Mohist Traces in the Early *Chunqiu fanlu* Chapters'. *Oriens Extremus* 48 (2009): 55–70.

Han Fei. *Han Fei Tzu. Basic Writings*. Translated by Burton Watson. New York: Columbia University Press, 1964.

Handelsman, Marceli. *Historyka. Zasady metodologji i teorji poznania* historycznego. Warszawa: Piotr Pyz i S-ka, 1928.

Harris, Eirik L. 'Legalism: Introducing a Concept and Analyzing Aspects of Han Fei's Political Philosophy'. *Philosophy Compass* 9, no. 3 (2014): 155–164.

Harris, Eirik L. *The Shenzi Fragments: A Philosophical Analysis and Translation*. New York: Columbia University Press, 2017.

Hartwell, Robert. 'Historical Analogism, Public Policy, and Social Science in Eleventh- and Twelfth-Century'. *The American Historical Review* 76, no. 3 (1971): 690–727.

Hatch, George. 'Su Hsun's Pragmatic Statecraft'. In *Ordering the World. Approaches to State and Society in Sung Dynasty China*, edited by Robert Hymes and Conrad Schirokauer, 59–76. Berkeley: University of California Press, 1993.

He Zhaowu. *An Intellectual History of China*. Beijing: Foreign Languages Press, 1991.

Hendrischke, Barbara. 'The Concept of Inherited Evil in the *Taiping jing*'. *East Asian History* 2 (1991): 1–30.

Hendrischke, Barbara. 'The Daoist Utopia of Great Peace'. *Oriens Extremus* 35 (1992): 61–91.

Holcombe, Charles. *In the Shadow of the Han: Literati Thought and Society and the Beginning of the Southern Dynasties*. Honolulu: University of Hawai'i Press, 1994.

Hou Wailu 侯外庐. *Zhongguo sixiang tongshi* 中国思想通史. Volume 4, shang. Beijing: Renmin chubanshe, 2011.

Hsiao, Kung-chuan. *History of Chinese Political Thought, Volume 1: From the Beginnings to the Sixth Century, A.D.* Princeton: Princeton University Press, 1979.

Hsieh, Shan-Yüan. *The Life and Thought of Li Kou (1009–1059)*. San Francisco: Chinese Materials Center, 1979.

Hsu Kwan-San. 'The Chinese Critical Tradition'. *The Historical Journal* 26, no. 2 (1983): 431–446.

Huang Chun-chieh 黄俊杰. *Rujia sixiang yu Zhongguo lishi siwei* 儒家思想与中国历史思维. Shanghai: Huadong shifan daxue chubanshe, 2016.

Huang Chun-chieh and John B. Henderson (eds.). *Notions of Time in Chinese Historical Thinking*. Hongkong: The Chinese University Press, 2006.

Huang Chun-chieh and Erik Zürcher (eds.). *Time and Space in Chinese Culture*. Leiden: Brill, 1997.

Huang Chun-chieh and Jörn Rüsen (eds.). *Chinese Historical Thinking: An Intercultural Discussion*. Göttingen/Taibei: V&R Unipress/National Taiwan University Press, 2015.

Hunter, Michael. *Confucius Beyond the Analects*. Leiden/Boston: Brill, 2017.

Hutton, Eric (ed.). *Dao Companion to Xunzi*. Dordrecht: Springer, 2016.

Ing, Michael. *The Dysfunction of Ritual in Early Confucianism*. New York: Oxford University Press, 2012.

Ivanhoe, Philip J. 'Heaven as a Source for Ethical Warrant in Early Confucianism'. *Dao. A Journal of Comparative Philosophy* 6, no. 3 (2007): 211–220.

Ivanhoe, Philip J. 'Chinese Theories of History', in *Routledge Encyclopedia of Philosophy*, edited by Edward Craig, 3577–3583. New York & London: Routledge, 1998.

Ivanhoe, Philip J. *On Ethics and History: Essays and Letters of Zhang Xuecheng*. Stanford: Stanford University Press, 2009.

Ivanhoe, Philip J. 'Lessons from the past: Zhang Xuecheng and the ethical dimensions of history'. *Dao: A Journal of Comparative Philosophy* 8, no. 2 (2009): 189–203.

Ivanhoe, Philip J. 'Historical Understanding in China and the West: Zhang, Collingwood and Mink', *Journal of the Philosophy of History* 8, no. 1 (2014): 78–95.

Jenkins, Richard. 'Disenchantment, Enchantment and Re-Enchantment: Max Weber at the Millennium'. *Mind and Matter* 10, no. 2 (2012): 149–168.

Jo-Shui Chen. *Liu Tsung-yüan and Intellectual Change in T'ang China, 773–819*. Cambridge: Cambridge University Press, 1992.

Jullien, François. *The Propensity of Things: Toward a History of Efficacy in China*. New York: Zone Books, 1999.

Kang-I Sun Chang. 'Liu Xie's Idea of Canonicity'. In *A Chinese Literary Mind. Culture, Creativity, and Rhetoric in the Wenxin Diaolong*, edited by Zong-qi Cai, 17–32. Stanford: Stanford University Press, 2001.

Keightley, David. 'The Oracle-Bone Inscriptions of the Late Shang Dynasty'. In *Sources of Chinese Tradition. Volume One*, edited by Wm. Theodore de Bary and Irene Bloom, 3–23. New York: Columbia University Press, 1999.

Kern, Martin. *The Stele Inscriptions of Ch'in Shih-huang: Text and Ritual in Early Chinese Imperial Representation*. New Haven: American Oriental Society, 2000.

Kern, Martin. 'Language and the Ideology of Kingship in the "Canon of Yao". In *Ideology of Power and Power of Ideology in Early China*, edited by Yuri Pines, Paul R. Goldin and Martin Kern, Leiden/Boston: Brill, 2015.

Kim, Youngmin. 'Cosmogony as Political Philosophy'. *Philosophy East and West* 58, no. 1 (2008): 108–125.

Kinney, Anne Behnke. *The Art of the Han Essay: Wang Fu's* Ch'ien-Fu Lun. Tempe: Center for Asian studies, 1990.

Klein, Esther. 'Constancy and the Changes: A Comparative Reading of *Heng Xian*'. *Dao: A Journal of Comparative Philosophy* 12, no. 2 (2013): 207–224.

Klein, Esther. *The History of a Historian: Perspectives on the Authorial Roles of Sima Qian*. PhD diss., Princeton University, Princeton 2010.

Knoblock, John and Jeffrey Riegel. *The Annals of Lü Buwei. A Complete Study and Translation*. Stanford: Stanford University Press, 2000.

Koselleck, Reinhart. *Zeitschichten: Studien zur Historik*. Frankfurt am Main: Suhrkamp, 2000.

Kroll, Paul W. *A Student's Dictionary of Classical and Medieval Chinese*. Leiden/Boston: Brill, 2017.

Kuukkanen, Jouni-Matti. *Postnarrativist Philosophy of Historiography*. London: Palgrave Macmillan, 2015.

Kwok, Daniel W.Y. 'Jia Yi: The Faults of the Qin'. In *Sources of Chinese tradition*, volume 1, edited by Wm. Theodore de Bary and Irene Bloom, 228–231. New York: Columbia University Press, 1999.

Le Blanc, Charles. *Huai nan tzu. Philosophical Synthesis in Early Han Thought: The Idea of Resonance* (Kan-ying) *With a Translation and Analysis of Chapter Six*. Hong Kong: Hong Kong University Press, 1985.

Lee, Thomas H.C. (ed.). *The New and the Multiple. Sung Senses of the Past*. Hong Kong: The Chinese University Press, 2004.

Legge, James. *The Chinese Classics. Vol. IV – Part II*. Hongkong/London: Lane, Crawford & Co./ Trübner & Co., 1871.

Leung, Vincent S. *The Politics of the Past in Early China*. Cambridge: Cambridge University Press, 2019.

Li Zhi. *A Book to Burn and a Book to Keep (Hidden): Selected Writings of Li Zhi*. Translated by Rivi Handler-Spitz, Pauline Lee and Haun Saussy. New York: Columbia University Press, 2016.

Li Yucheng 李玉诚. *Hanfeizi lishi sixiang yanjiu* 韩非子历史思想研究. PhD. diss., Shandong Daxue, Jinan 2014.

Liang Qichao 梁啟超. *Zhongguo lishi yanjiufa* 中國歷史研究法. Shanghai: Shanghai guji chubanshe, 1998.

Liu Fengchun 刘凤春. *Lishi zhexue shiyu xia de Kongzi ruxue sixiang yanjiu* 历史哲学视域下的孔子儒学思想研究. M.A. diss., Yanbian Daxue, Jilin 2009.

Liu Jiahe 刘家和. *Gudai Zhongguo yu shijie: yige gushi yanjiuzhe de sikao* 古代中国与世界：一个古史研究者的思考. Wuhan: Wuhan chubanshe, 1995.

Liu Liangjian 刘梁剑. *Wang Chuanshan zhexue yanjiu* 王船山哲学研究. Shanghai: Shanghai renmin chubanshe, 2016.

Liu, James T.C. *Reform in Sung China. Wang An-shih (1021–1086) and his New Policies*. Cambridge: Harvard University Press, 1959.

Liu, James T.C. *Ou-Yang Hsiu: An Eleventh-Century Neo-Confucianist*. Stanford: Stanford University Press, 1967.

Liu, JeeLoo. 'Is Human History Predestined in Wang Fuzhi's Cosmology?'. *Journal of Chinese Philosophy* 28, no. 3 (2001): 321–338.

Liu, JeeLoo. 'Wang Fuzhi's Philosophy of Principle (*Li*) Inherent in *Qi*'. In *Dao Companion to Neo-Confucian Philosophy*, edited by John Makeham, 355–379. Dodrecht et al.: Springer, 2010.

Liu Shu-hsien. 'Philosophical Analysis and Hermeneutics: Reflections on Methodology via an Examination of My Understanding of Chinese Philosophy' in *Two Roads to Wisdom? Chinese and Analytic Philosophical Traditions*, edited by Bo Mou, 131–152. Chicago/La Salle: Open Court, 2001.

Lo, Winston Wan. *The Life and Thought of Yeh Shih*. Hong Kong: The Chinese University of Hong Kong and the University Presses of Florida, 1974.

Loewe, Michael (ed.). *Early Chinese Texts. A Bibliographical Guide*. Berkeley: The Society for the Study of Early China, 1993.

Loewe, Michael, and Edward Shaughnessy. *The Cambridge History of Ancient China: From the origins of civilization to 221 BC*. Cambridge: Cambridge University Press, 2008.

Loewe, Michael. *Dong Zhongshu, a 'Confucian' Heritage and the* Chunqiu fanlu. Leiden/Boston: Brill, 2011.

Löwith, Karl. *Meaning in History*. Chicago and London: The University of Chicago Press, 1949.

Lu Xun 鲁迅. 'Wei-Jin fengdu ji wenzhang yu yao ji jiu zhi guanxi' 魏晋风度及文章与药及酒之关系. In *Eryi ji, Lu Xun Xuanji*, vol. 2, 377–405. Beijing: Renmin wenxue chubanshe, 1992.

Lu Yihan 路懿菡. *Xian Qin zhuzi lishi zhexue sixiang yanjiu* 先秦诸子历史哲学思想研究. MA diss., Liaoning Shifan Daxue, Dalian 2009.

Lü Zuqian. 'How to Study History'. Translated by Burton Watson. In *Sources of Chinese tradition*, volume 1, edited by Wm. Theodore de Bary and Irene Bloom, 659–660. New York: Columbia University Press. 1999.

Luo Guang 羅光. *Lishi zhexue* 歷史哲學. Taibei: Taiwan xuesheng shuju, 1996.

Dong Zhongshu. *Luxuriant Gems of the Spring and Autumn. Attributed to Dong Zhongshu*. Edited and translated by John Major and Sarah Queen. New York: Columbia University Press, 2016.

Makeham, John. 'The Formation of *Lunyu* as a Book'. *Monumenta Serica* 44, no. 1 (2016): 1–24.

McTaggart, John M.E. *The Nature of Existence*. Cambridge: Cambridge University Press, 1927.

Meisner, Thomas and Barbara Mittler. *Why China did not have a Renaissance – and why that matters*. Boston/Berlin: De Gruyter Oldenbourg, 2018.

Meisner, Maurice. *Li Ta-Chao and the Origins of Chinese Marxism*. Cambridge: Harvard University Press, 1967.

Mencius, *Mencius*. Trans. Irene Bloom, edited by Philip J. Ivanhoe. New York: Columbia University Press, 2001.

Meyer, Dirk. *Philosophy on Bamboo. Text and the Production of Meaning in Early China*. Leiden/Boston: Brill, 2011.

Mithen, Nick. *History and the Han Fei Zi*. M.A. diss., Fudan Daxue, Shanghai 2014.

Mou Zongsan 牟宗三. *Lishi zhexue* 歷史哲學 (*Philosophy of history*). Taibei: Lianjing, 2003.

Mozi. *The Book of Master Mo*. Translated and edited by Ian Johnston. London: Penguin Books, 2013.

Munro, Donald J. *Individualism and Holism: Studies in Confucian and Taoist values*. Ann Arbor: University of Michigan Press, 1985.

Needham, Joseph. *Science and Civilisation in China. Vol. 2. History of Scientific Thought*. Cambridge: Cambridge University Press, 1956.

Ng, On-cho. 'A Tension in Ch'ing Thought: "Historicism" in Seventeenth- and Eighteenth-Century Chinese Thought'. *Journal of the History of Ideas* 54, no. 4 (1993): 561–583.

Niu Runzhen 牛润珍. *Zhongguo shixue sixiang tongshi. Sui-Tang juan shangxia* 中国史学思想通史。 隋唐卷上下. Hefei: Huangshan chushe, 2004.

Nivison, David S. 'Chang Hsueh-Ch'eng and Collingwood'. Unpublished manuscript, 1957.

Nivison, David S. *The Life and Thought of Chang Hsüeh-ch'eng (1738–1801)*. Stanford: Stanford University Press, 1966.

Nivison, David S. 'Mengzi as Philosopher of History', in *Mencius: Contexts and Interpretations*, edited by Alan Chan, 282–304. Honolulu: University of Hawai'i Press, 2002.

Nivison, David S. 'Philosophy of History', in *Encyclopedia of Chinese Philosophy*, edited by Antonio Cua, 540–554. New York & London: Routledge, 2003.

Nylan, Michael. *The Five 'Confucian' Classics*. New Haven: Yale University Press, 2001.

Ong, Chang Woei. 'The Principles Are Many: Wang Tingxiang and Intellectual Transition in Mid-Ming China'. *Harvard Journal of Asiatic Studies* 66, no. 2 (2006): 461–493.

Owen, Stephen. *Readings in Chinese Literary Thought*. Cambridge: Harvard University Press, 1992.

Pang Tianyou 庞天佑. *Zhongguo shixue sixiang tongshi. Wei-Jin, Nan-Beichao juan* 中国史学思想通史。 魏晋南北朝卷. Hefei: Huangshan chushe, 2003.

Perkins, Franklin. 'The *Laozi* and the Cosmogonic Turn in Classical Chinese Philosophy'. *Frontiers of Philosophy in China* 11, no. 2 (2016): 185–205.

Petersen, Jens Østergård. 'The Anti-Messianism of the *Taiping Jing*'. *Studies in Central and East Asian Religions* 3 (1990): 1–41.

Pines, Yuri. 'Political mythology and dynastic legitimacy in the *Rong Cheng shi* manuscript'. *Bulletin of SOAS* 73, no. 3 (2010): 503–529.

Pines, Yuri. 'From Historical Evolution to the End of History: Past, Present and Future from Shang Yang to the First Emperor'. In *Dao companion to the philosophy of Han Fei*, edited by Paul R. Goldin, 25–45. New York: Springer, 2013.

Pines, Yuri. 'Dating a Pre-Imperial Text: The Case Study of the *Book of Lord Shang*'. *Early China* 39 (2016): 145–184.

Pines, Yuri and Gideon Shelach. '"Using the past to serve the present": Comparative perspectives on Chinese and Western theories of the origins of the state'. In *Genesis and regeneration: Essays on conceptions of origins*, edited by Shaul Shaked, 127–163. Jerusalem: The Israel Academy of Science and Humanities, 2015.

Platt, Stephen. *Provincial Patriots: The Hunanese and Modern China*. Cambridge: Harvard University Press, 2007.

Pokora, Timotheus, *Hsin-lun (New Treatise) and other writings by Huan T'an (43 BC–28 AD)*. Ann Arbor: Center for Chinese Studies, 1975.

Popper, Karl R. *The Poverty of Historicism*. Boston: The Beacon Press, 1957.

Puett, Michael. *To Become a God: Cosmology, Sacrifice, and Self-divinization in Early China*. Cambridge: Harvard University Press, 2002.

Puett, Michael. *The Ambivalence of Creation: Debates concerning innovation and artifice in early China*. Stanford: Stanford University Press, 2001.

Puett, Michael. 'Listening to Sages: Divination, Omens, and the Rhetoric of Antiquity in Wang Chong's *Lunheng*'. *Oriens Extremus* 45 (2005/06): 271–281.

Puett, Michael. 'Humans, Spirits, and Sages in Chinese Late Antiquity: Ge Hong's *Master Who Embraces Simplicity (Baopuzi)*'. *Extrême-Orient, Extrême-Occident* 29 (2007): 95–119.

Puett, Michael. 'The Belatedness of the Present: Debates over Antiquity during the Han Dynasty'. In *Perceptions of Antiquity in Chinese Civilization*, edited by Helga Stahl and Dieter Kuhn, 177–190. Heidelberg: Würzburger Sinologische Schriften, 2008.

Puett, Michael. 'Sages, Creation, and the End of History in the *Huainanzi*'. In *The Huainanzi and Textual Production in Early China*, edited by Sarah Queen and Michael Puett, 269–290. Leiden/Boston: Brill, 2014.

Pulleyblank, Edwin. 'Neo-Confucianism and Neo-Legalism in T'ang Intellectual Life, 755–805'. In *The Confucian Persuasion*, edited by Arthur Wright. Stanford: Stanford University Press, 1960.

Pulleyblank, Edwin. 'Chinese Historical Criticism: Liu Chih-Chi and Ssu-ma Kuang'. In *Historians of China and Japan*, edited by William Beasley and Edwin Pulleyblank, 135–166. London: Oxford University Press, 1961.

Qian Mu 錢穆. *Qian Bingsi xiansheng quanji* 錢賓四先生全集. Vol. 15. Xinbei: Lianjing chuban, 1998.

Qiu Hansheng 邱汉生. 'Lun Zhu Xi 'huigui yili' de lishi zhexue' 论朱熹'回归一理'的历史哲学. *Zhexue yanjiu* 6 (1982): 51–57.

Queen, Sarah. *From Chronicle to Canon. The hermeneutics of the* Spring and Autumn, *according to Tung Chung-shu*. Cambridge: Cambridge University Press, 1996.

Quirin, Michael. 'Scholarship, Value, Method, and Hermeneutics in *Kaozheng*: Some Reflections on Cui Shu (1740–1816) and the Confucian Classics'. *History and Theory* 35, no. 4 (1996): 34–53.

Ren Jiyu 任继愈. *Zhongguo zhexue shi* 中国哲学史. Beijing: Renmin chubanshe, 1985.

Ren Jiyu 任继愈. *Zhongguo zhexue fazhan shi* 中国哲学发展史. Beijing: Renmin chubanshe, 1998.

Robinson Richard. *Early Madhyamaka in India and China*. Wisconsin: Madison University Press, 1967.

Rodziński, Witold. *Historia Chin*. Wrocław: Ossolineum, 1974.

Rogacz, Dawid. 'In the Shadow of the Decay. The Philosophy of History of Mencius and Xunzi'. *Asian Studies* 21, no. 1 (2017): 147–171.

Rogacz, Dawid. 'The Motif of Legendary Emperors Yao and Shun in Ancient Chinese Literature'. In *Rethinking Orient. In Search of Sources and Inspirations*, edited by Adam Bednarczyk, Magdalena Kubarek, and Maciej Szatkowski, 113–125. Warsaw: Peter Lang, 2017.

Rogacz, Dawid. 'The birth of enlightenment secularism from the spirit of Confucianism'. *Asian Philosophy* 28, no. 1 (2018): 68–83.

Rogacz, Dawid. '"Spring and Autumn Annals" as Narrative Explanation'. In *Towards a Revival of Analytical Philosophy of History. Around Paul A. Roth's Vision of Historical Sciences*, edited by Krzysztof Brzechczyn, 254–272. Leiden-Boston: Brill-Rodopi, 2018.

Rogacz, Dawid. 'The Virtue of a Historian. A Dialogue between Herman Paul and Chinese theorists of history'. *History and Theory* 58, no. 2 (2019): 252–267.

Roth, Harold and Sarah Queen. 'The Huang-Lao Silk Manuscripts (*Huang-Lao boshu*)'. In *Sources of Chinese tradition*, volume 1, edited by Wm. Theodore de Bary and Irene Bloom, 241–256. New York: Columbia University Press, 1999.

Satō, Masayuki. *The Confucian Quest for Order: The Origin and Formation of the Political Thought of Xun Zi*. Leiden/Boston: Brill, 2003.

Schaberg, David. 'Foundations of Chinese Historiography: Literary Representation in *Zuo Zhuan* and *Guoyu*'. PhD diss., Harvard University, Harvard 1996.

Schinköthe, Ailika. *Liu Zhiji's* Shitong *and its Revival in Ming Dynasty – Pacing Historiography Anew*. PhD diss., Eberhard Karls Universität Tübingen, Tübingen 2017.

Schirokauer, Conrad. 'Chu His's Sense of History'. In *Ordering the World. Approaches to State and Society in Sung Dynasty China*, edited by Robert Hymes and Conrad Schirokauer, 193–221. Berkeley: University of California Press, 1993.

Schirokauer, Conrad. 'Hu Hong as a Historian'. In *The New and the Multiple. Sung Senses of the Past*, edited by Thomas C. Lee, 121–162. Hong Kong: The Chinese University Press, 2004.

Shang Yang. *The Book of Lord Shang*. Translated by J.J.L. Duyvendak. Londres: Arthur Probsthain, 1928.

Shang Yang. *The Book of Lord Shang. Apologetics of State Power in Early China*. Translated by Yuri Pines. New York: Columbia University Press, 2017.

Sharf, Robert. *Coming to Terms with Chinese Buddhism. A Reading of the* Treasure Store Treatise. Honolulu: University of Hawai'i Press, 2002.

Shaughnessy, Edward. *Unearthing the Changes: Recently discovered manuscripts of the Yi Jing (I Ching) and related texts*. New York: Columbia University Press, 2014.

Shaughnessy, Edward (ed.). *New Sources of Early Chinese History: An Introduction to the Reading of Inscriptions and Manuscripts*. New Haven: The Society for the Study of Early China, 1997.

Shaughnessy, Edward. 'History and Inscriptions, China.' In *The Oxford History of Historical Writing. Volume One. Beginnings to AD 600*, edited by Andrew Feldherr and Grant Hardy, 371–393. Oxford: Oxford University Press, 2011.

Skonicki, Douglas. *Cosmos, State and Society: Song Dynasty Arguments concerning the Creation of Political Order*. PhD diss., Harvard University, Cambridge 2007.

Skonicki, Douglas. 'The Authority of the Classics: A Comparative Analysis of the Hermeneutics of Ouyang Xiu and Ogyū Sorai'. *Sungkyun Journal of East Asian Studies* 11, no. 1 (2011): 17–36.

Sloterdijk, Peter. *Rage and Time: A psychopolitical investigation*. New York: Columbia University Press, 2012.

Smuts, Jan Christian. *Holism and Evolution*. London: MacMillon and Co. Ltd, 1926.

Strange, Mark. 'Representations of Liang Emperor Wu as a Buddhist Ruler in Sixth-and Seventh-century Texts'. *Asia Major* 24, no. 2 (2011): 53–112.

Sunzi. *The Art of War: Sunzi bing fa*. Translated by Lionel Giles. Berkeley: Ulysses Press, 2007.

Tan Sor-hoon. 'Balancing Conservatism and Innovation: The Pragmatic *Analects*'. In *Dao Companion to the Analects*, edited by Amy Olberding, 335–354. Dordrecht: Springer, 2013.

Tian Chenshan. *Chinese Dialectics. From Yijing to Marxism*. Lanham: Lexington Books, 2005.

Tillman, Hoyt C. *Utilitarian Confucianism: Ch'en Liang's Challenge to Chu Hsi*. Cambridge/London: Harvard University Press, 1982.

Tillman, Hoyt C. *Confucian Discourse and Chu His's Ascendancy*. Honolulu: University of Hawai'i Press, 1992.

Tillman, Hoyt C. *Ch'en Liang on Public Interest and the Law*. Honolulu: University of Hawai'i Press, 1994.

Tillman, Hoyt C. and Stephen West (eds.). *China Under Jurchen Rule: Essays on Chin Intellectual and Cultural History*. New York: State University of New York Press, 1995.

Topolski, Jerzy. *Metodologia historii*. Warszawa: Państwowe Wydawnictwo Naukowe, 1984.

Tucker, Aviezer (ed.). *A Companion to the Philosophy of History and Historiography*. Malden: Wiley-Blackwell, 2010.

Twitchett, Denis. *The Writing of Official History Under the T'ang*. Cambridge: Cambridge University Press, 1992.

Valmisa, Mercedes. 'Is the ideology of the 'Mandate of Heaven' already present in Western Zhou bronze inscriptions?' Unpublished paper. Available at: https://www.academia. edu/11319002/ Is_the_Ideology_of_the_Mandate_of_Heaven_already_present_in_ Western_Zhou_Bronze_Inscriptions.

van den Stock, Ady. *The Horizon of Modernity. Subjectivity and Social Structure in New Confucian Philosophy*. Leiden/Boston: Brill, 2016.

Wagner, Rudolf. *A Chinese Reading of the Daodejing. Wang Bi's Commentary on the Laozi with Critical Text and Translation*. New York: State University of New York Press, 2003.

Wang Can 王灿. 'Shangshu lishi sixiang yanjiu' 尚书历史思想研究. PhD diss., Shandong Daxue, Jinan 2011b.

Wang Gaoxin 汪高鑫. *Zhongguo shixue sixiang tongshi. Qin-Han juan* 中国史学思想通史。秦汉卷. Hefei: Huangshan shushe, 2002.

Wang Gaoxin 汪高鑫. *Dong Zhongshu yu Handai lishi sixiang yanjiu* 董仲舒与汉代历史思想研究. Shanghai: Shangwu yinshuguan, 2012.

Wang Jilu 王记录. *Zhongguo shixue sixiang tongshi. Qingdai juan* 中国史学思想通史。清代卷. Hefei: Huangshan shushe, 2002.

Wang Mingsun 王明蓀. 'Jindai shiren zhi lishi sixiang' 金代士人之歷史思想. *Xingda Lishi Xuebao* 11 (2000): 1–25.

Wang Mingsun 王明蓀. 'Wang Ruoxu zhi shixue piping' 王若虛之史學批評. *Xingda Lishi Xuebao* 2 (1992): 59–70.

Wang Mingsun 王明蓀. *Wang Anshi* 王安石. Taibei: Dongda tushu gongsi, 1994.

Wang Shounan 王寿南. *Zhongguo lidai sixiangjia: Han* 中国历代思想家：汉. Beijing: Jiuzhou chubanshe, 2011.

Wang, Q. Edward and On-cho Ng. *Mirroring the Past. The Writing and Use of History in Imperial China*. Honolulu: University of Hawai'i Press, 2005.

Wang, Zhihe. 2013. *Process and Pluralism: Chinese Thought on the Harmony of Diversity*. Landkreis Offenbach: Ontos Verlag.

Wawrzynowicz, Andrzej. 'Znaczenie refleksji historiozoficznej w rozwoju polskiej myśli społeczno-politycznej XIX i XX w.' *Filo-Sofija* 28, no. 2 (2015b): 53–64.

Wawrzynowicz, Andrzej. *Spór o mesjanizm. Tom 1. Rozwój idei*. (Warszawa: Fundacja Augusta hrabiego Cieszkowskiego, 2015a).

Wells, Marnix. *The Pheasant Cap Master and the End of History: linking religion to philosophy in early China*. St. Petersburg: Three Pines Press, 2013.

White, Hayden. *Metahistory: The Historical Imagination in Nineteenth-century Europe*. Baltimore: Johns Hopkins University Press, 1973.

Wichrowski, Marek. *Spór o naturę procesu historycznego: od Hebrajczyków do śmierci Fryderyka Nietzschego*. Warszawa: Wydawnictwo Naukowe Semper, 1995.

Wu Huaiqi 吳怀祺. *Zhongguo shixue sixiang tongshi. Song-Liao-Jin juan* 中国史学思想通史。 宋辽金卷. Hefei: Huangshan shushe, 2002.

Wyatt, Don J. *The Recluse of Loyang. Shao Yung and the Moral Evolution of Early Sung Thought.* Honolulu: Hawai'i Press, 1996.

Wyatt, Don J. 'Chu Hsi's Critique of Shao Yung: One Instance of the Stand Against Fatalism'. *Harvard Journal of Asiatic Studies* 45, no. 2 (1985): 649–666.

Wyatt, Don J. 'Shao Yong's Numerological-Cosmological System'. In *Dao Companion to Neo-Confucian Philosophy*, edited by John Makeham, 17–37. Dordrecht et al.: Springer, 2010.

Wyatt, Don J. 'The Transcendence of the Past. Objectivity, Relativism and Moralism in the Historical Thought of Shao Yong'. *Monumenta Serica* 61, no. 1 (2013): 203–226.

Xiang Yannan 项燕楠. *Zhongguo shixue sixiang tongshi. Ming juan* 中国史学思想通史。 明卷. Hefei: Huangshan shushe, 2002.

Xie Xuanjun 谢选骏. *Zhouyi de lishi zhexue* 周易的历史哲学. Raleigh: Lulu, 2015.

Xu Fuguan 徐复观. *Liang Han sixiang shi* 两汉思想史. Vol. II. Shanghai: Huadong Shifan Daxue chubanshe, 2002.

Xu Wentao 徐文涛. 'Xian Qin Rujia lishi zhexue yanjiu – yi Kong, Meng, Xun sixiang wei zhongxin' 先秦儒家历史哲学研究——以孔孟荀思想为中心. PhD diss., Shandong Daxue, Jinan 2006.

Xu Elina-Qian. *Historical Development of the Pre-Dynastic Khitan.* PhD diss., University of Helsinki, Helsinki 2005.

Xunzi. *A Translation and Study of the Complete Works.* Vol. I, II, III. Transl. John Knoblock. Stanford: Stanford University Press, 1988, 1990, 1994.

Xunzi. *Xunzi: The Complete Text.* Trans. Eric Hutton. Princeton: Princeton University Press, 2016.

Yan Buke 閆步克. 'Yueshi yu Ru zhi wenhua qiyuan' 乐师与儒之文化起源. *Beijing daxue xuekan* 5 (1995): 46–54.

Yang, Jui-Sung. *Body, Ritual and Identity: A New Interpretation of the Early Qing Confucian Yan Yuan (1635–1704).* Leiden/Boston: Brill, 2016.

Yao, Xinzhong. *An Introduction to Confucianism.* Cambridge: Cambridge University Press, 2000.

Yeung Man Shun 楊文信. *The historical writings of Wang Shizhen, 1526–1590.* PhD diss., University of Hongkong, Hongkong 1992.

Yi Ning and Wang Xianhua. 'Historical Identity in the *Shangshu*'. *Journal of Chinese Philosophy* 40, no. 1 (2013): 185–194.

Zhang Linxiang 張林祥. *Shangjunshu de chengshu yu sixiang yanjiu* 商君书的成书与思想研究. Beijing: Renmin chubanshe, 2008.

Zhao Wenyu 赵文宇. 'Cong *Hanshu* kan Wang Mang de lishi sixiang' 从汉书看王莽的历史思想. *Jiamusi Daxue Shehui Kexue Xuebao* 30, no. 1 (2012): 120–123.

Zheng Jixiong 鄭吉雄. 'Chen Liang de shigong zhi xue' 陳亮的事功之學. *Taida Zhongwen Xuebao* 6 (1994): 257–290.

Zheng Wangeng. 'Tracing the source of the idea of time in *Yizhuan*'. *Frontiers of Philosophy in China* 5, no. 1 (2010): 51–67.

Zhuangzi. *The Complete Works of Zhuangzi.* Translated by Burton Watson. New York: Columbia University Press, 2013.

Ziporyn, Brook. 'Spatio-Temporal Order in Yang Xiong's *Taixuan jing*'. *Early Medievel China* 2 (1995): 40–85.

Index

Lightning Source UK Ltd.
Milton Keynes UK
UKHW020211190422
401705UK00002B/38